Brand Management

M000250406

For more than three decades it has been argued that the brand is an important value creator and should be a top management priority. However, the definition of what a brand is remains elusive.

Brand Management: Research, Theory and Practice fills a gap in the market, providing an understanding of different 'schools of thought' in brand management and offers deep insight into the opening question of almost every brand management course: 'What is a brand?'

This comprehensive second edition offers an exhaustive scientific analysis of various approaches to brand management developed over the past thirty years. It also delivers a thorough understanding of the strategic and managerial implications of different brand perspectives.

Tilde Heding and **Charlotte F. Knudtzen** both consult businesses on communication issues and brand value creation. They also lecture on strategic brand management at Copenhagen Business School as well as other institutions.

Mogens Bjerre is an associate professor at Copenhagen Business School and has published widely in the areas of franchising, key account management, strategic relationship marketing and retailing.

'Without question, branding is a complex management area that deserves study from a variety of different perspectives and academic traditions. By providing a multidisciplinary approach, this book provides a welcome and invaluable resource for thoughtful students, scholars, and practitioners who want to fully understand branding and brand management.'

Kevin Lane Keller, Tuck School of Business, Dartmouth College, USA

'At last a book that cuts through the clutter about understanding brand and so clearly clarifies the brand concept. This book superbly bridges the academic domain and enables practitioners use it to build brand equity.'

Leslie de Chernatony, Aston Business School, UK

'We think this is an excellent treatment of our topic. Thorough and complete, yet concise and very readable. We love the design and structure, both with regards to the seven approaches as well as the four layers within each approach.'

Albert M. Muñiz, Jr., DePaul University, USA and Thomas O'Guinn, University of Wisconsin, USA

'The theory of branding is an exciting but complex field, and this is the perfect guide – it's accessible, comprehensive, brilliantly structured, and bang up-to-date.'

Robert Jones, Head of New Thinking, Wolff Olins and Visiting Professor, UEA, UK

'Like any strong brand this book provides a smart, unique and holistic perspective on brand management. It elevates branding from a marketing concept to a strategic discipline that impacts the entire organization.'

Sara Riis-Carstensen, Head of Global Brand Development, LEGO Group, Denmark

Brand Management

Research, theory and practice

Second Edition

**Tilde Heding,
Charlotte F. Knudtzen
and Mogens Bjerre**

Routledge
Taylor & Francis Group

LONDON AND NEW YORK

First published 2009

Second edition 2016
by Routledge
2 Park Square, Milton Park, Abingdon, Oxon OX14 4RNAnd by Routledge
7 1 1 Third Avenue, New York, NY 10017

Routledge is an imprint of the Taylor & Francis Group, an informa business

© 2016 Tilde Heding, Charlotte F. Knudtzen and Mogens Bjerre

The right of Tilde Heding, Charlotte F. Knudtzen and Mogens Bjerre to be
identified as author of this work has been asserted by them in accordance
with sections 77 and 78 of the Copyright, Designs and Patents Act 1988.

All rights reserved. No part of this book may be reprinted or
reproduced or utilised in any form or by any electronic, mechanical,
or other means, now known or hereafter invented, including photocopying
and recording, or in any information storage or retrieval system,
without permission in writing from the publishers.

Every effort has been made to contact copyright holders for their permission
to reprint material in this book. The publishers would be grateful to hear from
any copyright holder who is not here acknowledged and will undertake to
rectify any errors or omissions in future editions of this book.

Trademark notice: Product or corporate names may be trademarks
or registered trademarks, and are used only for identification
and explanation without intent to infringe.

British Library Cataloguing in Publication Data
A catalogue record for this book is available from the British Library

Library of Congress Cataloging in Publication Data
A catalog record for this book has been requested

ISBN: 978-1-138-80468-5 (hbk)
ISBN: 978-1-138-80469-2 (pbk)
ISBN: 978-1-315-75279-2 (ebk)

Typeset in Bembo and Helvetica Neue
by Florence Production Ltd, Stoodleigh, Devon, UK

Contents

List of figures   vii
List of tables   ix
List of boxes   x
Foreword   xii
Preface   xiii
Acknowledgements   xv

PART I
Setting the scene   **1**

1   Introduction   3

2   Overview: brand management 1985–2015   9

3   Taxonomy of brand management 1985–2015   18

PART II
Seven brand approaches   **25**

4   The economic approach   27

5   The identity approach   45

6   The consumer-based approach   85

7   The personality approach   120

8   The relational approach   158

9   The community approach   193

10 The cultural approach   227

PART III
Other perspectives
269

11 Other categorizations of brand management   271

12 Keywords in brand management   280

    Author index   299
    Subject index   301

Figures

1.1 The logic of the approach chapters 5
1.2 A reader's guide 7
3.1 Taxonomy of brand management 1985–2015 20
3.2 The logic of the approach chapters 23
4.1 The brand-consumer exchange of the economic approach 31
4.2 Supporting and core theories of the economic approach 35
4.3 Relation between price and demand 38
4.4 The academic evolution of the economic approach 41
5.1 Sources of brand identity: the corporation is pivotal for the creation of brand equity in the identity approach 52
5.2 Theoretical framework of the corporate identity approach 55
5.3 Brand identity: the supporting and core theory of the identity approach 60
5.4 Manifestations of organizational identity (culture) 67
5.5 Aligning identity, vision and culture 71
5.6 The academic evolution of the identity approach 80
6.1 The brand resides in the mind of the consumer 88
6.2 The computer is the central metaphor of man in cognitive psychology 89
6.3 Supporting and core theories of the consumer-based approach 90
6.4 Simple associative network spreading from the node Volkswagen 91
6.5 Dimensions of brand knowledge; adapted from Keller (1993) 95
6.6 Associations spreading from the node '7-Up' 98
6.7 '7-Up' brand associations adapted to the customer-based brand equity framework 99
6.8 Dualistic mechanisms of the consumer-based approach influencing the managerial implications 105
6.9 The academic evolution of the consumer-based approach 115
7.1 Brand personality construct 124
7.2 Supporting and core theories of the personality approach 126
7.3 Consumer self construct; based on Sirgy (1982), Sirgy and Johar (1991) 129
7.4 The brand-self exchange of symbolic brand value in the market place 133

7.5   US Dimensions and traits of brand personality; adapted from
      Aaker (1997)   134
7.6   Theoretical framework of the personality approach: brand
      personality   135
7.7   Creating brand personality in accordance with the consumer self
      construct   147
7.8   Example of a sincere brand personality dimension, traits and
      behaviour   149
7.9   The academic evolution of the personality approach   153
8.1   'Dyadic' brand-consumer relationship: brand management is
      perceived as an ongoing meaning-based process   165
8.2   Supporting and core theory of the relational approach   166
8.3   Layers and facets of brand relationship quality and stability;
      adapted from Fournier (1998)   175
8.4   The academic evolution of the relational approach   188
9.1   The 'brand triad': a brand community exists only when there is
      interaction between at least two consumers   196
9.2   Networks of consumers create brand meaning independently of
      the marketer   199
9.3   Theoretical framework of the community approach   199
9.4   Conceptualization of the community in the sociological tradition 201
9.5   Brand community construct (with examples from the Saab
      community)   202
9.6   The marketer as observer of a brand community   216
9.7   The academic evolution of the community approach   222
10.1 The core and supporting theories (cultural consumption), the
      societal comment on brand icons (the No Logo movement)
      and the future brand scenario (the citizen-artist brand)   230
10.2 Scope of the cultural approach   231
10.3 Movement of meaning from culture to consumer good to
      individuals create brands; adapted from McCracken (1988)   236
10.4 Research methods of the cultural approach   247
10.5 Gather cultural knowledge to build a cultural brand strategy   248
10.6 The academic evolution of the cultural approach   261
11.1 Four brand paradigms along two dimensions; adapted from Louro
      and Cunha (2001)   274

Tables

2.1   Received view and emergent paradigm   11
5.1   Characteristics of product and corporate branding   50
5.2   The supporting theories uncovering internal and external
      elements of brand identity   60
5.3   Three perspectives on organizational culture   66
5.4   Detecting identity gaps   73
5.5   Aligning identity gaps   75
6.1   A simple version of a matrix array   101
8.1   Differences between the information-processing and the
      experiential consumer perspective   163
8.2   Eight relationship forms inspired by communal versus exchange
      relationships   171
8.3   Relationship forms   172
9.1   Variations of brand community (community in the original
      understanding)   204
9.2   Three forms of community affiliation   205
9.3   Typology of online creative consumer communities   207
10.1 A comparison between the mindshare branding model and the
      cultural branding model   237
10.2 Iconic brands are brands that have become cultural icons   238
10.3 The postmodern and the post-postmodern branding paradigm   257
11.1 The role of brands   273
11.2 Four brand management paradigms   276
11.3 A comparison across four branding models   277
11.4 Comparison of brand management categorizations   278

Boxes

2.1	Learning objectives	9
2.2	Overview of brand management 1985–2015	16
3.1	Learning objectives	18
4.1	Learning objectives	28
4.2	Regression analysis	38
4.3	You are not done!	42
5.1	Learning objectives	47
5.2	Visual and behavioural identity from marketing	49
5.3	From product to corporate branding at Lego	51
5.4	Is identity enduring? Shifting paradigm	53
5.5	Culture in the identity approach	57
5.6	Misaligned identities: the case of Body Shop	63
5.7	How to do a brand identity study	69
5.8	Brand identity throughout the value chain	76
5.9	Living the brand: all about the people of Quiksilver	76
5.10	Dos and don'ts of the identity approach	77
5.11	You are not done!	80
6.1	Learning objectives	86
6.2	Memory representations	92
6.3	Heuristics are important in low-involvement categories	93
6.4	How to structure brand associations	98
6.5	Projective techniques	102
6.6	Map out customers' brand associations yourself	103
6.7	Things to consider when choosing the right brand name	107
6.8	Six managerial guidelines	109
6.9	Dos and don'ts of the consumer-based approach	111
6.10	You are not done!	115
7.1	Learning objectives	121
7.2	Ideal Self: Oil of Olay – female consumers' hopes and dreams	131
7.3	Archetypes and brand personality	136
7.4	Ordinal scales applied	140
7.5	Interval scales applied	140
7.6	'Six steps' method of exploring and measuring brand personality	142

7.7	Dove and the actual self	145
7.8	Brand personality defines consumers' interpretation of behaviour	151
7.9	Dos and don'ts of the personality approach	152
7.10	You are not done!	154
8.1	Learning objectives	159
8.2	Customer relationship management and brand relationship theory	160
8.3	Background of the brand relationship theory	169
8.4	Different personalities strike up different relationships	176
8.5	Depth is preferred to breadth	178
8.6	Stories can be helped along	179
8.7	Conduct a long interview yourself	180
8.8	You are not done!	188
9.1	Learning objectives	194
9.2	Who owns the Apple brand now?	197
9.3	Getting too close?	209
9.4	Solving the insider/outsider dilemma	210
9.5	Quantitative triangulation of qualitative data	211
9.6	How to do an ethnographic study of a brand community	212
9.7	Libresse: the community principles applied to fast-moving consumer goods	214
9.8	Insights from the Volkswagen 'Beetle' community	215
9.9	Dos and don'ts of the community approach	220
9.10	You are not done!	222
10.1	Learning objectives	228
10.2	Macro-level culture defined	230
10.3	How Snapple became an iconic brand	240
10.4	The case of Clearblue pregnancy tests	243
10.5	Doing semiotics	244
10.6	Doing a cultural study yourself	246
10.7	The versatile brand manager of the cultural approach	250
10.8	Just another legal case or an early warning sign?	252
10.9	Does CSR benefit all brands?	254
10.10	A citizen-artist brand?	258
10.11	Dos and don'ts in the cultural approach	260
10.12	You are not done!	262
11.1	Learning objectives	271

Foreword

Given the research I have undertaken over the years helping managers understand the nature of their brand and the opportunities for strategically growing brands, I am delighted to write the foreword for this insightful and most timely book. The authors have done an extremely thorough job, diligently working through the brand research literature to devise seven perspectives from diverse schools of thought about perceptions of brands. From this typology, among other things, they consider how the all-important brand equity is created and managed. The authors are to be congratulated on grounding this text so expertly in the literature yet still enabling management implications to be wisely crystallized.

Seeking to elucidate the nature of a brand is a daunting task, since brands are like amoeba, constantly changing. At the most basic, brands start life in brand planning documents, evolving as pan-company teams revise their ideas. Ultimately, after being finessed by stakeholders in the value chain, brands reside in the minds and hearts of consumers – hopefully in a form not too dissimilar from that desired by the firm. The research neatly synthesized in this text coherently brings more understanding to the challenge of understanding a corporation's brand and managing its growth trajectory. It is clear from the authors' work why diverse interpretations exist about the nature of brands.

From this well-argued text, it can be appreciated that one of the challenges managers face is finding a suitable metaphor to ensure common understanding of the firm's brand. Without this, supporting brand resources may not be coherently integrated. Furthermore, under the service dominant logic paradigm, it is more widely recognized that brands are co-created through stakeholder interactions. Managers not only have to understand each other's understanding and inputs to brand building, but also to recognize the way brand communities want to shape the brand. Again, the authors helpfully elucidate the importance of brand communities.

There is much in this book that makes it an inspirational read.

Leslie de Chernatony
Honorary Professor of Brand Marketing
Aston Business School

Preface

> There are numerous strengths of this book. First, the authors have been very brave
> to take a recent time period, to divide it up into phases and to then identify
> management types that have been employed to build brand. There are those who
> will question this particular typology; however, unless someone makes a start at
> putting forward such a typology, we will not see advancement in terms of the topic
> of brand management.
>
> Source: anonymous

We received this comment from one of the 'blind' reviewers contributing to the
lengthy process of turning a lot of our thoughts, knowledge and words into a real,
tangible book. The overall approach of this book is quite different compared to
how other brand management books communicate the scope of brand management, and we sure hope that the typology will be a subject of discussion. We,
however, also hope that it is a step in the right direction when it comes to creating
a solid and serious foundation for the evolution of brand management, both
academically and in practice. Our motivation for writing this book has from day
one been to provide clarity and equip students and practitioners with insights and
tools to deal with brand management in a valid and insightful way.

The book offers its readers a new chest of drawers. The seven drawers are filled
with the assumptions, theories and concepts that are presented higgledy-piggledy
in many other brand management books. Some will probably disagree with the
content of the individual drawers, while many hopefully will enthuse in the structure
and clarity they provide. The three authors have tested the material at lectures at
the Copenhagen Business School and concluded that by far the majority of students
belong to the latter category. The seven approaches seem to provide clarity and
answer many of the questions left unanswered in other brand management books;
meanwhile, they also spur great discussions of what a brand is and how it can be
managed. The communication of brand management as seven ideal types of
different brand approaches – with the necessary chopping of toes and squeezing
of heels – hopefully will also lead to independent and critical thinking!

Keeping our ears to the ground, we sense that typology and scientific clarity
are sought more and more in brand management, and it seems to us that brand
management is about to enter a new era where a deeper understanding of the

many aspects of the brand is needed. Since the mid-1980s it has been argued over and over again that corporations should make brand management a top priority in order to sharpen their competitive edge. That message has sunk in and things are now cooking when it comes to understanding the nature of the brand better and turning brand management into a management discipline as scientifically valid as comparable disciplines.

We hope that the book will be of value to students, academics and practitioners alike, and believe that the book has both valuable pedagogical potential and can be of great help to practitioners who demand validity and thorough analysis as a foundation for brand strategy in practice.

Acknowledgements

First, we would like to thank Amy Laurens, commissioning editor for Business and Management, and Nicola Cupit, editorial assistant for Business and Management, at Routledge for their faith in the project and help along the way. We appreciate the opportunity to write and publish the second edition of this book.

We are truly honoured that some of the most inspirational people in brand management research have agreed to contribute to the book with their valuable thoughts and insights. We gratefully acknowledge Professor Leslie de Chernatony (Aston University) for writing the foreword and Professor Majken Schultz (Copenhagen Business School); visiting Professor Emerita Mary Jo Hatch (Copenhagen Business School); Adjunct Professor Joseph Plummer (Columbia Business School); E. B. Osborne; Professor Kevin Lane Keller (Tuck School of Business, Dartmouth College); Professor Susan Fournier (University of Boston); Professor of Marketing, Albert M. Muniz, Jr (DePaul University); Professor Thomas C. O'Guinn (University of Wisconsin) and former Professor Founder and President of Cultural Strategy Group, Douglas B. Holt for writing comments for the approach chapters.

On a personal note, Tilde would like to thank her parents Mette and Troels Heding for once a week taking me to the library bus as a child. My most heartfelt thanks go to my husband Flemming Pedersen for his admirable patience, love and support. For my part, I dedicate this book to the lights of my life – our children Iris, Marie and Erik.

Personally, Charlotte would also like to thank her parents Jytte and Børge Knudtzen for always supporting my not always straight path to my goals and dreams. Fulfilling this dream would never have been possible without the support, love and constructive criticism from my darling husband Michael F. Knudtzen. I dedicate this book to you and our kids Vega and Sander.

Jointly, we dedicate this book to the memory of philosopher of science Thomas Kuhn (1922–1996).

Part I

Setting the scene

1   Introduction

'As markets change, marketing theories must also change to accommodate them'
(Kozinets *et al.* 2010, p. 71)

Brands are interesting from many different perspectives. Corporations spend millions planning and implementing brand activities. New research is published and frameworks are developed on a daily basis in the attempt to find the holy grail of brand management. Since the mid-1980s, in particular, researchers and practitioners alike have explored the domain, scope and potential of the brand. Many different concepts, theoretical frameworks and ideas have seen the light of day and, as a result, a wide spectrum of different perspectives on how a brand ought to be conceptualized and managed is in play today. Therefore, to obtain an overview of the field of brand management is an overwhelming task.

This book provides a complete overview of brand management by taking you through seven brand approaches. These seven 'schools of thought' represent fundamentally different perceptions of the brand, the nature of the brand–consumer exchange and how brand equity is created and managed. Understanding the seven brand approaches separately provides a deep insight into the strengths and weaknesses of each approach, and hence the potential of brand management as a whole. This comprehensive understanding will enable the reader to create customized brand strategies matching the unique challenges and possibilities facing a brand at any time.

The seven approaches are:

- *the economic approach*: the brand as part of the traditional marketing mix;
- *the identity approach*: the brand as linked to corporate identity;
- *the consumer-based approach*: the brand as linked to consumer associations;
- *the personality approach*: the brand as a human-like character;
- *the relational approach*: the brand as a viable relationship partner;
- *the community approach*: the brand as the pivotal point of social interaction; and
- *the cultural approach*: the brand as part of the broader cultural fabric.

The identification of the seven approaches is based on an extensive analysis of the most influential brand research articles published between 1985 and 2015 (500+

articles from the *Journal of Marketing, Journal of Marketing Research, Journal of Consumer Research, Harvard Business Review* and *European Journal of Marketing*). This body of literature is supplemented with key non-research literature, which has shaped the field of brand management since the mid-1980s. The analysis has been conducted using a methodology uncovering the development of scientific knowledge. The methodology is based on a theory developed by American philosopher of science Thomas Kuhn (Kuhn 1996, Berthon *et al.* 2003, Bjerre *et al.* 2008) (read more about the methodology in Chapter 3). Since (scientific) knowledge is in constant development, new brand approaches most likely will emerge in the future.

Traditionally, brand management textbooks offer an introduction to main concepts and a wide array of theories, but often fail to discriminate between how different approaches result in very different outcomes and why. It is important for us to stress that the aim of this book is to deconstruct brand management to enhance understanding and reflection on the differences. The different approaches to brand management draw on many different scientific traditions such as economics, strategic management, organizational behaviour, consumer research, psychology and anthropology just to mention a few. We believe that understanding this will equip students and practitioners with a more precise understanding of brand management. A complete overview of brand management hence requires multidimensional thinking. Most textbooks take on this multidimensionality through the integration of several perspectives in all-encompassing frameworks. If you look at the list of brand approaches, you will most likely recognize many of the brand elements (e.g. personality, relation and consumer) that are encompassed in the classical textbook models (e.g. see Aaker's brand identity model (Aaker and Joachimsthaler 2002), Kapferer's brand prism (Kapferer 1997) and Keller's customer-based brand equity pyramid (Keller 2003)). The integrated frameworks are, however, not necessarily ideal when it comes to understanding and getting an overview of the field of brand management. Integration tends to blur the differences and similarities between different approaches in brand management and leaves the reader rather confused. Still, the integrated frameworks have the advantage that a strategist can take into consideration all relevant aspects, without losing oneself in details.

This book can be read in two ways: either as a stand-alone textbook or as a supplement to the textbooks by the above-mentioned authors. Read as a supplement, the book offers the inquiring reader the opportunity to understand the components of the traditional models in depth. Read alone, the book offers the opportunity to evaluate the most important schools of thought in brand management and create his or her brand management model featuring the components that are most relevant for the challenge at hand. Furthermore, it provides a chronological account of 30 years of brand management and marketing theory.

Resting on a comprehensive analysis of brand management as a scientific discipline, *Brand Management: Research, Theory and Practice* offers the reader a scientifically grounded overview of the main schools/approaches in brand management, and of their managerial implications. *Brand Management: Research, Theory and Practice* presents each approach separately and as an 'ideal type' based on the conviction that understanding the exact content of each approach and its origin will better equip the reader to combine different approaches, being in an educational or a managerial setting.

The four layers of an approach

The seven 'schools of thought' are 'clusters' of literature sharing distinct brand perceptions. In each cluster, there is coherence between assumptions, theories and methods/data. The three 'scientific layers' (assumptions, theories and methods/data) add up to managerial implications. The structure of the seven approach chapters is guided by this coherence between assumptions, theories, methods/data and managerial implications.

Assumptions are not to be understood in a high-flown sense of the word. Each approach holds its own implicit view of the nature of the brand and the premises of the brand–consumer exchange. Clarifying these assumptions facilitates the understanding of the theories, methods and managerial implications of each approach. Assumptions also illuminate the intangibles inherent in the nature of the brand.

The 'theory' layer represents the concepts, models and figures, which are key to the understanding of each brand approach. The third layer of 'methods and data' provides insight into what data to look for and how to collect them when researching the content of a specific brand strategy. These three scientific layers

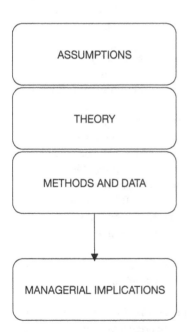

Figure 1.1 The logic of the approach chapters

add up to managerial implications guiding how the assumptions, theories and methods of each approach can be converted into a brand management strategy. The four layers comprising an approach are thus closely interconnected. The scientific clarification and the practical implications of the approaches will enable the reader to reflect on the compatibility of different elements of brand management strategies and ensure the creation of more accurate brand management.

True to its objective, *Brand Management: Research, Theory and Practice* does not provide one 'how to' solution meaning that we refrain from being normative when it comes to the overall management of a brand. Still, we are normative within each approach and leave it to the reader to reflect upon how different situations and circumstances require different means of action. It is our hope that this book will equip readers with an overview and a deeper understanding that will enable them to create splendid customized brand management strategies, and that this somewhat different approach to the communication of brand management will provide a sound platform for anyone interested in the field.

It is our hope that this book will provide its readers with a critical as well as a creative sense to be activated the next time they are presented with an easy-peasy solution to create a strong brand. Branding is indeed a complex management discipline and deserves attention and thoroughness for its potential to be fully unfolded.

A reader's guide

The chapters of this book fall into three parts.

Part I, 'Setting the scene', consists of three chapters: Introduction (Chapter 1), Overview: brand management 1985–2015 (Chapter 2) and Taxonomy of brand management 1985–2015 (Chapter 3).

Chapter 1: Introduction. The reader is introduced to the seven brand approaches, the literature analysis they stem from, and arguments supporting the importance of understanding these approaches separately before combining them in real-life brand management strategies.

Chapter 2: 'Overview: brand management 1985–2006' provides an overview of the chronological development brand management has undergone since it became a management priority in the mid-1980s and until 2006. The seven brand approaches are presented in a contextual and chronological setting. This overview facilitates the further reading of the seven brand approach chapters.

Chapter 3: 'Taxonomy of brand management 1985–2015' presents a precise overview of the chronological development of brand management. It is an overview as well as a checklist. The chapter will, through comparison, give a clear picture of the differences and similarities of the seven approaches.

Part II, 'Seven brand approaches', consists of seven chapters, one for each brand approach. Chapters 4–10 follow the structure presented below:

- There is a short introduction, followed by the assumptions of the approach.
- The theoretical building blocks of the approach are presented. This presentation is divided into supporting themes and core theme. Supporting themes clarify

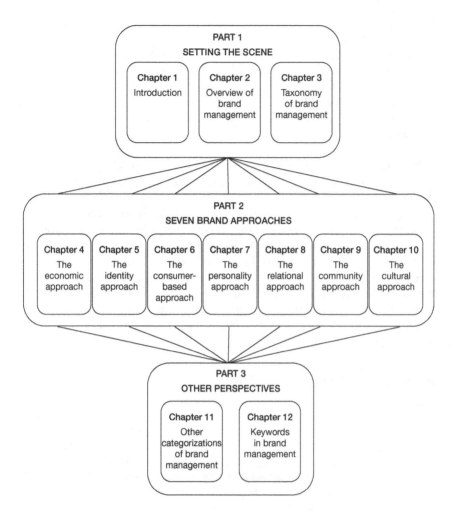

Figure 1.2 A reader's guide

the concepts that brand management 'borrows' from other disciplines, making up the core theme. The core theme clarifies the theoretical building blocks in a brand management context.

- Methods and data are reviewed. The approaches stem from different scientific traditions, which are all associated with specific methods and perceptions of validity. Understanding the methods associated with each approach enables the reader to request the best data possible.
- The managerial implications associated with the assumptions, theories, methods and data of each approach will round off the approach chapters. The assumed role of the marketer is explained as well as the managerial 'do's' and 'don'ts'.

- Each chapter is rounded off with a short overview of the academic evolution of the approach.
- Each chapter also features a text box overview focusing on present scope and future directions of the approach by one or two of its academic 'founding fathers'.
- You will find online supplementary material for each chapter on the book's accompanying website; for example, student questions, cases, supplementary reading.

Part III, 'Other perspectives', consists of two chapters: Chapter 11: 'Other categorizations of brand management' and Chapter 12: 'Keywords in brand management'.

Chapter 11: 'Other categorizations of brand management', provides a comparison between the proposed taxonomy of this textbook and other brand categorizations.

Chapter 12: 'Keywords in brand management'. The reader is provided with an introduction to key elements in brand management and brand management strategy. Being familiar with these elements is essential when reading the seven approach chapters, since each approach implies a distinct take on these elements. Besides the basic vocabulary of brand management, ideas from the approach chapters, which are important although not crucial to the understanding of the approach, are explained.

References and Further Reading

Aaker, D. A. and Joachimsthaler, E. (2002), *Brand Leadership*, Sydney: Free Press Business.

Berthon, P., Nairn, A. and Money, A. (2003), 'Through the paradigm funnel: Conceptual tool for literature analysis', *Marketing Education Review*, 13 (2): 55–66.

Bjerre, M., Heding, T. and Knudtzen, C. F. (2008), 'Using the dynamic paradigm funnel to analyse brand management', in K. Tollin and A. Caru (eds), *Strategic Market Creation: A New Perspective on Marketing and Innovation Management*, Chichester: Wiley, pp. 27–48.

Kapferer, J-N. (1997), *Strategic Brand Management: Creating and Sustaining Brand Equity Long Term*, London: Kogan Page.

Keller, K. L. (2003), *Strategic Brand Management: Building, Measuring, and Managing Brand Equity*, Upper Saddle River, NJ: Prentice Hall.

Kozinets, R. V., de Valck, K., Wojnicki, A. C. and Wilner, S. J. S. (2010), 'Networked narratives: understanding word-of-mouth marketing in online communities', *Journal of Marketing*, 74: 71–89.

Kuhn, T. S. (1996), *The Structure of Scientific Revolutions*, Chicago, IL: University of Chicago Press.

2   Overview

Brand management 1985–2015

Box 2.1 Learning objectives

The purpose of this chapter is to:

Provide an overview of brand management

- How brand management as a scientific discipline has evolved between 1985 and 2015.

Provide insight into the different paradigms in brand management 1985–2015

- A positivist paradigm ruled brand management in the first period of time.
- An interpretive paradigm surfaced over the course of the 1990s and has kept evolving in the new millennium.

Introduce the seven brand approaches

- The reader is introduced to the seven brand approaches before they are explored in detail in Part II of the textbook.

Understand three distinctly different periods of time

- The overall evolution of brand management can be divided into three periods of time.
- Each period displays different approaches in brand management.

This chapter provides an overview of how brand management has developed from its first academic conceptual beginning in 1985 and onwards (until early 2015 which is the time of revision). As described in the introduction, we have identified seven brand approaches forming the backbone of this book. But before going into detail with the seven approaches in Part II, we will present them briefly and explore the overall evolution that has taken place in brand management between 1985 and 2015. Weaknesses of one approach often lead to the development of a new one, and this interconnectedness of the seven brand management approaches is briefly introduced in this chapter. This overview of how brand management has evolved, the seven approaches, and the environmental drivers and changes that have triggered this evolution will facilitate the further reading and enable the reader to understand how the seven brand approaches are interconnected.

The seven approaches can be seen as links in a continuous evolution that slowly but surely has changed the field of brand management. It is important for us to stress that the birth of one approach does not imply the end of the 'previous' one(s), rather they complement each other. All the approaches have evolved and continue to do so. When we claim that an approach becomes important in a given period of time, it does not necessarily mean that it becomes dominant, but rather that it is novel, and that the research behind it is strong enough to constitute a new school of thought. Some of the older approaches are easy to criticize because much effort has been put into creating new, and more suitable, methods to explain consumption phenomena, such as brand loyalty and buying behaviour to name a few, since their day. Still, we believe that valuable things can be learned from all seven approaches. The first edition of this book was finished in 2008, while this edition was revised in early 2015. It is interesting that all seven approaches have been developed with publications of new research. In that respect, all approaches are still relevant and none can be deemed irrelevant.

In this introductory chapter, we will first describe the two brand management paradigms that have been present between 1985 and 2015. Thereafter, the seven brand approaches will be described. It makes sense to break the period of time down into three main periods. The periods are distinctively different and form the backdrop of the seven approaches. Understanding the dynamic movement from one period to another provides insight into the development of the body of research literature constituting the academic discipline of brand management.

Two brand management paradigms

Perhaps due to the elusive nature of the brand, the term 'brand paradigm' is often used at random in the branding discipline. The analysis of brand management that has provided the seven approaches framework or categorization of brand management presented in this book is based on the philosophy of science by Thomas Kuhn, who is one of the most influential contributors to knowledge about 'paradigms'. Without going into too much detail with the paradigm concept, we will touch briefly upon the paradigmatic development of brand management. From 1985 to 2015, two overriding paradigms have been present in the academic world of brand management: one with a positivistic point of departure and one of a constructivist or interpretive nature. The positivistic stance implies a notion of the brand being 'owned' by the marketer, who controls the communication to a passive recipient/consumer. Brand equity is perceived to be something created by the marketer, and the brand is seen as: 'A manipulable lifeless artefact (product plus that is created by its owners/managers and that can be positioned, segmented and used to create an image)' (Hanby 1999, p. 12).

The interpretive paradigm reflects on the nature of the brand and the value of brand equity as something created in the interaction between a marketer and an active consumer: 'As holistic entities with many of the characteristics of living beings' (Hanby 1999, p. 10), and 'As a living entity (with a personality with which we can form a relationship and that can change and evolve over time)' (Hanby 1999, p. 12).

A paradigm shift takes place in brand management over the course of the 1990s. It does not happen overnight but is an incremental process changing the discipline. The birth of the relational approach is an important indicator of the shift from a positivist paradigm with the more functionalistic brand perspective to an interpretive paradigm with a constructivist perspective on the brand and how it should be managed.

The same evolution is described in 'Brands and their meaning makers' by authors Chris T. Allen, Susan Fournier and Felicia Miller (2008) who categorize the development of brand management into two overarching paradigms, a 'received view' and an 'emergent paradigm'.

Table 2.1 Received view and emergent paradigm

	Received view	*Emergent paradigm*
Brands	Informational vehicles that support choice processes; risk reduction tools and simplifying heuristics	Meaning rich tools that help people live their lives
Guiding metaphor	Information	Meaning
Role of context in research	Context is noise	Context is everything
Central constructs of interest	Knowledge-based cognitions and attitudes	Experiential and symbolic aspects of consumption
Focal research domain	Purchase	Consumption
Guiding tenets	Simplification and control	Co-creation and complexity
Marketer's role	Owner and creator of brand assets	One of several brand meaning makers
Brand positioning assumptions	Consistency, constancy, simplicity	Complexity, mutability
Primary units of analysis	Individual consumers	Individuals, people in groups, consumers in cultures, cultural production mechanisms
Consumer's role	Passive recipients of marketer information	Active contributor to brand mechanisms
Consumer's central activity	Realizing functional and emotional benefits	Meaning making

Source: Adapted from Allen *et al.* (2008)

This distinction is based on a literature analysis and 'The received view on branding is squarely grounded in the disciplines of psychology and information economics' (Allen *et al.* 2008, p. 783) – hence related to the dominant consumer-based approach. 'The emergent paradigm' encapsulates the relational, community and cultural approaches (in our terminology), and the development towards the interpretive paradigm: 'By all counts we are living in a different branding world. Co-creation, collaborations, complexity, ambiguity, dynamism, loss of control, multivocality: such are the tenets of the new marketing world to which our brands must be held responsible' (Allen *et al.* 2008, p. 814).

Seven brand approaches

Analysing thirty years of brand management has been a fascinating journey, and the seven brand approaches can be described as the mountain peaks we have encountered along the way. Despite the above quote, none of the approaches can be declared dead. All are still developing and growing with new research and publications by researchers representing the branding perspective in question. An approach is not a paradigm in itself (at least not in the original Kuhnian sense of the word) but a particular 'school of thought' governing the global understanding of the nature of the brand, the consumer perspective and the methods associated with the scientific tradition behind the approach. Under the umbrella of a paradigm, different approaches are able to coexist.

The seven approaches are presented in the chronological order in which they have appeared in the data set of our analysis (please refer to Chapter 3 for the methodology and data set behind the taxonomy of this textbook). Going through the period of time we have studied, it makes sense to divide it into three sections. The first period of time is 1985–92, the second is 1993–99 and the last one begins in 2000 and onwards.

In the first period, brand management focused on the company behind the brand and the actions the company would take to influence the consumer. In the next period of time, the receiver of brand communication is the main point of interest, and brand management adopts a human perspective on the nature of the brand. In the last period, it is the contextual and cultural forces behind consumption choices and brand loyalty that are investigated in the groundbreaking articles and new literature.

In this section, we will briefly describe the three periods, explain how the seven approaches are anchored in them and touch upon the dynamic development leading from one period to the next.

1985–1992: company / sender focus

In the infancy of brand management, the research focuses on the company as sender of brand communication. This focus forms the background of the two first approaches in brand management: the economic approach and the identity approach.

The research of the economic approach is centred on the possibilities of the company to manage the brand via the marketing mix elements: product, placement, price and promotion, and how these factors can be manipulated to affect consumer brand choice. Quantitative data are the principal rule in this period. Researchers often use either data from supermarket scanner systems or laboratory experiments as the empirical basis of data. In the identity approach, research focuses on how the identity of the company as a whole can shape a coherent brand message that is communicated to all shareholders.

It is assumed that the brand is 'owned' by the company, but influenced by multiple stakeholders, and that the brand is communicated in a linear fashion from the company to the consumer.

The economic approach: the brand as part of the traditional marketing mix

The point of departure for brand management is that it is a breakaway discipline from the broad scope of marketing. Hence, the discipline starts out with a research environment marked by traditional marketing mix theory (the Four P's). The creation of brand value is investigated as influenced by changes in, for example, distribution channels, price modifications and promotions. A functionalistic brand perspective applies, as does a consumer perspective based on the notion of the 'economic man'. The economic consumer bases consumption decisions on rational considerations, and the exchange between the brand and the consumer is assumed to be isolated tangible transactions. Laboratory settings and scanner data are illustrative of the methodologies and (always quantitative) data. The marketer is definitely in charge of brand value creation, and hence consumers are believed to 'receive' and understand the messages 'sent' to them from the marketer exactly as intended.

The identity approach: the brand as linked to corporate identity

The economic approach lays the foundation for brand management as an independent scientific discipline, but one more stream of research is also influential during the first decades of this inquiry. The identity approach behind the notion of corporate branding is still very influential and under constant theoretical development. Especially, in the European research environment, the brand as linked with corporate identity is a very influential school of thought. Focusing on corporate identity, the brand is also primarily perceived as an entity 'owned' by the marketer (even though that perception has changed to encompass multiple stakeholders as the approach has evolved). Integration of the brand on all levels within and outside the organization is key in the management of the brand. The marketer (as corporation) is in charge of brand value creation. Processes of organizational culture and corporate construction of identity are key processes.

1993–99: human/receiver focus

The shift in attention towards the receiver of brand communication instigates a new period of time entirely different from the period 1985–93. New and groundbreaking research articles investigate the receiver of communication, and knowledge from different veins of human psychology is adapted to brand management theory. The human perspective is two-sided: the consumer is investigated closely and different human brand perspectives are coming into play. The humanistic and individualistic approaches – namely the consumer-based approach, the personality approach and the relational approach – see the light of day in these years.

During 1993–99, data collection becomes 'softer'; quantitative and qualitative, as well as mixed research designs are applied to the studies of the brand–consumer exchange. The relational approach is the first approach founded on an entirely qualitative study.

The consumer-based approach: the brand as linked with consumer associations

In 1993, Kevin Lane Keller founded a completely new approach to brand management. The brand is perceived as a cognitive construal in the mind of the consumer. It is assumed that a strong brand holds strong, unique and favourable associations in the minds of consumers. In this fashion, attention shifts from the sender towards the receiving end of brand communication. The consumer is the 'owner' of the brand in this approach, but still an assumption of linear communication applies. The consumer perspective of this approach is rooted in cognitive psychology, and in this tradition, the computer is the main metaphor for man as a consumer. This consumer perspective implies linear communication because the marketer is perceived to be able to 'program' the consumer into intended action. This school of thought has since become very dominant in brand management especially in the United States.

The personality approach: the brand as a human-like character

Another mountaintop in brand management was established in 1997, when a research study into brand personality was published. This study shows that consumers have a tendency to endow brands with human-like personalities. It is the 'human' brand perspective and the symbol-consuming consumer that are in the spotlight in this approach. Consumers endow brands with personalities and use these personalities in a dialogue-based exchange of symbolic value for their individual identity construction and expression. The personality approach is rooted in human personality psychology and uses quantitative scaling techniques in a combination with more explorative methods to identify and measure brand personality. The personality approach is a prerequisite for, and very much associated with, the relational approach.

The relational approach: the brand as a viable relationship partner

The idea of a dyadic relationship between brand and consumer profoundly changed the academic discipline of brand management. The notion of the brand being a viable relationship partner builds on the same human brand metaphor as the personality approach. The approach extends the dialogue-based approach to brand management as instigated in the personality approach. The relational approach is rooted in the philosophical tradition of existentialism and the methods are of a phenomenological nature. These roots imply that a paradigm shift is taking place because they are so fundamentally different from the roots of research methods used in the first approaches to brand management.

2000–2015: cultural/context focus

Profound theoretical changes emerge both from academic discussions and from significant environmental changes affecting how humans consume brands. Environmental changes often imply a development of our theoretical frameworks because new phenomena arise that cannot be explained by means of the existing theories. A need for new theoretical tools to explain new phenomena is very much the driver behind the two newest approaches (the community approach and the cultural approach). Technological and cultural changes have profoundly changed the rules of the game in brand management in the last period of time.

The new phenomena calling for new theories are phenomena such as autonomous consumers, brand icons, anti-branding movements and Internet-based brand communities. The most novel and innovative research looks at these new consumption patterns through new lenses trying to explain the context of brand consumption.

Two approaches can be identified in this period of time: the community approach and the cultural approach. The community approach brings influences from anthropological consumption studies, socio-cultural influences and consumer empowerment. The cultural approach explores how brands are an inherent part of our culture and explains how playing an active role in mainstream culture can turn a brand into an icon. Hence, cultural and contextual influences add new perspectives to the discipline of brand management from 2000 to 2015.

The community approach: the brand as the pivotal point of social interaction

The community approach is based on anthropological research into so-called brand communities. Brand value is created in these communities where a brand serves as the pivotal point of social interaction among consumers. This approach thus adds an understanding of the social context of consumption to the overall picture of brand management. This understanding has become a prerequisite for managing many brands, especially after the Internet has profoundly changed the market place. In the community approach, the marketer deals with 'autonomous' groups of consumers who are able to collectively influence marketing actions and potentially 'take over' the brand and take it into a direction not at all intended by the marketer. The field of brand management has come a long way from the assumptions of linear communication behind the earlier approaches to accepting the chaotic autonomous consumer forces in this approach.

The cultural approach: the brand as part of the broader cultural fabric

Just like the community approach, the cultural approach emanates around the millennium. The brand is seen as a cultural artefact in this approach and has as its backbone a theory of how to build an iconic brand. The approach borrows from the scientific tradition of cultural studies and makes use of a wide variety of qualitative methods. The attention has shifted from the transaction between a marketer and a consumer (or groups of consumers) to a macro perspective. The approach both explains how embedding the brand in cultural forces can be used strategically to build an iconic brand as well as take ideological issues into account.

It is important for us to stress that none of the approaches is obsolete and, hence, only of historical interest. At the time of writing (early 2015), there is academic activity in all of the seven approaches.

Summary

In marketing research, seven brand management approaches have been identified during 1985–2015: the economic approach, the identity approach, the consumer-based approach, the personality approach, the relational approach, the community approach and the cultural approach. These approaches reflect a development where the focus has shifted from the sending end of brand communications in the first period of time; they have then turned their attention to the receiving end in the second period and finally have addressed contextual and cultural influences on the brand to the global understanding of brand consumption.

Somewhere around the birth of the relational approach in 1998, a paradigm shift is instigated in brand management (see the above distinction between the received view and the emergent paradigm), with an implied shift from quantitative to qualitative methods, an acknowledgement of consumers' ownership of the brand, and an embrace of the more chaotic forces in consumer culture.

Box 2.2 Overview of brand management 1985–2015

Two paradigms	Three periods of time	Seven brand approaches
Positivistic	Company/sender focus	The economic approach
The identity approach
	Human/receiver focus	The consumer-based approach
The personality approach
Constructivist/ interpretive	Cultural/context focus	The relational approach
The community approach
The cultural approach

Box 2.2 depicts how the paradigm shift has taken place somewhere around the birth of the relational approach, and how the three periods of time form the background of the seven brand approaches. This is only a brief introduction to a fascinating journey into the world of brand management. The interconnected web of assumptions, brand perspective, consumer perspective, theories and methods of each approach will be explained in Part II of this book.

References

Allen, C. T., Fournier, S. and Miller, F. (2008), 'Brands and their meaning makers', in C. P. Haugtvedt, P. M. Herr and F. R. Kardes (eds), *Handbook of Consumer Psychology*, New York: Lawrence Erlbaum Associates, pp. 781–822.

Hanby, T. (1999), 'Brands dead or alive', *Journal of Market Research Society*, 41 (1): 7–19.

3   Taxonomy of brand management 1985–2015

Box 3.1 Learning objectives

The purpose of this chapter is to:

Provide an introduction to the Kuhn-based taxonomy of brand management 1985–2015.

Provide an overview of the seven brand approaches.

After the short introduction to the seven brand approaches, in this chapter, we provide an overview of the different perspectives on key subjects in brand management reflected in the seven approaches to brand management. The taxonomy (Figure 3.1) sums up the key learning points from the seven approach chapters. The background of this book and taxonomy is a systematic analysis of 500+ brand management research articles spanning the period of 1985–2015. The analysis has been executed in accordance with the logic of the methodology in the Dynamic Paradigm Funnel (Berthon *et al.* 2003, Bjerre *et al.* 2008). The Dynamic Paradigm Funnel is based on theory about how science evolves: the philosophy of science developed by Thomas Kuhn. As mentioned briefly in Chapter 1, this proposed taxonomy of 30 years of brand management is based on an analysis of 500+ articles from the most influential marketing journals (*Journal of Marketing, Journal of Marketing Research, Journal of Consumer Research, Harvard Business Review* and *European Journal of Marketing*). The journals are selected due to their academic influence (Hult *et al.*1997) (the first four) and the last one to add a European perspective to the data set. The criteria for selecting the articles are that they feature the words 'brand' or 'branding' in either the title or abstract (as we wanted a dedicated focus on the subject). These 500+ articles emerging in this search became our data set and are thus not chosen on a subjective basis. According to the Kuhnian logic, the 500+ articles were then assigned a number:

* 1: the main focus of the research article is empirical observations. The existing set of assumptions, theories, methodologies are not questioned in the article;

- 2: methodologies are questioned;
- 3: theories are questioned;
- 4: assumptions are questioned.

Low numbers reflect paradigmatic calm in the academic community. Rising numbers reflect rising instability and paradigmatic turbulence in the research community – anomalies are observed 'in nature' and the community does not have the right tools (methodological, theoretical or assumption-wise). The level 4 articles are very few, but the ones offering something are completely new – often a groundbreaking article with a whole new perspective as a possible solution to unexplainable anomalies (Berthon *et al.* 2003).

An example is the meaningful, brand-related interaction among drivers of vintage Saabs in the United States, written vividly about by researchers Albert Muñiz, Jr and Thomas O'Guinn in their 'founding father' comment on Chapter 7. No theoretical framework could describe this interaction (the anomaly) and hence they began researching 'brand communities'. The rest is brand management history – they came up with a groundbreaking new theory (a number 4 article) and laid the groundwork for a new approach. When a new perspective is presented, other researchers join in establishing the approach. Some articles question the perspective, some validate it and some provide new theoretical insight and thereby expand the theoretical knowledge (without questioning the assumptions). And in that process, a 'school of thought' is founded.

Taxonomy of brand management 1985–2015

In Figure 3.1, the most significant traits of each approach are presented side by side. By going through the characteristics of each approach, a clear overview of the seven brand approaches is gained. It is important to notice that each approach is presented as an 'ideal type'. We emphasize the ideal type of each approach rather than eventual nuances and similarities, because it enables us to understand the differences between the mindsets underlying each approach. For example, the perception of the brand–consumer exchange in the identity approach has evolved over time from a perception of linear communication towards an assumed co-creation of brand value. In practice, most of the approaches have evolved and often embraced new developments and accommodating critique. The differences between the approaches in practice are hence more blurred than they are as presented in the framework of this book. The most important developments and discussions are included in each approach chapter, but we have chopped a toe and squeezed a heel in order to provide our readers with as much clarity as possible. In the following, we will go through the main categorizations of the model.

The time of origin (or academic conceptualization) of each brand approach is more or less precise. Some of the approaches are born from a specific, ground-breaking article introducing a whole new brand perspective. These approaches can be dated to a specific publication. Others emerge incrementally and from the hands of several researchers, they can only be dated approximately. The seven approaches

	The economic approach	The identity approach	The consumer-based approach
			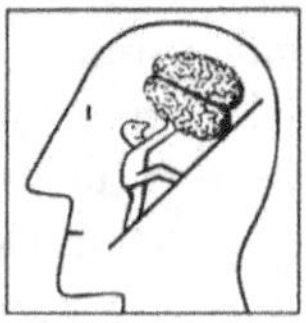
Time of origin	Before 1985	Mid-1990s	1993
Key reading	McCarthy, E. J. (1964), *Basic Marketing, a managerial approach*, Richard, D. Irwin, Inc. Borden, N. (1964), 'The concept of the marketing mix', in G. Schwartz (ed.) *Science in Marketing*	Hatch, M. J. And Schultz, M. (1997) 'Relations between organizational culture, identity and image', *European Journal of Marketing*	Keller, K. L. (1993), 'Conceptualizing, measuring and managing customer-based brand equity', *Journal of Marketing*
Keywords	The economic man, transaction theory, marketing mix (Four P's)	Corporate branding, identity, organizational culture, vision, image	Customer-based brand equity, brand image, brand associations
Brand perspective	Functional	Corporate	Cognitive construal
Consumer perspective	Economic man	Stakeholder	Computer
Scientific tradition	Positivism, empiricism	Socio-economic constructivism/ interpretivism	Cognitive psychology
Methods	Scanner panel data, laboratory setting, quantitative data	Organizational culture studies and organizational values, heuristic methods and storytelling	Cognitively based association maps, interviews, projective techniques
Managerial keyword	Control	Linear communication	Programming
Supporting theories	The economic man, marketing mix	Organizational identity, corporate identity, image, reputation	Cognitive psychology the information processing consumer
Brand value creation	Marketer ↓ Consumer	Marketer ↓ Consumer	Marketer ↑ Consumer

Figure 3.1 Taxonomy of brand management 1985–2015

The personality approach	The relational approach	**The community approach**	The cultural approach
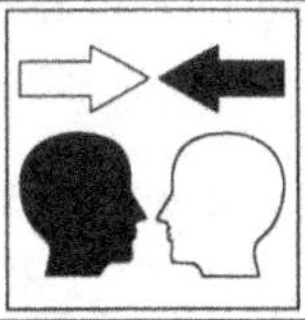			
1997	1998	2001	Around 2000
Aaker, J. L. (1997), 'Dimensions of brand personality', *Journal of Marketing Research*. Plummer, J. (1985) 'How personality makes a difference', *Journal of Advertising Research*	Fournier, S. (1998) 'Consumers and their brands: developing relationship theory in consumer research', *Journal of Consumer Research*	Muñiz, A. M. Jr, and O'Guinn, T. C. (2001), 'Brand community', *Journal of Consumer Research*	Holt, D. B. (2002) 'Why do brands cause trouble? A dialectical theory of consumer culture and branding', *Journal of Consumer Reasearch*
Personality, self, congruity, archetypes	Dyadic brand – consumer relationship, brand relationship quality	Brand communities, brandfests, the brand triad, Web 2.0	Globalization, popular culture, brand icons, ideology
Human	Human	Social	Cultural
Psychological	Existential being	Tribe member	Homo mercans
Human personality, psychology	Existentialism, phenomenology	Anthropology, micro-perspective	Cultural studies
A mix of quantitative and qualitative methods, scaling techniques	Depth interviews, life story method	Ethnography, netnography	Macro-level analysis on micro-level data
Symbolic exchange	Friendship	Discretion	Bird perspective
Personality, comsumer self, brand self-congruity	Animism, relationship theory	Community theory, subcultures of consumption	Cultural consumption, doppelgänger brands, anti-branding discourse, CSR, global ideoscapes
Marketer ↕ Consumer	Marketer ↕ Consumer	Marketer ↗↖ Con-sumer ↔ Con-sumer	Marketer → Culture Consumer ↑

Figure 3.1 Continued

are presented in a chronological order reflecting when the approaches were conceptualized in the context of brand management. In the cases of the easy-to-date approaches, the ground-breaking articles are identified as key readings. In the other approaches, key readings are research articles central to and representative of the approach; written by the most important and influential researchers constituting the approach.

Key words are the main concerns of the approach. The brand perspective describes the overall 'take' on the brand in the given approach. We have focused not only on clarifying the different brand perspectives, but also on the different consumer perspectives associated with the different brand perspectives.

Each brand approach can be traced to a specific scientific tradition. The clarification of the respective traditions implies differences in consumer perceptions and methods and also hints towards differences in philosophical standpoints. These aspects of the proposed taxonomy might seem difficult and over the top, but in our experience, it actually facilitates the understanding of the discipline to add the assumed, 'taken for granted' stuff, as it guides the overall concerns of each approach: what is investigated; which methods are presumed valid; view of man (as consumer) and so on. When it comes to methods, the model makes it very clear that the methods formally applied to brand management research have developed from a focus on quantitative methods to the use of a wide variety of methods, and that they are primarily qualitative in the later approaches.

At the heart of brand management is the ability to create brand value. The arrows reflect the implied perception of the brand value creation in the brand–consumer exchange. The managerial implications of each approach are complex, but we have tried to sum them up in seven different words. The managerial key words evolve from reflecting control with the process of brand value creation to key words reflecting a perception of the brand manager having to acknowledge the influence of other forces on the brand value creation. In the theoretical building blocks of each approach, we have presented core themes and supporting themes. The supporting themes form the backdrop of the main theory of the approach, and reflecting upon them should facilitate the understanding of each approach.

The model also contributes with an overview of how it is assumed that brand management can endow brands with value. The two first approaches (economic and identity) assumed that brand value is created in the domain of the marketer. This brand value creation shifted in the third approach (consumer-based approach), where it is a thorough understanding of the consumer who is presumed to be at the heart of superior brand value creation. In the personality approach and the relational approach, the creation of brand value is presumed to be dialogue-based and takes place in a dyadic exchange between the consumer and marketer. The community approach adds the triadic brand–consumer relationship to the assumptions of what drives brand value creation: making the arrow point in three different directions, because real brand value is assumed to be created not so much in the interaction between marketer and consumer, as was the case in the previous approaches, but in the interaction between consumers. In the last approach, the addition of macro-level culture makes the assumed brand value creation very complicated, because the marketer is assumed to be dependent on macro and consumer culture more than on the exchange with one or more consumers.

Concluding remarks

This book is a revised version of a 2008 publication based on an analysis of a data set covering the period 1985–2006. The period from 2007–2015 has added 200+ new articles to the data set, which has resulted in thorough updates of each approach. New approaches have not emerged, but publication of interesting new insights within all seven approaches has resulted in thorough updates of all chapters. As a new feature of this edition, we have added a timeline at the end of each approach chapter providing a fast overview of the development of the approach. Where do the ideas come from, when was the founding theory published and which significant new studies have developed the approach? These timelines are based only on the research articles from the data set – not supplementary literature.

The taxonomy provides much detail to enhance understanding of brand management, both when it comes to width and when it comes to depth. The fact that the taxonomy proposes seven approaches to brand management provides a very detailed insight into the subject. Furthermore, the chosen background of research articles and Kuhnian philosophy of science has provided the taxonomy with a detailed and logical structure based on the interconnectedness between assumptions, theories, methods and data and managerial implications. This structure

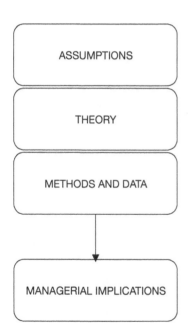

Figure 3.2 The logic of the approach chapters

provides the reader with a thorough and deep understanding of brand management as an academic discipline, and it is our hope that it is a step in the direction of understanding the elusive nature of the brand better.

References and further reading

Berthon, P., Nairn, A. and Money, A. (2003), 'Through the paradigm funnel: conceptual tool for literature analysis', *Marketing Education Review*, 13 (2): 55–66.

Bjerre, M., Heding, T. and Knudtzen, C. (2008), 'Using the dynamic paradigm funnel to analyse brand management', in K. Tollin and A. Caru (eds), *Strategic Market Creation: A New Perspective on Marketing and Innovation Management*, Chichester: Wiley, pp. 27–48.

Hult, G. T. M., Neese, W. T. and Bashaw, E. R. (1997), 'Faculty perceptions of marketing journals', *Journal of Marketing Education*, 19 (1): 37–52.

Kuhn, T. S. (1996), *The Structure of Scientific Revolutions*, Chicago, IL: University of Chicago Press.

Tellis, G. J., Chandy, R. K. and Ackerman, D. S. (1999), 'In search of diversity: The record of major marketing journals', *Journal of Marketing Research*, 36 (1): 120–31.

Part II

Seven brand approaches

4   The economic approach

Fast-moving consumer goods manufacturer Procter & Gamble gave birth to the first management practices of brand management with their product management approach. The theories underlining the way this multinational producer of fast-moving consumer goods during the 1930s dealt with brand management were mainly borrowed from neoclassical economics and classical marketing theory. The fast-moving consumer goods industry has since played a major role in the evolution of brand management research and practice, and the ideas are reflected in the economic approach.

The economic approach builds on one of the most fundamental concepts in marketing, namely the idea that the right marketing mix will generate optimal sales. Neil Borden first introduced the marketing mix concept when he deducted twelve factors that management should consider when planning and implementing marketing strategy. One can argue that the whole idea of brand management really rests on his initial factor theory of marketing (Borden 1964). The twelve elements reflected internal considerations and relevant market forces in relation to marketing strategy.

E. Jerome McCarthy later narrowed Borden's framework down into the Four P's framework we know today (McCarthy 1960). The Four P's (product, place, price and promotion) have since been immortalized by numerous marketing books and become everyday marketing practice in countless marketing departments around the world and often make up the first introduction students get to marketing and brand management.

Brand management adopted the Four P's concept from marketing. The analysis behind the taxonomy of this textbook begins in 1985 and the literature from this time is dominated by this worldview. During the mid and late 1980s, much research was focused on exploring how different factors of the marketing mix affect consumers' brand choice. During the late 1990s and the turn of the millennium, research into marketing mix elements has evolved from measuring how marketing mix elements influence brand performance based on sale to how the marketing mix elements affect brand equity in the long run.

This chapter provides the reader with an overview of the assumptions, theoretical building blocks and concepts that have shaped the economic approach. Finally, we will assess its applicability in practice.

Box 4.1 Learning objectives

The purpose of this chapter is to:

Understand assumptions: Consumption choices are rational and brand–consumer exchange linear

- Consumers base consumption decisions on rational parameters and the exchange between brand and consumer is perceived to be linear, functional and transaction-based.

Understand theory: Transaction theory and marketing mix

- The supporting theories – transaction theory and marketing mix (the Four P's) – make up the theoretical framework of the economic approach.

Understand methods: Large-scale scanner panel and quantitative studies

- The economic approach primarily uses quantitative methods to explore how manipulating elements of the marketing mix affects consumer brand choice and the long-term effects on brand equity.

Learn how to manage with the Four P's

- The marketing mix can help the brand manager plan and execute a brand strategy within the economic approach.

- An overview of the strengths and weaknesses of the economic approach and the key points of critique to this perspective on branding.

Understand the academic evolution of the economic approach

- The economic approach builds on marketing mix and the Four P's.

- Perspectives have evolved from short-term perspective on sales figures to also measuring brand performance.

The economic approach is the first approach to branding described in this book and is thereby the approach upon which the consecutive brand management approaches rest. Since the economic approach represents the foundation for how brands have been (and are) managed, it is important to understand the line of thought behind assumptions, theoretical framework, methods and the management of a brand according to these. It is also important for us to stress that, even though this approach is the oldest one in this context, it is still academically and managerially relevant and new research is still being published in 2015 based on this brand perspective.

The marketing mix – or the Four P's – of the economic approach is one of the first attempts at categorization in the early days of marketing. It put order to the discipline and helped conceptualize it, making it possible to test, validate and alter theoretical frameworks (Van Waterschoot and Van Den Bulte 1992). The Four P's are based on certain assumptions about how consumers choose products and what marketers can do to facilitate that choice. It is important to understand this background in depth, because it will enable the reader to get an idea of the strengths and weaknesses of the economic approach and how these strengths and weaknesses, among other parameters, have influenced the evolution of brand theory over the years.

The chapter is divided into four main sections, according to the structure laid out in the introduction: assumptions, theoretical framework, methods and data and management considerations and guidelines. The assumptions describe the implicit view of the nature of the brand and the premises of the brand–consumer exchange. The theoretical framework describes the concepts and models key to the economic approach. Methods and data provide insight into what data to look for and how to collect it. These three scientific layers add up to a managerial 'how-to' guide for how the assumptions, theories and methods of the approach can be converted into a brand management strategy in practice.

The economic approach is the first identified approach in brand management and it serves as a prerequisite for planning and execution of brand management strategies still today. But branding has both scientifically and in practice evolved drastically and the assumptions of how and why consumers choose brands and the brand–consumer exchange as a linear mechanism has been subject to much criticism. Therefore, this chapter will be rounded off with a discussion of the key points of critique, which serves as a natural point of departure for understanding the development of the forthcoming approaches in brand management.

Assumptions of the economic approach

In the economic approach, a key assumption is that the brand can be controlled and managed by the sender (company). If management gets the marketing mix right (the Four P's), then the brand will be successful and strong. Consumers, who perceive and evaluate brand messages rationally, are perceived to be more or less passive receivers of marketing messages. This perception of the consumer originates from the concept of the economic man and transaction theory about the exchange of goods.

Microeconomics and the economic man

The assumptions and premises of the economic approach have their origin in the ideas of exchange from microeconomic theory. The model of exchange in microeconomics is purely theoretical, which means that the assumptions and key models are the result of theorizing rather than empirical research. In *The Wealth of Nations*, Adam Smith (1937) argued that if one would let market forces govern the allocation of resources and the exchange of goods, then an 'invisible hand' would allocate resources in a way that optimizes both the individual and societal beneficial use of available resources. In this perception of market forces lies an assumption that individuals pursue self-interest and attempt to maximize their own revenue or functional utility.

The principle of the 'invisible hand' assumes that resources are allocated according to where they will give the highest possible functional outcome or revenue, because efficient methods of production will be adopted by manufacturers in order to accommodate the utility-maximizing behaviour displayed by the individual. Marketing is an academic discipline stemming from microeconomics, just as brand management stems from marketing. Thereby, it is very logical that these assumptions govern the first brand management approach.

The economic man is a key concept in this line of thinking and the concept most often used to describe these assumptions about human behaviour:

- Human behaviour is guided by rational parameters.
- Consumers have 'perfect information' about the available alternatives.
- The exchange between two parties is perceived as an isolated event.
- Consumers are constrained by limited income, which forces them to find ways of maximizing the utility of their income.

The logic is hence applicable both at the level of the market and the individual. In a consumption and brand management context, this means that a consumer will always go for the deal that provides the best functional utility related to the price of the product.

'Perfect information' is another keyword in this approach. The economic man is not only assumed to be able to oversee all available choices, but also able to evaluate all of them and choose the best functional deal. Thereby we are dealing with a consumer able and willing to take in 'perfect information' in order to make the most rational choice in any situation.

The economic approach rests upon a positivist research ideal. This line of thought is very much in opposition to the stream of qualitative research methods that have become more and more dominant in marketing research in recent decades. In the quantitative methods, objectiveness is important and phenomena are presumed to be measurable. The objectivity of data is important for validity, and closeness to the subject of research is not essential.

The brand–consumer exchange and transaction cost theory

Transaction cost theory is closely linked to the neoclassical microeconomic logic explained above and defines the firm theoretically in relation to the marketplace. The theory of transaction costs builds on the same assumption as the principle of the 'invisible hand' that all actors involved in the exchange of goods will exhibit behaviour of optimization. From a manufacturer point of view, not only is it important to supply the best deal, but from a marketing perspective, it is equally important to reduce the transaction costs associated with the search, purchase and consumption of a product. It is on these assumptions of behaviour of optimization and minimization of transaction costs that the theories of the economic approach to brand management are based.

Consumers search for the best possible deal and are assumed to consider every transaction cost before choosing the right brand or product. If the barrier of transaction costs is too high – if, for example it is too difficult to find and buy the product – then the consumer might choose another product even though it might not deliver maximum utility compared to other products, or in relation to price.

In the economic approach, it is therefore crucial that transaction costs are minimized. The marketer can do this by ensuring that the right product, at the right price, is made known and accessible to consumers through adequate distribution (place) and promotion. This will ensure that consumers are always aware of the product whenever they need it and that they have easy access to purchasing the product. Hence branding aims at minimizing consumers' transaction costs and facilitates consumers' decision processes because it diminishes the barriers to an 'economic man' brand choice behaviour. The exchange between the brand and the consumer is hence perceived to be of a transaction-like nature, where the consumer acts as an economic man who rationally evaluates all available choices and chooses the best available offer. The communication between the brand and the consumer is perceived to be linear and functional, where consumers will act according to market stimuli with a certain predictable brand choice behaviour.

Consumption is hence perceived to be the result of consumers' insatiable desire for goods and services and is not influenced by social interaction, culture or the well-being of others. Brands are regarded as signals that can reduce uncertainty and barriers associated with any transaction. Hence the economic approach does not, like the other approaches described in this book, include consumers' hedonic consumptions satisfying more emotional and symbolic wants and desires. Furthermore, the brand–consumer exchange is perceived merely as an exchange of goods through isolated transactions, as opposed to the other approaches, where the exchange between brand and consumer is perceived more broadly as a relationship with different characteristics, depending on the specific approach. So what does this difference in the perception of the brand–consumer exchange imply? It means that transactions are analysed as isolated events, as opposed to a lasting relationship, because the primary goal is to achieve the next transaction – or sale.

In the theoretical models, there is hence no interaction between the brand and the consumer. It is assumed that brand choice is based on a linear communication, where the marketer sends off brand messages in the shape of a product, price, a placement and promotions, and consumers receive these messages and act on them

Figure 4.1 The brand-consumer exchange of the economic approach

accordingly (see Figure 4.1). The brand–consumer exchange is hence perceived to consist of a predictable isolated transaction without interactivity. The brand can be managed and controlled entirely by the company.

Summary

The assumptions of the economic approach are based on neoclassical micro-economics of how market forces allocate resources most efficiently through the principle of the 'invisible hand' and classic marketing theory. The consumer is assumed to be able to make rationally based brand consumption choices that maximize functional utility – and always choose whatever brand delivers the best utility value compared with the price. The theoretical apparatus is based on the basic ideas from transaction marketing, where it is assumed that the exchange between brand and consumer consists of isolated transactions rather than an ongoing relationship. The primary goal of brand communication is hence to ensure that consumers are aware of the fine qualities of the brand at the right time and place and for the right price through linear communication from the brand to the consumer.

Supporting theories of the economic approach

The economic approach builds on traditional economic theory of exchange where the principles of the invisible hand and the economic man, and transaction cost theory guide behaviour. This section will account for each of the supporting theories that make up the theoretical framework. The supporting theories of the economic approach to brand management consist respectively of transaction cost theory, it describes the transaction-based perspective on exchange between brand and consumer, and the second, the marketing mix, classification scheme adopted from marketing, the 4P configuration of actions and measurements used when building a brand strategy.

Supporting theory: transaction cost

The principle of the invisible hand and the perception of the consumer as an economic man imply that any consumption choice is the result of a reasoning process, where the involved partners will choose whatever will maximize their own profit or functional utility. There are however some exceptions to this rule, because consumers do not always display utility-maximizing consumption choice behaviour. Consumers, for example, do not have perfect information and access-ibility to all the choices available, or consumers can have switching costs when shifting from one brand to another. Transaction cost theory explains these exceptions and barriers to the 'perfect' exchange. Transaction costs are barriers to utility maximization, and the goal for brand management in the economic approach is to eliminate these transaction costs and facilitate that transactions will take place. The next transaction is the ultimate goal in the economic approach. A good measurement of whether or not a brand strategy is efficient is measuring the number of transactions – or sales figures. The transactional perspective has a rather short-term time perspective, because transactions are perceived to be isolated events, and the primary focus for the marketer is the next transaction rather than relationship building. Price and the functional product quality are believed to be important parameters for consumers. Managerial efforts for companies operating in a trans-actional momentum are often directed to the rather tactical management and improvement of the marketing mix, to target large numbers of consumers with mass communication, and ensuring product quality, sold in the right place, for the right price (Hultman and Shaw 2003).

The barriers to transactions, described in the transaction cost theory, impede consumers' ability to act rationally because prior to any exchange or transaction they are limited by bounded rationality. With the concept of bounded rationality, it is acknowledged that consumers are not able to have a complete overview of options and to cognitively grasp all information about available alternatives. Because consumers are not able to make perfect rationally based consumption decisions, it is crucial that the marketer facilitates transactions by providing the consumer with the right information about the product, sets the right price and ensures that it is available at all relevant points of contact. Transactions barriers are hence the instigator of the next theoretical building block: the concept of marketing mix also known as the Four P's.

Supporting theory: The Four P's

The marketing mix originally offered a managerial planning tool to facilitate transactions and exchange of goods. According to the American Marketing Association in 1985: 'Marketing is the process of planning and executing the conception, pricing, promotion and distribution of ideas, goods and services to create exchanges that satisfy individual and organisational objectives' (Hultman and Shaw 2003, p. 37). The objective with the marketing mix is, through analysis, to ensure profitable spending of marketing resources adhering not only to marketing but also to other functions that have an influence on the effectiveness of the relation between the company and its markets. In this line of thought, the function of the marketer is described as:

> an empiricist seeking in any situation to devise a profitable 'pattern' or 'formula' of marketing operations from among the many procedures and policies were open to him. If he was a 'mixer of ingredients', what he designed was a 'marketing mix'.
>
> (Borden 1964, p. 9)

The term marketing mix refers to the mixture of elements useful in pursuing a certain market response and an efficient connection between the company and the market place by employing attributes related to the Four P's (product, price, place and promotion). Brand managers are assumed to be able to control consumers' brand choice behaviour by ensuring an optimum mix between the four main elements of the marketing mix and they are key instruments for understanding and facilitating transactions between the company and the market. The logic is that a brand will succeed only if the manufacturer of that brand is able to produce a product that delivers high-utility benefits, then sells it at the right price, in the right places, and promotes it to such an extent and in such a way that spurs consumer awareness. The Four P's – product, place, price and promotion – are hence key denominators of a brand's success.

The marketing mix quickly became an unchallenged basic model of marketing, and the Four P's have gone their course of victory across the world of marketing: 'since its introduction, McCarthy's (1960) description of a marketing mix comprised of product, price, promotion and place has widely become regarded as an "infallible" guide for the effective planning and implementation of marketing strategy' (Grönroos 1994b, p. 4).

Product

The product represents the tangible, physical product itself and the benefits that the consumer can gain from buying the brand. It includes the design, brand name, functionality, quality, safety, packaging and so on. The product encompasses all the tangible aspects of the product a manufacturer offers. The primary aim of the product is to be able to satisfy a functional demand – the functionality of the product, as such, is very important and the first prerequisite in the economic approach. In research of marketing mix elements post 2000, the introduction of new products have been an important part of the equation, because a significant number of studies have pointed out that new product introductions are a powerful predictor; they positively affect the long-term effectiveness of marketing promotions. Having something new to say increases the effectiveness of promotional actions (Slotegraaf and Pauwels 2008).

Price

The price is based on the total cost of manufacturing the product, the distribution and advertising cost. These direct and indirect production costs combined with a competitive analysis, and perhaps uncovering how much consumers are willing to pay for the product, make up the input for the analysis of what the price of the product should be. The price element of the marketing mix is closely linked to promotion. Since promotions are often used as a way to increase awareness or boost sales, pricing strategies are often planned based on scanner panel data from supermarket checkouts measuring how promotions affect the overall demand for the brand. Price is affected by actions adhering to the remaining P's, and research has documented that price-elasticity is decreased by discounting, but increased by advertising and product line length. In a significant study published in 2010, Ataman Heerde and Mela analysed the weekly performance of 70 brands in 25 categories over 5 years, with the aim to identify how marketing-mix strategies correlate with growth in brand sales. The result demonstrated a positive correlation from product and distribution and very limited positive performance effect from discounts and advertising in the long run (Ataman, Heerde and Mela 2010).

Place

Place in the marketing mix refers to the distribution of the product from the manufacturer to the end consumer. In short, it is about making goods available in the right quantities at the right locations. It is essential here to consider which distribution channels will be most effective for the brand and to develop a supply chain strategy that fits with the attributes of the brand and the demand of the consumers. This supply chain strategy implies the identification of the right channel partners, inventory management basically ensuring that all steps from when the brand leaves the production site until it reaches the consumer are geared and optimized.

Promotion

Promotion is the various elements a marketing plan can consist of when promoting a brand, and encapsulates two basic functions and goals: communication and persuasion. The higher goal of communication is to raise awareness and knowledge of products and covers everything from advertising, campaigns and general information about brands and products. Persuasion covers all activities that are more directly linked to facilitating the sale and can consist of everything from sales promotion, in store features or personal selling. Promotion hence covers all efforts to bring the sale forward and is recognized as a potent tool for managing brands, with in-store displays, feature advertising and temporary price reductions, which are key components of a traditional promotional mix (Blattberg and Neslin 1990). The increased accessibility of scanner panel and market data has made research into the short- and long-term effects of promotion on sales, and brand equity a key topic not only in research but also in practice in many sales and marketing departments.

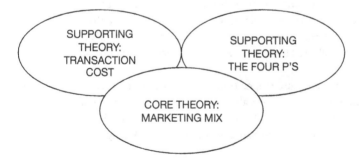

Figure 4.2 Supporting and core theories of the economic approach

Core theory: marketing mix

The premises of the brand in the economic approach is hence that it operates in a market, where the consumer is assumed to make primarily rational consumption decisions; interactions with consumers are linear and standalone isolated events rather than an ongoing relationship. Consumers evaluate brands on their functional utility against their price, and the Four P's is the mix of marketing actions that makes the transaction with consumers possible; getting to the right mix is essential for the success of a brand (see Figure 4.2).

Summary

The theoretical framework of the economic approach consists of two theoretical building blocks: transaction cost theory and the concept of the marketing mix. Transaction cost theory describes the barriers that can impede transactions taking place according to the principles of the invisible hand and the economic man, and transactions as isolated events. The primary aim is to achieve the next transaction by eliminating or breaking down the barriers that inhibit the transaction from taking place. These barriers to transactions must be overcome. The tool used in the economic approach to overcome these barriers is the marketing mix, or the Four P's. Using the toolbox of the Four P's can ensure that the right product is available to consumers at the right price, in the right locations, and that it is promoted by using advertising and promotion to make consumers aware of and interested in purchasing the product.

Methods and data of the economic approach

The aim of data collection in the economic approach is to gather data that delivers insights to guide the marketer in defining the marketing mix that will deliver optimal brand performance – increase the number of transactions. Post 2000 research has also been directed towards long-term effects of marketing mix actions on brand equity. The overall objective of research and data collection in the economic approach is to investigate how manipulating one or more factors of the marketing mix will affect consumers' brand choice. It is the investigation of the causal effects between two or more variables relating to the marketing mix that is primarily studied. The methods used are quantitative, and there are extensive amounts of data that are usually collected to demonstrate causal effects marketing activities have on demand.

Since the Four P's are rather operational and tactically focused, the methods used in the economic approach are also very output and managerially oriented, where results can be applied directly and used for decision making and problem solving in relation to the planning and execution of a marketing strategy.

Data and analysis in the economic approach

The types of studies in the economic approach require a combination of extensive access to data and the right analytical set up, dealing with the extensive data and the endogeneity[1] of marketing, making sure that the statistical modelling will capture and uncover the right causal effects. The big data samples are used to deduce correlations between variables and are suitable because of the need for data and results to be replicable and generalizable. The disadvantage is that it is difficult to gain a sound understanding of why variables are correlated, because the data are sampled broad instead of deep. As opposed to qualitative research methods, where smaller samples deliver rich and descriptive conclusions, the results of quantitative research designs are often expressed in tables or other statistical representations of data.

As explained in the assumptions section, the approach rests upon a positivistic paradigm, which is also visible in the suggested data collection methods. Data such as scanner panel data from cash registers at supermarkets and laboratory experiments are considered valid. The data are then subjected to different kinds of statistical analysis that often consist of regression analysis or multivariate dynamic linear models that captures and links brand sales to marketing strategy actions.

To accommodate the need for investigating different marketing mix variables that affect different factors of consumer brand choice behaviour, such as brand switching or brand market shares, customized regression models are often developed to fit the exact problem at hand.

Summary

The methods of the economic approach are mainly quantitative and focus on exploring how consumers' brand choice behaviour is affected by changes in one or more factors of the marketing mix. The data used are very factual and measurable in statistical models. Data are often derived from scanner panel data or other factual, statistical data. The method of analysis mostly focuses on the construction of mathematical regression models that can be used to measure the causal effects of how changing a variable in the marketing mix of a brand will affect consumer brand choice behaviour. The replicability of results is important because results are mostly used for decision making and problem solving on a general basis in practice.

Managerial implications

The 4 P's marketing mix classification is offered in the early stages of marketing as a management discipline, a clear classification and overview of instruments available, which allows one to judge and evaluate the effectiveness of marketing actions and continuously develop best practice for how to best facilitate sale. In the economic approach, the primary focus of the brand manager is to eliminate the barriers to exchange and facilitate the next transaction. The marketing mix is considered to be the best toolkit for this transactional approach to brand

Box. 4.2 Regression analysis

Regression analysis is a statistical tool for the investigation of relationships between variables. Any regression study sets out with a hypothesis that the investigator formulates, e.g. when a brand is on promotion (the price is lower than usual) the demand will increase. After having formulated the hypothesis the researcher assembles data on the variables of interest – data on price levels over time and data of demand levels over time. The data are then subjected to regression analysis that estimates the quantitative effect or correlation between the variables. Hereby, it is possible to ascertain the causal effect of one variable upon another; hence how a price cut in the shape of a promotion affects sales. The illustration reflects the correlation between how price promotions affect demand (the x axis reflecting the price and the y axis illustrating the fluctuations in demand). It is clear that whenever the product has been on promotion – sold at a reduced price – the demand for the product is higher.

Once a correlation between two variables has been established the statistical significance of the estimated relationships can be seen. In Figure 4.3 the relation between price and demand is reflected: whenever the product or brand is on promotion, it is reflected in the sales figures – the demand for the brand is higher.

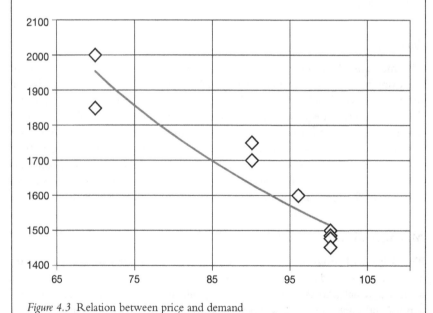

Figure 4.3 Relation between price and demand

management. Brand managers hence have the Four P's at their disposal to optimize brand performance. Because of the rather operational nature of the theoretical building blocks, this section will not, as is the case in the other approach chapters, elaborate extensively on how to manage the marketing mix variables, since the key issues have already been explained in the theoretical building blocks. Rather, it will focus on the strengths and weaknesses of using the economic approach as a basis of brand building. It will also summarize the main points of critique that the approach has been subject to since its foundation and application in the context of brand management.

As mentioned earlier, the idea of the marketing mix has in many ways dominated the marketing environment and become an indisputable paradigm. The economic approach and the transactional approach to brand management represents a 'push' approach to the marketing of brands, whereas the newer approaches represent a more pull-oriented approach to brand strategy (refer to Chapter 12 for elaboration and additional literature on push versus pull marketing). This way of managing brands has been subject to critique since its foundation, but it is important to keep in mind that the economic approach is the foundation of how brand management has evolved until today. Understanding the premises of the approach will enable the reader to critically evaluate how the approach is still relevant for some key problems in brand management, while insufficient for others. The managerial branding focus of the economic approach is, as mentioned, individual transactions, and branding is considered to be a management problem that can be solved through managerial tasks of analysing, planning and implementing marketing activities with the purpose of selling as many products as possible. In the research literature and in management practice, the tools of the economic approach, for example the Four P's and the marketing mix and how it can affect consumers' brand choice behaviour, are still widely researched.

In practice, managing a brand according to the theory of the marketing mix means that companies believe that by manipulating a series of interrelated marketing decisions the marketing manager can target and position products within a defined market segment which will respond in a planned and desirable manner – the consumer reacts to the marketing mix and does not engage in any interaction with the company as such. This lack of consideration for the interactivity consumers have with brands is a key point of critique of the economic approach.

> the marketing process consists of analysing market opportunities, researching and selecting target markets, designing marketing programs, and organising, implementing, and controlling the marketing effort . . . [and] to transform marketing strategy into marketing programs marketing managers must make basic decisions on marketing expenditure, marketing mix, and marketing allocation.
>
> (Kotler 1997 p. 86–7)

Originally, using the marketing mix as the primary marketing tool and measuring performance through sales figures solely can result in a rather short-term focus because of the extensive emphasis on the next transaction. The marketer is concerned with 'hooking new clients' and sales figures, and the exchange between the brand and the consumer is reduced to the isolated transaction. The brand-building qualities, where the interaction with the consumer is perceived as an ongoing relationship rather than isolated transactions and individual exchanges, is not really captured in the paradigm and scope of the economic approach. However, it is important to understand the economic approach as the foundation of contemporary brand management. The more long-term perspective, the focus on emotional and cultural issues, and the qualitative data collection methods will be thoroughly reviewed in subsequent approach chapters.

The other main critique stems from the inability to portray the world of consumption adequately with the functional and transactional exchange paradigm. In the real world, consumers do not have perfect information about available products and brands. Furthermore, individual preferences often violate utility theory – different people have different preferences, which cannot be explained by theories of maximization – and these considerations are not incorporated in the theoretical apparatus of the economic approach. Hence, the very nature of the Four P's as manageable, controllable factors combined with the intrinsic lack of market input in the model is in contrast with the ideals of market orientation implying that all marketing activities should be based on the identification of consumer needs and wants, which are very much in line with the widely accepted brand management theory.

The thoughts behind the economic approach serve as the foundation for brand management and from here, the discipline evolves into still more complex and specialized theories of consumer behaviour and brand consumption. One can say that the following approaches all accommodate the shortcomings of the economic approach as they each explain brand and consumption perspectives not accounted for in the economic approach.

Summary

The value of the tools of the economic approach for the planning and imple-mentation of marketing plans short-term are, however, great and a prerequisite in brand management, but the strategic value and potential for brand building of the marketing mix tools is questionable. The economic approach is hence a suitable planning and execution tool in brand management, but it cannot stand alone if one wishes to reap the full potential of brands and brand management reflecting how consumers in the new millennium consume brands.

Academic evolution of the economic approach

In this concluding section of the chapter, we outline the evolution of the economic approach in brand management academia (see Figure 4.4). This outline is based on the primary data of the taxonomy of this textbook – articles from the top market-ing journals with a primary focus on the brand (read more about methodology and data set in Chapter 2). The supplementary literature included in this chapter is hence not included in this section.

Prior to the late 1990s, research focus in the economic approach was directed towards how marketing actions related to one or more of the Four P's would affect sales figures. The increasing availability of large quantitative data pools from supermarket scanner panels made it possible to conduct real-life studies of how promotional actions, shelf space or visual features and campaigns, for example, would affect the price elasticity of a product and demand. Measurement of performance was primarily based on short-term sales figures, and hence tactical in nature. Post 2000, a growing number of 'marketing mix' research articles published

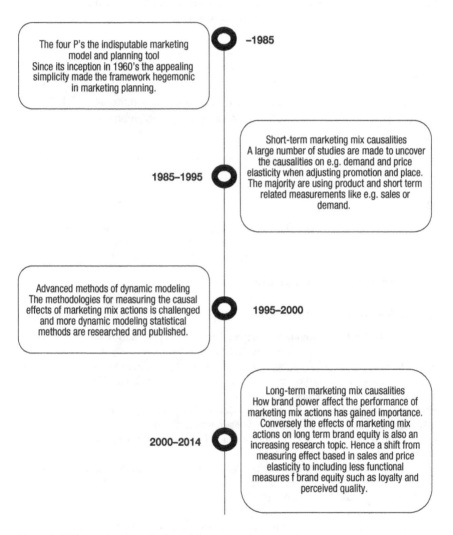

Figure 4.4 The academic evolution of the economic approach

shifted measurement focus and scope. From a narrow product to brand equity and from short-term tactical to long-term effects of, for example, discounts on brand equity. This new research substantiated the importance of the brand in generating differential effects from marketing mix actions. For example, higher-equity brands are able to generate higher immediate returns from their marketing-mix efforts (Slotegraaf *et al.* 2003), and higher-loyalty brands generate greater stockpiling from promotions (Bell *et al.* 1999; Slotegraaf and Pauwels 2008; Ataman *et al.* 2010; Stahl *et al.* 2012). Hence expanding the paradigmatic boundaries of the economic approach, research initiatives have since the turn of the millennium aimed at lifting the use of scanner panel data from a tactical level (price level – short term) to a long-term strategic level also considering how marketing mix actions are determinants of how brand equity evolves in the longer run.

Box 4.3 You are not done!

Don't forget to visit the website for supplementary material such as case examples, student questions and supplementary literature.

Note

1   Endogeneity refers to changs caused by other variables within a model. Endogenous variables are variables determined by other variables in the system.

References and further reading

Key readings are in bold type

Ackerman, F. (1997), 'Consumed in theory: Alternative perspectives on economics of consumption', *Journal of Economic Issues*, 31 (3): 651–64.

Ailawadi, K. L., Lehman, D. R. and Neslin, S. A. (2001), 'Marketing response to major policy change in the marketing mix: Learning from Procter & Gamble's value pricing strategy', *Journal of Marketing*, 65 (1): 44–61.

Ataman, M. B., Van Heerde, H. J. and Mela, C. F. (2010), 'The long-term effect of marketing strategy on brand sales', *Journal of Marketing Research*, 47 (5): 866–82.

Bath, S. and Reddy, S. K. (1998), 'Symbolic and functional positioning of brands', *Journal of Consumer Marketing*, 15 (1): 32–43.

Bell, D. R., Chiang, J. and Padmanabhan, V. (1999), 'The decomposition of promotional response: an empirical generalization', *Marketing Science*, 18 (4): 504–26.

Blattberg, R. C. and Neslin, S. A. (1990), *Sales Promotion: Concepts, Methods and Strategies*, Englewood Cliffs, NJ: Prentice Hall, pp. 349–50.

Borden, N. (1964), 'The concept of the marketing mix', in G. Schwartz (ed.), *Science in Marketing*, New York: Wiley, pp. 2–7.

Bucklin, R. E., Gupta, S. and Han, S. (1995), 'A brand's eye view of response segmentation in consumer brand choice behavior', *Journal of Marketing Research*, 32 (1): 66–74.

Bucklin, R. E. and Gupta. S. (1999), 'Commercial use of UPC scanner data: Industry and academic perspectives', *Marketing Science*, 18 (3): 247–73.

Carpenter, G. and Lehman D. R. (1985), 'A model of marketing mix, brand switching, and competition', *Journal of Marketing Research*, 22 (3): 318–29.

Constantinides, E. (2006), 'The marketing mix revisited: Towards the twenty-first century marketing', *Journal of Marketing Management*, 22: 407–38.

Deleersnyder, B. and Koll, O. (2012), 'Destination discount: A sensible road for national brands?' *European Journal of Marketing*, 46 (9): 1150–1170.

Demirdjian, Z. S. and Turan, S. (2004), 'Perspectives in consumer behavior: Paradigm shifts in prospect', *Journal of American Academy of Business*, 4 (1/2): 348–53.

Erdem, T., Swait, J. and Valenzuela, A. (2006), 'Brands as signals: A cross-country validation study', *Journal of Marketing*, 70 (1): 34–49.

Gardner, B. B. and Levy, S. J. (1955), 'The product and the brand', *Harvard Business Review*, 33 (2): 33–9.

Grönroos, C. (1994a), '*Quo vadis*, marketing? Toward a relationship marketing paradigm', *Journal of Marketing Management*, 10 (5): 347–60.

Grönroos, C. (1994b), 'From marketing mix to relationship marketing: Towards a paradigm shift in marketing', *Management Decision*, 32 (2): 4–26.

Hasegawa, S., Nobuhiko, T. and Allenby, G. M. (2012), 'Dynamic brand satiation', *Journal of Marketing Research*, 49 (6): 842–53.

Hultman, C. M. and Shaw, E. (2003), 'The interface between transactional and relational orientation in small service firms' marketing behavior: A study of Scottish and Swedish small firms in the service sector', *Journal of Marketing Theory and Practice*, 11 (1): 110–12.

Keller, K. L., Heckler, S. E. and Houston, M. J. (1998), 'The effects of brand name suggestiveness on advertising recall', *Journal of Marketing*, 62 (1): 48–57.

Kirmani, A. and Rao, A. R. (2000), 'No pain, no gain: A critical review of the literature on signaling unobservable product quality', *Journal of Marketing*, 64 (2): 66–79.

Kotler, P. (1965), 'Competitive strategies for new product marketing over the life cycle', *Management Science*, 12 (4): 104–19.

Kotler, P. (1997), *Marketing Management: Analyses, Planning, Implementation, and Control*, Upper Saddle River, NJ: Prentice-Hall.

McCarthy, E. J. (1960), *Basic Marketing: A Managerial Approach*, Homewood, IL: Irwin.

Mela, C. F., Gupta S. and Lehman D. R. (1997), 'The long-term impact of promotion and advertising on consumer brand choice', *Journal of Marketing Research*, 34 (2): 248–61.

Mehta, N. and Ma, Y. (2012), 'A multicategory model of consumers' purchase incidence, quantity, and brand choice decisions: Methodological issues and implications on promotional decisions', *Journal of Marketing Research*, 49 (4): 435–51.

Nelson, J. A. (1998), 'Abstraction, reality and gender of "economic man"', in J. G. Carrier and D. Miller (eds), *Virtualism: A New Political Economy*, Oxford: Berg, pp. 75–94.

Papatla, P. and Krishnamurthi, L. (1996), 'Measuring the dynamic effects of promotion on brand choice', *Journal of Marketing Research*, 33 (1): 20–35.

Park, C. W., Jaworski, B. J. and MacInnis, D. J. (1986), 'Strategic brand concept–image management', *Journal of Marketing*, 50 (4): 135–45.

Rahinel, R. and Redden, J. P. (2013), 'Brands as product coordinators: Matching brands make joint consumption experiences more enjoyable', *Journal of Consumer Research*, 39 (6): 1290–1299.

Shugan, S. M. (1987), 'Estimating brand positioning maps using supermarket scanning data', *Journal of Marketing Research*, 24 (1): 1–18.

Shultz, D. E. (2001), 'Marketers: Bid farewell to strategy based on old Four Ps', *Marketing News: American Marketing Association*, 35 (4): 7–8.

Slotegraaf, R. J. and Pauwels, K. (2008). The impact of brand equity and innovation on the long-term effectiveness of promotions, *Journal of Marketing Research*, 45 (3) 293–306.

Slotegraaf, R. J., Moorman, C. and Inman, J. J. (2003), 'The role of firm resources in returns to market deployment', *Journal of Marketing Research*, 40 (3): 295–309.

Smith, A. (1937[1776]). *An Inquiry into the Nature and Causes of the Wealth of Nations*. New York: Modern Library.

Stahl, F., Heitmann, M., Lehmann, D. R. and Neslin, S. A. (2012), 'The impact of brand equity on customer acquisition, retention, and profit margin', *Journal of Marketing*, 76 (4): 44–63.

Steenkamp, J. B. E., Van Heerde, H. J. and Geyskens, I. (2010), 'What makes consumers willing to pay a price premium for national brands over private labels?', *Journal of Marketing Research*, 47 (6): 1011–1024.

Van Waterschoot, W. and Van den Bulte, C. (1992), 'The 4P classification of the marketing mix revisited', *The Journal of Marketing*, 56 (4): 83–93.

Vargo, S. L. and Lusch, R. F. (2004), 'Evolving a new dominant logic for marketing', *Journal of Marketing*, 68 (1): 1–17.

Vilcassim, N. J. and Dipak, C. J. (1991), 'Modeling purchase-timing and brand-switching behavior incorporating explanatory variables and unobserved heterogeneity', *Journal of Marketing Research*, 28 (1): 29–41.

Yudelson, J. (1999), 'Adapting McCarthy's Four Ps for the twenty-first century', *Journal of Marketing Education*, 21 (1): 60–7.

Zaichkowsky, J. L. (1991), 'Consumer behavior: Yesterday, today and tomorrow', *Business Horizons*, 34 (3): 51–8.

5 The identity approach

with a commentary by Professor Majken Schultz, Copenhagen Business School, and Professor Emerita Mary Jo Hatch, University of Virginia

In 1907, AEG appointed Peter Behrens to be, what at the time was called, an 'Artistic Consultant'. His job turned out to be the first corporate engagement in the conscious management of identity. Peter Behrens's philosophy was simple – the products, design and communication should express one unified identity. To accomplish this, he created products, logos, advertising material and company publications with a consistent, unified design. This unified design and visual expression of identity made Peter Behrens and AEG the founders of the rationale behind the corporate identity concept and corporate identity management programmes in practice.

Originally based on the assumption that a strong brand is created through consistent and reliable communication of the corporation behind the brand, the identity approach was based on a sender perspective on the brand–consumer exchange, and in that sense comparable to the economic approach. However, this approach is a much more all-encompassing idea of how to manage the brand, since it involves the whole organization (in terms of incorporating the organization, it can be argued that it is the most far-reaching brand approach of this taxonomy).

In the late 1980s and early 1990s, the line of thought originating with AEG and the design school began to take shape in brand management academia, laying the ground for the identity approach. Abratt (1989) elaborated on the conceptual development of the approach by adding an in-depth study of the dimensions that link the interior processes (corporate identity) with the exterior-focused activities (corporate image). A new stream of research (especially in a European context) has during the 1990s led to a conceptualization of brand identity, where the interplay between corporate identity, organizational identity, image and reputation provides the elements to explore and create a strong brand within this approach.

After the millennium, the theoretical constructs, frameworks and methodologies have been evaluated, altered and refined, and scope was further expanded to entail larger networks of stakeholders and additional sources of identity. Recently, the impact of social media and open source developments on brand identity is a trending topic, exploring the ambiguity of organizing brand identity versus the volatile dynamics of social media.

This chapter offers an overview of the identity approach, by providing insights into the assumptions, theoretical frameworks and methodologies that can be used to gather data and study corporate brand identity. Finally, it describes and discusses the managerial guidelines that can be accumulated from the most prominent research publications and key non-research literature, supplemented with illustrative cases of how companies have dealt with the management of brand identity in practice. It is important to note that, even though this approach stems from the early 1990s, it is still under development with many new publications.

In brand management, the identity construct has grown increasingly popular, because it is a powerful and complex concept with the potential of strengthening competitive power significantly. Most companies today build and manage identity to ensure that the brand identity expresses an exact set of values, capabilities and unique sales propositions.

Unlike several of the other brand management approaches described in this book, the conceptualization and evolution of the identity approach is primarily practitioner-led. This means that the core definitions and conceptualization of the identity approach are not the result of a single comprehensive breakthrough study (as is the case in the consumer-based, the personality, the relational and the community approaches) but rather based on practical experience from the use of the identity concept as a management tool. There are, however, many influential scholars, articles and books worth mentioning in relation to the identity approach. We will refrain from listing the complete selection but mention two collections that in particular have set the scene in the recent perspectives on brand identity. *The Expressive Organization* by Schultz *et al.* (2000) is a selection of articles exploring the identity domain from multiple academic fields, with the aim of discussing the relational differences between identity, image and culture in organizations with the aim of clarifying and articulating the theoretical domain of identity (Schultz *et al.* 2000). *Revealing the Corporation: Perspectives on Identity, Image, Reputation, Corporate Branding, and Corporate-level Marketing* (Balmer and Greyser 2003) is another important collection guiding the reader through influential classics and contemporary academic articles shedding light on different perspectives on identity, image, reputation and corporate branding.

The brand identity approach has evolved over the years, from its original focus on creating and managing coherent identity to a post year 2000 focus on the balancing act of corporate identity drawing on and balancing multiple sources of identity. Post 2005 research articles in the data set have granted more and more focus on empirical challenges of how to deal with the fragmentation of the brand identity, where the brand identity is fragmented into a variety of formal identities such as, for example, a corporate brand, an employer brand and the formation of a social brand identity (Hatch and Schultz 2009, Da Silva and Alvi 2008). Another post 2005 research focus is the challenges of maintaining and passing on corporate brand identity through more and more complex value chains – both up and downstream for supply and though to all sales channels (Anisimova and Mavondo 2010, Morhart *et al.* 2009, Hughes and Ahearne 2010, Sirani *et al.* 2013). The shifting focus over the years since the late 1990s in the research articles studying brand identity demonstrates a displacement in how the paradigm and approach to

Box 5.1 Learning objectives

The purpose of this chapter is to:

Understand the assumptions of the identity approach

- The brand should express one unified and coherent identity, internally as well as externally, by using the visual and behavioural identity of the corporation to build the brand. Consumers' perception of a brand equals the sum of their total experience with a company.

Understand the theoretical framework of the corporate identity approach

- The four supporting theories of corporate brand identity: corporate identity, organizational identity, image and reputation.
- The two key normative theoretical frameworks, the corporate brand toolkit and the AC4ID model, are useful for the alignment of corporate identity, organizational identity, image and reputation to create a coherent brand identity.

Provide insights into the methods of the identity approach

- In the identity approach, a mix of methods is used. Internally, focus is on corporate identity (visual and strategic) and organizational identity (behaviour and culture) rooted in ethnographic and anthropological methods. Externally, the element's image and reputation combine methods from cognitive and social psychology.

Understand the managerial implications

- Understand the complexity of managing corporate brand identity by ensuring alignment of corporate identity, organizational identity, image and reputation. How to ensure brand identity throughout the value chain and take into account how to avoid the potential fragmentation of brand identities.

Understand the academic evolution of the approach

- Brand identity initially focused on visual and symbolic brand identity.
- Focus shifted to corporate identity and the framework we know today was conceptualized encompassing corporate vision, organizational culture and stakeholder perspective.
- Recent research has evolved to also explore how brand identity can be ensured throughout complex value chains and sales channel setups along with how social media affects the creation of brand identity.

branding have evolved and matured. Most articles of the late 1990s and turn of the millennium struggled to define and develop the theoretical construct of brand identity, and post 2005 an increasing number of articles have elaborated on the managerial challenges of brand identity. Hence, there has been a shift from theory development to managerially oriented research articles.

Assumptions of the identity approach

In the economic approach, attributes related to the Four P's of marketing (product, price, placement and promotion) are the main mechanisms behind the creation and management of brand equity.

The identity approach brings into focus the creation of a unified, visual and behavioural identity. It is assumed that consumers attribute identity characteristics to companies, and that people form images of companies based on the total experience of the company. This places the corporation and its employees at the centre of brand equity creation, and hence adds the corporate brand identity to the domain of brand management.

The identity perspective

The identity concept has a long history from the field of marketing (both in research and in practice) and many of the concepts used and studied in marketing have been applied to the corporate identity concept in brand management. The identity approach is multidimensional and draws on very diverse strategic, visual and behavioural scholarly fields such as graphic design and strategic management, stakeholder management, organizational culture studies and behaviour. Before seeking a proper understanding of the assumptions underlying the identity approach, it is therefore necessary to know how the identity concept has been played out in the field of marketing prior to its adaptation to a brand management context.

In a brand management context, the key assumption of the identity approach is that all marketing and communication activities should be integrated, aligned and elevated from a product-focused and tactical level to a strategic, corporate level. Only in that way will it be possible to create a coherent company experience for consumers. It is from that assumption that the idea of corporate branding and integrated market communication stems. The notion of identity is applicable to the individual brand level, but corporate-level branding plays a vital role in the identity approach because alignment of all communications in one unified identity and managing the total customer experience across all touchpoints requires strategic-level brand management. Identity is something that is initiated from inside the company. Some of the questions corporations need to ask themselves are in the identity approach. Who are we? What do we stand for? What do we want to become? Brand value creation is hence dependent on finding the right answers to these questions and implementing them in every aspect of the business. Only that will ensure a coherent total experience for consumers.

Box 5.2 Visual and behavioural identity from marketing

There were two main streams of practice and research in the identity concept in marketing prior to its adaptation in a brand management context. One focused on visual identity while the other focused on behavioural identity.

Visual identity

Wally Olins is an identity pioneer. In his first big publication about corporate identity, *The Corporate Personality: An Inquiry into the Nature of Corporate Identity* (1978), he described the rationale of the identity concept and advocated the importance of identity for corporate entities. Olins poses two questions that are still pivotal in the corporate identity approach today: *What are we?* And *who are we?* Olins answers these questions primarily through a visual expression of identity. He acknowledges that identity is not only about appearance but also about behaviour, but his subject area has been visual identities. Olins advocates that corporations use a visual identification system to build identity and use the visual identity as a communication vehicle. Consistency is the key in Olins' approach, as he emphasizes that communication should uphold a consistent visual expression while ensuring that the brand remains fashionable by undergoing continual adaptation to emergent changes.

Behavioural identity

Kennedy laid the ground for the conceptualization of behavioural identity in 1977 in marketing. She hypothesized that consumers base consumption decisions on their perceptions of company personality to a much greater extent than on a rational evaluation of product attribute functionality. Consumer perception of identity is, according to Kennedy, based on the total experience of the company that consumers form through all the contacts consumers have with the brand/company over time. This line of thought adds the employees and their behaviour as a key contributor to corporate brand identity.

From product to corporate branding

Traditionally, the general notion of the classic brand management system has been that each individual product must have an individual and distinct brand identity. The textbook models of brand identity, for example David Aaker and Kapferer, refer to this notion of brand identity. Hence, Aaker's brand identity system or the brand identity prism developed by Kapferer are both models and construals for exploring and analysing layers of brand identity. They are textbook models of

how to analyse brand identity. In the identity approach, identity refers to the corporate brand identity (refer to Chapter 12 for elaboration and additional literature
about brand architecture) and the internal and external elements that contribute
to the corporate brand identity. Hence, brand identity is uncovered and described
as a school of thought in brand management and is not to be confused with textbook
and analytical models of brand identity.

The idea of corporate branding is the assumption that creating one unified (at
corporate level) message across all functions will elevate brand management from
a tactical operational discipline involving only the marketing and sales department
to a strategic, corporate level involving the whole organization. Creating one unified
message across functions hence requires one unified corporate identity. Corporate
branding implies deserting product branding with its narrow marketing-driven focus
on tactical, functional processes. Product branding has been criticized for having
a too narrow, external perspective, detached from the organization behind the
products. Corporate branding is an attempt to accommodate these weaknesses.
Product branding is based on short-term advertising ideas, while corporate branding
is based on a long-term brand idea. Corporate branding also expands the parameters
of differentiation by enabling companies to use their rich heritage actively to create
strong brands. Corporate branding involves the whole organization and emphasizes
the pivotal role employees play in the creation of a strong corporate brand. Values

Table 5.1 Characteristics of product and corporate branding

	Product branding	*Corporate branding*
Foundation	Individual products	The company/organization
Conceptualization	Marketing, outside-in thinking	Cross disciplinary, combines inside-out and outside-in thinking
Brand receivers	Consumers	All stakeholders
Core processes	Marketing and communication	Managerial and organizational processes
Difficulties	Create and sustain differentiation Involvement of employees and use of organizational cultural heritage Limited involvement of other stakeholders than consumers	Alignment of internal and external stakeholders Create and communicate credible and authentic identity Involvement of multiple subcultures internally, and multiple stakeholders externally
Brand equity comes from	Superior product attributes, good advertising and communication	The visual and behavioural identity of the corporation

Source: Adapted from Schultz *et al.* (2005)

and beliefs held by employees are key elements in the differentiation strategy. Corporate branding is a 'move towards conceiving more integrated relationships between internal and external stakeholders linking top management, employees, customers and other stakeholders' (Schultz *et al.* 2005, p. 24).

This is why organizational and managerial processes are in focus in corporate branding: only in that way can the distinctive identity of the corporate brand be reflected in and nurtured by the way the organization works. Strategy making in corporate branding should take a multidisciplinary approach, because it involves not only marketing but multiple functions and departments.

> Alignments between the origin and everyday practices of the organization [organizational culture]; where the organization aspires to go [strategic vision]; how the organization is perceived by external stakeholders [images]; all nested in perceptions of who the organization is [identity].
>
> (Schultz *et al.* 2005, p. 24)

Corporate branding focuses on developing distinctive features of the organization through organizational and managerial processes. Breaking down the silos between marketing (externally focused) and organizational development (internally focused) and using internal organizational resources to build brand identity, image, reputation and corporate branding have increasingly become an integral part of brand management, and practitioners ascribe corporate culture as one of the most important aspects when conceptualizing the domain of identity. The case of how Lego has shifted from a focus on product branding to corporate branding is a good example of how this shift can be done in practice.

Box 5.3 From product to corporate branding at Lego

In the mid-1990s, Lego was caught in a general decline in the toy market. For most people, Lego is synonymous with the Lego brick, which was also the focus internally. The product focus was perceived as an impediment to growth. Lego had to reinvent the company by implementing a shift from product branding to corporate branding. The identity (internally) and image (externally) of Lego underwent analysis. It was found that the image of Lego was indeed strong among many stakeholders as a producer of toys enhancing creativity and learning. The strategic vision of the company had to be aligned with this image. Management moved away from defining themselves as producers of Lego bricks to defining themselves as leaders in the business of creativity and learning.

Adapted from Hatch and Schultz (2001) and
Schroeder and Salzer-Mörling (2006)

The 'brand–consumer' exchange

In the identity approach, a reliable image and reputation are assumed to be key determinants of consumers' brand choice. In the other six brand approaches, the brand–consumer exchange is key. In the identity approach, brand–consumer exchange is expanded to focus on all potential stakeholders, and not only inter-action with consumers. Hatch and Schultz describes this wider scope as enterprise branding, providing a broader focus and altered perception of who contributes to the creation of corporate brand identity (Hatch and Schultz 2009) (see Figure 5.1).

There have been countless discussions of the extent to which communication between brand and receiver (here all stakeholders) is linear or the result of a dialogue, with a traditional sender–receiver model describing the exchange. Or rather that communication is formed by multiple sources and that it is interactive and dynamic in nature. The reason for the discussion probably can be explained by the fact that scholars and practitioners involved in the field of brand identity often come from very different academic backgrounds, entailing a variety in perspective and emphasis. Getting an overview of these different points of views will clarify the assumption battle of the brand–stakeholder exchange in the identity approach:

- The exchange between brand and stakeholder from a visual and strategic point of view (corporate identity) derives its mindset from marketing, graphic design and strategic management. The concept of corporate identity focuses on the creation of a coherent visual identity. The key determinant of success is the ability to control all communication, with the aim of creating an enduring, distinctive and stable brand identity that is communicated linearly to all stakeholders.
- Research into the more behavioural aspects of brand identity (organizational identity) has its origin in academic disciplines like sociology, anthropology and organization studies. The concept of organizational identity focuses on how behaviour affects brand identity. Identity is believed to be context-dependent and both socially and individually created – hence a social constructivist view of identity, where it is assumed that identity is the result of a co-creation between brand and stakeholder.
- Image is defined as the mosaic of brand associations held by stakeholders, hence implying the stakeholder perspective of the exchange. Here the communication may be linear, but stakeholders' reactions are perceived to be a central element in the formation and management of identity.

Figure 5.1 Sources of brand identity: the corporation is pivotal for the creation of brand equity in the identity approach

- Reputation is a more long-term gathering of impressions and evaluations of image stored in the long-term memory of consumers and stakeholders. Reputation focuses more on relation building than linear communication.

In a recent research of brand identity, a multidimensional approach has been adopted where the four perspectives mentioned above are combined. The construction of the brand in the identity approach is hence, in its original form, assumed to be linear, but a social constructionist perspective with a more interaction-based notion has come to take up a more and more dominant role in the identity approach in the recent years. The perception of how brand equity is created has evolved from a linear perception of the brand consumer exchange (in its origin), to a wider scope and also a more dynamic and interactive perception of the creation of corporate brand identity.

In that sense, the brand identity approach to branding has evolved from a rather static, narrow concept focusing on graphic design to a much more dynamic, complex and social constructivist perception of identity. Hence, when identity is context-dependent and socially constructed, it follows that the linear communication process originally characterizing the 'brand–stakeholder exchange' is also challenged. These behavioural, cultural and in nature social constructivist perspectives on corporate identity imply that identity is not just formed inside a company and then sent to consumers, who perceive the message exactly as intended.

Box 5.4 Is identity enduring? Shifting paradigm

In 1985, Albert and Whetten defined organizational identity by three key characteristics:

- *Central character*. It captures the essence of the organization.
- *Claimed distinctiveness*. It distinguishes the organization from others.
- *Temporal continuity*. It exhibits continuity over time (it is stable and enduring).

These three characteristics went unchallenged until the late 1990s, when an increasing number of researchers challenged that corporate identity is enduring and stable, arguing that corporate identity is indeed relatively fluid, dynamic and not stable at all. Indeed, the fluidity and flexibility of identity is the strength of many organizations, because it enables them to accommodate rapid environmental changes (Gioia *et al.* 2000). This new perception of organizational identity as context-dependent and socially constructed introduces a new and more dynamic perspective on identity. It spurred a paradigmatic shift and a new stream of research and practice for building and managing brand identity, incorporating the dynamic and fragmented nature of organizational identity.

In the dynamic view of corporate brand identity, it is perceived that identity is co-created and evolves in an interaction between multiple internal and external stakeholders. This co-creation of identity resulted during the 1990s in a new area of research, namely the research on how to ensure alignment between the internal corporate identity and organizational identity and the external expressions of brand identity image and reputation: 'To get the most out of corporate brand strategy, three essential elements must be aligned: vision, culture, and image. Aligning these strategic stars takes concentrated management skill and will. Each element is driven by a different constituency' (Hatch and Schultz 2001, p. 131).

Summary

The identity approach assumes that a strong and coherent brand identity is pivotal for brand value creation and acknowledges that balancing multiple identities is key (due to its fragmented nature). The corporate brand identity is the result of a continuous journey exploring and answering 'who we are' as an organization in order to facilitate the expression of one coherent identity to all stakeholders. Attention has shifted from a focus on the visual representation of product brands to a focus on how organizational behaviour affects identity, and ultimately image and reputation. The perception of the consumer in the identity approach has also evolved. Scope and perception of the brand consumer exchange has shifted from the idea that brand identity could be managed and controlled by the corporation, and a linear perception of the exchange between the brand and the consumer, to a much broader perception, where it is acknowledged that identity is not enduring but context-dependent; it can hence not be communicated linearly, but is the result of negotiation between internal and external shareholders.

Theoretical framework of the identity approach

The supporting theories of the corporate identity approach have changed and broadened along with the shift in focus from product to corporate branding. The ever-continuous evolution of the conceptualization of brand identity has led to a considerable volume of concepts and frameworks of a multidisciplinary nature. Concepts are often used interchangeably, and it can be difficult to gain a clear overview of the key constructs, how they relate to each other and how they can be combined.

The theoretical framework is composed by four supporting theories: *organizational identity, corporate identity, image* and *reputation* (see Figure 5.2).

These supporting theories can be divided into two main categories: the internal and the external elements of brand identity. Two 'internal' supporting theories: corporate identity and organizational identity, describe the creation, maintenance and research of brand identity internally. The two supporting theories, image and reputation, describe the theoretical constructs used to build, manage and research corporate brand identity externally. One can say that the multifaceted nature is

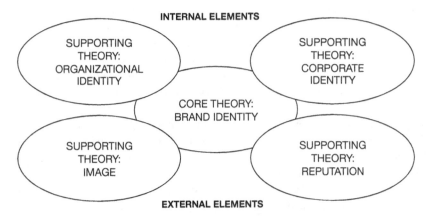

Figure 5.2 Theoretical framework of the corporate identity approach

reflected in the supporting theories – as they describe the different aspects and sources of corporate identity.

How to study, analyse and activate the supporting theories (the different sources of identity) is yet another story that requires an additional layer to gain a complete overview of the theoretical constructs and frameworks of the brand identity approach. Fortunately, prominent scholars have supplied us with two key frameworks that do exactly that, setting up guidelines for how to ensure coherence, alignment and balance in the multiple and complex sources of identity. In the following, we will present these two frameworks as guiding theories of the approach.

The VCI (vision, culture, image) model is the corporate brand toolkit by Hatch and Schultz. It came out in 2001 and provided the theoretical construct and managerial model for how to align sources of identity and the perception of identity different stakeholders have. The AC4ID framework (Balmer and Soenen 1999) is the key framework; it focuses on the interface between seven identity types (actual, communicated, conceived, covenanted, cultural, ideal and desired). These two frameworks have become the most influential – academically and in practice – and despite their differences, they both approach and identify the problem of alignment and balance between multiple identities as key when building corporate brand identity.

Supporting theory: corporate identity (internal)

The first internal supporting theory is corporate identity. Corporate identity comprises two facets of identity internally: first, *visual representations of identity* and second, *how the strategic brand vision influences brand identity*. Corporate identity is an assembly of visual, physical and behavioural cues representing the company, making it immediately recognizable to consumers and other stakeholders.

Ideally, the visual identity is the outward expression through visual cues, signs and symbols of the inward commitment and promise that an organization can deliver. The visual perspective focuses on tangible visual manifestations of the brand identity and on how these manifestations can affect leadership behaviour and company structure and vice versa. It has its origin in graphic design, where focus is on the creation and management of logo, the name, colour, sound, touch and smell in a way that ensures optimum reflection of brand identity. From this visual perspective, corporate identity is aligned through graphic design, by using a visual identification system, for example a design/brand manual. These systems help the management of the brand, but they can also act as catalysts for change and as vehicles of communication, and they are vital tools to ensure that the visual expression of brand identity is up to date. The visual school has often been criticized for being too narrowly conceived and misunderstood in practice because of too much focus on design, name and logo. However, working with the aspects of visual identity should also encompass the merging of behaviour and the visual identity; it is only when behaviour and appearance are linked that a strong corporate brand identity emerges. This link is underpinned by one of the frontrunners of brand identity, Wally Olins.

> The fact of the matter is that when an organization has a clear idea about itself, what its business is, what its priorities are, how it wants to conduct itself, how it wants to be perceived, its identity falls fairly easily in place.
>
> (Olins 1979, p. 60)

The visual expression of brand identity becomes much easier if identity is also embedded in a common corporate behavioural standard. Signs and symbols of identity are merely myths, but they can become reality if they also act as catalysts for change and guide behaviour. Hence corporate identity cannot be confined merely to the visual expressions of brand identity, it also refers to the way employees and other stakeholders involved in delivering brand identity to consumers think, behave and work. The focus is to ensure the right expression outwards as opposed to the organizational identity, where the goal and focus are to ensure the right behaviour, culture and expression inwards.

The strategic perspective of corporate identity focuses on the central idea of the organization (mission, vision and philosophy) and hence links the corporate strategy with brand identity. It provides answers to key strategic questions such as: who they are; what are the core competences; and how can these be utilized to ensure that they are embedded in all aspects of brand identity?

Corporate identity hence contributes to brand identity in two ways. First, it ensures that input from strategic management – the vision, mission and strategic direction of the corporation – is in line with the creation and management of brand identity. Second, it ensures that brand identity is represented visually through management of product design, logo, name and so on, encompassing all visual representations of brand identity. The acknowledgement of the importance of behaviour has been underpinned by research pointing out how difficult it can be to translate managerial and strategic vision into brand identity. To ensure that this process is done accurately, deep insight into organizational behaviour and culture is needed. The next theoretical building block of the identity approach describes how the theoretical construct of organizational culture and behaviour is activated in the identity approach.

Supporting theory: organizational identity (internal)

The second supporting theory of brand identity is organizational identity: it refers to the *behavioural and cultural aspects of brand identity*. Key concepts are organizational behaviour, culture and structure; these are all elements affecting how organizational members perceive *who they are* and *what they stand for* as a company or organization. The organizational identity provides a cognitive and emotional foundation on which organizational members build attachment. It also sets the scene for how employees create meaningful relationships with their organization. Organizational culture is closely linked to employee commitment and performance, which is why organizational identity is so pivotal for consumers' evaluation of brand identity, because corporate image and reputation directly depends on the ability of employees to deliver on brand content and promise. This notion makes employees a pivotal instrument for brand management and it is especially prevalent in industries, where people or the employees are key bearers of the brand (for instance in the service industry or in retailing).

The 'living the brand' construct is often used to describe organizational identity. The concept describes how organizational members can become so attached to the brand that it becomes an important part of the creation and enhancement of brand equity. Employees will 'live the brand' and act as brand ambassadors and co-creators of brand equity. The brand is brought to life in the interaction between

---

Box 5.5 Culture in the identity approach

In the identity approach, culture is defined at micro-level (while the cultural approach highlights branding in the context of macro-level culture). In the micro-level culture definition of the identity approach, organizational culture is to be understood as a concept that provides a local context or frame for the organizational identity. The organizational culture contributes with symbolic material to the construction of corporate identity. Culture is regarded as the expression of everyday life in an organization – the values (the 'taken-for-granted assumptions'), the behaviour ('the way we do things around here') and the formal internal and external communication, as well as the more informal communication of internal organizational stories.

Source: Hatch and Schultz (2000)

consumer and employee, demanding a high level of commitment to the brand from the employee. In an ideal world, organizational culture is altered and nursed by embedding certain values in the culture and behaviour using tools such as storytelling, internal training and employee branding. This process aligns employee behaviour with the brand vision and brand identity. Since employees increasingly demand empowerment and a meaningful workplace, and companies demand committed employees, this approach seems like a win–win situation for both employees and companies. But unfortunately in reality it is often difficult to achieve; the proven effect of internal employee branding (the storytelling and value-based management tools used to alter organizational culture) is questionable. Several studies conclude that the majority of employees do not really buy into internal branding efforts long term (Karmark 2005). Once activities have died down, resistance to change and old routines win the battle. Hence, managing brand identity through the creation and enhancement of organizational identity is not an easy task, but if done with success, the result can be an unbeatably strong and unique brand identity. The methods of how to go about creating an organizational culture as a brand manager and some of the problems and how to overcome them are further explained in 'methods' (p. 65) and 'managerial implications' (p. 71).

Reseller brand identification – bringing the brand to life outside

Many corporations are dependent on resellers and retailers outside the organizational boundaries to deliver brand identity and pass on the unique stories and features of the brand. Hence, the formation of brand identity is not only dependent on employees' ability to live the brand, but also on interactions that customers have with people outside the organization anywhere in the value chain who can potentially have great impact on customers' evaluation of brand identity. Hatch and Schultz refer to this as the enterprise of the brand: 'The brand is not just developed by the corporation but by the network of stakeholders, that take part in the creation of the brand or the network that the corporation is part of' (Hatch and Schultz 2009).

Post 2005, an increasing number of research articles from the data set have explored how distributors, reseller and retailers can be encouraged to pass on brand identity. The role of retailers and salespersons is pivotal in winning consumers' hearts. Brand identification is the theoretical construct used to describe how resellers identify with their employers (distributor identification) or with a brand (brand identification) from a supplying manufacturer. It is conceptualized as a social construction that involves the integration of perceived brand identity into the self-identity of the reseller (Morhart *et al.*, 2009, Hughes and Ahearne 2010, Sirani *et al.*, 2013). The challenges of ensuring that brand identity is brought to life by people anywhere in the value chain outside the formal control of the organization is from a managerial viewpoint an area of growing interest and will be elaborated in the section of this chapter on how to build and manage brand identity.

Supporting theory: corporate image (external)

The concept of corporate image represents and uncovers the external aspects of brand identity, measuring brand impact among brand receivers. The aim is to project one coherent image to all stakeholders, ensuring a consistent perception of brand image among stakeholders. Corporate image is all about perception, and it is formed by a mosaic of impressions derived from a variety of formal and informal signals projected by the company. From this mosaic, the recipient pieces together the corporate image. The corporate image does not necessarily equal what the company projects and communicates, but rather it exists in the mind of the receivers – how they at either individual or group level perceive brand identity. Corporate image is the result of a mosaic of attitudes commencing within the company with the employees and their perception of the company. Continuously measuring the corporate image is an important way to keep track of how consumers and other stakeholders perceive and value brand identity. Image refers to an instant image at a given point in time. The counterpart of image to measure stakeholder perception is reputation, the next external theoretical building block of the identity approach.

Supporting theory: reputation (external)

Some scholars argue that the research and literature about reputation can be categorized as one of the schools of thought on how to create and manage the corporate image. We define the concept of reputation in a category by itself, because the mechanisms applying to this field are quite different from the mechanisms that apply to the theoretical construct of image.

During the 1990s, the concept of reputation gained popularity particularly in practice. As opposed to the image concept *reputation is built and formed over a longer period of time*. It is based on what the company has done over time and how it has behaved, rather than being a result of short-term communication and advertising as is the case for the formation of image. The corporate reputation construct is mainly used externally to measure consumer evaluations of brand identity, but can also be used internally to guide employee behaviour. Corporate reputation can also reveal the standards that govern organizational behaviour. So how does a company ensure a good reputation? Too often it does not – because reputation management is often not considered unless it is threatened.

The key drivers of reputation are public relations (PR) and the communication of corporate success stories and corporate social responsibility. Reputation can be enhanced through corporate communication, but is more effective when communicated by an independent third party. This is one of the reasons why increasingly higher percentages of company expenditure are invested in the building of PR and good relations with key players in the media or lobbying influencing political interests.

Core theory: brand identity

An in-depth understanding of the four theoretical building blocks adds up to the theoretical framework of the identity approach; namely brand identity. By combining all components in Figure 5.3 and Table 5.2, you will gain a clear picture of the components of brand identity.

After having gained a sound understanding of the elements that comprise the brand identity construct, the next section will elaborate on how these elements, in interplay, can be managed to construct and enhance brand identity. 'Alignment' is the key word if the management of all four elements is to result in a unified communication of a coherent brand identity to all shareholders.

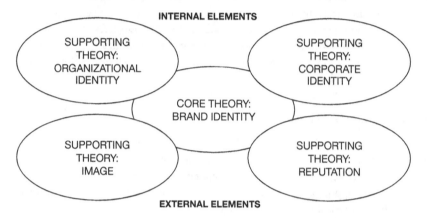

Figure 5.3 Brand identity: the supporting and core theory of the identity approach

Table 5.2 The supporting theories uncovering internal and external elements of brand identity

	Corporate identity	*Organizational identity*
Internal	• visual expression of brand identity • strategic vision of brand identity • top management	• behavioural aspects of brand identity • organizational culture • employees
	Image	*Reputation*
External	• short term • mosaic of stakeholder associations • exists entirely in the minds of stakeholders	• long-term evaluation of brand identity • stakeholder evaluations of brand actions • key tools: personal relations and lobbying

Aligning brand identity

The two frameworks selected and described here have been chosen because they are the most influential and express the key concern that most recent frameworks for the management of brand identity have in common, namely the alignment of identity, culture, image and reputation. This alignment is the pivotal task in the brand identity management process.

The *corporate brand toolkit* developed by Hatch and Schultz is based on research and data from more than 100 companies during a time span of more than 10 years. The toolkit was published in *Harvard Business Review* in 2001.

Balmer and Greyser developed another influential framework, the *AC4ID framework*. It has its origin in the late 1990s, where Balmer and Soenen first published the ACID test framework in *Journal of Marketing Management*. Balmer has since extended the framework to incorporate seven identity types. Like the corporate brand toolkit, it focuses on the identity types present in a company and how these identity types should be managed in order to ensure alignment. The AC4ID framework is based on extensive research in the corporate industry field, but has also incorporated trends and findings from research and academic literature.

The corporate brand toolkit

The corporate brand toolkit identifies strategic vision, organizational culture and stakeholders' images as the strategic stars of the organization.

- *Strategic vision*: central idea behind what the company does. The strategic vision expresses future management aspirations.
- *Organizational culture*: internal values and beliefs. Basic assumptions that embody the heritage of the company are manifested in the ways employees feel about the company across rank and are reflected in behaviour.
- *Stakeholders' images*: how external stakeholders perceive the company. In other words, it is the outside world's overall impression of the company.

These elements are comparable to the four supporting themes: strategic vision equals corporate identity, organizational culture and organizational identity share a common perspective, and stakeholder images are equivalent to the two external supporting themes, image and reputation. The alignment of these stars is the means to the creation of a strong and successful corporate brand identity. This alignment requires that attention be paid to all three elements simultaneously. Misalignments can be detected by a series of diagnostic questions to all stakeholders internally as well as externally.

The aim with this series of questions is to uncover gaps between either of the elements, represented by, respectively, employees, management and external stakeholders. It is a way to see whether the strategic vision of top management is in line with consumer demands and if there is sufficient internal employee support for the strategic vision. Analysis of identity gaps should ideally be conducted concurrently to ensure ongoing alignment of the strategic elements, which are key to the creation of brand identity.

After having identified any identity gaps, it is essential that the information gathered is used to make an action plan for how vision and image can undergo a process of realignment. If the problem is misalignment between vision and organizational culture, then the consequences could be a brand identity promising too much compared with what employees are prepared or able to deliver. This type of misalignment problem requires that either the strategic vision is downplayed or that an organizational culture in line with the strategic vision of the company is nurtured and developed. The identification and analysis of gaps between the strategic stars of brand identity lay the foundation for a customized strategy for aligning identified gaps that can ensure the continuous alignment of the elements of brand identity (Hatch and Schultz 2001).

The AC4ID framework

The AC4ID (Balmer 2010) framework focuses on the alignment of seven identity types in the corporation that affect the creation of brand identity. The assumption is similar to that of the corporate brand toolkit, namely that multiple corporate identities must be continually aligned to ensure a strong brand identity. Dissonance between the seven identity types will weaken the overall brand identity and ultimately corporate brand performance. AC4ID is an acronym for the seven identity types to be aligned:

- *Actual*: the actual identity, organizational behaviour and everyday reality of the corporation;
- *Communicated*: the brand identity expressed through all sources of communication;
- *Conceived*: refers to the image/reputation of the corporation – how do stakeholders conceive brand identity?
- *Covenanted:* refers to an explicit set of promises and relationships associated with a corporate level brand identity;
- *Cultural*: refers to the collective feeling employees have in relation to the corporate brand; derived from the values, beliefs and assumptions relating to the corporate brand including its historical roots;
- *Ideal*: represents the optimum positioning of the organization in the market at any given time;
- *Desired*: lives in the hearts and minds of the corporate leaders – equivalent of the strategic vision.

In the AC4ID framework, the four theoretical building blocks are also reflected; the desired, covenanted and communicated identity cover the same topics as the supporting theory corporate identity (here defined as visual and strategic). The actual and cultural identity is comparable to what we define as organizational identity and the conceived identity and ideal identity cover the external elements equivalent to the supporting theories image and reputation. Management should on a continuous basis ensure that these identities are aligned, meanwhile also updating the ideal and desired identity according to changes and developments in the business environment. Not monitoring and aligning the multiple identities of a brand can have fatal consequences.

The AC4ID framework can assist top management in the research and management of multiple identities and guide the company through identity changes and realignment processes needed to ensure a consistent and coherent brand identity, essential if the organization is to be capable of delivering a unified total brand experience to consumers. Especially in situations where identity is challenged (e.g. mergers or acquisitions), brand identity management is crucial.

Summary

The theoretical framework of the identity approach consists of four supporting theories. Corporate identity and organizational identity describe internal identity elements, while image and reputation explain the external sources of brand identity. These four supporting theories each contribute to the theoretical brand identity construct. Pivotal in the recent theoretical frameworks for the management of brand identity is the alignment of the multiple identities of the corporation. Two key frameworks are the *corporate brand toolkit* focusing on the

---

Box 5.6 Misaligned identities: the case of Body Shop

The founder of the Body Shop, Anita Roddick, from the beginning ran the Body Shop according to her environmental and socially responsible values. Her personal values (desired identity) had a significant influence on the positioning and branding of the Body Shop as a socially responsible company against animal testing and so on. An investigation of whether the actual practices of the corporation could live up to these values led to accusations that it did not. This is clearly a case of misalignment of the desired identity in relation to the actual identity. Media attention led to consumer suspicion, with the result that the conceived identity also became misaligned with the desired identity. The misalignment of identities in the case of Body Shop is a good example of what often happens when small companies grow fast, and the growing distance between the ideals and dreams of the founder and the actual behaviour is inevitable if well-managed brand identity-building activities are not in place to make up for this lack of presence in everyday procedure by the founder.

Adapted from Balmer and Greyser (2003)

alignment between vision/organizational culture and image. The *AC4ID framework* works with the alignment of seven identity types present in the organization.

Methods and data of the identity approach

The methods and data used in the identity approach reflect the diverse academic school of the theoretical framework and hence have their origin in different research traditions, matching the different focus (internal and external) and origins of the four theoretical building blocks in the brand identity construct. The methods used to collect data about organizational identity stem from anthropological and culture studies, while the study of corporate identity draws on heuristic methodologies from strategic management, exploring the visual expression and history of a corporation. Researching the image element of brand identity requires insights into the cognitive processes that consumers and stakeholders go through when evaluating a brand identity, and requires methods from cognitive psychology. Finally, the reputation element requires a study of the long-term interaction between the brand and the consumer, or stakeholder. In the attempt to make an overview of these diverse methods more comprehensible, the section is divided into two main parts. The first part accounts for the methods and data used, when researching corporate identity and organizational identity. The second part offers an overview of the methods and data used to research image and reputation.

The internal elements of brand identity: methods for the study of corporate identity and organizational identity

How to uncover corporate identity

Corporate identity is an expression of a strategic vision for the brand or the corporation as a whole. The corporate identity also refers to the visual identity of the brand. The methods for gathering data about the two differ:

- When uncovering the strategic perspective on corporate identity, it is mainly historical sources about the development of the vision and strategy of the company and brand specific historical records that are used to get an overview of the corporate identity and its development. Semi-structured interviews, storytelling methods and heuristic analysis are specific methods used as a supplement to the formal records of how the strategic vision has developed over time.
- Data about how the visual expression of the corporate identity has evolved over time must also be researched when uncovering corporate identity. The strength of the visual identity can also be a part of this aspect of assessing brand identity – measuring and comparing how the visual expressions reflect the positioning of a brand relative to the competition.

Having uncovered the sources of visual and strategic identity representing the more formal aspects of identity expressed by the company, the behavioural and cultural aspects of identity must also be uncovered. Organizational identity consists of a much higher degree of informal cues and symbols, hence a completely different set of methods are adequate to use when uncovering how organizational identity influences the corporate brand identity.

How to uncover organizational identity

Research into organizational identity (organizational culture and behaviour) draws on methods from various research traditions (such as anthropology, sociology, cultural and organizational studies). In the academic milieu there has been a fierce discussion about how organizational culture ought to be perceived and studied. However, during the last decade methods using a multi-paradigm approach (combining the different views and starting points) have emerged. High-performing brands often share the characteristic that they use organizational culture as a tool to nurture high employee commitment and loyalty. A strong organizational culture is consistent over time and the organizational values and norms rather than control schemata guide action and communication. There are several sources of a strong organizational identity: the style of top management, everyday organizational behaviour, organizational stories and myths, and embedded norms and values. How these elements contribute to organizational identity is the subject of analysis when uncovering organizational culture.

The basic perception of organizational identity has evolved from static and functionalistic to a more dynamic constructivist view. In the functionalist view, understanding culture is about identifying and categorizing cultural stereotypes. From a symbolic and dynamic perspective, culture is embedded in and expressed through people's actions and language. In a latter constructivist view, organizational culture is much more volatile and the strength of an organizational culture is found in its ability to learn, change and adapt to market demands. This evolution is reflected in the recent multi-paradigm methods of studying organizational culture. One of the key frameworks for the study of organizational culture offers a three-perspective approach. The three perspectives reflect the inherent ambiguity and forces of organizational culture (see Table 5.3).

The *integration* perspective represents the functionalist perspective and the forces in the organization oriented towards consensus and consistency. This perspective is usually found in the messages and activities initiated by top management to create and enhance organizational culture.

The *differentiation* perspective represents a more interpretive approach. The differentiation perspective assumes that cultural consensus exists within different subcultures and groupings, but not on an organization-wide level. The manifestations of organizational culture are hence not consistent throughout the organization. Ambiguity and the drivers of organizational culture are to be found in the consistency within subgroups and in the ambiguity distinguishing these different subgroups.

Table 5.3 Three perspectives on organizational culture

Characteristics	Integration	Differentiation	Fragmentation
Level of consensus	Organization-wide consensus	Subcultural consensus	Consensus appears only temporarily in clusters
Consistency of cultural manifestations	Consistent	Inconsistent	Complex
How ambiguity is perceived	Ambiguity is excluded and avoided	Ambiguity between subcultures is acknowledged	Ambiguity rather than consensus is assumed
The primary creators of culture	Founder or top management	Groups of subcultures	Individuals
Where to look for organizational culture	The formal culture dispersed by top management	The different levels of culture are played out in different functions or other groupings: a mix of formal and informal culture	Culture exists at an individual level
How to uncover organizational culture	Join all meetings and go through all internal communication and formal activities for employees	Get in deep with every function/ department or subculture to learn how they are diverse	It is by getting to know the individual employee that culture can be uncovered because it is assumed that there are as many interpretations of organizational culture as there are individual employees

Source: Adapted from Martin (2002)

In the third, and last, perspective of fragmentation, the more constructivist perspective is represented. Here, it is assumed that an organizational culture can display a multitude of views. In the fragmentation perspective, there is no consensus, and the relation between manifestations of organizational culture is complex. Only a combination of the three levels – the whole organization, subgroups and individual level of research – can give an accurate and complete snapshot of the cultural web and drivers of organizational culture.

In practice, the data collection focuses on the manifestations of organizational culture expressed through a combination of different elements. These elements illustrate that not only is it essential to encompass different perspectives in a research plan to ensure a deep and full understanding but grasping organizational culture also requires breadth. The manifestations form the cultural web of manifestations, which in combination define a specific organizational culture.

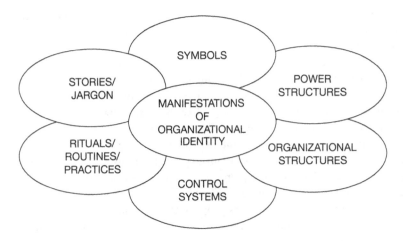

Figure 5.4 Manifestations of organizational identity (culture)

Organizational culture is best studied qualitatively and through embedding oneself in the cultural settings. The researcher must seek detailed and holistic descriptions based on intensive fieldwork to ensure understanding of how the cultural manifestations express a certain organizational identity. Since intensive fieldwork can be time-consuming, the ethnographic approach can adopt a clinical perspective, where qualitative interviews are the main research instrument. But in order to really understand a culture and interpret manifestations correctly, interviews and observation may not always be enough. Interaction with and immersion into the culture can be necessary to ensure the right interpretation (refer to Chapter 9 for a fuller description of ethnographic methods).

The external elements of brand identity: methods for the study of image and reputation

The object of analysis when collecting data and learning about image and reputation is, on the one hand, the positioning of the company image in relation to competitors and, on the other hand, research of image from the receivers' point of view. When studying the image and reputation of a brand in relation to competitors, surveys and laddering techniques are frequently used. But in order to get a deep understanding of how and why consumers associate a certain image with a brand, methods from cognitive and social psychology are used to investigate consumer perceptions and evaluations of image and reputation. Attitudes and perceptions are key elements when uncovering the formation of brand image and the mechanisms behind how image and reputation can be studied:

- *Perception.* Human beings perceive through sensory processes involving sight, sound, taste and hearing. After having absorbed inputs with our senses, it is time to perceive them. Perception is the process of meaning creation where the brain identifies input patterns and recognizes certain elements as being intertwined.

- *Cognition.* Before being able to think about sensory inputs and messages, they must be perceived and recognized. Consumers construct mental representations (images) and develop an understanding of what they have perceived – recognition process. This process takes place through abstract cognitive units rather than in language based units. These cognitive units are created through the use of images, words and symbols. Cognitive units link object (apple) and attribute (green), and action (donation of money to charity) to subject (a corporation). The cognition process is hence mental images capturing spatial relationships and ensuring recognition.
- *Attitudes* are the general evaluations people make of themselves, other people, objects and issues. Attitudes are emotional and influence how people behave. Attitudes can make people react. (In brand management it is important to know exactly which brand initiatives make consumers react i.e. consume.) It is difficult to predict to what extent attitudes affect action, but one thing is sure: people are more predisposed to act when some kind of change of circumstance causes them to evaluate their attitudes.

Understanding how cognitive units work and what makes consumers change their attitudes and maybe change consumption patterns is very valuable when researching brand image and reputation. Any research design for the investigation of the external elements of brand identity should reflect this knowledge about how consumers perceive, form attitudes and ultimately act. Image is the result of short-term advertising or other communication efforts, and reputation is formed based on a more long-term evaluation of brand actions and how the consumer interprets these and the motives behind them. Analysis of the contact points between brand and receiver is more important when collecting data about reputation. However, no matter whether the subject of analysis is image or reputation, knowledge about how consumers perceive and ultimately evaluate brand interaction is essential. There is an overlap of methodologies described here to uncover image and reputation and the methods used in the consumer-based approach, hence Chapter 6 provides a more in-depth explanation of cognitive methods to uncover consumers' perception and attitudes towards brands.

Summary

The methods used and the data collected in the identity approach vary depending on which of the four supporting themes is the subject to be studied. Data about corporate identity are collected with the use of heuristic methods. The aim is to study the historical and current strategic development and visual expression of brand identity. When researching organizational identity, the methods draw on inspiration from anthropology and cultural studies, where participation, immersion and

Box 5.7 How to do a brand identity study

- Since the four elements of brand identity are studied with very different methods, make sure that you differentiate and carefully select the right methods to study each of the four elements of brand identity.
- Initiate a long-term continuous research of reputation. Use a combination of surveys, questionnaires and in-depth interviews.
- For the study of image, initiate the research with explorative qualitative methods, where free association methods subtract all potential feedback and associations. Finalize and make the results useful to guide managerial decisions by using quantitative methods to uncover the salience of the complete list of feedback until narrowed down to a few central insights.
- For the study of the internal elements, plan the research, ensure full access to all meetings and processes. Without full access you will not get a complete and accurate picture of the organizational identity or the corporate identity.
- Immerse yourself in the everyday environment of the objects: watch, listen, learn and act.
- Initiate the process of changing the object that is observed (mainly organizational identity) according to the observations made already. Changes should not be stand-alone activities, but should be implemented in everyday processes.
- Observe how existing routines or other manifestations of organizational identity are affected.
- Make sure to include all levels and functions in all actions and observations, not only in the process of collecting data, but also in the data interpretation process. This will ensure a more accurate and deep understanding of organizational identity and its interplay with the corporate identity.
- Reflect on how the initiated changes were received, what can be done differently to improve results. What have you learned about the organizational culture that is new and requires new methods of observation and maybe new actions?
- Make sure that all the four elements are studied simultaneously and that the results from the four studies are merged in an overall plan for how to respond to the results.

extensive fieldwork are a prerequisite for gaining the deep and rich insights necessary to understand the underlying drivers of the cultural manifestations. Image is best studied by using a combination of qualitative methods for the explorative phase, supplemented by a quantitative phase making the results managerially useful. The methods originate from cognitive and social psychology and the focus is on consumer/stakeholder perception, cognition and attitudes formed in the process of a continuous evaluation of brand image and reputation.

Managerial implications

A strong brand identity can be the source of competitive and financial strength. However, building and managing brand identity is a complex and difficult management task. Research and management of the four supporting themes adding up to brand identity require very diverse data collection methods and a variety of skills and processes to implement in practice, because they respond to very different constituencies. This underpins the need for a carefully planned strategy and sensitive approach when managing brand identity.

Where most companies fail, is getting the organizational identity right and aligned with the remaining three sources of brand identity – the corporate identity (visual and strategic), image and reputation. Not dealing with identity issues can be devastating for business; 'ignoring issues of identity is not a feasible option, particularly for managers. Indeed, it only tends to exacerbate the problem. Identity does not go away, and can surface with a vengeance' (Balmer and Greyser 2003, p. 34). The involvement of employees in the co-creation of brand identity is extremely difficult and requires extraordinary skill and persistence. This section introduces the reader to the managerial guidelines of how the four theoretical building blocks – corporate identity, organizational identity, image and reputation and the two normative frameworks – *AC4ID* and *the corporate brand toolkit* – can guide managers to build and align the multiplicity of sources into a coherent brand identity.

Aligning vision and culture in practice

Any management process and activity, big or small, requires the right insight into the elements that are to be managed. In the case of brand identity, the goal is not to get information about the theoretical building blocks separately, but rather to observe and analyse the interplay between them. As mentioned and explained in the theory of brand identity, their alignment is the key to a strong brand identity. In practice, these four elements have different constituencies and different drivers; top management drives the strategy and formal visual identity (corporate identity), while employees are the drivers of culture and behavioural aspects (organizational identity). Finally, the drivers of image and reputation are all stakeholders. These different constituencies require that information is gathered from multiple sources and a variety of methods are used before misalignments or opportunities are uncovered.

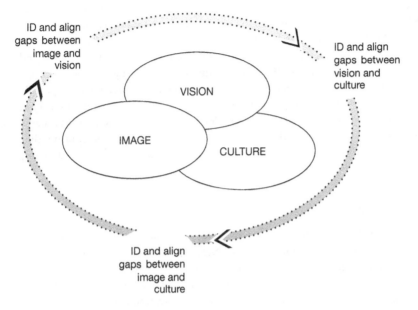

ID and align
gaps between
image and
vision

ID and align
gaps between
vision and
culture

VISION

IMAGE

CULTURE

ID and align
gaps between
image and
culture

Figure 5.5 Aligning identity, vision and culture

Gaps between vision and culture occur when the strategic vision that top management plans for the organization is too far from the reality (organizational identity) of the corporation – when employees are not able or willing to live up to the ambitious goals set by management. To uncover these gaps between vision and culture, it must be investigated if and to what extent employees support the visions planned by top management. It is also essential to uncover if all functions or subcultures (from R&D across production, marketing and eventually the sales force and pre-sales service function) in the organization approve and support the vision. If not all subcultures or groupings of an organization work to achieve the same goal it is very difficult to build a coherent brand identity. Vision and culture are essential for brand identity because they are the primary drivers of difficult-to-imitate differentiation, it is hence important to investigate how the vision and culture of the corporation stand out compared to the competition. This will deliver important managerial insights of to what extent corporate and organizational identity deliver sufficient grounds for the differentiation of brand identity. A general tendency is that management practices have evolved from focus on control mechanisms and extensive identity programme manuals to focus more on empowerment, the use of experience and storytelling to build commitment and cultural affiliation. In a 2009 publication, Hatch and Schultz elaborate on the corporate branding models and argue a move from corporate to enterprise branding, where a whole network of stakeholders contribute to the creation of brand identity.

A consequence of this development can be a fragmentation of brand identity, where, for example HR independently of the corporate brand develops an employer brand (Hatch and Schultz 2009) or where the voice of the brand on social media and its direct response and interaction with stakeholders must be weighed and managed while maintaining the agility required when dealing with social media (Young 2013). This is a good example of how marketing and branding – especially brand identity – are challenged by the increasing specialization and multiplicity of stakeholders within the field of marketing. It challenges the organizational structural management of branding and marketing to accommodate the voices of multiple stakeholders both internally and externally, while not losing the way and ending up with a fragmented brand identity.

Detecting identity gaps

Gaps between image and culture occur if employees do not deliver on the brand promise and thereby disappoint consumer expectations. Here, the focus of investigation is on the extent to which employees' perception of brand identity is in line with stakeholder associations and evaluations of brand image and reputation. It is vital to uncover how brand stimuli and the interaction between employees as carriers of brand identity and stakeholders contribute to the formation of brand image. Finally, gaps between image and vision are an expression of a situation where top management is alienated from what consumers expect and perceive of the brand identity. Misalignments between vision and image can result in consumers rejecting new product launches or marketing activities if they do not feel that it is the right direction for the brand. Misalignment between vision and image is serious and can be a symptom of inertia or lack of sufficient consumer intelligence. As a consequence, the company will miss out on market potential and consumer loyalty. To detect whether there are dangers of misalignment between vision and image, it must be identified who the primary stakeholders of the brand are and what these stakeholders expect from the brand identity. Frontline employees can play an important role in gathering information about how consumers react to new products or brand activities, a rich source of information that can provide, otherwise hard to attain, first hand impressions of consumer perceptions (see Table 5.4).

Aligning identity gaps

In practice, brand managers can use knowledge about the multiple identities and their alignment to manage the brand in a direction that is in line with consumers' perceptions of image, the strategic visions and hopes for what the brand should achieve in the future, the actual behaviour and organizational culture of the brand. After having uncovered the state of the image, corporate identity and the organizational identity and their respective alignment issues or gaps, a process must pave the way for realignment. This process can be divided into five cyclical steps:

Table 5.4 Detecting identity gaps

Theoretical elements	Corporate identity and organizational identity	Organizational identity and image	Image and corporate identity
Gaps between (according to the corporate brand toolkit)	Vision/Culture	Culture/Image	Image/Vision
Gaps between (according to the AC4ID framework)	Desired/ideal identity misaligned with the actual identity	The actual identity *misaligned* with the communicated and conceived identity	The conceived identity misaligned with the desired and ideal identity
Constituencies	Top management and employees	Employees and stakeholders	Stakeholders and top management
Questions	• Does the everyday reality reflect the values the vision requires? • Is the vision supported by all functions and subcultures? • Are vision and culture sufficiently differentiated from competition?	• What perception of image do stakeholders express? • How do employees perceive company image? • How do stakeholders and employees interact?	• Who are the stakeholders of the company? • What do the stakeholders want and expect from the company? • How well is knowledge about stakeholders' images communicated to top management and vice versa?
How to solve misalignment	Ensure that not only communication but also out-of-the-box activities and continuous training ensure that employees understand and support the corporate identity	Set up organizational identity in a way that supports the image and reputation of the brand identity. Measure all contact points between stakeholders and employees against image and reputation	Make sure that top management is informed by customer insights and new tendencies are detected. Avoid inertia and irrelevant brand launches or activities by taking image or perceptions seriously

- *Stating.* State the vision and identity of the corporate brand. (Who are we and what do we want to become?) Articulating core values and identity behind brand *establishes the corporate identity*.
- *Organizing.* Link vision with culture and image practices. How can we reorganize to achieve fit? Cross-functional structure and process changes establish the frame for developing the appropriate organizational identity.
- *Involving.* Involve stakeholders through culture and image. Engage employees in execution and involve consumer images. Get input from multiple sources.
- *Integrating.* Integrate culture and image around a new brand identity. Align the organization behind the brand. *Align the multiple identities across internal functions*.
- *Monitoring.* Track corporate branding gaps and brand performance (see Table 5.5).

The challenges of building brand identity

Brand-building activities based on the line of thought behind the identity approach are often criticized for being an ego-stroking waste of time with no relevance for either consumers or stakeholders. To avoid this identity trap and enhance the probability of success, the objectives of the brand identity building campaign must be defined and the results carefully measured against objectives. Is the objective to create awareness, the creation of favourable attitudes or the enhancement of organizational identity, and why? Is the goal externally oriented or is the focus more internal, with the aim to increase employer motivation and attract better recruits? No matter what the goal is, it is important to be very clear on why brand identity activities are needed and what the company wishes to achieve with such activities.

It is also necessary to consider whether the organizational structure of the company suits the aims of brand identity. It is important to understand the forces that drive particular types of organizations. Having established goals and organizational structure, it is time to involve employees in the brand identity project. Often, too much energy is used on attempts to change employee attitudes and behaviour in practice. Best-practice cases show that efforts should focus on the translation of brand values into real-life experiences, which can be used on any occasion. It is often difficult to get all the employees to actively support brand identity programmes.

A good way to ensure daily involvement and commitment can be to give employees 'out of the box' experiences on a regular basis through events and sponsorships; this can provide real-life experiences, building commitment and sharing. Instead of trying to implement and align identities through communication only, these real-life experiences can inspire employees to activate the brand promise in their everyday working environment. Sharing of real-life experiences among employees is a good way to bring the brand identity to life internally and ensure that employees live the values and the organizational identity of the brand.

The cultural and historical heritage of a company can also be used to build brand identity. The company does not necessarily need to have been in business for many years before it is able to use history or culture actively in the building of brand identity. Also a unique organizational identity or a charismatic CEO can be the source of corporate and organizational identity.

Table 5.5 Aligning identity gaps

Activity	Cycle 1: State	Cycle 2: Organize	Cycle 3: Involve	Cycle 4: Integrate
Key process	State the identity for the corporate brand and link this identity to corporate vision	Link corporate vision to organizational culture and the image	Involve stakeholders through organizational culture and the image	Integrate corporate vision, organizational culture and the image around the new brand identity
Key question	Who are we as an organization and what do we stand for?	How can we reorganize the corporate brand?	How can we involve internal and external stakeholders in the corporate brand?	How can we integrate corporate vision, organizational culture and the image of the corporate brand?
Key concerns	• Make company-wide audit of brand expression • Revisit brand cultural heritage • Analyse brand images among stakeholders	• Create a coherent brand organization • Provide Managerial foundation for implementation processes	• Does the company have a shared cultural mindset? • Ensure active inclusion of global stakeholders perceptions	• Integrate the brand across markets and business areas

Source: Adapted from Schultz et al. (2005)

Box 5.8 Brand identity throughout the value chain

Brand power of the front

The managerial challenge of ensuring that all stakeholders in the value chain enhance and not devaluate brand identity has become a growing research concern since 2005 in the identity approach. The influence that resellers, retailers and other front-line employees have on brand success is immense. Therefore, the value of branded service encounters and how they affect brand performance has led to an increasing research and managerial focus. It is the battle to ensure that front-line employees, sales channel partners and other stakeholders throughout the value chain are engaged and ready to deliver on brand identity.

Brand identification with resellers

In line with the enterprise branding perspective put forward by Hatch and Schultz (2009), where the whole network of stakeholders and their stake in the creation of brand identity is acknowledged, an increasing number of articles advocate that companies should prioritize spending resources on building psychological connections with resellers – or other upstream value chain personnel. In a retail setting especially, the success of a brand heavily relies on the ability of this stakeholder group to identify with the brand. According to Hughes and Ahearne (2010), the psychological identification is more effective than brand control schemes. This requires that managers will do much better by empowering resellers, to make them feel part of the articulation and delivery of brand identity to consumers. They should be given the opportunity to act as role models and the freedom to individually interpret their roles as brand representatives. It is a fine line of balancing standardized brand experiences and front-line employee empowerment (Sirani *et al*. 2013, Zeithaml *et al*. 2013).

Box 5.9 Living the brand: all about the people of Quiksilver

'Living the brand' is a construct that describes brands building on ideas so powerful that employees engage to such an extent that they are not only employed by a corporation or a brand, they 'live the brand'; the power of the brand builds unforeseen employee involvement and commitment. Employees internalize brand values: brand values, symbols and stories keep employees' behaviour aligned with the values of the brand. This enables them to deliver the brand promise to consumers, hence acting as key co-creators of brand equity. The companies succeeding in this benefit in terms of higher productivity, enhanced financial performance and greater intellectual capital.

Australian surfers Alan Green and John Law founded Quiksilver in 1970. Green and Law's vision was to redesign the surfer's board-riding shorts by using a fabric that dried rapidly, with Velcro and snap closure. These features were exactly what board riders demanded and the product became a huge success. The founders had insights into the needs of board riders because they themselves were part of that environment and their insights were what laid the foundation for the company. This foundation and the founders' engagement in the environment of their consumers is still a priority. Today, Quiksilver calls themselves a board-riding company, where employees share the passion for board riding. Consumer involvement is underpinned by much sponsorship of surfers and of board-riding events that Quiksilver supports or arranges around the world. Employees at Quiksilver live the Quiksilver brand, and they are actively involved in board-riding communities.

Box 5.10 Dos and don'ts of the identity approach

Do	*Don't*
Disperse shared vision to all stakeholder groups within and outside the organization	Don't neglect diverse interpretations and loose vitality and dynamics
Aim at building a shared organizational culture and behavior	Don't get stuck in the pitfall of group-think and path dependence
Management should be strong, visible, and provide behavioral guidance	Don't neglect subcultures and diverse organizational functions
Be cross-functional, involve the whole organization	Don't cut off innovation and new ideas that require deep insight and exploration of new paths
Listen to the market and be open to co-creation of brand identity	Don't jeopardize the distinctiveness of brand identity
Embed brand identity management strategically	Don't go with short-term market trends and lose core competences
Align corporate identity, organizational identity, image and reputation continuously	Don't leave brand management to top management solely

Make sure that brand identity evolves continuously	Don't revolutionize brand identity
Run campaigns internally before they are run externally	Don't fail to communicate and activate to ensure real life experiences internally before brand activities are initiated externally
Ensure to also empower frontline employees	Don't solely use control schemes to create and manage standardized brand encounters

Summary

The primary task of the brand manager in the brand identity approach is to ensure that consumers and stakeholders experience a strong and coherent brand identity through all contacts with it. In order to achieve this, it is essential that the identity types or the theoretical building blocks of organizational identity, corporate identity, image and reputation are aligned. This requires a multi-dimensional approach where gap detection and identity alignment can take place across all functions and subcultures in the organization. *The corporate brand toolkit* or the *AC4ID test* are two normative frameworks suitable for detecting and balancing multiple identities. After careful analysis of identity gaps, the brand identity can be developed and enhanced through a process of cyclical steps. In this process, the brand identity is stated, more information about identity types is gathered and core values are articulated. Second, the brand identity is organized – how can the stated brand identity be implemented to kick in all identity types? The third process ensures that all stakeholders are involved in the creation and implementation of brand identity through dispersing information and brand identity-building activities. The final process integrates all the identity types in one coherent brand identity.

The academic evolution of the identity approach

Brand identity was in its earlier days led by so-called design consultants, and the focus was in how to make business strategy visible through symbols and graphic design. Wally Olins, a pioneer in the identity school, advocated visual identity programmes to manage and ensure coherent brand identity (Olins 1979). During the 1990s, focus in research of identity shifted focus from product to corporate level brand identity, paving the way for a multidisciplinary approach incorporating organizational culture and behaviour, as well as consumer images.

A very influential stream of research and managerial orientation of brand identity emerged led by pioneers in the field: the duo of Hatch and Schultz, as well as Balmer. Under their influence, the brand identity scope evolved to encompass multiple identity types. Furthermore, constructs and tools incorporating internal and external sources of brand equity were developed. Despite differences, all with the higher aim of incorporating alignment and balance of multiple identities into one coherent brand identity (Balmer and Soenen 1999, Hatch and Shultz 2001).

Especially in a European context, the theoretical constructs, frameworks and methodologies to comprehend, analyse and manage these large amounts of data and sources of identity were evaluated, altered and refined after the millennium, and the scope was further expanded to entail larger networks of stakeholder and additional sources of identity (Balmer 2008, Balmer 2012, Hatch and Schultz 2009). Post 2005, a significant number of articles addressing the challenge of ensuring a coherent brand identity throughout the value chain and in particular with front-line employees have been published. They explore constructs and frameworks to ensure employee brand identification and the balance between control schemes and empowerment when managing and aiming at standardized branded service encounters and customer experiences (Anisimova and Mavondo 2010, Hughes and Ahearne 2010, Morhart *et al.* 2009, Sirani *et al.* 2013).

Most recently, the impact of social media and open source developments on brand identity are a trending topic, exploring the ambiguity of organizing brand identity versus the volatile dynamics of social media (Da Silva and Syed Alwi 2008, Young 2013).

Comments from the 'founding fathers'

The value of the identity approach to the study and management of brands

Majken Schultz, Copenhagen Business School and Mary Jo Hatch, University of Virginia

Branding is constantly on the move, both in theory and in practice. Since the early days, when it was rooted in the marketing discipline, branding has become a strategic concern for corporations, which requires a much more integrative approach than marketing alone can provide. A range of different disciplines and organizational functions need to be engaged and inspired so that the organization is motivated to deliver the brand promise throughout all activities. The recent development of what here is called the identity approach is an example of this shift in the foundation for analysing and managing brands.

Originating from corporate identity with its focus on the expressive side of branding, the identity approach draws on insights from organization studies, social psychology and stakeholder theory. Through these influences, the approach embraces the relational and dynamic nature of identity, claiming that, when corporate branding works, it is intimately tied into the organization's identity, continuously arcing between the poles of 'Who am I?' and 'What do others think about me?' Knowing what creates the sense of 'we' allows organizations to authentically tell others what they stand for. But knowing who you are also requires intimate knowledge of how stakeholders see your organization. This is because

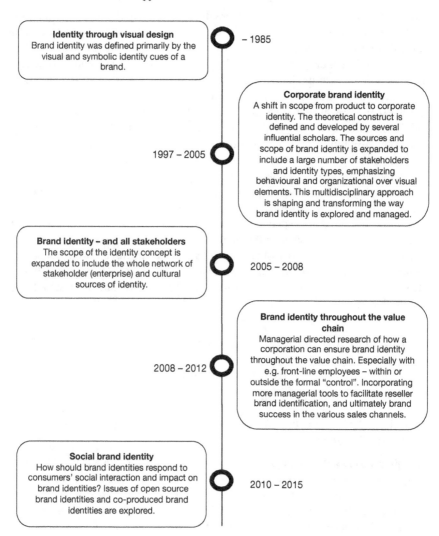

Figure 5.6 The academic evolution of the identity approach

Box 5.11 You are not done!

Don't forget to visit the website for supplementary material such as case examples, student questions and supplementary literature.

external images interact with the ways in which employees think about their organization and the organizational culture that helps them make sense of what they hear and know about the organization. Together, what they know themselves to be through direct experience and contact with the images of others creates an identity dialogue that provides the foundation for branding.

We claim that strong brands are based in the alignment between strategic vision, organization culture and stakeholder images. This is represented in Chapter 5 as the corporate branding toolkit. As with most conceptual models, this is an ideal to aim for. The reality for most companies is that they continually struggle to maintain alignment through most of their lives, at times confronting significant gaps in the relationships between vision, culture and images, which require more radical intervention. It is our experience that what makes the difference between leading brands and the rest is their willingness and ability to pose questions to their corporate brands – and use the answers in their continuous development of their vision, their culture and their images. This is a process that never ceases.

Meanwhile, as a practice and a field of study, branding continues to evolve from its roots in product thinking and its further development as a corporate-wide endeavour. As a consequence the ways in which companies engage in brand management continue to change. Branding began as a marketing endeavour to create and manage the relationship between *products and consumers*. This might have worked well at the product level, but it implied that corporate brands often were treated as if they were giant economy-sized product brands, which can be created with advertising campaigns.

When the term *corporate* started to receive more attention in corporate branding, brand management became a multi-functional activity. This meant that HR, corporate communication, investor relations and all the other communication functions joined with marketers to manage the corporate brand. This ultimately spawned cross-functional task forces and teams whose job was to co-ordinate all the corporate brand efforts going on around the company and to bring corporate brand thinking to other projects and programmes as well. Corporate branding led to such innovations as employer brands and a plethora of brand activation and renewal programmes – each designed, orchestrated and led by different groups within the corporation. Over time, this activity contributed to fragmentation and confusion as different groups claimed their piece of the branding puzzle and the resources that came along with them.

In the context of the stakeholder society, a new wave of *enterprise* branding is evolving to respond to these gathering forces and balance the identity conversation by positioning the corporate brand to be the voice, not just of the company, but of the stakeholders who comprise the enterprise. This newly emerging framework holds out hope not only that corporate branding will resolve internal integration problems, but that it will reaffirm the strategic approach to managing the expectations of those stakeholders who make up the enterprise of which the company is but a part.

As a result, the next generation of brand managers will spend increasing amounts of time looking at the brand through the eyes of their multiple stakeholders.

Participation in brand community events will feature prominently on their schedules, and every interaction inside the firm and out will become much more of a two-way communication process. Brand managers will bring some of these stakeholders into the management process, making use of their ideas and skills in internal company activities. They will design new activities that get employees to work alongside even more stakeholders doing things that give all of their lives greater meaning.

References and further reading

Key readings are in bold type

Aaker, D. A. (1991), *Managing Brand Equity*, New York: Free Press Business.

Aaker, D. A. and Joachimsthaler, E. (2000), *Brand Leadership*, New York: Free Press Business.

Abratt, R. (1989), 'A new approach to the corporate image management process', *Journal of Marketing Management*, 5 (1): 63–76.

Albert, S. and Whetten, D. (1985), 'Organizational identity', *Research in Organizational Behavior*, 7 (1): 263–95.

Anisimova, T. and Mavondo, F. T. (2010), 'The performance implications of company–salesperson corporate brand misalignment', *European Journal of Marketing*, 44 (6): 771–95.

Argenti, P. A. (1998), 'Strategic employee communications', *Human Resource Management*, 37 (3–4): 199–207.

Balmer, J. M. T. (1995), 'Corporate branding and connoisseurship', *Journal of General Management*, 21 (1): 24–46.

Balmer, J. M. T. (1998), 'Corporate identity and the advent of corporate marketing', *Journal of Marketing Management*, 14 (8): 963–96.

Balmer, J. M. T. (2001a), 'The three virtues and seven deadly sins of corporate brand management', *Journal of General Management*, 27 (1): 1–17.

Balmer, J. M. T. (2001b), 'Corporate identity, corporate branding and corporate marketing; seeing through the fog', *European Journal of Marketing*, 35 (3–4): 248–91.

Balmer, J. M. T. (2008), 'Identity based views of the corporation: Insights from corporate identity, organizational identity, social identity, visual identity, corporate brand identity and corporate image', *European Journal of Marketing*, 42 (9/10): 879–906.

Balmer, J. M. T. (2010), 'Explicating corporate brands and their management: Reflections and directions from 1995', *Journal of Brand Management*, 18 (3): 180–96.

Balmer, J. M. T. (2012), 'Strategic corporate brand alignment: Perspectives from identity based views of corporate brands', *European Journal of Marketing*, 46 (7/8): 1064–1092.

Balmer, J. M. T. and Greyser, S. E. (2003), *Revealing the Corporation: Perspectives on Identity, Image, Reputation, Corporate Branding, and Corporate-level Marketing*, London: Routledge.

Balmer, J. M. T. and Soenen, G. B. (1999), 'The acid test of corporate identity management™', *Journal of Marketing Management*, 15 (1–3): 69–92.

Berens, G., van Riel, C. B. M. and van Bruggen, G. H. (2005), 'Corporate associations and consumer product responses: The moderating role of corporate brand dominance', *Journal of Marketing*, 69 (3): 35–48.

Bernstein, D. (1984), *Company Image and Reality: A Critique of Corporate Communications*, Austin, TX: Holt, Rinehart and Winston.

Collins, J. C. and Porras, J. I. (1994), *Built to Last: Successful Habits of Visionary Companies*, New York: Harper Business.

Da Silva, R. V. and Syed Alwi, S. F. (2008), 'Online brand attributes and online corporate brand images', *European Journal of Marketing*, 42 (9/10): 1039–1058.

De Chernatony, L. (1999), 'Brand management through narrowing the gap between brand identity and brand reputation', *Journal of Marketing Management*, 15 (1–3): 157–9.

Fombrun, J. C. and van Riel, C. B. M. (1998), 'The reputational landscape', *Corporate Reputation Review*, 1 (1): 5–13, reprinted in J. M. T. Balmer and S. Greyser (eds) (2003), *Revealing the Corporation: Perspectives on Identity, Image, Reputation, Corporate Branding, and Corporate-level Marketing*, London: Routledge.

Gioia, D. A., Schultz, M. and Corley, K. G. (2000), 'Organizational identity, image and adaptive instability', *Academy of Management Review*, 25 (1): 63–81.

Gotsi, M. and Wilson, A. (2001), 'Corporate reputation management: Living the brand', *Management Decision*, 39 (2): 99–104.

Gray, E. R. and Balmer, J. M. T. (2001), 'The corporate brand: a strategic asset', *Management in Practice*, 4: 1–4.

Gray, E. R. and Schmeltzer, L. R. (1987), 'Planning a face-lift: Implementing a corporate image programme', *Journal of Business Strategy*, 8 (1): 4–10.

Grunig, J. (1993), 'Image and substance: From symbolic to behavioral relationships', *Public Relations Review*, 19 (2): 121–39.

Hackley, C. (2003), *Doing Research Projects in Marketing, Management and Consumer Research*, London: Routledge.

Hatch, M. J. and Schultz, M. (1997), 'Relations between organizational culture, identity and image', *European Journal of Marketing*, 31 (5–6): 356–65.

Hatch, M. J. and Schultz, M. (2000), 'Scaling the tower of Babel: Relational difference between identity, image and culture in organizations', in M. Schultz, M. J. Hatch and H. Larsen (eds), *The Expressive Organization: Linking Identity, Reputation and the Corporate Brand*, Oxford: Oxford University Press, pp. 11–35.

Hatch, M. J. and Schultz, M. (2001), 'Are the strategic stars aligned for your corporate brand?' *Harvard Business Review*, 79 (2): 128–34.

Hatch, M. J. and Schultz, M. (2003), 'Bringing the corporation into corporate branding', *European Journal of Marketing*, 37 (7–8): 1041–1064.

Hatch, M. J. and Schultz, M. (2008), *Taking Brand Initiative: How Companies can align Strategy, Culture, and Identity through Corporate Branding*, San Francisco, CA: Wiley.

Hatch, M. J. and Schultz, M. (2009), 'Of Bricks and Brands: From Corporate to Enterprise Branding', *Organizational Dynamics*, 38 (2): 117–30.

Hatch, M. J. and Schultz, M. (2010), 'Toward a theory of brand co-creation with implications for brand governance' *Journal of Brand Management*, 17 (8): 590–604.

Hughes, D. E. and Ahearne, M. (2010). Energizing the reseller's sales force: The power of brand identification, *Journal of Marketing*, 74 (4): 81–96.

Ind, N. (1992), *The Corporate Image*, London: Kogan Page.

Ind, N. (1997), *The Corporate Brand*, New York: New York University Press.

Ind, N. (1998), 'An integrated approach to corporate branding', *Journal of Brand Management*, 6 (5): 323–9.

Ind, N. (2001), *Living the Brand*, London: Kogan Page.

Kapferer, J-N. (1997), *Strategic Brand Management: Creating and Sustaining Brand Equity Long Term*, London: Kogan Page.

Karmark, E. (2005), 'Living the brand', in M. Schultz, Y. M. Antorini and F. F. Csaba (eds), *Corporate Branding: Purpose, People, Process*, Copenhagen, Denmark: Copenhagen Business School Press, pp. 103–24.

Keller, K. L. (1997), *Strategic Brand Management: Building, Measuring, and Managing Brand Equity*, Englewood Cliffs, NJ: Pearson.

Kennedy, S. H. (1977), 'Nurturing corporate images', *European Journal of Marketing*, 1 (3): 119–64.

King, S. (1991), 'Brand building in the 1990s', *Journal of Marketing Management*, 7 (1): 3–13.

Martin, J. (2002), *Organizational Culture: Mapping the Terrain*, Thousand Oaks, CA: Sage Publications.

Mitchell, C. (2002), 'Selling the brand inside: You tell customers what makes you great. Do your employees know?' *Harvard Business Review*, 80 (1): 99–106.

Mitchell, A. (2004), 'Getting staff to live the brand: Work in progress', *Marketing Week*, 2 September, p. 30.

Morhart, F. M., Herzog, W. and Tomczak, T. (2009), 'Brand-specific leadership: Turning employees into brand champions', *Journal of Marketing*, 73 (5): 122–42.

Olins, W. (1978), *The Corporate Personality: An Inquiry into the Nature of Corporate Identity*, London: Design Council.

Olins, W. (1979), 'Corporate identity - the myth and the reality', *Royal Society of Arts Journal*, 127 (5272): 208-23.

Olins, W. (1989), *Corporate Identity: Making Business Strategy Visible through Design*, Boston, MA: Harvard Business School Press.

Olins, W. (2001), 'How brands are taking over the corporation', in M. Schultz, M. J. Hatch and M. H. Larsen (eds), *The Expressive Organization: Linking Identity, Reputation and the Corporate Brand*, Oxford: Oxford University Press, pp. 51–65.

Petty, R. E. and Cacioppo, J. T. (1986), *Communication and Persuasion: Central and Peripheral Routes to Attitude Change*, New York: Springer.

Schmitt, B. and Simonson, A. (1997), 'Looks count', *Entrepreneur*, 25 (9): 166–70.

Schroeder, J. E. and Salzer-Mörling, M. (ed.) (2006), *Brand Culture*, London and New York: Routledge.

Schultz, M., Hatch, M. J. and Larsen, M. H. (eds) (2000), *The Expressive Organization: Linking Identity, Reputation and the Corporate Brand*, Oxford: Oxford University Press.

Schultz, M., Antorini, Y. M. and Csaba, F. F. (2005), *Corporate Branding: Purpose, People, Process*, Copenhagen, Denmark: Copenhagen Business School Press.

Scott, W. A., Osgood, D. W. and Peterson, C. (1979), *Cognitive Structure: Theory and Measurement of Individual Difference*, New York: Wiley.

Sirianni, N. J., Bitner, M. J., Brown, S. W., and Mandel, N. (2013), 'Branded service encounters: Strategically aligning employee behavior with the brand positioning', *Journal of Marketing*, 77 (6): 108–23.

Vinhas Da Silva, R. and Faridah Syed Alwi, S. (2008), 'Online brand attributes and online corporate brand images', *European Journal of Marketing*, 42 (9/10): 1039–1058.

Young, J. (2013), 'A conceptual understanding of organizational identity in the social media environment', *Advances in Social Work*, 14 (2): 518–30.

Zeithaml, V. A., Bitner, M. J. and Gremler, D. D. (2013), *Services Marketing: Integrating Customer Focus Across the Firm* (6th edn), New York: McGraw-Hill.

Websites

www.aeg.com
www.lego.com/en-us
www.quiksilver.com

6   The consumer-based approach

with a commentary by Professor Kevin Lane Keller, Tuck School of Business, Dartmouth College

> In communication, as in architecture, less is more. You have to sharpen your message to cut into the mind. You have to jettison the ambiguities, simplify the message, and then simplify it some more if you want to make a long-lasting impression.
>
> *Ries and Trout (2001), p. 8*

In the early years of brand management the focus was on the 'sender end' of brand communication. Still, in the accompanying scientific discipline of consumer research, a new view of the consumer was being thoroughly investigated in the 1980s. The idea of the information-processing consumer (Bettman 1979) as well as the ideas about positioning (Ries and Trout 1983, 2001) paved the way for a radically new brand perspective. In 1993, brand management was profoundly shaken by one research article in particular. Kevin Lane Keller published the article 'Conceptualizing, measuring, and managing customer-based brand equity' in the *Journal of Marketing* and thereby instigated a major change in the field of brand management. Customer-based brand equity is based on the premise that the brand resides in the minds of consumers as a cognitive construal, which is why we have chosen to name it the consumer-based approach. Consumer research was, at this point in time, very much influenced by cognitive psychology and the related information-processing theory of consumer choice. Insights from these veins of literature were adapted to brand management theory with the birth of the consumer-based approach.

This brand perspective has been tremendously influential in the shaping of brand management and is still considering a pivotal point in the discipline. The publication of research-based literature exploring this brand perspective is still significant; the more recent research tries to understand and explain how *context* is influencing our memory processes, brand evaluations and consumption choices. Hence, the new research tries to understand one of the basic premises of this brand perspective; that we are living in an over-communicated society.

Box 6.1 Learning objectives

The purpose of this chapter is to:

Understand the assumptions of the consumer-based approach

- The brand is a cognitive construal in the mind of the consumer.
- The brand resides in the mind of the consumer, but the marketer is still able to control brand value creation.

Understand the theoretical building blocks and how they are connected

- The cognitive consumer perspective.
- The information-processing theory of consumer choice.
- Customer-based brand equity.

Provide insights into the variety of methods used to enquire into the cognitive aspects of the consumer

- Input–output methods to understand how consumer decisions change if stimuli are changed.
- Process-tracing methods to understand the process of brand choice.
- Measuring customer-based brand equity.

Understand the managerial implications

- The 'dualist' nature of the approach.
- Superior outside–in capabilities.
- The marketer should stress brand congruency and consistency.

Understand the academic evolution of the approach

- The consumer-based approach is inspired by theories about positioning and the information-processing consumer.
- The CBBE framework constituted the approach in 1993.
- Recent development is characterized by research into memory and decision of memory processes and displays an increasing focus on context.

The 1993 article introduced a new brand and consumer perspective, thus giving birth to a new brand management approach. Besides that, it also played an extremely important role as it discussed and clarified some central notions of brand management. At that time, the discipline of brand management suffered from a lack of independence in relation to the parent discipline of marketing. Research articles on branding were often difficult to tell from articles on advertising research and other marketing phenomena. The key notion of brand equity was often not even mentioned, and certainly not defined. All in all, the academic discipline of brand management appeared rather immature and scientifically incomplete. All this changed after the introduction of customer-based brand equity. One of the very important contributions of the Keller publication was that the article instigated a new way of relating to the more and more independent scientific disciplines of brand management by its thorough discussion of the key term of brand equity. Before 1993, academic articles rarely mentioned brand equity, while the vast majority of post-1993 articles start out by relating their subject of choice to different definitions of brand equity (read about brand equity in Chapter 12).

Since the launch of the consumer-based approach, the mindset behind it has been widely adopted and become a very influential way of thinking about brands and branding: 'Keller's exposition of the customer-based brand equity model offers the most widely accepted and comprehensive treatment of branding in American marketing' (Holt 2005, p. 277). The initial impact of the theory as presented in 1993 has been followed up by the great importance of Keller's book *Strategic Brand Management: Building, Measuring, and Managing Brand Equity* (1998, 2003 and 2012).

Since it is our aim to make a side-by-side presentation of the seven schools of thought in brand management, they are presented as ideal types. Therefore, we focus on the original cognitive brand and consumer perspective in this approach (by focusing on the founding article and the literature relating to it). How the approach has further developed will be discussed and compared with the new approaches in the two final sections; one section about the way this brand perspective has been supplemented with insights from other approaches (presented in numerous textbooks) and one section about how the approach is developing in brand management academia.

Assumptions of the consumer–based approach

The two prior approaches – the economic approach and the identity approach – are both primarily focused on the *sender side* of brand communication. The economic approach (Chapter 4) focuses on the way a marketer can influence brand value creation through adjusting the components of the traditional marketing mix. The primary focus of the identity approach (Chapter 5) is the brand from an organizational perspective. In the consumer-based approach, the brand is analysed as residing *in the mind of the individual consumer* as a *cognitive construal*.

The consumer has thus become the main point of interest in this approach. He or she is considered the 'owner' of the brand. Where the two prior approaches stressed an inside–out perspective on brand value creation, the consumer-based approach introduces an outside–in approach to brand management. The consumer-based approach hence embraces external strategy formation, as opposed to the internal strategy formation focus of the two prior approaches and requires a more adaptive mindset (Louro and Cunha 2001).

Brand value creation takes place by moulding the brand associations held in the consumers' minds. Understanding the consumer is hence central in this take on brand value creation, but it is important to notice that the approach implies a specific view of the consumer. The consumer is analysed by means of theories adopted from cognitive psychology and the information-processing theory of consumer choice.

The 'brand–consumer exchange' and the cognitive perspective

In this section, we will introduce the consumer-brand exchange and consumer perspective jointly. In the consumer-based approach, brand strength equals strong, unique and favourable associations in the minds of its consumers. The fact that the brand is a cognitive construal in the mind of the consumer makes one jump to the conclusion that the consumer 'owns' the brand and thereby controls brand value creation (see Figure 6.1).

That is not the case; the marketer is on the contrary assumed to be very much in control with brand communication as the approach rests upon an assumption of the consumer as a *cognitive man*. The consumer is seen and analysed through a lens grounded in cognitive psychology and information economics. As we describe in further detail in the next section, the cognitive perspective implies a view of man that still grants managers control over brand image creation. Even though the brand is analysed as a mental construal in the mind of the consumer, it still makes sense to talk about the communication of intended meaning. This notion of linear communication means that the recipient of a message understands the message as intended by the sender. In cognitive psychology, the dominant man metaphor is that of the computer and the human mind is supposed to process sensory data in much the same way a computer processes binary data.

In cognitive psychology, an 'if–then' logic applies. *If* the marketer feeds the 'consumer computer' with the most appropriate information, *then* the consumer will do as intended and choose the brand. One is able to program a computer into doing the same thing every time and this is the logic that applies to the brand–consumer exchange. In other words, the consumer is the focal point, but the marketer is still assumed to control the brand in the consumer-based approach. A linear response to sensory input → consumer → brand choice is hence assumed.

At a first glance, the consumer appears to be all-powerful in the brand–consumer exchange, but the consumer 'ownership' of the approach is paradoxical; even though the consumer 'owns' the brand, he or she is still treated as a generic entity that the skilled communicator is able to 'program' into intended action. The chaotic, unpredictable and 'autonomous' aspects of consumer behaviour that are taken into consideration in the later approaches (the relational, the community and the cultural approaches) are not considered in this consumer perspective.

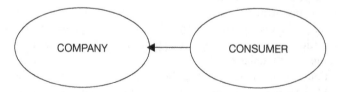

COMPANY   CONSUMER

Figure 6.1 The brand resides in the mind of the consumer

Summary

The consumer-based approach assumes that the brand is a cognitive construal residing in the mind of the consumer.

This assumption indicates that the consumer is very much in control of the brand–consumer exchange. This is, however, not entirely the case. The consumer is seen through a lens borrowed from cognitive psychology and the main metaphor for man in this perspective is that of the computer.

And just like a skilled computer programmer is able to program the computer into doing as intended, the marketer who is willing to map out the brand construal in the mind of the consumer will be able to choose exactly the right brand elements and communicate them to a consumer, who will respond accordingly. These, seemingly contradictory, assumptions are what lie behind the consumer-based approach.

Theoretical building blocks of the consumer-based approach

As mentioned in the introduction, the consumer-based approach is founded on one research article presenting the customer-based brand equity framework. This framework is the core theory of the consumer-based approach.

Behind the framework is the information-processing theory of consumer choice, and *behind* this theory we find the cognitive consumer perspective. In this section, we will move forward, starting out with a brief introduction to the cognitive consumer perspective (see Figure 6.2). From here, we move on to a short review of the information-processing theory of consumer choice. Both topics are extremely comprehensive and quite complicated and going into depth with them is beyond the scope of this book. Having become acquainted with important characteristics of these two topics, the reader will be better equipped to fully understand the core theory: customer-based brand equity.

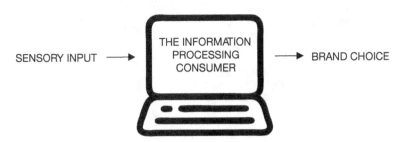

Figure 6.2 The computer is the central metaphor of man in cognitive psychology

Figure 6.3 depicts how the customer-based brand equity framework builds on insights from both the cognitive consumer perspective and the information-processing theory of consumer choice and that this theory also draws on the cognitive consumer perspective.

The cognitive consumer perspective

In the assumptions, the key characteristics of cognitive psychology were introduced. The main metaphor for man (the consumer) is that of a computer; cognitive psychology focuses on the process where a consumer is exposed to stimuli from his or her environment (input, information), how these stimuli enter the mind via the senses and how they lead to action (choice). It is also fundamental to understand the 'if–then' logic that applies to this consumer perspective.

Cognitive psychology is concerned with the higher cognitive processes, namely memory, language, problem solving, imagery, deduction and induction. In other words, the cognitive research tradition deals with aspects such as reasoning, intelligence and learning, and tries to answer questions like 'How do we learn?' 'How do we remember?' 'What makes us pay attention?' 'What makes us react?' As we grow up, we develop greater cognitive structure, meaning that we become still better at discriminating among stimuli and organizing stimuli into meaningful constructs.

Relevant to the consumer-based perspective is how we store knowledge, how we remember and how our attention is captured. The sum of these processes is to understand how it leads to action, in our line of interest: namely brand choice. The cognitive research tradition deliberately neglects emotional factors as well as historical and cultural aspects when studying how human beings function, behave and respond.

We store enormous amounts of knowledge in our memory. Memory is activated (by a sensory input) and spreading activities begin. Thereby, knowledge is retrieved from memory. Knowledge in memory consists of nodes and links and is structured

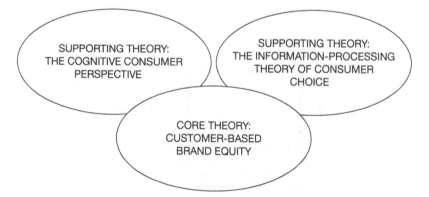

Figure 6.3 Supporting and core theories of the consumer-based approach

into associative networks. Nodes are the stored information connected by links in associative networks. The nodes vary in strength; some associations are stronger than others. Environmental stimuli (e.g. a commercial message) trigger a node that through the 'spreading activity' triggers new nodes associated with the first one. An example of this spreading activity might be the word Volkswagen. The retrieval of the node Volkswagen triggers a spreading activity that potentially could look like Figure 6.4. The associations can continue spreading in all directions until they have lost relevance for the node Volkswagen. The fact that some links are emphasized shows that some associations are more direct and are thus retrieved more easily than others (they are *stronger* associations).

A node is a mental representation. Cognitive research aims at deepening the understanding of mental representations as a level of description, separable from, respectively, neurological and socio-cultural aspects. Mental representations are

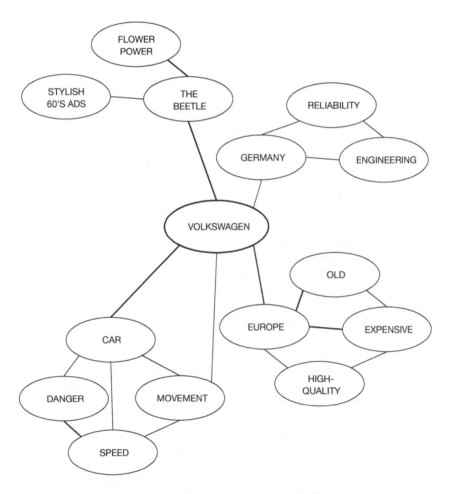

Figure 6.4 Simple associative network spreading from the node Volkswagen

abstractions we all perform at any given time as a way of 'stocking' information in memory. We cannot 'stock' items the way they really are, and therefore we 'catalogue' them in certain systems. (We cannot mentally store the phenomenon of a 'Volkswagen' in its totality.) One of the fundamental challenges of cognitive psychology is that human beings under study have to 'translate' their memory representations into language even though we do not necessarily 'stock' memories by means of language.

In cognitive psychology, memory is considered very durable. Things we store in memory tend to stay there for a long time. In cognitive consumer research, repeated exposure to a commercial message is therefore considered very important. Perceptual enhancement of a concept can actually lead to more or less permanent memory nodes.

Box 6.2 Memory representations

Understanding how memory works is important in the consumer-based approach. Memory representations fall into different categories: direct, non-verbal representations (sensory), propositional representations (abstract interpretations) and linguistic representations.

- **Direct or analogous representations** are direct (non-verbal) sensory sensations such as: what does a brand look like or how does it feel? They include stimuli of all senses: visual images, auditory representations, tactile experiences with the brand, tastes and smells. Sensory representations also include how packaging and advertisements look. For example a Volvo is a large, rather square car and most often a station wagon.
- **Propositional representations** are interpretations of the brand (symbolic meanings). They are non-sensory, abstract brand meanings derived from the sensory brand experiences described above. For example a Volvo is often interpreted as a car for a well-off and rather intellectual family.
- **Linguistic representations** are words and sentences used to express brand meaning and experiences with the brand. These can be lengthy accounts or so short that they almost become analogous representations of the brand. For example Volvo = safety.

These three categories add up to the brand and are worth considering when investigating brand associations in the memories of consumers as important brand associations emanate on all levels.

Source: Franzen and Bouwman (2001)

This brief introduction to cognitive psychology is by no means exhaustive but has introduced the key characteristics that are most important for understanding the background as well as the implications of the consumer-based approach.

The information-processing theory of consumer choice

The information-processing theory of consumer choice has cognitive psychology as its point of departure and focuses on explaining how consumers process information before reaching a consumption choice. Here, choice provides the focal point: 'the consumer is characterized as interacting with his or her choice environment, seeking and taking in information from various sources, processing this information, and then making a selection from among some alternatives' (Bettman 1979, p. 1).

Consumers make an enormous number of choices, and make choices at many different levels. Should I buy a particular brand? Should I examine info or not? When should I make the purchase? Where should I make the purchase? How should I pay for it? These are examples of the countless number of choices we all go through before leaving a store with a purchase. A key assumption in this theory is that choice is a process. The marketer should seek an understanding of these choice processes in order to fine-tune marketing communication to make the consumer choose as intended. (Read about process-tracing methods in the methods and data section.)

In this theory, the following factors – processing capacity, motivation, attention, perception, information acquisition and evaluation, memory decision processes and learning – influence the process. The information-processing theory of consumer

---

Box 6.3 Heuristics are important in low-involvement categories

Consumers take more brand alternatives into consideration during a consumption choice process if either the perceived risks or the perceived benefits are high.

Choosing a mundane, low-involvement brand involves a simpler process of choice where heuristics are more easily applied.

Heuristics take on different forms. Below are two examples:

- *Lexicographic* heuristic: 'I buy the least expensive brand.'
- *Familiarity* heuristic: 'I buy the brand most familiar to me.'

Especially in low-involvement categories, it is hence worthwhile investigating which heuristics are typically applied in choice processes.

Source: Kardes (1994)

choice displays a belief that behaviour is caused and hence (in principle) explainable (the if–then logic of cognitive psychology).

In the economic approach, the consumer was supposed to be an economic man, able to take into consideration all relevant information and rationally evaluate different options in a choice situation. The view of the consumer in the information-processing theory of consumer choice is somewhat different. The consumer is assumed exposed to a constant information overload and the mind an inadequate container in an over-communicated society full of commercial messages. 'The computer' is in other words not capable of processing all the data that are fed to it. Therefore, the human mind economizes on processing capacity by choosing not to process all information. These simplifying strategies that economize on processing capacity (heuristics) are also central to understanding the information-processing theory of consumer research and the further implications for and of the customer-based brand equity framework.

Customer-based brand equity

'Customer-based brand equity is defined as the differential effect of brand knowledge on consumer response to the marketing of the brand' (Keller 1993, p. 2). It is also a conceptual model of brand equity seen from the perspective of the individual consumer: The 'marketing' of the above definition relates to the marketing mix, but the point of view is reversed in comparison with the economic approach (Chapter 4) – it is consumer reactions to marketing actions that are in focus.

The global understanding of the brand in the mind of the consumer is conceptualized as 'brand knowledge', which is divided into 'brand awareness' (brand recall and brand recognition) and 'brand image' (the set of associations linked with the brand). Memory principles and structure from cognitive psychology are the background of brand knowledge. As explained in the above sections, memory and knowledge consist of a set of nodes and links. Nodes are stored information and links are what bind them together. The links vary in strength depending on how well the association is stored in long-term memory (see Figure 6.5).

In order to measure whether a brand has customer-based brand equity, brand knowledge has to be mapped, implying that brand awareness and brand image – in the mind of the individual consumer – have to be measured. Brand awareness is a prerequisite for customer-based brand equity. Brand awareness consists of brand recognition and brand recall.

- Brand *recognition*. Does the consumer recognize the brand name? The consumer must confirm having had prior exposure to the brand.
- Brand *recall* is a bit more demanding of the consumer. Here, the brand has to be recalled on the mention of a cue (e.g. the product category).

But being able to retrieve the brand from memory is only the foundation for having customer-based brand equity. A thorough conceptualization of brand image is also a part of customer-based brand equity. Brand image is 'perceptions about a brand as reflected by the brand associations held in consumer memory. Brand

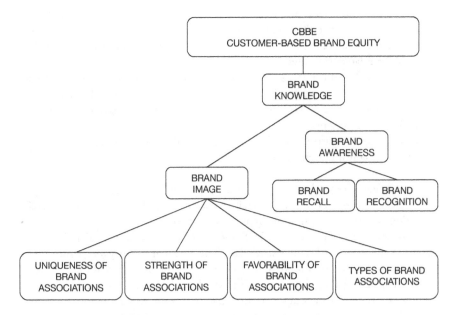

Figure 6.5 Dimensions of brand knowledge; adapted from Keller (1993)

associations are the other informational nodes linked to the brand node in memory and contain the meaning of the brand for consumers' (Keller 1993, p. 3).

Until 1993, the term brand image became increasingly used and the need for managing the brand image over time became emphasized: 'The relationship between a brand's concept and its image must be managed throughout the life of the brand' (Park *et al.* 1986, p. 137). Despite growing interest, it was quite unclear what brand image was. In the customer-based brand equity framework, the associations related to brand image consist of several *types of associations* relating to *attributes*, *benefits* and *attitudes*.

Attributes are descriptive features characterizing a product or a service.

- Product-related attributes are associations directly associated with the product or the service. It could be the physical appearance of a car and the feel of driving it.
- Non-product-related attributes are external aspects related to its purchase or the consumption of it. There are four groups of non-product-related attributes that are taken into account: price information, packaging, user imagery (an impression of the type of person that consumes the brand) and use image (impressions of the context of brand use).

Benefits are personal values attached to the brand by the consumer. They are idiosyncratic evaluations or expectations of what the brand can do for the consumer. Benefits fall into three categories: functional, experiential and symbolic.

- *Functional* benefits are personal expectations of what the product can do for consumers. They correspond to the product-related features but are more personal evaluations; the functional benefits are thus less objective than the product-related attributes.
- *Experiential* benefits relate to the sensory experience of using the brand. What does it feel like to use the brand? What kind of pleasure will I obtain from consuming the brand? This aspect provides variety for the consumer and satisfies hedonic consumption needs.
- *Symbolic* benefits are about self-expression and the way we signal to others by means of consumption objects.

Brand attitudes are the last class of brand associations in the map of brand image. Brand attitudes are consumers' overall evaluations of the brand. This overall evaluation is very important as it often guides brand choice.

To recapitulate, a brand (of which the consumer is aware) is a node in an associative network of brand knowledge. The brand name triggers a spreading activity and associations pop up. Some associations pop up faster and more immediately than others; they are connected to the brand node by a stronger link and are, thus, more powerful associations than the ones connected more loosely to the main node. The associations appear as different kinds of mental representations, as all associations are interpretations made by our cognitive mindsets. Some associations are of a more visual nature and some are of a more verbal nature than others.

The basis for talking about customer-based brand equity is, as already mentioned, brand awareness. If brand awareness can be stated, the further process is to create a map of consumer associations consisting of the above-mentioned elements. These customer associations paint an accurate picture of the content of brand image.

Content is one thing, but customer-based brand equity also expresses a value that can be measured against that of competitors. For a brand to have *high* customer-based brand equity (in other words to be a strong brand), the consumer associations need to be more *favourable, strong* and *unique* than the image associated with competing brands.

- *Favourability* corresponds to whether the consumer's overall brand associations are more or less favourable than those associated with competing brands. Is the overall brand attitude so favourable that it will likely affect consumption behaviour?
- *Strength* of brand associations corresponds to the way associations spread in the associative web activated by the brand as node. Strong associations appear fast (the accentuated links in Figure 6.4 – Volkswagen association map) and demand attention. (Make the consumer pay attention to the information stored in the association.)
- *Uniqueness* of associations. A brand with desirable customer-based brand equity can also claim some unique associations. Some central associations should ideally not be shared by competing brands. Unique associations are the unique selling point of the brand.

Customer-based brand equity has a comparative framework and can also be negative:

> a brand is said to have positive (negative) customer-based brand equity if consumers react more (less) favourably to the product, price, promotion, or distribution of the brand as they do to the same marketing mix when it is attributed to a fictitiously named or unnamed version of the product or service.
>
> (Keller 1993, p. 8)

As the customer-based brand equity is a conceptual model, it does not build on a research project, but is rather an application of the established knowledge about consumer behaviour to branding. It gives birth to a new approach to brand management (which to date has proven the most tenacious) and opens up for a clarification of brand image and brand equity. Now:

> [. . .] brand equity should be thought of as a multidimensional concept that depends on (1) what knowledge structures are present in the minds of consumers and (2) what actions a firm can take to capitalize on the potential offered by these knowledge structures.
>
> (Keller 1993, p. 14)

Summary

Cognitive psychology applied to consumer research, and the associated information-processing theory of consumer choice, serve as supporting theories for the core theory of customer-based brand equity. In cognitive psychology, man is presumed to function much like a computer and the focus is on how knowledge (in the form of mental representations) is stored in and can be retrieved from memory.

The information-processing theory of consumer choice focuses on explaining the process of choice. Man is supposed to have limited processing capacity, which is why, the marketer should be aware to make the most efficient communication.

The customer-based brand equity framework is a brand management theory that draws upon the two above theories. This framework maps brand knowledge as a cognitive construal. In order to be able to talk about customer-based brand equity, brand awareness has to exist in the minds of consumers. The brand has to be recalled and recognized. If this is the case, brand image can be mapped. Brand image consists of consumer associations depicting tangible as well as intangible aspects of the brand, also depicting attributes, benefits and attitudes. Customer-based brand equity is a comparative framework by which the favourability, strength and uniqueness of brand association can be measured against those of competing brands.

Methods and data of the consumer-based approach

As described in the introduction to this chapter, the cognitive consumer perspective and the consumer-based approach have become very dominant both in the fields

Box 6.4 How to structure brand associations

The association map below depicts associations spreading from the node '7-Up'. The map is based on a limited number of interviews of Dutch consumers and the brand name is the only stimulus (Franzen and Bouwman 2001). The stronger associations are emphasized, but whether the associations are *strong*, *favourable* and *unique* is not investigated, nor is brand awareness measured. Therefore the association map is a 'messy' picture of brand image. Below, the association map is structured according to the brand image elements.

The process of structuring association maps arranges the content of brand image. It becomes clear which associations are linked with the product, and which are more abstracted. In the case of user imagery, it

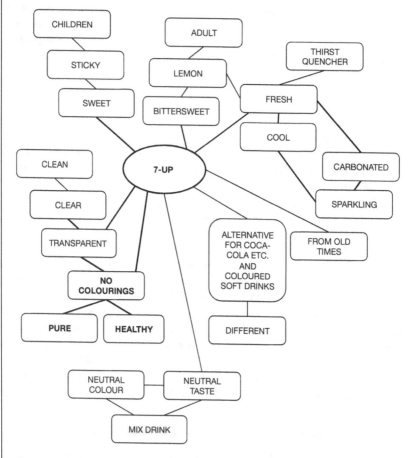

Figure 6.6 Associations spreading from the node '7-Up'

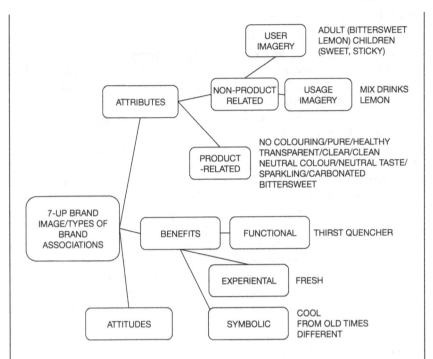

Figure 6.7 '7-Up' brand associations adapted to the customer-based brand equity framework

is interesting that the 'children' association is linked with 'sweet' and 'sticky', while the 'adult' user imagery is linked with 'bittersweet' and 'lemon'. In that sense, the association map turned into brand image provides great insights to be elaborated on in the further planning of marketing activity.

of consumer research and brand management. Therefore, there is an abundance of methods that can be used for researching consumers along this line of thought. In this section, we will present a few of the most widely applied methods for gathering knowledge of the cognitive consumer and his or her choice processes. These methods provide an insight into the way consumers are investigated when the researcher aims at understanding the cognitive mechanisms activated during consumption choices.

The customer-based brand equity framework also encompasses methods and directions for measuring customer-based brand equity. These methods will conclude this section.

Gathering data in the information-processing consumer perspective

As described in the sections on assumptions and theoretical building blocks, the theories based on the cognitive consumer perspective try to explain how stimuli entered into the 'computer' consumer are economically processed and then lead to a consumption choice. In order to map out these processes, two main categories of methods are applied; namely *input–output* and *process-tracing* approaches.

Input–output methods are experiments where input factors are manipulated and the change in the output of the process is then measured. These methods correspond to the 'If–then' logic that is so fundamental to the cognitive consumer perspective. There are in effect no limits to which inputs can be altered in order to test output. The respondent can be presented to different advertising methods, consideration sets can be differentiated, different price information can be applied to the same brand and so on. By testing consumer reactions to different inputs, the best (most predictable) marketing action can be planned.

In the information-processing theory of consumer choice, choice is seen as a process following explainable paths in consumers' minds. The *process-tracing* approaches aim at understanding and explaining this process. They are attempts to monitor the sequence of information, the data acquired and the choices they lead to. There are many different ways of understanding this process, below are some examples:

- *Verbal protocols.* The respondent thinks out loud during the performance of an actual task. For instance, a consumer goes shopping equipped with a voice recorder. Thoughts are verbalized and recorded as they occur. In this fashion, the process of making a brand choice is recorded. For the researcher, this technique is rather time-consuming as he or she has to sort through large amounts of data.
- A similar method is the *prompted protocol*. A consumer is (willingly) video-filmed during a shopping experience. After the shopping experience, the consumer comments on the video film, and thereby explains which decision processes he or she went through during the shopping experience.
- *A matrix array* is another way of understanding a choice process. Here, a matrix is constructed reflecting as many of the factors as possible, which are parts of a choice process. For example, the matrix can be constructed with brands in rows and attributes in columns. In each case of the matrix, the respondent can take an information card (e.g. the price of the Toyota on information card n, or the size of the engine of the Fiat on information card t; a few examples are provided in Table 6.1). This method simulates the examination of choices a consumer goes through – one at a time – leading to the final choice. The consumer researcher will get as data the sequence of cards selected and the amount of information acquired before the consumer feels ready to commit to a choice. The data will contain rich information providing insight into central processes of choice and will answer questions like 'How many information cards are necessary before making a choice?' 'Which cards are the most important?' 'Are some information cards revisited?' 'Which piece of

information turns out to be the decisive one?' Imagine the matrix in Table 6.1 as a mini-bookcase with information cards on the shelves. The respondents then pick the cards necessary for reaching a consumption choice at their own pace.

- *Chronometric analysis* is an analysis of response time. The cognitive consumer perspective is much occupied with understanding the pace of memory. In a chronometric analysis, the respondent is asked to complete certain tasks: answering questions or finding associations. The time it takes to complete these tasks is then measured. Mapping out the time between the presentation of a stimulus and the response to that stimulus is beneficial in order to understand the pace of memory as well as understanding how easily associations are retrieved (the 'thickness' of the links in Figure 6. 6).

These are some of the methods that can be applied when wanting to understand the choice processes that take place in the mind of the 'computer' consumer. Customer-based brand equity can also be measured; how, will be explained in the forthcoming section.

Measuring customer-based brand equity

There is a direct and an indirect approach to measuring customer-based brand equity. For an optimal result, these two approaches should be complemented. The indirect approach measures brand knowledge (brand awareness and brand image, Figure 6.5) by assessing its sources (consumers' associations). The direct approach measures customer-based brand equity by measuring consumer responses to the brand's marketing actions.

The indirect approach implies measuring customer-based brand equity *without* measuring it against something else. Here, the sources of brand knowledge and

Table 6.1 A simple version of a matrix array

	Colour	Safety	Price	Engine
Volkswagen	Information card a: Black	Information card f: 5 Euro NCAP stars	Information card k	Information card p
Ford	Information card b: Grey	Information card g: 4 Euro NCAP stars	Information card l	Information card q
Audi	Information card c: Red	Information card: 5 Euro NCAP stars	Information card m	Information card r
Toyota	Information card d: Green	Information card i	Information card n	Information card s
Fiat	Information card e: Orange	Information card j	Information card o	Information card t

pattern of associations are identified through mapping out consumers' brand knowledge. Keller recommends that several methods are applied in order to capture as many aspects of customer-based brand equity as possible. Remember that associations are stored in the memory as different mental representations. Some methods are more suited for bringing out some representations than others.

- *Brand awareness* is assessed through aided as well as unaided memory measures. To start with is the brand name recognized? The brand should be correctly discerned by the consumer as previously seen or heard. Brand recall can be tested through testing which brand is 'top of mind' in a brand category. The brand should be correctly identified given for instance a product category. Response times for both recall and recognition can be measured in order to depict the ease with which the brand comes to mind, reflecting attitude strengths.
- *Brand associations* can be captured in many ways. Free association tasks can be performed either individually or in focus groups to lay out the association maps fundamental to the customer-based brand equity framework. Probing (in terms of asking 'how', 'why', 'what' questions) and projective techniques can be applied in order to help reluctant respondents along. Examples of suitable projective techniques are sentence completion, picture completion and filling in speech balloons. Individual interviews can also be conducted in order to understand the formation of associations.

Box 6.5 Projective techniques

Using projective techniques is a way to let the respondents' unconscious speak. Respondents are assumed to hold things back in order to protect their self-image in a research situation. When investigated by means of projective techniques, focus is moved away from the respondent and 'projected' at hypothetical others. Thereby, respondents are supposed to open up to the interviewer and actually reveal more about themselves than if asked directly. Below are listed different projective techniques.

- *Sentence completion*: Respondents are presented with an unfinished sentence and asked to complete it.
- *Picture completion*: In the same fashion, respondents are asked to complete an unfinished picture.
- *Speech balloons*: An empty speech balloon is filled out by the respondent.

The sentences, the pictures and the drawings forming the backgrounds of the speech balloons should all carefully depict a situation that is relevant to the brand in question.

The direct approach to measuring customer-based brand equity implies measuring *against* the customer-based brand equity of other brands. Here, consumer reactions to the marketing strategies of the brand are compared with reactions to the same strategies ascribed to a fictitious or unnamed brand. In these blind test scenarios, different elements of the marketing mix are compared between a named brand and an unnamed 'rival' brand. Any marketing element will do, for example the marketer can test perceptions of taste, feel, product quality, packaging and advertising. The majority of these results show that the connotations of the known brand affect the perception of all marketing methods (negatively or positively). This comparative approach to measuring customer-based brand equity can be used for all kinds of marketing methods, but it is a challenge to secure valid results from these tests. Ideally, the whole sequence of mapping brand knowledge is performed in two or more simultaneous groups where group members are exposed to exactly the same material. Remember that brand associations are mental representations of all kinds of sensory input (Box 6.2) and the research design should therefore try to accommodate the fact that some representations are more linguistic than others. The more abstract associations should also count as important data.

Having listed a number of suitable research methods aimed at the practical use of this brand management approach, we will round this section off with a note on the methods used in the academic research that is still investigating this take on the brand and the consumer, and thereby developing the consumer-based approach. It is remarkable how quantitative research methods are still dominant in this approach. The relational approach (Chapter 8), the community approach (Chapter 9) and the cultural approach (Chapter 10) all embrace qualitative methods and thereby move brand management into the interpretive paradigm. Still, it is worth noting that research grounded in positivism is still strong and influential in the

---

Box 6.6 Map out customers' brand associations yourself

- Start out by asking your respondents if they recognize the brand name.
- In another respondent pool, ask which three brands come to mind when you mention the given product category or industry.
- Ask your respondents to draw association maps.
- Expose your respondents to an appropriate set of projective techniques (e.g. finishing sentences, filling out blank speech balloons).
- Interview individual respondents and make them rate their associations.
- Ask respondents what they consider to be unique about the brand.
- Compare result patterns across as many respondents as possible.
- Do the same routine with the brand's closest competitors.
- Now, compare the analyses in order to know exactly which associations of your brand are the most strong, favourable and unique.

Source: Keller (1993)

academic world of brand management. Read more about recent research in the concluding section about the academic evolution of the consumer-based approach.

Summary

Building on the 'if–then' logic of cognitive psychology and the way choice is seen as an accurate process in the information-processing perspective, the methods applied to investigate the cognitive aspect of the consumer can be divided into input–output and process-tracing approaches. In the first category, input is changed and changes in output are measured in order to capture how the human 'computer' works. In the latter approach, different choice scenarios are monitored by means of (for example) verbal protocols, prompted protocols and chronometric analysis.

Measuring customer-based brand equity can be done indirectly as well as directly. Applying the indirect techniques, brand knowledge is mapped by consumers. The results should be combined with direct comparative analyses of the brand and competing brands or through blind-testing marketing actions against a fictitiously named or unnamed brand.

The academic studies driving the approach forward are characterized by quantitative studies, which is remarkable in the overall context of brand management presented in this textbook (read the final section about the academic evolution of the consumer-based approach).

Managerial implications

In the understanding assumptions section, we discussed the ownership of the brand in the consumer-based approach, which implies that brand value creation is measured in the mind of the consumer, but the view of man behind the approach still allows the idea of linear communication. This duality is reflected in the managerial implications of the approach. One aspect of the implications is a seemingly 'all power to the people' assumption, the other an assumption that the marketer is still able to control (linear) communication.

The first aspect requires closeness to the consumer. The marketer's budget should prioritize constant market monitoring in order to be at the leading edge of consumers' development. This 'market sensing' priority implies a functional or market-centred organizational form – the consumer-based marketers must possess superior outside–in capabilities in order to succeed.

The other aspect of the consumer-based approach is that the marketer should create the optimal brand communication in order to create the strongest brand. The most skilled marketer is the best 'programmer' of the mind. It is all about making the brand known to consumers, making consumers pay attention to the brand by choosing the right brand elements and positioning the brand through consistency in brand communication. The marketer should also consider the brand a strategic corporate priority and see all marketing actions as influencing the brand in the future. Therefore, step 2 in Figure 6.8 leads to the need for a new step 1, and so on and so on. Finally, it should be considered if brand image is balanced with brand identity.

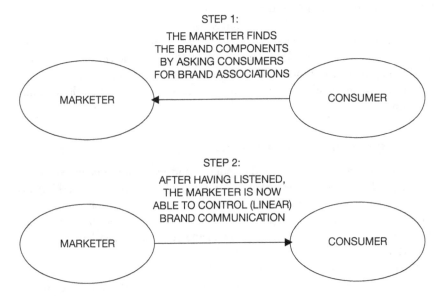

Figure 6.8 Dualistic mechanisms of the consumer-based approach influencing the managerial implications

Make consumers aware of your brand

The fact that the brand name ideally should spur high levels of awareness means that consumers should be exposed to the brand name repeatedly. Customer-based brand equity starts with brand awareness, building awareness is one of the important first steps to take when marketing a brand along the consumer-based line of thought. In the section about the cognitive consumer perspective, we mentioned that memory is assumed to be very durable. As knowledge we store in memory tends to stay there for a very long time, repeated exposure to a commercial message is considered very important. Perceptual enhancement of a concept can lead to permanent memory nodes.

Brand awareness might be the most important use of heuristics (the simplifying strategies) where consumers choose the well-known brand because it facilitates the choice process. The consumer seems to be willing to pay a premium price and accept lower-quality goods for the same brand if it is a brand with high awareness. Consumers display a tendency to accept more advertising repetition by a familiar brand than from an unknown one and pioneering brands have tremendous advantages, when it comes to conquering the permanent positive memory nodes. So building the highest possible degree of brand awareness or familiarity is crucial for a successful brand in the consumer-based approach.

When establishing brand awareness, the marketer might also want to pay some attention to whether brand recognition or brand recall is the most important goal for the brand in question. The recall aspect is most important in high involvement categories and when the purchase decision is made outside the store. When it comes to low-involvement categories and the purchase decision primarily is taken in-store, a high level of recognition might be enough. Here, the consumer does not need to be able to recall the brand in order to make a purchase decision. When a low-involvement brand is recognized in the supermarket, it is often the one that gets chosen.

Make consumers pay attention to your brand

After meticulously investigating and mapping brand associations, the marketer will be equipped with the tools to choose the right brand elements. The marketer has an exact overview of the types of associations held in the minds of consumers, as well as the favourability, strength and uniqueness of these associations. Also, the marketer will get an impression of whether the consumer-based brand equity is positive or negative.

Equipped with this knowledge, the marketer is able to make a detailed brand strategy by having the answers to the following questions and many more: Which elements are the most central? Which are the strongest? Which are more unique? Which associations lack in favourability? Thereby, the marketer can accurately plan where to make an effort and along which parameters the brand is the strongest. In this fashion, the marketer is able to create a detailed and well-founded work schedule for how to strengthen the brand.

Some elements might require special attention. The marketer can organize investigations of key elements in order to further fine-tune brand communication to accommodate the mechanisms of the cognitive consumer. Box 6.7 provides insight into the many considerations that might be taken into account before choosing the brand name. The right brand name is only one of the many important elements a marketer has to decide.

Position your brand

In the process of building customer-based brand equity, it is also important to identify the maximum level of congruence between brand associations. Congruence means that it is beneficial to build the communication platform around the associations that are the most similar. Congruence among the different brand associations determines the cohesiveness of the brand image. A coherent brand image facilitates the spreading activity in the mind of the consumer. In other words, the 'computer' is better able to process data that it does not have to retrieve in too many different places.

The need for congruence is related to the question of heuristics in the information-processing theory of consumer choice. The consumer has a limited processing capacity and lives in a world of a million commercial messages; 'consumers encounter many more brands than people in an average day.' (Fitzsimons *et al.*

Box 6.7 Things to consider when choosing the right brand name

The brand name is a very important brand element as it is most often the key node activating the spreading activity in the associative network of brand knowledge. The brand name spurs brand awareness, which is the pre-requisite for talking about brand image and customer-based brand equity in the first place.

In *Dimensions of Consumer Expertise* researchers Alba and Hutchinson (1987) list things to consider when choosing the right brand name adjusted for easy recognition.

- *The brand name should be easily read.* Consumers scan shelf displays rapidly when in a supermarket and do not take time to read carefully each name on display. In order to test the readability of a word, respondents can be exposed to the word extremely briefly or can be exposed to a name with letters missing.
- *The brand name should be easily recognized.* Studies show that pseudo-words (nonsense) words are more difficult to recognize than real words (meaning something). But as the number of exposures increases the difference seems to diminish.
- *Consider a frequently used word as brand name.* Frequently used words are more easily remembered than infrequently used words.

In 'The sound of brands' Argo *et al.* (2010) test what constitutes a successful brand name. They find that the rhetorically deviant figure of repetition affects people positively. The positive effect is emphasized when read aloud. Coca-Cola is an example of a brand name containing repetition – and the positive effect of this name will be enhanced if communicated orally, meaning that media containing sound (e. g. radio, cinema, television) are preferable to enhance this brand element. Staff might also be encouraged to speak the brand name aloud and not be afraid to repeat it.

Gunasti and Ross (2010) investigate the effect of alphanumeric names, names consisting of a mix of letters and names. These names are often used for sub- or model brands and influence our preferences and buying decisions. The researchers differentiate between low-need-for-cognition consumers (LNCs) and consumers with a high-need-for-cognition (HNCs) and conclude that LNCs tend to go by the idea of 'the higher, the better' assuming that the model X-4000 is superior to the model X-3000. The HNCs are more thorough and spend time getting to know the different features of the product. Thereby, they are not as prone to the logic of the alphanumeric names.

Other criteria apply when it comes to recalling a brand name. The inquiring reader should turn to the original source, as the above list is by no means exhaustive and meant only to indicate how many details the marketer can go into when managing the brand in the consumer-based approach.

Sources: Alba and Hutchinson (1987); Argo *et al.* (2010);
Gunasti and Ross (2010)

2008, p. 21). Therefore, the consumer only pays attention to the incoming information that captures attention *and* starts a relatively easy spreading activity.

Consistency in communications is also a key aspect of the consumer-based approach. Once having established high brand awareness and the right congruent brand associations, it is assumed risky to change course. These aspects of the consumer-based approach share many characteristics with the idea of *positioning* (Ries and Trout 1983, 2001). This hugely popular theory rests upon the same key assumptions about the human mind being a computer with limited processing capabilities in an over-communicated society, which is why the clever marketers are the ones repeating over and over again the commercial messages that are fine-tuned to establish a lasting mental territory for the brand. This very important aspect of the consumer-based approach is what associates it with terms like Unique Selling Proposition, brand DNA, brand mantra and 'owning associations'.

Marketing a brand according to the consumer-based approach also requires identifying the most relevant competition. As customer-based brand equity is defined as being either positive or negative compared with competitors, there is essentially only one brand in each category with positive customer-based brand equity. In order for the marketer to make the most relevant brand strategy, it is worthwhile thinking about which competitors are the real threat and then conducting the comparative analyses and formulating the brand strategy in relation to them.

An emphasis on strategy

In 1993, when the idea of customer-based brand equity was first put forward, it was often difficult to distinguish between brand research and ad research. The idea of brand management being a central area of interest in corporations seemed years away. We have mentioned earlier that the publication of customer-based brand equity was extremely important in itself, and that it also had some valuable side effects, such as shedding light on the topic of brand equity and brand image. Furthermore, it lifted the brand to being a strategic priority and something, else and, more than advertising. In the 1993 article Keller outlines specific managerial guidelines. The guidelines are explained in Box 6.8 and their implications are that the brand should be managed in a continuous process, on a strategic level, and should be conceived as much more than advertising.

Box 6.8 Six managerial guidelines

- *Adopt a broad view of marketing decisions.* Think in broad terms when you consider the many marketing actions and the many aspects of brand knowledge that can be activated and that could influence sales.
- *Define the desired knowledge structures.* The marketer should be razor-sharp when making a plan for which knowledge structures will be most important to customers, and thus will build the stronger brand. Looking at the filled-out association map, which parts of the knowledge structure need the most attention?
- *Evaluate alternative tactical options regarding communication channels.* Consider the whole spectrum of potential consumer touchpoints and activate them systematically so that they add to the congruence and consistency of the chosen brand identity.
- *Take a long-term view of marketing decisions.* Think ahead! Every marketing action influences future marketing actions and, as the consumer is supposed to have a very long memory, every action may influence brand associations for a very long time.
- *Employ tracking studies over time.* As all marketing actions are seen as a long chain of interrelated events influencing the brand, tracking studies should be applied on a continuous basis. Here, gaps between the intended and the real brand knowledge can be detected and marketing actions can be adjusted.
- *Evaluate potential extension candidates.* Management ought to consider and evaluate potential brand extensions in order to benefit from the obtained brand equity. The brand image of the main brand may serve as an efficient information base for the new product. On the other hand, associations that differ too much between the main and the extended brand may damage the main brand severely.

Source: Keller (1993)

Balancing brand image with brand identity

The consumer-based approach is born and becomes influential over the same course of years as the identity approach. These two approaches are interesting to compare as they are based on completely opposite perceptions of where the brand should find its true nature, inspiration and energy. Because they are so opposite in assumptions, they illustrate each other's weaknesses neatly. In the identity approach, the brand is found inside the organization, and strategic force and inspiration hence stem from within the organization behind the brand. The main problem of managing a brand according to this approach is the risk of organizational 'narcissism' and a lack of market sensing.

It goes without saying that consumer-based management depends on superior abilities when it comes to market sensing and customer knowledge. The main problem of managing the brand according to this approach is that the focus on the consumer leads to a lack of organizational vision. Even though there is no doubt that there is some truth in the assumption that the brand exists in the mind of the consumer, the marketer should also consider that the process of listening only to consumer associations is essentially backward-looking. Consumers relate to previous marketing initiatives and hence are not visionary. Hereby, the vision for the brand stemming from the brand corporation risks a lack of future perspective: 'Brand management is enacted as a tactical process of cyclical adaptation to consumers' representations of the focal brand whereby brand image gradually supplants brand identity' (Louro and Cunha 2003, p. 863).

Summary

Managing a brand according to the principles of the consumer-based approach requires acknowledging that the brand is something residing in the minds of consumers and that listening to consumers is a prerequisite for skilled brand management. Still, the marketer is seen as in charge of communications as an assumption of linear communication applies to the cognitive consumer perspective.

The marketer should start by making sure that consumers are sufficiently aware of the brand. Once an adequate level of brand awareness is obtained, brand image has to be communicated and the brand has to be positioned. The brand image should be built around the most relevant and congruent consumer associations. The elements should be tested for their cognitive suitability before application to brand image.

The brand should be positioned through consistency in communications. As memory is believed to be very durable in cognition, permanent memory nodes can be obtained by remaining on the same course communications-wise.

The consumer-based approach also implies that the brand should be a strategic priority and all marketing actions should be seen as a long chain of events, all influencing the brand image. The marketer might consider balancing the strong sides of the consumer-based approach with the strong sides of the identity approach as founding the brand solely on consumer associations might lead to a lack of vision for the brand.

Development of the consumer-based approach and later approaches

As mentioned in the introduction, the consumer-based approach has in a US context become the most dominant approach of the seven we present in this book. Therefore, we have chosen to round off this chapter with a few comments on how the consumer-based approach has developed since the 1990s – reflecting our presentation, and how other approaches define themselves against it.

Box 6.9 Dos and don'ts of the consumer-based approach

Do	*Don't*
Inquire consumer associations meticulously	Don't neglect the true owners of the brand (the consumers)
Use consumers' brand associations to determine the content of the brand	Don't believe you can formulate the brand strategy yourself
Find congruency in brand associations	Don't apply a scatter-gun technique
Communicate brand image consistently	Don't change brand communications too often
Think ahead in brand communications	Don't think that there are marketing actions that will not affect the brand
Identify your real competitors	Don't forget your brand's unique selling proposition
Consider if listening to customers drives your brand forwards in a visionary fashion	Don't forget that closeness to the market is your strongest asset

---

As mentioned in the introduction, it is our goal to present the roots of each approach, the founding publications and main theories, methods and data and its managerial implications. In each approach chapter, we try to balance emphasis on the roots with the newest research-documented developments.

Due to the fact that the consumer-based approach in many ways has developed into *the* textbook treatment of brand management, the development of the approach has moved in an all-encompassing direction. Therefore, we have emphasized the roots of the approach in the chapter description and somewhat neglected its further development. We will, however, try to make up for this choice by explaining how this brand perspective has developed here, where we will provide an overview of how the approach has evolved respectively in textbooks and in academia.

In this chapter, we have spent the majority of our space introducing the reader to the quintessential cognitive brand and consumer perspective. It should, however, be noted that Keller has embraced the later approaches in his more recent publications (read also the 'founding father' comment by Keller at the very end of this chapter). The consumer-based approach is concerned with brand knowledge, and when you think of it, there is nothing that cannot be seen as part of consumers' brand knowledge. In that way, all approaches of this book can be added to brand knowledge.

Keller and Lehmann (2003) claim that branding is all about understanding the customers' mindset. According to Keller and Lehman, the mindset consists of five dimensions: awareness, associations, attitudes, attachments and activity. The first three dimensions can be recognized as components of the customer-based brand equity framework. The fourth dimension (attachment) is about loyalty and resistance to change. This dimension resembles the relational approach somewhat, while the latest dimension (that of activity) reminds us of the community approach, as it relates to consumer interaction.

In a 2003 article, Keller took stock of brand management theory. J. Aaker's work on brand personality (Chapter 7), Fournier's brand relationship theory (Chapter 8) and Muñiz and O'Guinn's conceptualization of brand communities (Chapter 9) are mentioned as important contributions to the academic discipline. Still, they are added to the term 'brand knowledge'.

> These studies and others similar in spirit are noteworthy for their ability to use novel research methods to uncover overlooked or relatively neglected facets of consumer brand knowledge that have significant theoretical and managerial implications.
>
> (Keller 2003, p. 596)

Looking at brand management from the cognitive perspective implies that everything can be added to brand knowledge. Keller, however, recognizes that he looks at the brand from a specific angle:

> Important perspectives on branding and brand knowledge obviously can, and have been, gained from other disciplinary viewpoints, for example, anthropological or ethnographic approaches. Part of the challenge in developing mental maps for consumers that accurately reflect their brand knowledge is how best to incorporate multiple theoretical or methodological paradigms.
>
> (Keller 2003, p. 600)

The consumer-based approach can thus be hard to negotiate with as brand knowledge can be said to be all-encompassing. As Keller states in the two above-mentioned examples, the new approaches can be added to brand knowledge, and in that sense, you can say that the consumer-based approach suffices.

One of the goals of this book is to deconstruct the field of brand management seen from a perspective rooted in the philosophy of science. And in this context, it is necessary to regard the latter approaches as something more than merely new additions to brand knowledge. As we have mentioned in the section about the cognitive consumer perspective, the cognitive tradition deliberately neglects emotional and cultural parameters in its search for explanations of human behaviour. Later approaches embrace the emotional and cultural factors that the cognitive tradition neglects in their search for explanations of human behaviour. Therefore, the purpose of fitting all kinds of brand knowledge into the same mould instead of understanding them separately can be questioned.

The significant influence of the consumer-based approach is difficult to evaluate. The seven approaches of this book represent profoundly different brand and consumer perspectives, some more compatible than others. Still, it is unusual that one approach defines itself in opposition to another approach. But the consumer-based approach seems to be more deliberately challenged than the other approaches. The challenges come from two sides: the relational approach (of Chapter 8) and the cultural approach (of Chapter 10).

The relational approach does not explicitly define itself in opposition to the consumer-based approach. The relational approach, however, is influenced by phenomenology, which is a scientific and philosophical tradition stressing the 'inner reality' of consumers. In the world of brand management and consumer research, the phenomenological view of the world defines itself in opposition to the information-processing view (see Table 8.1). Thereby, the consumer-based and the relational approach represent very different points of departure when it comes to understanding the consumer and managing the brand.

The cultural approach (or its most important author, Douglas B. Holt) is much more explicit in his critique of the consumer-based approach. Holt defines four different branding models (see Table 11.3) and stresses 'the mindshare model' (comparable to the consumer-based approach) as the dominant one. The cultural approach is then neatly formulated as a viable alternative to the consumer-based approach stressing its Achilles heel of emphasizing consistency in communication. In the cultural approach, the brand is seen as a cultural artefact influenced by changes in time and culture (see a comparison between the two branding models/brand approaches in Table 10.1).

Academic evolution of the consumer-based approach

In this concluding section of the chapter, we outline the evolution of the consumer-based approach in brand management academia. This outline is based on the primary data of the taxonomy of this textbook – articles from the top marketing journals with a primary focus on the brand (read more about methodology and data set in Chapter 3). The supplementary literature included in this chapter is hence not included in this section.

The main theory was introduced in 1993 and was inspired by ideas about positioning and the information-processing consumer. Building on these ideas – in short – that we live in an over-communicated society and that consumers have limited processing capability – the CBBE framework offered an entirely new way of translating these ideas into an approach to the brand along with new managerial implications.

As already mentioned, this brand perspective (in a translated, more all-encompassing version) has become the foundation of the major US brand management textbooks. In the academic milieu, that approach is also alive and vibrant; a considerable amount of research has been published over the years in the academic journals constituting the data set of this textbook.

The more recent academic articles are still concerned with expanding the understanding of the basic tenets of the consumer-based approach; decision processes (Ng and Houston 2009 – an examination of brand-level versus product-level storage of information; see also Wan *et al.* 2009), the mechanisms of memory and evaluation processes (e.g. Muthukrishnan and Chattopadhyay 2007 – a comparison between memory-based and stimulus-based evaluations), perception (Janakiraman *et al.* 2009) and the effects of stimuli (e.g. Sweldens *et al.* (2010) – a comparison between direct and indirect affective stimuli; see also Argo *et al.* (2010), which is mentioned in Box 6.7). The literature behind the consumer-based approach has always been focused on brand extensions and the nature of the fit between brand and extension. Shine *et al.* (2007) and Milberg *et al.* (2010) are examples of recent research in this phenomenon. It is also a fundamental idea in the consumer-based approach that once a certain set of associations is stored in long-term memory, it is almost impossible to un-store (forget) it. Two studies examine what this mechanism does to the chance of repositioning an established brand. Gibson (2008) concludes that it is much more difficult to reposition a mature brand compared to an immature one. Lee and Shavitt (2009) conclude the same in a study of changing the associations of McDonald's. Hence, fortifying the basic assumptions of the consumer-based approach.

Another stream of research is expanding the idea of information into the idea of experience as the outcome of encounters with the brand (Brakus *et al.* 2009) and it seems to be the most radical evolution, pushing the boundaries of the approach forward.

Furthermore, there is an overall trend in a new focus on the context of consumers and consumption (and the implied decision processes). As mentioned in the section about data collection methods, the recent research primarily uses quantitative methods, and the literature reviews are based on literature with a point of departure in economics and marketing (e.g. Janakiraman *et al.* 2009). Hence, the approach is still heavily linked to a more positivistic paradigm. The 'laboratory' research ideal of positivism is hence challenged or nuanced by this new trend.

Examples are:

- Collaborative context: Lindsey and Krishnan (2007) examine the decision processes of consumers in groups versus as individuals. What happens with the process when you recall and decide on a given brand within a group of friends? How are target brands retrieved in a group compared to the process of an individual?
- Evaluation context: Nam and Sternthal (2008) examine what the 'company' of a given brand advertised in a magazine means. Does an Armani ad on the left-hand page 'rub off' on the Honda ad on the right-hand page?
- Decision context (Meyvis *et al.* 2012). When evaluating brand extensions, the context of the evaluation (presence of visual information and presence of competing brands) influences consumers and tends to shift attention from 'fit' to 'quality'.

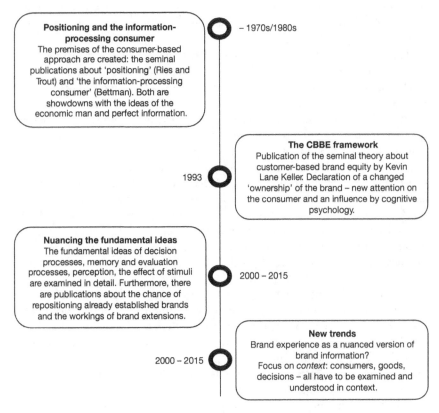

Positioning and the information-processing consumer
The premises of the consumer-based approach are created: the seminal publications about 'positioning' (Ries and Trout) and 'the information-processing consumer' (Bettman). Both are showdowns with the ideas of the economic man and perfect information.

– 1970s/1980s

The CBBE framework
Publication of the seminal theory about customer-based brand equity by Kevin Lane Keller. Declaration of a changed 'ownership' of the brand – new attention on the consumer and an influence by cognitive psychology.

1993

Nuancing the fundamental ideas
The fundamental ideas of decision processes, memory and evaluation processes, perception, the effect of stimuli are examined in detail. Furthermore, there are publications about the chance of repositioning already established brands and the workings of brand extensions.

2000 – 2015

New trends
Brand experience as a nuanced version of brand information?
Focus on *context*: consumers, goods, decisions – all have to be examined and understood in context.

2000 – 2015

Figure 6.9 The academic evolution of the consumer-based approach

---

Box 6.10 You are not done!

Don't forget to visit the website for supplementary material such as case examples, student questions and supplementary literature.

Comments from the 'founding fathers'

The value of consumer-based approaches to the study of branding and brand management

Kevin Lane Keller, Tuck School of Business, Dartmouth College

Without question, branding is a complex management area that deserves study from a variety of different perspectives and academic traditions. By providing a multidisciplinary approach, this book provides a welcome and invaluable resource for thoughtful students, scholars and practitioners who want to fully understand branding and brand management.

This chapter introduced some of the key tenets of the consumer-based approach. As any good brand researcher will admit, any approach to the study of branding and brand management will have its advantages and disadvantages. Part of the power of a consumer-based approach is that it squarely focuses on the consumer as being at the heart of brand equity. Consumer-based approaches, if properly invoked and interpreted, are extremely versatile and can provide detailed insights as to how consumers make all kinds of brand-related choices.

Consumer-based approaches capitalize on the numerous researches and industry advances in the study of consumer behaviour – how consumers think, feel and act towards brands, products, services, companies, other consumers and so on. Consumer-based approaches can provide the foundation for how and why consumers forge relationships with brands and form communities with others; how culture is manifested in consumer consumption behaviour and how brands take on meaning that transcends physical products and services and strict service specifications.

As a note of caution, it is important to *not* narrowly view consumer-based approaches in terms of just information processing models. Although such models can be extremely useful to understand how consumers learn about brands and how that knowledge, in turn, affects how they respond to any aspect of marketing, researchers adopting a consumer-based approach to the study of branding and brand management have successfully introduced or adapted many other concepts related to non-cognitive issues and concerns.

The best consumer-based researchers recognize that branding and brand management are an art and science and that the strongest brands have achieved their success by being able to affect consumers both in their head and in their heart. Like the best marketing practitioners, consumer-based researchers adopt a broad view of how to think about consumers and strive to keep abreast of key cultural trends that suggest new areas of consumer behaviour to study.

In my own research, I have found that focusing on consumer brand knowledge structures provides a comprehensive, cohesive foundation for analysis and a common denominator by which many different topics and issues can be addressed. Fundamentally, the question becomes: how does any marketing action or any other event or trend that occurs in the marketplace affect how consumers think, feel and act about brands? Defining customer-based brand equity as the 'differential effect that brand knowledge has on how consumers respond to marketing activity' has allowed me to conceptualize sources and outcomes of brand equity in great detail and provide specific managerial guidelines based on this conceptualization.

With a consumer-based approach, concepts, theories and findings from diverse areas such as learning, memory, emotions, behavioural decision theory and consumer decision making – to name just a few – can all be brought to bear to better understand how brands should be optimally built and managed. With such dramatic changes in the marketing environment due to increased globalization, technological advances, environmental concerns and many other factors, the power of the consumer-based approach to flexibly apply a variety of conceptual tools to address a variety of managerial concerns in brand management is truly invaluable.

References and further reading

Key readings are in bold type

Aaker, J. L. (1997), 'Dimensions of brand personality', *Journal of Marketing Research*, 34 (3): 347–56.

Aaker, D. A. and Keller, K. L. (1990), 'Consumer evaluations of brand extensions', *Journal of Marketing*, 54 (1): 27–41.

Alba, J. W. and Hutchinson, J. W. (1987), 'Dimensions of consumer expertise', *Journal of Consumer Research*, 13 (4): 411–54.

Allen, C. T., Fournier, S. and Miller, F. (2006), *'Brands and their Meaning Makers'*, in C. P. Haugtvedt, P. M. Herr and F. R. Kardes (eds), *Handbook of Consumer Psychology*, Mahwah, NJ: Lawrence Erlbaum Associates, pp. 781–822.

Anderson, J. R. (1983), *The Architecture of Cognition*, Cambridge, MA: Harvard University Press.

Argo, J. J., Popa, M. and Smith, M. C. (2010), 'The sound of brands', *Journal of Consumer Research*, 74 (4): 97–109.

Bahn, K. D. (1986), 'How and when do brand perceptions and preferences first form? A cognitive developmental investigation', *Journal of Consumer Research*, 13 (3): 382–93.

Bettman, J. R. (1979), *An Information Processing Theory of Consumer Choice*, Reading, MA: Addison-Wesley.

Bettman, J. R. (1986), 'Consumer psychology', *Annual Review of Psychology*, 37: 257–89.

Brakus, J. J., Schmitt, B. H. and Zarantonello, L. (2009), 'Brand experience: What is it? How is it measured? Does it affect loyalty?', *Journal of Marketing*, 73 (3): 52–68.

Campbell, M. C. and Keller, K. L. (2003), 'Brand familiarity and advertising repetition effects', *Journal of Consumer Research*, 30 (2): 292–304.

Fitzsimons, G. M., Chartrand, T. L. and Fitzsimons, G. J. (2008), 'Automatic effects of brand exposure on motivated behavior: How Apple makes you "think different"', *Journal of Consumer Research*, 35 (1): 21–35.

Fournier, S. (1998), 'Consumers and their brands: Developing relationship theory in consumer research', *Journal of Consumer Research*, 24 (4): 343–73.

Franzen, G. and Bouwman, M. (2001), *The Mental World of Brands: Mind, Memory, and Brand Success*, Henley on Thames, UK: World Advertising Research Centre.

Gade, A. (1997), *Hjerneprocesser: Kognition og neurovidenskab*, Copenhagen, Denmark: Frydenlund.

Gardner, H. (1985), *The Mind's New Science: A History of the Cognitive Revolution*, New York: Basic Books.

Gibson, B. (2008), 'Can evaluative conditioning change attitudes towards mature brands? New evidence from the implicit association test', *Journal of Consumer Research*, 35 (1): 178–88.

Gross, R. and McIlveen, R. (1997), *Cognitive Psychology*, London: Hodder & Stoughton.

Gunasti, K. and Ross, W. T. Jr (2010), 'How and when alphanumeric brand names affect consumer preferences', *Journal of Marketing Research*, 47 (6): 1177–1192.

Holt, D. B. (2005), 'How societies desire brands: Using cultural theory to explain brand symbolism', in S. Ratneshwar and D. G. Mick (eds), *Inside Consumption: Consumer Motives, Goals, and Desires*, London: Routledge, pp. 273–91.

Hoyer, W. D. and Brown, S. P. (1990), 'Effects of brand awareness on choice for a common, repeat-purchase product', *Journal of Consumer Research*, 17 (2): 141–8.

Janakiraman, R., Sismeiro, C. and Dutta, S. (2009), 'Perception spillovers across competing brands: A disaggregate model of how and when', *Journal of Marketing Research*, 46 (4): 467–81.

Kardes, F. R. (1994), 'Consumer judgement and decision processes', in R. S. Wyer and T. K. Srull (eds), *Handbook of Social Cognition*, Mahwah, NJ: Lawrence Erlbaum Associates, pp. 399–466.

Keller, K. L. (1993), 'Conceptualizing, measuring, and managing customer-based brand equity', *Journal of Marketing*, 57 (1): 1–22.

Keller, K. L. (2003), 'Brand synthesis: The multidimensionality of brand knowledge', *Journal of Consumer Research*, 20 (4): 595–600.

Keller, K. L. (2005), 'Branding short cuts', *Marketing Management*, 14 (5): 18–23.

Keller, K. L. and Lehmann, D. R. (2003), 'How do brands create value?', *Marketing Management*, 12 (3): 26–31.

Lee, K. and Shavitt, S. (2009), 'Can McDonald's ever be considered healthful? Metacognitive experiences affect the perceived understanding of a brand', *Journal of Marketing Research*, 46 (2): 222–33.

Lindsey, C. D. and Krishnan, H. S. (2007), 'Retrieval disruption in collaborative groups due to brand cues', *Journal of Consumer Research*, 33 (4): 470–8.

Louro, M. J. and Cunha, P. V. (2001), 'Brand management paradigms', *Journal of Marketing Management*, 17 (7–8): 849–75.

Malaviya, P. and Sternthal, B. (2009), 'Parity product features can enhance or dilute brand evaluation: The influence of goal orientation and presentation format', *Journal of Consumer Research*, 36 (1): 112–21.

Meyvis, T., Goldsmith, K. and Dhar, R. (2012), 'The importance of the context in brand extension: How pictures and comparisons shift consumers' focus from fit to quality', *Journal of Marketing Research*, 49 (2): 206–17.

Milberg, S. M, Sinn, F. and Goodstein, R. C. (2010), 'Consumer reactions to brand extensions in a competitive context: Does fit still matter?', *Journal of Consumer Research*, 37 (3): 543–53.

Mitchell, A. A. (1982), 'Models of memory: implications for measuring knowledge structures', *Advances in Consumer Research*, 9 (1): 45–51.

Muñiz, A. M. Jr, and O'Guinn, T. C. (2001), 'Brand community', *Journal of Consumer Research*, 27 (4): 412–31.

Muthukrishnan, A. V. and Chattopadhyay, A. (2007), 'Just give me another chance: The strategies for brand recovery from a bad first impression', *Journal of Marketing Research*, 44 (2): 334–45.

Nam, M. and Sternthal, B. (2008), 'The effects of a different category context on target brand evaluations', *Journal of Consumer Research*, 35 (4): 668–79.

Ng, S. and Houston, M. J. (2009), 'Field dependency and brand cognitive structures', *Journal of Marketing Research*, 46 (2): 279–92.

Park, C. W., Jaworski, B. J. and MacInnis, D. J. (1986), 'Strategic brand concept–image management', *Journal of Marketing*, 50 (4): 135–45.

Payne, J. W., Bettman, J. R. and Johnson, E. J. (1993), *The Adaptive Decision Maker*, Cambridge: Cambridge University Press.

Ries, A. and Trout, J. (1983, 2001), *Positioning: The Battle for your Mind*, New York: McGraw-Hill.

Robertson, T. S. and Kassarjian, H. H. (1991), *Handbook of Consumer Behavior*, Englewood Cliffs, NJ: Prentice-Hall.

Shine, B. C., Park, J. and Wyer, R. S. Jr (2007), 'Brand synergy effects in multiple brand extensions', *Journal of Marketing Research*, 44 (4): 663–70.

Sweldens, S., van Osselaer, S. M. J. and Janiszewski, C. (2010), 'Evaluative conditioning procedures and the resilience of conditioned brand attitudes', *Journal of Consumer Research*, 37 (3): 473–89.

Wan, E. W., Hong, J. and Sternthal, B. (2009), 'The effect of regulatory orientation and decision strategy on brand judgments', *Journal of Consumer Research*, 35 (6): 1026–1038.

7   The personality approach

with a commentary by Adjunct Professor Joseph Plummer, Columbia Business School

In 2006, Apple launched the first of three new television advertisements for Mac laptops. A young man dressed in casual clothes introduces himself as a Mac ('Hi, I am a Mac'). An older, more conservative-looking man enters the scene, introducing himself as PC. The two, clearly very different personalities, act out a brief vignette in which the capabilities and attributes of 'Mac' and 'PC' are compared. The PC is represented as a formal and stuffy person overly concerned with work – often being frustrated by the superior abilities of the more laid-back Mac. The two, the casual Mac and the more uptight PC, discuss some of the everyday difficulties of the PC and how the Mac does not have these problems.

The Mac versus the PC personality is a very literal example of how personality can be used to position and differentiate a brand against competing brands in the same product category, while also connecting with target users communicating explicitly the personality traits in play for consumers brand personality and self-congruity.

Creating a so-called brand personality has been a well-known trick in the advertising industry for decades. In 1997, one article stirred the pot and set a new agenda in brand management. The validated theoretical construct of brand personality entered brand management academia by Jennifer Aaker's article 'Dimensions of Brand Personality', which presented a whole new theoretical framework and method.

The publication of this research introduced a new brand perspective in brand management, inspired by human personality psychology and with a new dialogue-based brand-consumer exchange as a major implication.

Since then, Aaker's brand personality framework, scales and methodologies has been validated and adjusted by numerous studies. A few studies have failed to replicate the results and pose critique about the methodology and the assumption of homogeneous perceptions of brand personality (Azoulay and Kapferer 2003, Freling and Forbes 2005, Ivens and Valta 2012). A significant number of research articles have tested and supported the framework and it remains key in describing and studying how brand personality can be used to create emotional attachment between brands and consumers (Yorkston, Nunes and Matta 2010).

Box 7.1 Learning objectives

The purpose of this chapter is to:

Understand the expression of consumer self and personality are key to the assumptions

- Consumers express self through consumption of brands and ascribe personality traits to brands. A brand with a strong personality effectively 'speaks' to consumer self is an important driver of the emotional bonding between brand and consumer.

Understand personality, self and congruity comprise the theoretical framework

- The personality approach builds on three supporting theories: personality, consumer self and self-congruity.
- Personality draws on theory from psychology about the categorization of human personality.
- The personality construct can, in interplay with consumer expression of self, be a driver of strong consumer–brand relationships. Self-congruity describes the extent to which there is a match between consumer and brand personality.

Understand a mix of methods can be used to explore and establish generalizable data

- Gain an overview of the mix of qualitative and quantitative methods that can be used to uncover brand personality and get an introduction to scaling techniques used in the personality approach.

Understand how to build and manage brand personality

- Understand how a brand personality can be created and managed by using direct and indirect sources of brand personality.
- Get an overview of the academic evolution of the personality approach, from the evolution of the theoretical framework to more focus on brand-self congruity and its influence on brand personality performance.

The idea and development of the brand personality construct will be reviewed in this chapter.

Consumers automatically ascribe personality to brands. This process is a central aspect of consumers' symbolic consumption and construction of self. The personality approach in brand management explains how and why people choose brands with certain personalities, and how imbuing brands with personality can be a powerful tool to create and enhance brand equity. The assumptions, theories and methods of the personality approach borrow from related academic fields such as human psychology, sociology, personality research and consumer behaviour.

Understanding consumers' attraction to brand personalities has long been an area of interest in consumer behaviour, where research has focused on how brand personality enables consumers to express 'self' through the symbolic use of brand personality. This focus has been prevalent in an advertising context until the mid-1990s. Since the publication of 'Dimensions of Brand Personality', the personality contrast has also been immersed in a brand management context academically. Practitioners have viewed brand personality primarily as a way to position and differentiate the brand from other brands in the same product category, as a driver of consumer preference, and as a common denominator that can be used across national cultures.

Research into how personality affects consumer choice of brands and how personality can lead to stronger brands began in the field of consumer and advertising research. Adjunct Professor Joseph Plummer was one of the first to undertake substantial research into how personality plays a role in advertising, and how it affects consumer behaviour. His studies were based on conceptual models and mechanisms from human psychology (Plummer 1985). These early studies of personality primarily focused on the product-related personality.

If one wants to understand the idea of brand personality, one also has to understand the idea of consumer self (how the two are related will be explained later). Alongside the emerging knowledge about brand personality, a growing and increasingly influential stream of research evolved in consumer behaviour research focusing on consumer self. Russell W. Belk established a framework, describing how possessions are perceived as an extension of self, focusing on the emotional and symbolic roles played by possessions in people's lives (Belk 1988). Joseph M. Sirgy followed up with several articles exploring how self-congruity (the similarity between the product's functional and value-expressive benefits and consumer self) plays an important role in predicting consumers' brand attitudes (Sirgy and Johar 1991, Sirgy and Johar 1992, Sirgy *et al.* 1992).

Going back to brand personality, several research articles have expanded the applicability of the Aaker framework and empirically tested the structure of personality dimensions across, for example national cultures, firm stereotypes and gender, also the importance of category versus product level personality has been subject to empirical testing (Sung and Tinkham 2005, Batra *et al.* 2010, Grohman 2009, Vohs and Mogilner 2010).

Along with the significant number of research publications focusing on brand personality dimensions and scales, the notions of self-concept and self-congruity have been studied in greater detail. Especially the different layers of self (ideal, actual, individual and social) and their relative impact on consumers' perception of brand personality have been studied and accounted for in further detail. Different aspects of activating brand personality in relation to the social self-concept, such as user imagery, social in/out group belongings, have also been studied in greater detail, and the positive correlation between brand personality and self-congruity – both individually and socially, has been studied and documented by several studies from early 2000 until 2014 (Malär *et al.* 2011, Haarhoff and Kleyn 2012).

This chapter offers an overview of the personality approach by providing insights into the assumptions, key theoretical framework and methodologies underlying the personality approach. Finally, this chapter describes and discusses the managerial guidelines and recommendations that can be deduced from literature, supplemented with cases describing how companies manage brand personality in practice.

Assumptions of the personality approach

Previous approaches in brand management have placed the Four P's, the identity of the corporation or the consumer at the heart of brand equity creation. In the personality approach, it is assumed that consumers' need for identity and expression of self is a key driver of brand attitudes, choice and consumption. Consumers are believed to also – apart from the physical and functional characteristics of a brand – consume brands due to the symbolic benefits provided by brands:

> [T]herefore, like the multi-attribute model, which sheds insight into when and why consumers buy brands for utilitarian purposes, a cross-category framework and scale can provide theoretical insights into when and why consumers buy brands for self-expressive purposes.
>
> (Aaker 1997, p. 348)

Furthermore, it is assumed that if these symbolic benefits are expressed by imbuing the brand with a human-like character, then the brand will be strengthened significantly. A strong and attractive brand personality can, if well executed, serve as an important source of differentiation and brand power. Furthermore, consumers more easily relate to and bond with brands that are imbued with a brand personality as opposed to brands without brand personality. The rationale is that consumers 'see' themselves in the personality of the brand and use the brand personality in their construction and expression of identity and self. The more consumers perceive the brand personality as a reflection of their own personality, the stronger the brand personality and brand performance. The function of a brand personality is, however, not limited to consumers' personal inward use as a source of construction of self. Brands with an attractive brand personality are also chosen and consumed due to their outward symbolic signalling value. The use of brand personality as a symbolic signal or source of self/identity construction can be based on the brand personality itself or the personality of the ideal/actual users of a brand. This mechanism is referred to as 'brand personality and self-congruity' and has since the millennium been subject to an increasing number of research projects aiming to uncover details of how brand personality and self-congruity affect brand performance parameters such as consumers' brand preference, attitudes and loyalty. The personality approach hence places the personality of the brand and the personality of its stereotypical or ideal user at the heart of brand management.

The basic assumptions of the brand in the personality approach are depicted in Figure 7.1; it illustrates how brands are endowed with human-like personalities, which are activated in a continuous reciprocal, dialogue-based exchange between brand and consumer.

In the personality approach, the emotional bond between the brand and the consumer is hence strengthened significantly if the brand is imbued with an attractive and relevant brand personality. For consumers, brands with a brand personality are hence appealing because they serve as a means of identity/self construal and self-expression. For companies brand personality can serve as an important source of differentiation, positioning and a tool to build emotional bonds with consumers.

The personality perspective

The brand personality approach draws on theories and insights from the academic fields of human psychology, sociology and consumer behaviour. From human psychology, the personality approach borrows different categorizations of human character, human personality dimensions and traits. From sociology and consumer behaviour research, knowledge about how consumers use brands in their construction and expression of self is in play. The underlying assumption is that there is a high level of homogeneity among consumers' perception of the personality of brands, meaning that the majority will have a similar perception of the human-like personality dimensions and traits that can be used to describe a specific brand. The primary function of the brand is hence to express a personality that consumers can relate to and use for their own construction and expression of self. The primary subjects of analysis are respectively brand personality, consumer self and self-congruity. It is the relation between brand personality and consumers' perception, construction and expression of self.

In human psychology, personality is perceived as the pattern in which individuals can be divided according to how consistently they react to different environmental situations. In a brand management context, the construct of brand personality refers

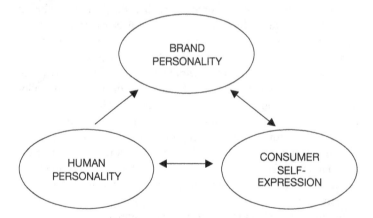

Figure 7.1 Brand personality construct

to 'the set of human characteristics associated with a brand' (Aaker 1997, p. 347). Personality traits associated with a brand are assumed to be enduring, distinct and stable. These traits offer self-expressive values to consumers. Therefore, it is assumed that the distinctiveness of the brand personality influences brand attractiveness and ultimately brand performance and thereby equity. In the field of consumer behaviour, it has long been acknowledged that consumers use brands for symbolic consumption and as means to express themselves by selecting brands with a particular brand personality. The level of consumers' identification with the personality of the brand determines the degree to which the consumers evaluate the brand as suitable or not for their own self-expression and construction of identity.

Strategically, the extent to which consumers are able to use the specific brand as a point of reference for their own construction and expression of identity is the rationale and basis for differentiation of the brand from other brands in the same category. Hence, in the personality approach, a really powerful and differentiated brand is perceived by the consumer as a brand that contributes to the consumer's individual and social construction and expression of self. For the company, the brand personality and insights into consumers' self-concepts can therefore be a strategic source for positioning, differentiation and a driver of loyalty. The brand personality construct enables companies to imbue intangible symbolic cues into the 'behaviour' and communication of the brand. These symbolic cues enhance consumers' attraction to and relation with the brand and hence serve as an important driver of competitive advantage and brand loyalty.

The 'brand–consumer exchange'

The personality approach introduces a strong emotional bond between the brand and the consumer, based on consumers' use of the brand personality for the inward construction and outward expression of self. The nature of the brand–consumer exchange in the personality approach is interactive and dyadic, and revolves around the exchange of symbolic benefits. These symbolic benefits (in this case brand traits) are evaluated by the consumer based on the extent to which they contribute to their construction and expression of identity, referred to as self-congruity. High self-congruity, when there is a high match between the brand personality and the self-concept, which this personality matches (being on an actual, ideal, individual or social level).

The unit of analysis is the individual consumer and the focus is hence as in the previous approaches individual. The nature of the relation is dyadic. It is this symbolically charged interaction between the brand and the consumer that motivates consumers to choose one brand over another. Because a brand personality sets off a process of social identification between the brand and the self of the consumer, it is assumed in the personality approach that the fulfilment and expression of self is one of the strongest basic driving forces that predispose consumers to act on and consume brands. The creation of brand personality is hence a dynamic cyclical process that sets off from the company and then, in an interactive process between consumer and brand, creates and enhances a certain brand personality. Consumers evaluate a brand personality based on their observations of the brand behaviour over time. These evaluations add up to a general assessment of the brand, and the self-congruence between brand and consumer enhances attitudinal and behavioural consumer responses to the brand. (Aaker 1999, Grohman 2009, Chaplin and John 2005, Park and John 2010).

Summary

In the personality approach, human personality and consumers' identity construction, as well as expression is the pivotal point of brand equity creation. It is the symbolic benefits a brand can provide to consumers expressed through a certain brand personality that are assumed to be the key drivers of brand strength. The level of analysis is the individual consumer, and the subject of analysis is consumer self and identity. The main function of the brand is not to provide utilitarian attributes and benefits as in the economic approach, but to enable consumers' construction and expression of self by providing symbolic signal value. The strength of the brand is determined by the extent to which there is congruity between the brand personality and the personality or self of the consumer.

Theoretical framework of the personality approach

In this section, the theoretical framework and building blocks of the personality approach and their interrelation will be explained. The supporting theories of brand personality that make up the theoretical framework are: personality, consumer self and self-congruity (see Figure 7.2). The personality construct has its origin in

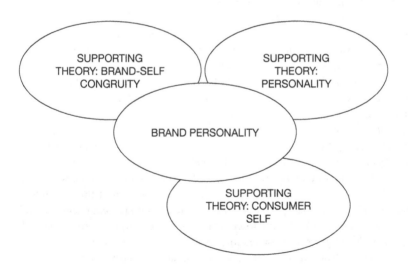

Figure 7.2 Supporting and core theories of the personality approach

theory from cognitive and social psychology about human personality. The self-concept refers to consumers' construction and expression of self. The self-concept is widely studied in the field of consumer behaviour, but also borrows from the field of psychology about the construction of identity. The last supporting theory, self-congruity, is derived from the field of social psychology and describes the social identification process consumers engage in with brands they consume. The three supporting theories in the personality approach are all explained in the context of brand management and provide theoretical input to understanding the theoretical framework as a whole – brand personality.

Supporting theories: personality

The concept of personality has its origin in the field of human psychology. The personality is one of the most significant manifestations of a human being's self-concept and has been an area of research in human psychology since the 1930s.

In human psychology, the personality construct focuses on the development of frameworks for the categorization of human beings according to their personality. These frameworks define people according to different personality types defined by certain personality traits. It hence assumes that personality traits describe internal characteristics of human beings from which their behaviour in different situations can be predicted and explained. Personality traits can be described with adjectives such as 'talkative', 'organized', 'imaginative' or 'responsible'.

There are several theoretical frameworks used in the field of psychology for the categorization of personalities, but one of the most influential is the framework of the 'Big Five'. This framework reduces the number of adjectives describing human personalities to five by which human beings can be categorized. If the person's behaviour can be described by adjectives as 'talkative', 'active', 'energetic' and 'outgoing', the dominant dimension is 'extroversion'.

The personality of human beings not only determines how they will react to different situations, or behave in general, it also influences how humans are able to connect with other human beings and the role that people with different personalities play in relationship and interaction with other people, individually or in groups.

Supporting theory: consumer self

The first step in understanding how and why consumer self plays a role in the personality approach implies insight into the way human beings attach meaning to possessions (almost as if they are a part of own self). This meaning is key in the understanding of consumption patterns and the drivers that motivate consumers' symbolic consumption of brands. Belk, a pioneer in the conceptualization of the self-concept, quotes William James (founder of the modern conceptions of self (1890, pp. 291–2)), in his quest for a conceptualization of how possessions affect the formation and expression of self:

The sum total of all that he *can* call his, not only his body and his psychic powers, but his clothes and his house, his wife and children, his ancestors and friends, his reputation and works, his lands and yacht and bank-account.

(Belk 1988, p. 139)

According to the modern conceptions of self, material possessions are thought to be an extension of our identity – and are defined as an important part of the so-called 'extended self'. The extended self is hence the extensions of self that humans produce through their relations with other people, family members, achievements and last – but in this context of brand management, certainly not least – our possessions. The nature and the importance of different possessions as contributors to the extended self fluctuate over time. Consumers hence neglect old possessions and seek new ones when the possessions no longer fit the consumers' actual or ideal self-images. Even though consumers' needs for material possessions decrease with age, the need to define and express self through possessions remains high throughout life.

It seems an inescapable fact of modern life that we learn, define, and remind ourselves of who we are by our possessions. . . . Our accumulation of posses-sions provides a sense of past and tells us who we are, where we have come from, and perhaps where we are going.

(Belk 1988, p. 160)

Apart from using possessions to enhance own sense of self, consumers also use possessions to express self to others. Consumers hence use brands to define themselves to others, demonstrate group affiliation or to tell the story of who they are, and what they stand for. Consumers' self is structured in terms of two dimensions:

- *Attributes*. A person can be tall, lucky or can appreciate family values.
- *Narratives*. The attributes are linked to key events in life structured as stories.

Consumers use brands to express their own attributes and to play out personal narratives about their lives and identities, positioning themselves in relation to other people, groups, culture and society. Objects or brands that people love are particularly important for the creation, maintenance and expression of self: 'Loved objects serve as indexical mementos of key events or relationships in the life narrative, help resolve identity conflicts, and tend to be tightly embedded in a rich symbolic network of associations' (Ahuvia 2005, p. 179). In the personality approach, these mechanisms are essential because they contribute to understanding the interplay between how consumers use brand personality in the creation and expression of attributes and narratives of their life.

Layers of consumer self

According to Sirgy, one of the key contributors to describing the self-concept in a marketing and advertising context, the consumer self-construct consists of two 'branches': an individual and an interdependent one (see Figure 7.3).

The individual aspect refers to a self-concept, where objects are consumed because they carry a symbolic significance for the consumer on an individual basis. The individual self can be further divided into actual and ideal self. The actual self is the objective and authentic representation of self. The ideal self is a representation of consumer aspirations and dreams of something that the consumer would like to become (Sirgy 1982, Sirgy and Johar 1991, Malär *et al.* 2011). Hence, the consumption of brands and consumers' emotional attachment and formation of attitudes towards brands partly stem from consumers' need to create and maintain self at an individual level.

The consumer self also has a social aspect – that is, the expression of self to others. This symbolic consumption of objects serves to express self to others at a social group level. Here brands are consumed to either demonstrate belonging or distance to certain social or cultural groupings. For outgroup behaviour, consumers will use brands to demonstrate that they are not part of, or do not support certain social or subcultural groups. Ingroup behaviour describes a situation, where consumers by consuming certain products demonstrate belonging or support of certain groups. These mechanisms can take place on a small scale – among teenagers in school, demonstrating belonging by wearing certain brands – or it can be played out on bigger scales, where psychological distance or belonging to certain subcultures and larger social groupings is demonstrated through the consumption of certain brands. Also at the social/group level, brands can appeal to either actual or aspirational (ideal) selves (Erdem and Sun 2002, Choi and Winterich 2013).

Brands contribute to the construction of self in various ways. They can help consumers achieve goals motivated by the ideal self, meet needs for self-expression

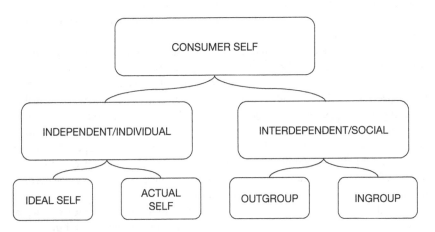

Figure 7.3 Consumer self construct; based on Sirgy (1982), Sirgy and Johar (1991)

either socially or individually, or serve as a tool for connecting with the past events. They can be symbols of personal achievement, an expression of individuality, or they can help people through life transitions. The self-expressive values and the distinctiveness of the brand personality have a significant effect on how attractive the brand personality is as perceived by the consumer. But the self-expressive value is far more important than the distinctiveness. The self-expressive value of a brand personality depends on the level of consistency between the brand personality and the self-image of the consumer – the brand self-congruity. The third theoretical building block of the personality approach is hence the construct of social identification between brand and consumer – the match between brand personality and consumer self.

Supporting theory: self-congruity

When experiencing brands with different personalities, consumers engage in a matching process to identify brands that are congruent with their own self-images. This process is here referred to as self-congruity and can be described in three steps. First, consumers form associations about brands that can be related to their self – in the context of brand personality, it will often be in the form of certain personality traits. Second, consumers' representations of self are activated – either actual, ideal or social self. Third, consumers engage in a matching process between their perception of associations derived from the brand and their representation of self, determining the match between the brand personality and consumer self. This process of self-congruity ultimately has great significance for consumers' formation of attitude, emotional attachment, brand choice and loyalty.

The brand self-congruity construct has its origin in the concept of social identification from the field of psychology. This construct proposes that consumer behaviour is determined partly by the consumer's comparison of own perception of self (either individual: actual/ideal, or their social: out-group or in-group as illustrated in Figure 7.3) and the personality of the brand. Self does not necessarily refer to the actual self; the brand personality can also be congruent with the ideal self of the consumer.

Hence, brands can have different functions in relation to how they activate consumers' self – for either construction or expression of self, consumers use brand personalities in relation to self in two ways on an individual level: (1). They either try to preserve their own self-concept by consuming brands with a personality matching their actual self, or (2) they use the symbolic consumption of brands with a certain personality to enhance their self-concept, by consuming brands with a personality that is congruent with their ideal self, representing hopes, aspirations and dreams of the consumer. Consumers also use the brands as an expression of social self, here the mechanism for consumers is to position themselves according to social or cultural reference groups in society.

Recent research has sought to explore the relative importance of the actual versus the ideal self for consumers' emotional attachment to brands, and the results indicate that the actual self is becoming more important for consumers' emotional brand attachment. As a consequence, it is more effective to build a brand personality appealing to the actual self rather than an ideal self. This is often referred to as authentic branding and has spurred a growing stream of both research and practice that focuses on the actual self and authenticity rather than aspirational, hard to live-up-to ideal representations of reality (Gilmore and Pine 2007, Malär *et al.* 2011).

Box 7.2 Ideal self: Oil of Olay – female consumers' hopes and dreams

Deep insight into consumer motivation and self-brand relations is crucial when developing brand personality. In 1985, Joseph Plummer made an investigation of consumers' associations with the Oil of Olay brand that could be used to describe the brand personality of Oil of Olay. The result was rather surprising and illustrates well how brands can appeal not only to the actual self of consumers but also to the ideal self of consumers. Consumers were asked to associate how they would describe Oil of Olay with other abstract descriptions, apart from it being a lotion. Consumers associated Oil of Olay with:

- an animal: a mink
- country: France
- occupation: secretary
- fabric: silk
- magazine: *Vogue*.

These associations brings to mind a French secretary wearing mink and silk reading *Vogue* while relaxing somewhere on the French Riviera. This elegant woman uses Oil of Olay every morning and evening to stay beautiful. The stereotypical user of Oil of Olay at the time had a personality far from the personality consumers associated with the Oil of Olay brand. She could be described as:

- down-to-earth
- practical.

All in all, very different from the personality described as the personality of Oil of Olay, which was described as more up-scale, exclusive and sophisticated. These differences illustrate very well how some brands in their communication must address not necessarily the actual self of the stereotypical consumer but rather the desired or ideal self.

Adapted from Plummer (1985)

At the social level, brand personality serves to signal belonging to certain social groupings or subcultures. In that case, consumers reject brands and brand meaning that are not consistent with the references and images of the reference group the consumer is or would like to be a part of and use brands that are in accordance with their aspirations. At the individual level, the brand can fulfil a need from the independent self to differentiate from groups of people and thereby demonstrate individual image and self. Research of how consumers use brands in relation to their social self indicates a correlation with other social constructs such as moral identity and self-esteem, and their causal effect on social self-congruity. These insights can be used for certain target groups (e.g. teenagers) and for products that are sensitive to either moral identity or subjects of self-esteem (Dommer *et al.* 2013, Choi and Winterich 2013). Hence when building a brand personality for products targeted at teenagers, where self-esteem and social self is important in their identity and self-construction and expression, mechanisms of belonging to the group can be used to build brand attachment and loyalty.

The development of self-congruity using brand personality is a dynamic two-way process. Consumers who prefer a particular brand because of its personality, endow and influence the brand personality with their own self and symbolic signalling, strengthening or weakening the brand personality. To ensure that this process will strengthen and not weaken the brand personality, it is essential for brand managers to ensure that the brand personality appeals to the right consumers (target group) and that their consumption of the brand underpins the desired brand personality. Getting this process right will consolidate and enhance the brand personality in the long run, because user images in flux with the intended brand personality enhance and build favourable brand associations. Selecting and appealing to the right group of consumers can hence strengthen the brand, whereas attracting the 'wrong' group of consumers can devaluate the brand personality and undermine the credibility of the brand. The interaction between the brand and the consumer can hence be described as a cyclical process, either strengthening or weakening the brand.

Congruence between self and brand personality positively affects brand loyalty directly and indirectly through functional congruity, product involvement and brand relationship quality. This underpins the paramount importance of self–brand congruity, not only in the battle to attract and appeal to certain groups of consumers, but also for the long-term nurturing of brand attitude, choice and loyalty in the efforts to create the right brand personality.

Theoretical framework: brand personality

Brand personality is hence made up of three key theories, categorizations of human personality – the 'Big Five' from human psychology, the concept of self and the matching mechanisms between brand personality and self – brand-self congruity. Hence, brand personality is twofold and refers to both the personality endowed in the brand by the company and the brand personality perceived by consumers. One aspect of brand personality is hence what the company wants the

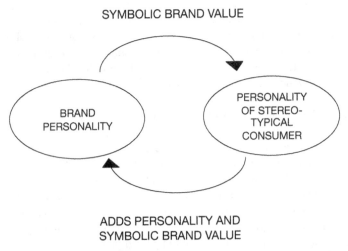

SYMBOLIC BRAND VALUE

BRAND
PERSONALITY

PERSONALITY
OF STEREO-
TYPICAL
CONSUMER

ADDS PERSONALITY AND
SYMBOLIC BRAND VALUE

Figure 7.4 The brand–self exchange of symbolic brand value in the market place

consumer to think and feel about the brand. The other perspective is what consumers perceive (the two are not necessarily the same) (see Figure 7.4).

As mentioned earlier, in 1997 Jennifer Aaker published the first research-based
conceptualization of the personality construct in a brand management context.
Her conceptualization of the personality construct builds on the theoretical and
methodological frameworks from psychology about the categorization of people
according to the salience of different personality dimensions. It focused on
investigating if and how the categorization of human personalities from psychology
also applies to brands. Aaker made an extensive study with the aim of identifying
which personality traits people associate with a wide range of brands. Aaker came
to the conclusion that it is possible to transfer the idea of personality dimensions
from human personality psychology to brands and brand management.

The study resulted in the Big Five of brand management (the five dimensions
of brand personality) (see Figure 7.6). They describe the five major groupings of
personalities consumers associate with brands and conclude that brands, in the same
way as humans, have unique personalities. In a complementary research following
the Aaker study, the five personalities have been proven viable not only in the
United States (where the study was originally made) but also in other Western
cultures. In Latin and Asian cultures, however, there seem to be some variations
in how the different personality dimensions are rated (Aaker *et al.* 2001, Sung and
Tinkham 2005).

The personality traits describe the characteristics that people associate with
each brand personality dimension. These traits should ideally be reflected in the
attributes of the brand and/or in the 'behaviour' of the brand. From the consumer
perspective, the brand personality can be uncovered by exploring consumers' brand
associations. From the company perspective, it can be uncovered by analysing the

product-related attributes such as brand name, logo, communication style, price, distribution, behaviour and so on. All these elements add up to the brand personality. Apart from the more product-specific attributes, the brand personality is also reflected in the characteristics attributed to the brand and in the associations, symbolic values and emotional responses to the brand or the emotional relationship with the brand. For a brand personality to be successful, it must be consistent and durable.

If the attributes or behaviour of the brand (marketing activities) are not consistent with the brand personality, consumers are likely to abandon the brand because the personality looses credibility. From the marketing perspective, brand personality is closely related to and an important driver of brand identity and is a useful management tool that can be used to benchmark brand personality within or across product categories. The brand personality framework can be used to materialize abstract, intangible brand ideas and provide direction for the implementation of the brand idea in the user imagery, advertising and more product-related aspects such as packaging. Succeeding in developing and implementing a strong, attractive and unique brand personality increases consumer preferences and evokes consumer emotions and bonding with the brand. This increases the level of trust and loyalty between brand and consumer. A key reason why brand personality can be such an effective tool for brand management is that consumers consume brands as a means in their identity construction projects – brands are important for consumers' construction and expression of self. The brand personality construct and

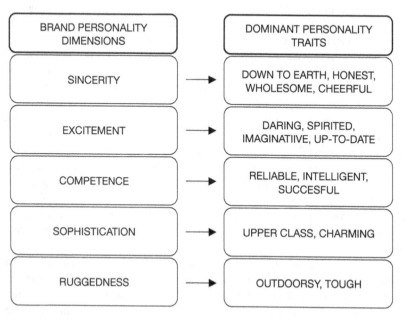

Figure 7.5 US dimensions and traits of brand personality; adapted from Aaker (1997)

consumers' expression of self are hence closely related. The framework of Aaker is the most up-to-date conceptualization of a personality framework for brand management, because it reflects the most recent insights into the mechanisms of human personality and brand personalities (see Figure 7.5).

In practice, other theoretical frameworks and foundations for imbuing personality into brands have been widely used (see Figure 7.6). The effectiveness of these tools and methods are, however, not supported by an extensive study such as the Aaker framework. Theory about archetypes and narrative structures is an example of these alternative foundations for brand personality tools that have been widely used, especially by advertising agencies, to build a brand platform or personality. The theory of archetypes represents a more deterministic and predetermined perspective on the drivers of human behaviour than the personality construct presented in this chapter because it bases the drivers of human consumption on universal predetermined behavioural patterns latent in all human beings. But archetypes is one of several other frameworks used to create and manage brand personality. On the company-side, as already mentioned, the advertising industry has for decades worked with personality as a way of linking products with consumers' lives. In that process, a personality statement is the strategic driver (the communication goals the company has for the brand) and reflected in the brand personality, serving as the guiding platform for the creation and enhancement of the brand in the long run. The personality statement also delivers important input to the creative strategy when creating advertising campaigns. Joseph Plummer, a key practitioner and scholar of the personality approach has worked with personality in an advertising context and he has done significant research and development with Young & Rubicam. They have co-developed frameworks and procedures for how to use brand personality strategically and as a driver of the creative process.

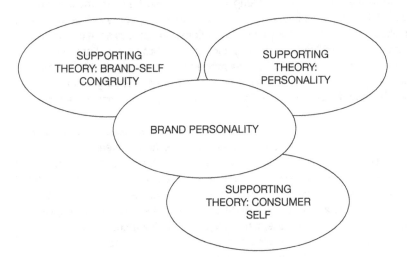

Figure 7.6 Theoretical framework of the personality approach: brand personality

An established framework still used by Young & Rubicam and many other practitioners is archetypes, see Box 7.3.

The Aaker framework is key in this book, because it from a scientific point of view is the first to establish a new school of thought and an entirely new theoretical framework for how to analyse and manage brand personality in a brand management context.

Box 7.3 Archetypes and brand personality

Carl Gustav Jung (1875–1961) was a Swiss psychiatrist. Among many important contributions to analytical psychology, he pioneered the theory about archetypes based on extensive psychological studies in the early 1900s. Jung built the theoretical notions of archetypes on an idea that all human beings share a collective unconscious (an even deeper layer than the 'id' proposed by Sigmund Freud). The collective unconscious is the root of our communication and consists of psychological codes that transcend time. The collective unconscious is, according to Jung, 'identical in all men and thus constitutes a common psychic substrate of suprapersonal nature which is present in every one of us'. This collective unconscious act as a communal well in the mind filled with psychic content that we all share' (*The Archetypes and the Collective Unconscious* (C.G. Jung, pp. 3–41) and *Building Brands and Believers: How to Connect with Consumers Using Archetypes* (K. Wertime 2002, p. 60)).

Archetypes are believed to be the basic mechanisms and source codes that enable people to communicate and connect at a rudimentary subconscious level. These codes are believed to be static, universal and deeply rooted in the human psyche. Jung further believed that the unconscious level of the human psyche is an active agent in people's lives and a significant factor that shapes everyday actions. Archetypes are expressions of the patterns of fundamental psychic content that we all share and are related to instinctively. They cover a range of basic elements in the human psyche such as evil, happiness, heroic and maternal feelings. In religion and culture archetypical expressions have been used for millennia to express universal truths.

In brand management, archetypical patterns can, according to Mark and Pearson (2001), provide fundamental, timeless and universal reference points, by using symbols and images tapping into the unconscious. In that way brand managers can ensure brands achieve symbolic significance for all consumers because they address the archetypical level of unconscious patterns that we all share. Mark and Pearson's framework for working with archetypes in brand management consists of twelve archetypical personalities. These twelve archetypes are believed to be able to fulfil different, subconscious, archetypical needs for consumers:

Basic archetypical need

- stability and control, and need to feel safe;
- belonging and enjoyment and a need to love and feel part of a community;
- risk and mastery and a need to achieve and perform well;
- independence and fulfilment and a need to find harmony and happiness.

Archetypical personality

- Creator
- Caregiver
- Ruler
- Jester
- Regular girl/guy
- Lover

- Hero
- Outlaw
- Magician
- Innocent
- Explorer
- Sage

A brand imbued with archetypical meaning is believed to enhance the creation of emotional affinity, which makes way for the rational arguments for buying a product. In the personality approach, archetypical symbols are path openers between brands and consumers. Get a Donna Karan dress and feel like a queen or see the Christmas ads from Coca-Cola and feel the innocence. Archetypes mediate between products and customer motivation by providing symbolic meaning. Archetypical meaning hence makes brands come to life and ensures that consumers can relate to the product or brand on an emotional level.

Source: Mark and Pearson (2001)

Summary

The theoretical framework of the personality approach consists of the three theoretical building blocks: personality, consumer self and self-congruity. Personality describes how the personality approach draws on the construct of personality from the field of human psychology, characterizing the main personalities that human beings can be categorized according to.

The concept of self describes how consumers consume and choose brands based on how these brands contribute to their construction and expression of self.

The construct of self-congruity describes the process of identification that takes place between the personality of a brand and the personality of the consumer. The greater the congruence between the personality of the brand and the personality of the consumer, the more likely it is that the brand personality is strong and performs well in creating emotional attachments between the brand and the consumer.

The core framework of the personality approach is brand personality. The framework 'Dimensions of brand personality' developed by Aaker (1997) consists of five dimensions that brands can be divided according to and an explanation of how these dimensions can be expressed in the communication of a brand personality by emphasizing certain traits or behaviours.

Methods and data of the personality approach

The methods and data used in the personality approach vary, depending on the focus and aim of the data collection and research at hand. The quantitative method developed by Aaker (1997) has gained support and has been widely used to uncover dimensions of brand personality, also across different national cultures, product brands and categories.

Research into the correlation between brand personality and consumers' expression of self and self-congruity is conducted using a mix of qualitative and quantitative methods. Mixed methods are used in the brand personality approach depending on the goal of the study. Quantitative methods are used for categorizing and uncovering brand personality and for the study of consumers' self-expression through brand personality; the focus is on rich and descriptive qualitative data. Qualitative data are necessary in order to gain understanding of the complex nature of consumer self and how it affects attitudes, consumption patterns and ultimately how brand personality can be used to enhance consumers' expression of self. Quantitative methods and advanced statistical models are used to uncover the salience and generalizability of brand personality across larger populations. The methods in the personality approach hence vary from quantitative statistical studies of brand personality at one end of the scale to longitudinal field studies of brand personality and consumer expression of self at the other extreme.

Quantitative methods for researching brand personality

Investigating brand personality takes place in the cross-field between psychology and consumer research. In psychology, quantitative methods dominate, while consumer research methods are becoming increasingly qualitative. The aim of quantitative methods is, simply put, reducing ambiguity by transforming perceptions into structured quantifiable categories – or, as in the case of methods for studying brand personality, reducing consumers' perceptions of how a brand can be characterized, described and perceived as a personality into a structured set of brand personality dimensions. Until 1997, a variety of methods were used to explore and measure brand personality, but none of them had been validated by research extensive enough to deliver reliable, valid and generalizable results.

In the 1997 study, the aim was to develop a framework that would be generalizable across brands and industries using an extensive (primarily) quantitative study of the dimensions of brand personality. Aaker collected personality characteristics from both psychology and practice. From psychology – 'the Big Five' was derived, from practitioners (advertising agencies, scholars and research agencies)

204 unique traits were uncovered, finally from a small-scale qualitative consumer study 295 were deduced. This procedure resulted in 309 non-redundant personality traits. These 309 personality traits were reduced further, by asking respondents to evaluate their importance on an ordinal scale. Factor analysis was used to narrow down findings and establish the five dimensions and related personality traits of the brand personality framework. Hence, the process of founding the theoretical framework also represents a good example of how mixed methods are adequate at different stages when uncovering and studying brand personality.

This quantitative method for measuring brand personality has subsequently been validated by several studies and is widely used today. The aim was to identify a limited (manageable) number of dimensions that can be used to categorize all brands. For this purpose, Aaker developed a method based on a structured quantitative measurement technique (scaling) combined with factor analysis of the large quantity of data generated in the study. To get a grip on what scaling techniques are all about, the most common scaling techniques used in marketing will be explained in the next section.

Questionnaires and scaling techniques

Questionnaires and scaling techniques are at the heart of methods for measuring brand personality. This short introduction will enable the reader to know the basics about scaling.

Scaling refers to the process of measuring or ordering entities according to the attributes or traits that characterize them. An example could be a scaling technique that could involve estimating individuals' levels of extroversion, or how consumers perceive the personality of a certain brand. There are different scaling methods that can provide different results suited for different objectives. Certain methods of scaling estimate magnitudes on a continuum, while other methods provide only the relative ordering of the entities.

In the personality approach, scaling techniques are used to determine the nature and strength of consumers' attitudes or opinions towards a specific brand personality. There are four types of scales: nominal, ordinal, interval and ratio. They have different properties suitable in different situations depending on the type of information needed.

- *Nominal scales* are the weakest form of scale. The numbers assigned to entities serve only to identify the subjects under consideration. Nominal scales are used only to categorize or label – the number has no mathematical properties. Examples are inventory codes or ISBN book codes.
- *Ordinal scales* seek to impose more structure on objects by rank-ordering them in terms of the subject's characteristics, such as weight or colour. As with nominal scales, identical objects are given the same number, but the ordinal scale has the added property that it can tell us something about the direction or relative standing of one object to another. An example is a preference ranking: to what extent does a consumer prefer one brand to another brand?

In order to be able to draw conclusions about differences between the numbers (reflecting how much a consumer prefers one brand over another), we must know something about the interval between the numbers. Since ordinal scales do not provide that, interval scales can be used.

- *Interval scales* are grounded on the assumption of equal intervals between the numbers, that is the space between 5 and 10 is the same as the space between 45 and 50 and in both cases this distance is five times as great as that between 1 and 2 or 11 and 12, and so on. Numbers indicate the magnitude of difference between items, but there is no absolute zero point. Examples are attitude scales and opinion scales – this scale would be able to measure how much a consumer prefers one brand to another.

Box 7.4 Ordinal scales applied

Ordinal scales express consumers' satisfaction or evaluation of one product or one brand, for example 'How satisfied are you with your current newspaper?'

Satisfaction   **Score 1–5**

- Not satisfied
- Neither satisfied nor dissatisfied
- Satisfied
- Very satisfied
- Extremely satisfied

Box 7.5 Interval scales applied

Interval scales express the standing of several brands in relation to each other, for example 'Assign the different beer brands according to the brand you prefer the most' (assign the number 1 to the brand you prefer and assign the number 5 to the brand you least prefer).

Brand   **Score 1–5**

Miller's
Coor's light
Carlsberg
Budweiser
Heineken

- *Ratio scales* are the most powerful and possess all the properties of nominal, ordinal and interval scales. In addition they permit absolute comparisons of the objects, for example 6 m is twice as high as 3 m and six times as high as 1 m. Numbers indicate magnitude of difference and there is a fixed zero point. Ratios can be calculated. Examples include: age, income, price, costs, sales revenue, sales volume and market share.

The brand personality scale

The Likert scale was adapted by Aaker to measure brand personality. This type of psychometric response scale is often used in questionnaires and in survey research. When responding to a Likert questionnaire item, respondents specify their level of agreement with a statement. In Aaker's brand personality study, a measurement scale for measuring brand personality was developed consisting of a five-point Likert scale measuring to what extent consumers agree that a personality dimension describes brand personality: from 1 (strongly agree) to 5 (strongly disagree). This scale was used to measure 42 dimensions of brand personality based on more than 1,000 respondents. After generating data, factor analysis was used to analyse data and statistically reduce the number of personality traits. Factor analysis is a statistical data reduction technique used to explain variability and factor correlation among random variables.

Methods for studying self-concept and self-congruity

The methods used for studying self consist of descriptive methodologies, where consumers are asked to determine to what extent a word or a symbol is self-descriptive. After that, the congruence between self and brand personality can be measured. It consists of a two-step procedure, where the initial step uncovers the personality traits consumers attribute to a certain brand and the second step determines to what extent these personality traits are congruent with the personality traits identified in the descriptive exploration of self. Most studies of brand personality and self mix qualitative, descriptive methods and the brand personality scaling method (as developed by Aaker 1997).

Apart from these rather quantitative methods, it can also be useful to include more qualitative methodologies such as free association methodology, photo sorting or autobiographical methods, where consumers describe their autobiographical memory related to certain stimuli that have a relation to the brand in question. These methods can provide a more detailed image of the self-concept and its various layers. Studies of self-congruity are often done by using a scale, where consumers rate their perceptions of own self according to the personality characteristics of the brand. Quantitative regression analysis can then be used to analyse the congruity between brand personality and the consumer's self-concept.

Mixing methods for better results

Quantitative scales tend to be developed under a laboratory setting and may not be the best survey tool for capturing the unconscious aspects of people's symbolic consumption of brands. Qualitative research is perceived to better capture the nature of consumption behaviour, which is why quantitative research methods are often used in combination with qualitative methods in the personality approach. Qualitative methods are used to ensure a deep understanding of the phenomena before doing the quantitative research with the aim of generating generalizable results. Aaker solved this problem by combining the quantitative study with qualitative methods in the exploratory phase – free association method was used to ensure that the personality trait list generated from the theoretical reviews of human personality theory was complete and accurate to explain brand personality. Free association methods, photo-sorting techniques or in-depth interviews are often combined with quantitative approaches in the personality approach to respond to the dilemma of commercial research into consumer behaviour and perceptions, as well as the need to generate generalizable results.

As mentioned previously, the notion of the archetype is as a field related to brand personality, and more qualitative methods for uncovering consumers' perception of brands in relation to archetypes have been developed. The memory elicitation method (Braun-Latour 2007) provides insight into the rich symbolism

---

Box 7.6 'Six steps' method of exploring and measuring brand personality

- Set up a qualitative study of the personality traits that people ascribe to the brand. Gather a complete list of all personality traits mentioned from all relevant shareholders.
- Reduce the number of relevant traits by narrowing down the field. This can be done by using a scaling technique where respondents are asked to judge how well a trait describes a brand on a seven-point scale ranging from 1 (not at all descriptive) to 7 (extremely descriptive). Select the traits with an average score of 6 or more.
- Use factor analyses to further reduce the number of traits for the aggregate database and identify the final number of personality dimensions.
- For every factor (personality dimension), a new factor analysis is done to identify traits that accurately describe each dimension in greater detail (to ensure rich description of each dimension and a more full description of personality).
- Confirm the test results with a new sample of respondents to ensure validity of both brand personality dimensions and the accuracy of how well the traits describe each dimension.
- If necessary, test the results across national cultures to ensure that the strategies developed based on the results are applicable internationally, or define possible adjustments due to the differences in national culture.

of archetypes and brand relationships. The methodology is presented in Chapter 8 about the relational approach.

Summary

Quantitative studies and questionnaires are at the heart of the data and methods used in the personality approach. The methods used to uncover brand personality are derived from psychology and involve measuring what kind of personality consumers attribute to brands by applying different scaling techniques. To gain insights into the self-concept and its relation to brand personality, quantitative methods are, however, not suitable. This is why the quantitative methods that have dominated the personality approach in recent years have been accompanied by more qualitative and loosely structured research methods to uncover the unconscious aspects of consumer self.

Managerial implications: how to manage brand personality

We have now learned how the personality approach assumes that brands are consumed because they contribute to their construction and expression of identity, and that they project humanlike personality traits to brands.

The managerial focus of the personality approach can be derived from these assumptions. The primary and most important task for the brand manager in the personality approach is to understand how the brand contributes to construction and expression of identity. After understanding these mechanisms, they must translate this understanding into a brand personality strategy, which delivers value and relevance for the consumer. The creation and management of brand personality can be described as a series of steps to uncover and consider, each of these steps is elaborated in this section.

The goal of brand personality is to describe a mix of perceptual reality from the consumer perception – they should reflect the way consumers feel about the brand rather than just expressing how the company would like the consumer to feel. The creation of brand personality consists of the following steps:

- *Identify personality*. Identify personality dimensions and personality traits to be communicated and built into the 'behaviour' of the brand. By narrowing down the relevant traits as described in the methods and data of the personality approach, it is possible to finally end up with the brand personality statement describing the traits and facets characterizing the brand personality.
- *Make sure it is appealing*. Make sure that the personality appeals to the consumer, by analysing the consumer self–brand exchange. Should adjustments be made to the brand personality based on an analysis of how consumers are to use the symbolic attributes of the brand?
- *Understand target groups*. Make sure that the right consumer groups are targeted, and the right brand endorsers are chosen. The typical consumer of a brand

can have an enormous impact on how the brand personality is perceived by other future consumers. This is why getting the target group right (early adopters) from the beginning can be crucial for the success of the brand personality.

- *Align the personality of the brand and the consumer.* Gather data and analyse the extent to which the brand is congruent with consumers' self and align the personality accordingly.
- *Develop the communication platform.* Having identified the personality dimensions that should characterize the brand, the final step is to develop an efficient communication platform and choose communication channels that underpin the developed brand personality.

The effectiveness and success of a brand personality depends on the extent to which management is able to imbue the brands with a personality that is attractive, relevant and enhances consumers' creation and/or expression of self. To master this process is not easy because it requires deep insight into consumers' identity construction and how this process lays the grounds for consumers' motivation for the consumption of brand personalities that will assist them in their construction and expression of self. This insight must be used to create a coherent personality through the wide array of brand activities, ensuring that the brand personality statement is expressed in the behaviour and communication of the brand across all channels and touchpoints.

The brand personality framework is also increasingly being used to explore, diagnose and develop segmentation, positioning and differentiation strategies. E.g. using the brand personality construct to categorize brands across a product category for instance, can sharpen and make the differentiation and brand positioning clearer, by tapping into the more psychological dimensions of the brand. The efforts to create a strong brand personality are worthwhile; several comparisons and studies point to the fact that brands with strong personalities outperform brands without. Furthermore, once created, a brand personality usually has a long 'life' and serves as an effective tool to build not only attitudes and consumption behaviour but also consumer loyalty.

Self and brand personality management

As explained, the basis of a strong brand personality starts with insight into how the symbolic benefits of the brand personality contribute to consumers' construction and expression of self. It is hence individual, psychological consumers' processes that lay the grounds for the managerial guidelines. Insight into what layer of the self-concept that is predominant for a specific brand is key, knowing exactly which level of self the brand appeals to is essential. Managerially these steps from understanding the mechanisms of self and construction of brand personality are accounted for – also explained in the consumer self construct (Box 7.6).

Exact knowledge about the mechanisms and focus of self for the particular brand in question is a prerequisite for the ability to develop a brand personality that is relevant and attractive to consumers. Since 2005, an increasing number of research articles have studied in detail how the layers of self (individual: actual, ideal; and social: ingroup, outgroup) play different roles in the creation of brand personality. Several articles have documented that consumers respond more to brand personalities 'speaking' to the actual self as opposed to an ideal self, representing consumer aspirations and dreams. Hence, where the majority of advertising and branding campaigns previously were built to address consumers' ideal self, research has pointed out that for most brands, it is more effective to 'speak' to consumers' actual self, giving grounds for reconsidering aspirational branding as a way of building emotional attachment with consumers (Malär *et al.* 2011). Also in practice, this move in focus is reflected: an increasing number of brands have begun to work on actual self-congruence when building brand personality. The 'actual self' seems to be growing in importance because consumers are more and more looking for reality and authenticity in marketing messages as opposed to the more ideal representations of reality traditionally used in advertising and brand communication (Gilmore and Pine 2007). Dove is a good example of a company that has taken the leap from ideal to actual self brand-congruence. The beauty industry has traditionally focused on building brand personalities appealing to consumers' ideal self.

The case of Dove is also a good example of how brands in practice play more than one string and cannot be boxed according to the schools of thought in this book. The way that Dove builds and activates a very strong brand that resonates with target consumers, can also be explained from a cultural branding perspective (read Chapter 10 about the cultural approach), where brands tap into cultural forces on a macro-level to build brand icons. Dove's problems with Photoshopping are also described in the community approach (Chapter 9).

Box 7.7 Dove and the actual self

In 2004, Dove launched The Campaign For Real Beauty addressing consumers' actual self, which was based in a big study made by Dove called The Real Truth about Beauty leading to insight into issues of beauty having become limited and unattainable for the majority of women. The Campaign For Real Beauty was a campaign where real non-Photoshopped women were used as the images of Real Beauty instead of picture perfect models with little or no realism for the average Dove consumer. The Real Beauty campaign was a great success with consumers and ignited a global conversation of how the beauty industry projects unreal images of beauty, negatively impacting the way average women perceive their own beauty. Dove has based all brand building and campaigns on the strategic driver of The Campaign for Real Beauty – actual self – instead of the hard to reach, artificial dreams and aspirations used as driver in the beauty industry in general.

Early adopters and brand self-congruity

Early adopters of a brand are critical for the alignment of brand personality, because they are the group of consumers that other consumers will identify with and use as a measure for the authenticity of the brand personality. This process takes place because, as explained in the sections on theoretical building blocks, consumers' self-expression has not only an individual but also a social dimension, where consumers seek inspiration from reference groups for brand consumption and use brands to demonstrate belonging to certain reference groups. The brand can hence be reinforced in a cyclical process if the right target group picks it up because it will serve as inspiration for other consumers who identify with or aspire to identify with the reference group that this target group represents. Early adopters can be used as a control group, to make sure that the brand actually expresses desired personally traits. If early adopters display personality traits that are similar to or in line with the personality of the brand, the brand personality will be reinforced and strengthened. If the group of early adopters, on the other hand, do not share personality characteristics with the brand personality communicated, then the brand personality will be weakened.

The greater congruity between the personality of the target consumer and the personality of the brand, the stronger brand personality. Early adopters are hence critical for aligning the brand personality and can be a useful tool when measuring and aligning brand self-congruity, and they can potentially reinforce the personality of the brand and can be used actively in the advertising campaigns and management of the brand. The brand self-congruity can be used as a measure for evaluation of how the brand personality interacts with the self of consumers. To what extent is there brand self-congruity? And how does this fit or lack of fit affect the brand personality? The results can lay the basis for continuous alignment of the brand personality and its appeal to the target consumer and use of personality endorsement (Klipfel *et al.* 2013).

Sources of brand personality

Once the consumer self has been uncovered, steps must be undertaken to construct or maintain the brand personality. The personalities that consumers attribute to brands can be divided along five main personality dimensions. These five dimensions serve as the template for creating brand personality. Personality traits are a more nuanced description of the behavioural character traits, built into the brand personality and expressed through the different sources and modes of communication that the brand uses to express personality. Personality traits are often translated into a strategic tool through a brand personality statement. It is more short-term and contains multiple and a more nuanced and rich personality trait description that can be altered over time and serve as a guide for how the brand should appear and behave more specifically. Below you will find an example of how a brand personality can be constructed in accordance with the consumer-self mechanisms using the brand personality framework (Figure 7.7).

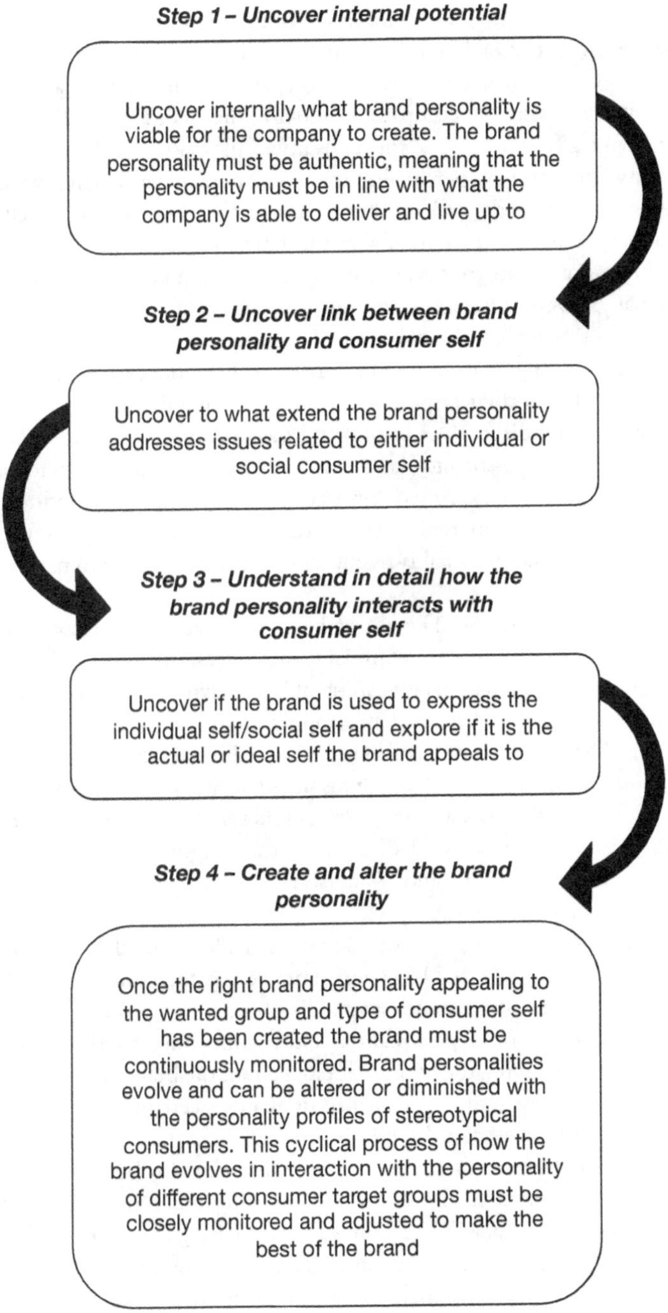

Step 1 – Uncover internal potential

Uncover internally what brand personality is
viable for the company to create. The brand
personality must be authentic, meaning that the
personality must be in line with what the
company is able to deliver and live up to

**Step 2 – Uncover link between brand
personality and consumer self**

Uncover to what extend the brand personality
addresses issues related to either individual or
social consumer self

**Step 3 – Understand in detail how the
brand personality interacts with
consumer self**

Uncover if the brand is used to express the
individual self/social self and explore if it is the
actual or ideal self the brand appeals to

**Step 4 – Create and alter the brand
personality**

Once the right brand personality appealing to
the wanted group and type of consumer self
has been created the brand must be
continuously monitored. Brand personalities
evolve and can be altered or diminished with
the personality profiles of stereotypical
consumers. This cyclical process of how the
brand evolves in interaction with the personality
of different consumer target groups must be
closely monitored and adjusted to make the
best of the brand

Figure 7.7 Creating brand personality in accordance with the consumer self construct

Consumer perceptions of a brand personality are formed and influenced by all the direct and indirect contacts the consumer has with the brand or other users of the brand, also named the sources of brand personality. The direct sources of brand personality are: the set of human characteristics associated with the typical user of the brand, the employees of the company producing the brand; the CEO, or endorsers of the brand also affect how the consumers ultimately will perceive the brand personality. In that way, personality traits of the people associated with that brand are transferred directly and unfiltered to the brand personality itself. Personality can also be transferred indirectly to the brand through the product-related attributes and product category associations, but also brand communication such as the brand name, logo, style, price and distribution channel affect how the brand personality will be perceived by consumers.

When developing a brand personality, brand managers have direct and indirect sources of brand personality at their disposal to create and shape the desired brand personality. The direct and indirect sources of brand personality shape in interplay the full picture of the brand personality, and it is important that the behaviour, signal value and symbolic clues expressed through both the direct and indirect sources of brand personality are coherent to ensure that the consumers experience, perceive and evaluate the brand personality as authentic and true to its own nature.

- *Direct sources of brand personality.* The set of human characteristics associated with the stereotypical brand user, company employees, the CEO, brand endorsers. These human characteristics can be of both a symbolic nature, such as sophistication, or they can have a demographic nature, such as age, social class and so on. The direct sources of brand personality are always 'person-based'. The founder of Virgin, Richard Branson, advocates new thinking and doing things differently through all the products inherent in the Virgin brand. His personality traits are transferred directly to the Virgin brand. Richard Branson is very visible as a CEO and his personality helps promote a certain Virgin brand personality to consumers.
- *Indirect sources of brand personality.* All the decisions made about the physical, functional and tangible aspects that can be experienced by the consumer, such as the tone of voice, visual style, price, shape, distribution and promotion, are the indirect sources of brand personality. They contribute to the brand personality indirectly by giving the consumer clues about the brand personality. A company with a strong brand personality does not need to have a very visible CEO advocating a certain brand personality, as is the case with the direct sources of brand personality. Brand personality can also be transferred indirectly from management to the brand, by choosing different vehicles of communication. For example, MTV is expressing an exciting brand personality through its events, sponsorships, website and advertising; the sources of brand personality are indirect, since a vehicle of communication is used.

Having uncovered the sources of brand personality and how these sources can be used actively to shape the personality of the brand, it is important to establish

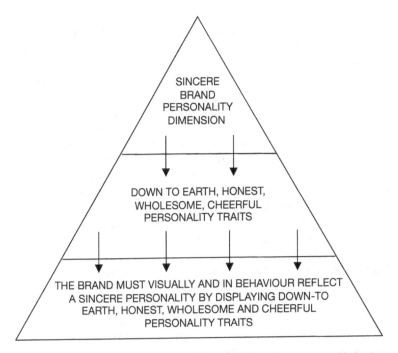

Figure 7.8 Example of a sincere brand personality dimension, traits and behaviour

an efficient communication platform that can launch the brand personality as distinctive and attractive, but also underpin the personality traits of the brand. The communication platform should not consist only of traditional marketing tools such as ads, website and so on. A distinctive brand personality cannot be built through communication only. The behaviour of the brand is also a necessary and important part of a brand personality (see Figure 7.8). To create an authentic and believable brand personality, the brand manager must engage in a wide range of branding activities, which express personality and create an emotional bond with the consumer. Activities like sponsorships, events or add-on consumer services matching the personality of the brand are essential to complete the picture. Too often companies fail on this because they emphasize short-term goals focused on reaching sales targets or they end up responding ad hoc or emulating competitors' strategies.

Brand personality and consumer–brand relationships

The next chapter is about brand relationships. The two constructs (of brand personality and brand–consumer relationships) are closely related. Generally, how a relationship evolves and the level of intimacy that can be achieved depends on the personalities of the partners involved in that relationship. In brand management, the brand personality influences the behaviour and how the brand interacts with the consumer – the brand relationship. Different brand personality types have different effects on the strength of the brand–consumer relationship. Brands with sincere personality traits encourage progressively stronger relationships compared with exciting brands. This is why sincere personalities are often valued as a more stable and better choice for a long-term relationship as opposed to exciting brand personalities.

In practice, considering and managing a brand personality is closely related to the management of the relationship that brands have with consumers. But it is not only in practice that these two concepts are becoming more and more intertwined. Some of the more prominent researchers of the personality approach (Jennifer Aaker) and the relational approach (Susan Fournier) along with Adam Brasel have joined forces and conducted an interesting study exploring how different personalities affect the interaction between the brand and the consumer as the relationship evolves. This study is elaborated in Box 7.7 and demonstrates how a mismatch between brand personality and brand behaviour can have serious consequences for the brand consumer relation.

The dynamic of how a brand personality and brand behaviour affects the consumer–brand relationship is essential to include in any brand management consideration. Key questions such as what personality dimensions and traits are more suitable for the brand in question, and whether the organization is able to deliver on the promise/expectations that, for example, a sincere brand personality sets out must be addressed. Hence the personality traits and the relationship roles that different brands can potentially play in consumers' lives are pivotal in the management of brand personality. Relationships with sincere brands deepen over time, and relationships with exciting brands have the evolutionary character of a short-lived fling. Research findings suggest that dynamic construal of brand personality is more accurate and useful for management in describing the potential of a brand personality. This interrupt events and relationship contracts between brand and consumer formed on the basis of the consumer–brand interaction can reveal much more about the strength of a brand personality than a more static perception of brand personality. In practice this is also why recently much research into brand personality overlaps research into the consumer–brand relationship. Read more about brand relationships in Chapter 8.

Summary

The primary focus for the brand manager in the personality approach is to build an attractive and relevant brand personality, which can serve as a strategic tool to ensure a deep and long-lasting emotional connection between brand and consumers. The prerequisites for creating the right brand personality are insights into how consumers use the specific brand in their construction and expression of self. Understanding these mechanisms can ensure that the right perpetual personality mix is created for the brand personality and that the right means of communication for that personality is used. The right platform for the brand personality requires that both direct and indirect sources of brand personality are considered. Target

Box 7.8 Brand personality defines consumers' interpretation of behaviour

The article 'When good brands do bad' explores the correlation between brand personality and consumer–brand relationships. For this purpose, Aaker *et al.* (2004) set up a field study: two online film processing companies, one with a sincere brand personality (expressed through pretested graphic element, tonality, font, content, and links to other sites), the other more exciting. The idea was to expose the customers of the two different brand personalities to the same transgression, followed by attempts to recover and excuse the transgression. Since transgressions according to theory are almost inevitable in long relationships, it is of major importance how consumers respond to them and so the damage can be limited. The evolution of the relationship would hence consist of comparable transgressions and attempts to resolve the situation. It turned out that the consumers were much more reluctant to forgive the online film processing company with the sincere brand personality than the exciting brand personality. The sincere brand showed no sign of recovery after reparation attempts, whereas the exciting brand character showed signs of a strengthened relationship after a transgression if recovery activities were attempted immediately after the transgression had occurred.

Aaker *et al.* (2004) conclude that the evolution and boundaries of consumer-brand relationships are to a great extent affected by what personality type the brand possesses. The study illustrates how transgression brands commit are perceived differently depending on what personality types that brand has. The study hence demonstrates the interrelation between brand personality and consumer–brand relationship. The study suggests that instead of interpreting and managing brand personality as a static construct, it could be valuable to have a more dynamic approach to brand personality that also includes the roles that different personalities are able to play in consumer–brand relationships. Brands with sincere personality traits encourage progressively stronger relationships than exciting brands. But sincere brand personalities are much more vulnerable to transgressions than exciting brands. Hence, depending on the personality of the brand, research indicates that if recovery attempts are initiated by the marketer after a transgression, then these can dilute the negative effects of failures (transgressions) and sometimes even drive the relationship to a satisfaction level beyond the level prior to the transgression incident.

Source: Aaker *et al.* (2004)

group users and early adopters can be used as control groups and a measure for the evaluation of whether the brand is on the right track and to ensure a continuous alignment of the brand self-congruity. Adopting a dynamic approach to brand personality including analysis of the relationship role different personalities are able to act out in the brand–consumer relationship is essential to gain the complete and full picture of how the brand personality and the consumers interact.

Box 7.9 Dos and don'ts of the personality approach

Do	*Don't*
Remember to uncover the complex ways the brand contributes to consumers self construction and expression. Consider how to achieve congruity with consumer selves?	Don't develop a brand personality without knowing the mechanisms of consumer selves this specific brand can address
Make a thorough personality statement that can guide brand-building activities	Don't limit the brand personality to being described by one personality dimension, also define traits, behaviour and how to express in direct or indirect sources
Consider how the brand personality sets the standard and boundaries for brand behaviour	Don't limit the question of brand personality solely to marketing; make sure the entire organization is ready.
Make sure to have the right plan for how to cope with transgressions that matches the brand personality type	Don't forget that the stereotypical user of the brand affects the brand personality
Make sure that the organization is able to deliver on the promise and expectations linked to the chosen brand personality	
Choose and acknowledge the role that early adopters can influence how the brand personality evolves	

Academic evolution of the personality approach

Research published in the journals from the data set used as primary data for this book indicates how the academic focus of the brand personality approach has started and developed with regards to assumptions, theory, methodology and managerial guidelines over time.

In the 1970s and 80s, the primary perspectives on personality were represented in research and practice by a strong focus in consumer research and advertising on self and personality. Plummer, Belk and Sirgy are some of the more prominent researchers and practitioners from this perspective. In 1997, Aaker published her

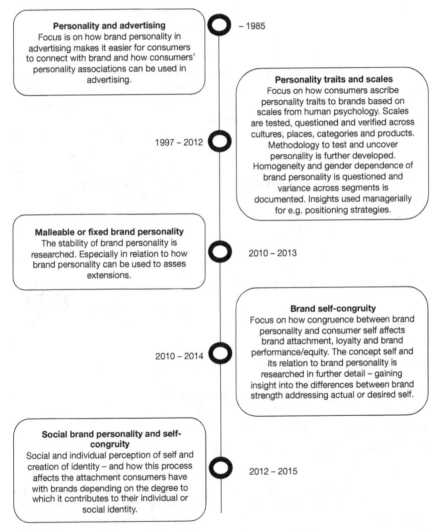

Figure 7.9 The academic evolution of the personality approach

brand personality scale, providing a theoretical framework and methodology for working with brand personality, valid and applicable across product categories. Since 1997, Aaker's brand personality scale has been tested and expanded in several empirical studies. A number of studies have focused on the effect of gender and cultural differences on the brand personality dimensions (Aaker *et al.* 2001, Krohmer *et al.* 2007, Grohman 2009, Pantin-Sohier and Breé 2004, Supphellen and Grønhaug 2003, Sung and Tinkham 2005). The homogeneity of brand personality has been questioned and it has been argued that the assumption of a homogeneous and fixed brand personality does not always hold (Freling and Forbes 2005, Ivens and Valta 2012). Consumers' perception of the malleability of brand personality traits and how this affects the ability of the brand to extend has also been a research subject, documenting a positive correlation between consumers' perceptions of the malleability of brand personality and consumers' acceptance of brand extensions (Yorkston *et al.* 2010, Batra *et al.* 2010).

In this context, the notion of self-concept has continuously gained increasing importance since 2005. The majority of these articles uncover a more detailed and in–depth understanding of how the multiple layers of self play a role in the creation of emotional attachment between brands and consumers though brand personality. A substantial number of articles also create a more detailed empirical documentation for the relation between brand personality, the self-concept and self-congruity (Kahn 2010, Lui *et al.* 2011, Malär *et al.* 2011). The social aspects of brand personality and the self-concept is also a research topic on the rise. The focus here is the study of how social layers of self through in/outgroup attitudes, moral identity and belong-ings affect the brand personality and to what extent consumers feel emotionally attached to brands and how this affects consumption choice (Choi and Winterich 2013, Dommer *et al.* 2013).

Box 7.10 You are not done!

Don't forget to visit the website for supplementary material such as case examples, student questions and supplementary literature.

Comments from the 'founding fathers'

Brands and personality: the origin

Joseph Plummer, Columbia Business School

As mass media evolved from print to electronic media in the 1940s, 1950s and 1960s, the battle for brand name recall and recognition became intense. Some agencies and advertisers created special ways to generate brand recall beyond simply spending more money – Leo Burnett in particular – with their ability to bring a brand name to life through memorable characters such as Tony the Tiger, the

Marlboro cowboy and the Jolly Green Giant. I was lucky to be a part of that period at Leo Burnett in the late 1960s and 1970s when these and other advertising icons were born.

One of my favourites that I worked on was Morris the Cat for Nine Lives cat food. Morris had an attitude, like most cats, and wouldn't accept any old brand – he liked Nine Lives and could 'persuade' his owners to serve it. The magic of this idea was that cat owners tend to 'humanize' their cats. They give them personalities, human feelings and ascribe a great sense of independence to them.

In 1979, I joined Young & Rubicam, where I was blessed to work with Frazier Purdy. In 1980, he and I were reviewing new campaigns for Dr Pepper, a challenger brand in the United States to Coca-Cola and Pepsi. Frazier rejected the three campaigns because he said they didn't 'capture the attitude of the brand'. That brilliant observation triggered my past experience with Morris and Nine Lives. If they could 'humanize' a cat, was it possible that consumers could 'humanize' a brand? Could a brand have attitudes – maybe even a personality? We undertook some very innovative research with the help of Howard Leonard of the Y&R research department to see if Dr Pepper had a personality, one that was perceptually different from Coca-Cola and Pepsi. The results were astonishing! Consumers could imagine and express different personalities of the three brands through choices of personality characteristics such as fun-loving, masculine and energetic, and a selection of symbols such as certain animals.

We were so encouraged by the initial results that we studied other agency brands such as Oil of Olay, Jell-O, Kentucky Fried Chicken and Merrill Lynch. All the brands had clear and measurable personalities. The journey then began to share this news with clients and integrate brand personality into the Y&R strategy process. Twenty-five years have passed since Frazier and I stumbled on to brand personality. It is used throughout the advertising industry worldwide today and the phenomenon has been studied carefully by leading academics such as Jennifer Aaker and Kevin Keller in the United States.

Source: Edited version of the preface to Marco Lombardi (ed.) *La marca, una come noi. La personalità di marca nell'era post spot*, Milan: Franco Angeli (2007)

References and further reading

Key readings are in bold type

Aaker, J. (1997), 'Dimensions of brand personality', Journal of Marketing Research, 34 (3): 347–56.

Aaker, J. (1999), 'The Malleable Self: The Role of Self-Expression in Persuasion', *Journal of Marketing Research*, 36 (1): 45–57.

Aaker, J. and Fournier, S. (1995), 'A brand as a character, a partner and a person: three perspectives on the question of brand personality', *Advances in consumer research*, 22: 391–405.

Aaker, J., Benet-Martinez, V. and Garolera, J. (2001), 'Consumption symbols as carriers of culture: A study of Japanese and Spanish brand personality constructs', *Journal of Personality and Social Psychology*, 8 (3): 492–508.

Aaker, J., Fournier, S. and Brasel, A. S. (2004), 'When good brands do bad', *Journal of Consumer Research*, 31 (1): 1–16.

Aaker, J., Vohs, K. D. and Mogilner, C. (2010), 'Nonprofits are seen as warm and for-profits as competent: firm stereotypes matter', *Journal of Consumer Research*, 37 (2): 224–37.

Ahmad, A. and Thyagaraj, K. S. (2014), 'Brand personality and brand equity research: Past developments and future directions', *IUP Journal of Brand Management*, 11 (3): 19.

Ahuvia, A. C. (2005), 'Beyond the extended self: Loved objects and consumers' identity narratives', *Journal of Consumer Research*, 32 (1): 171–84.

Azoulay, A. and Kapferer, J-N. (2003), 'Do brand personality scales really measure brand personality?' *Brand Management*, 11 (2): 143–55.

Batra, R., Lenk, P. and Wedel, M. (2010), 'Brand extension strategy planning: Empirical estimation of brand-category personality fit and atypicality', *Journal of Marketing Research*, 47 (2): 335–47.

Belk, R. W. (1988), 'Possessions and the extended self', *Journal of Consumer Research*, 15 (2): 139–68.

Braun-LaTour, K. A., LaTour, M. S. and Zinkhan, G. M. (2007), 'Using childhood memories to gain insight into brand meaning', *Journal of Marketing*, 71 (2): 45–60.

Chaplin, L. N. and John, D. R. (2005), 'The development of self-brand connections on children and adolescents', *Journal of Consumer Research*, 32 (1): 119–29.

Choi, W. J. and Winterich, K. P. (2013), 'Can brands move in from the outside? How moral identity enhances out-group brand attitudes', *Journal of Marketing*, 77 (2): 96–111.

Chung, K. K., Dongchul, H. and Seung-Bae, P. (2001), 'The effect of brand personality and identification on brand loyalty: Applying the theory of social identification', *Japanese Psychological Research*, 43 (4): 195–206.

Das, G., Guin, K. K. and Datta, B. (2012), 'Developing brand personality scales: A literature review', *The IUP Journal of Brand Management*, 9 (2): 44–63.

Diamantopoulos, A., Smith, G. and Grime, I. (2005), 'The impact of brand extensions on brand personality: Experimental evidence', *European Journal of Marketing*, 39 (1/2): 129–49.

Dommer, S. L., Swaminathan, V. and Ahluwalia, R. (2013), 'Using differentiated brands to deflect exclusion and protect inclusion: The moderating role of self-esteem on attachment to differentiated brands', *Journal of Consumer Research*, 40 (4): 657–75.

Durgee, J. F. (1988), 'Understanding brand personality', *Journal of Consumer Marketing*, 5 (3): 21–6.

Erdem, T. and Sun, B. (2002), 'An empirical investigation of the spillover effects of advertising and sales promotions in umbrella branding', *Journal of Marketing Research*, 39 (4): 408–20.

Escalas, J. E. and Bettman, J. R. (2005), 'Self-construal, reference groups and brand meaning', *Journal of Consumer Research*, 32 (3): 378–89.

Fournier, S. (1995), 'Toward the development of relationship theory at the level of the product and brand', *Advances in Consumer Research*, 22: 661–5.

Freling, T. H. and Forbes, L. P. (2005), 'An Empirical Analysis of the Brand Personality Effect', *Journal of Product and Brand Management*, 14 (7): 404–13.

Gilmore, J. H. and Pine, B. J. (2007), *Authenticity: What Consumers Really Want*, Cambridge, MA: Harvard Business Press.

Govers, R. C. M. and Schoormans, J. P. L. (2005), 'Product personality and its influence on consumer preference', *Journal of Consumer Marketing*, 22 (4): 189–97.

Grohmann, B. (2009), 'Gender dimensions of brand personality', *Journal of Marketing Research*, 46 (1): 105–19.

Haarhoff, G. and Kleyn, N. (2012), 'Open source brands and their online brand personality', *Journal of Brand Management*, 20 (2): 104–14.

Helgeson, J. G. and Supphellen, M. (2004), 'A conceptual and measurement comparison of self-congruity and brand personality: The impact of socially desirable responding', *International Journal of Market Research*, 46 (2): 205–33.

Ivens, B. and Valta, K. S. (2012), 'Customer brand personality perception: A taxonomic analysis', *Journal of Marketing Management*, 28 (9–10): 1062–1093.

James, W. (1890), *Principles of Psychology* (Vol. I), New York: Holt.

Johar, G. V., Sengupta J. and Aaker, J. (2005), 'Two roads to updating brand personality impressions: Traits versus evaluative inferencing', *Journal of Marketing Research*, 42 (4): 458–69.

Johar, J. S. and Sirgy, M. J. (1991), 'Value-expressive versus utilitarian advertising appeals: when and why to use which appeal', *Journal of Advertising*, 20 (3): 23–33.

Jung, C. G. (2014), *The Archetypes and the Collective Unconscious*. London: Routledge.

Khan, B. M. (2010), 'Brand personality and consumer congruity: Implications for advertising strategy', *The IUP Journal of Brand Management*, 7 (1): 7–24.

Kleine, R. E, III., Kernan, J. B. (1988), 'Measuring the meaning of consumption objects: An empirical investigation', *Advances in Consumer Research*, 15 (1): 498–504.

Klipfel, J. A. L., Barclay, A. C. and Bockorny, K. M. (2013), *'Self-Congruity: A Determinant of Brand Personality'*, (Doctoral dissertation, Northern State University).

Malär, L., Krohmer, H., Hoyer, W. D. and Nyffenegger, B. (2011), 'Emotional brand attachment and brand personality: The relative importance of the actual and the ideal self', *Journal of Marketing*, 75 (4): 35–52.

Mark, M. and Pearson, C. S. (2001), *The Hero and the Outlaw: Building Extraordinary Brands through the Power of Archetypes*, New York: McGraw-Hill.

Monga, B. A. and Lau-Gesk, L. (2007), 'Blending co-brand personalities: An examination of the complex self', *Journal of Marketing Research*, 44 (3): 389–400.

Orth, U. R. and Malkewitz, K. (2008), 'Holistic package design and consumer brand impressions', *Journal of Marketing*, 72 (3): 64–81.

Park, J. K. and John, D. R. (2010), 'Got to get you into my life: Do brand personalities rub off on consumers?', *Journal of Consumer Research*, 37 (4): 655–69.

Phau, I. and Lau, K. C. (2001), 'Brand personality and consumer self-expression: Single or dual carriageway?', *Journal of Brand Management*, 8 (6): 428–44.

Plummer, J. (1985), 'How personality makes a difference', *Journal of Advertising Research*, 24 (6): 27–31.

Puzakova, M., Kwak, H. and Rocereto, J. F. (2013), 'When humanizing brands goes wrong: The detrimental effect of brand anthropomorphization amid product wrongdoings', *Journal of Marketing*, 77 (3): 81–100.

Sirgy, M. J. (1982), 'Self-concept in consumer behavior: A critical review', *Journal of Consumer Research*, 9 (3): 287–300.

Sirgy, M. J. and Johar, J. S. (1992), 'Value expressive versus utilitarian appeals: a reply to Shavitt', *Journal of Advertising*, 21 (2): 53–4.

Smith, E. G., Van den Berge, E. and Franzen, G. (2003), 'Brands are just like real people', in F. Hansen and L. B. Christensen (eds), *Branding and Advertising*, Copenhagen, Denmark: Copenhagen Business School Press, pp. 22–43.

Sung, Y. and Tinkham, S. F. (2005), 'Brand personalty structures in the United States and Korea: Common and culture-specific factors', *Journal of Consumer Psychology*, 15 (4): 334–50.

Swaminathan, V., Oage, K. L. and Gürhan-Canli, Z. (2007), '"My" brand or "our" brand: The effects of brand relationship dimensions and self-construal on brand evaluations', *Journal of Consumer Research*, 34 (2): 248–59.

Swaminathan, V., Stilley K. M. and Ahluwalia R. (2009), 'When brand personality matters: The moderating role of attachment styles', *Journal of Consumer Research*, 35 (6): 985–1002.

Thomas, T. T. W. (2004), 'Extending human personality to brands: The stability factor', *Brand Management*, 11 (4): 317–29.

Wang, X., Yang Z. and Liu, N. R. (2009), 'The impacts of brand personality and congruity on purchase intention: Evidence from the Chinese mainland's automobile market', *Journal of Global Marketing*, 22 (3): 199–215.

Wertime, K. (2002), *Building Brands and Believers: How to Connect with Consumers using Archetypes*, Singapore: Wiley.

Wright, N. D., Claiborne, C. B. and Sirgy, M. J. (1992), 'The effects of product symbolism on consumer self-concept', *Advances in Consumer Research*, 19 (1): 311–18.

Yorkston, E. A., Nunes J. C. and Matta S. (2010) 'The malleable brand: The role of implicit theories in evaluating brand extensions', *Journal of Marketing* 74 (1): 80–93.

8 The relational approach

with a commentary by Associate Professor Susan Fournier, Boston University School of Management

'I wear Reebok running shoes. Me and my Reeboks. They are beat up by now. Want to see them? Like a favorite pair of jeans, you know? You go through so much together'.

The words stem from an interview with Karen who is a recently divorced mother of two young girls telling about brands that are important to her. For Karen, Reebok is a 'best friend' brand. In 1998, a new brand perspective was introduced in the *Journal of Consumer Research*. The concept of brand relationships was introduced by Susan Fournier and instigated an immense and immediate interest in a new phenomenon – the relationship between brand and consumer.

This new approach is closely related to the personality approach, but based on other scientific ideals and inspired by other disciplines. With the relational approach, brand research and conceptualization entered a new era characterized by phenomenology, deep analysis, inner experiences and individual life projects. The game shifted towards a hitherto unforeseen focus on the individual consumer and a holistic interest in his or her life. These new thoughts about brands and consumers have been instrumental in driving brand management forward. The new thoughts, the new research design, the leaving of traditional marketing thinking and entering a new explorative and curious approach understanding brands as part of the consumer's whole life made a mark and opened up new qualitative ways of understanding and investigating the nature of brands. This radically new way of doing research made the theory compelling enough to constitute a subsequent large and influential stream of literature.

The original text has been supplemented by a huge body of work focused on turning this powerful idea into managerially accessible theories and tools. It has proven difficult; the area is characterized by complex, yet deep and inspiring metaphors. So do not give up, it might be a bit more complicated than the other approaches, but a careful and patient read will pay off.

Brand relationship theory reached a wide brand management audience when 'Consumers and their brands: developing relationship theory in consumer research' by Susan Fournier was published in the *Journal of Consumer Research* (March of 1998). Drawing on theories about human relationships and the idea of brand

Box 8.1 Learning objectives

The purpose of this chapter is to:

Understand the assumptions of the relational approach

- The brand is perceived as a viable relationship partner and a 'dyadic' brand perspective is hence introduced in brand management.
- A view of the consumer as an existential being.

Understand the main theoretical building blocks and how they are connected

- Animism
- Human relationships
- The brand relationship theory
- Relationship forms
- Relevance and transgressions

Provide insights into the variety of methods used to research relationships

- Depth interviews
- Life story method
- Memory elicitation technique

Understand how to manage customer–brand relationships

- The brand has to act as a true friend
- Meaning-based brand management
- Customer front and centre
- Careful CRM (Customer Relationship Management)

Understand the academic evolution of the approach

- Inspired by relationship marketing
- Founding article published in 1998
- Types of relationships and transgressions
- Insights into brand love and brand relevance

personality, the study investigated one of the 'buzz words' of the 1990s: relationship marketing.

It also turned the whole idea of the brand upside down, which is why brand management was never the same after the introduction of this approach. The research focused on understanding the three respondents' lifeworlds fully – and in that process understanding which roles brands play in their lives. Previous research had focused more on respondents as consumers – not the holistic perceptions of the entire human beings in this research. The research also took place in the homes of respondents, not in either an artificial, neutral setting or in a situation of consumption. This primary and holistic focus on the *lives* of the consumers is still a challenge in the (practical as well as academic) world of brand management: 'our metrics suffer from firm-centricity, focusing on evaluation of the person's satisfaction with or depth of commitment to the brand relationship that is formed. But relationships that resonate have a different focal goal: they are engaged to make people's lives easier, better, or happier' (Fournier 2008, p. 9).

The brand is understood as a phenomenon. Vicki, Jean and Karen (the three respondents of the original research) experience relationships with certain brands and these relationships are closely linked to their life situations and values. Interesting and compelling! The challenge is that it does not necessarily make us cleverer when we have to market brand X. As stated in the introduction, the academic community of this line of thinking has done a lot to make it more accessible and we will do our best to present the managerial tools at the end of this chapter.

Brand relationship theory did not only shift its focus from the business to business (B2B) relationship to a business to consumer (B2C) setting, it also offered new insights about brand loyalty (refer to Chapter 12 for an elaboration and additional literature on brand loyalty). Loyalty is often closely linked with the sensation of a relationship. Loyal consumers are valuable consumers. Creating brand loyalty is all about managing the brand–consumer exchange long term instead of a short-term exchange focusing on the transaction. But while brand loyalty is an expression

---

Box 8.2 Customer relationship management and brand relationship theory

The term 'relationship marketing' was first introduced in the literature on services and then became an important notion in business-to-business markets, where the business relationships often are longer than in business-to-consumer markets. In the literature on services and relationships, a service encounter is defined as 'the dyadic interaction between a customer and service provider' (Bitner *et al.* 1990, p. 72).

Fournier's aim was to establish a thorough framework for the use of the metaphor of the relationship and apply it to consumers' brand relations; 'In a sense, the field has leapt ahead to application of relationship ideas and the assumption of relationship benefits without proper development of the core construct involved' (Fournier 1998a, p. 343).

Customer relationship management and brand relationship theory are hence not necessarily the same. Customer relationship management offers different tools to manage a customer relationship on a long-term basis instead of focusing on the singular transaction, while brand relationship theory goes to the root of the relationship metaphor.

Sources: Bitner *et al.* (1990) and Fournier (1998)

of *if* a consumer chooses the brand on a continuous basis, applying the brand relationship theory offers explanations of *how* and *why* brands are consumed by loyal consumers.

> In real life, people relate to one another in many different ways. The same is true as to how they relate to the brands they buy. To reduce it simply to a matter of loyalty or lack of loyalty is like saying that you either marry everybody you meet or they will never be a meaningful part of your life.
>
> (Fournier 1998b)

Brand relationships span a variety of different levels of loyalty and engagement – from the ultra-loyal relationships characterized by sensations of love and long-term friendship to much more practical (and sometimes unstable) relationships filling entirely other needs.

> Brand relationships can serve higher-order identity goals, addressing deeply rooted dialectical identity themes and enabling centrally held life projects and tasks. But they can also address functions lower on the need hierarchy by delivering against very pragmatic concerns.
>
> (Fournier 2008, p. 6)

Brand relationship theory builds on a comprehensive phenomenological study. Thereby, the scientific and philosophical tradition of phenomenology is added to the context of brand management. This addition implies a significant shift in the way brands and consumers are perceived and investigated.

Assumptions and academic implications of the relational approach

The relational approach is grounded in phenomenology. Phenomenology is a qualitative, constructionist research tradition emphasizing the accessing of an 'inner reality' and, as a consequence, the validity of 'lived experience'. The relational approach also is the first approach relying on purely qualitative research. Brand consumption is understood only through a deep and holistic understanding of the personal context in which the brand is consumed.

The relational approach implies a major paradigmatic shift in brand management and can be identified as the one approach leading brand management into the twenty-first century. As described in Chapter 3, the period of analysis (1985–2015) can be divided into three periods of time: the first focusing on the sending end of brand communication, the second with a focus on the receiving end and the third emphasizing the context of brand consumption. The relational approach belongs to the second period where the consumer is the pivotal point. The relational approach is, however, very different from the other two approaches emphasizing a deep understanding of the consumer (the consumer-based approach and the personality approach).

We have three reasons for identifying the relational approach as an important indicator of a paradigm shift. First, it is the first approach applying solely qualitative methods. Second, the approach is meaning-based. Third, it takes brand research into the domain of the consumer, emphasizing a holistic view of the consumer. The interest in consumers' lifeworlds is associated with a phenomenological research tradition. For these three reasons, we see the relational approach as a trailblazer for the two forthcoming approaches, namely the community approach and the cultural approach.

The concept of meaning is often opposed to the concept of information. Information is considered external stimuli to the consumer, while meaning stems from the inner reality, life and identity of the consumer: 'Phenomenology can conceive consumption not merely as behavioural response to external stimuli but as a meaning-directed behaviour driven by emotions, feelings and fantasies' (Hackley 2003, p. 112).

A phenomenological approach adapts a psychological view of the individual. Thereby, the relational approach is based on an idiosyncratic view of meaning creation, based on a basic idea that reality construction takes place in the mind. The notion of meaning is also central to the community approach and the cultural approach, but in these approaches, meaning is found in the social interaction with others and in the surrounding culture and society, respectively. In that sense, the relational approach is the first meaning-based approach of the three.

> What matters in the construction of brand relationships is not simply what managers intend for them, or what brand images 'contain' in the culture, but what consumers do with brands to add meaning in their lives. The abstracted, goal-derived, and experiential categories that consumers create for brands are not necessarily the same as the categories imposed by the marketers in charge of brand management. . . . This reality – that consumers' experiences with brands are often phenomenologically distinct from those assumed by the managers who tend them – commands a different conception of brand at the level of lived experience, and new, more complex approaches to the social classification of branded goods.
>
> (Fournier 1998a, p. 367)

Psychological phenomenology is about investigating how an individual interacts with external objects to learn about the structures that make up the individual's construction of reality. Phenomenology has special capabilities for uncovering non-rational aspects of consumption.

The phenomenological tradition features a distinctive take on the question of validity. The positivist research traditions assume an outer reality, a reality that can be touched, studied and measured. In this tradition, validity means that different studies performed by different researchers should end up with exactly the same result.

In the phenomenological tradition, 'lived' or 'felt' experience is considered valid, which depicts clearly how different the phenomenological tradition is from the positivist research ideal. Reality is not 'out there' to be touched and measured but is constituted within the individual respondents. How we perceive and feel about a phenomenon constitutes the phenomenon – the world is inseparable from the subject, and vice versa. Phenomenological perspectives will thereby be subjectivist and the first person perspective is an important prerequisite in phenomenology for generating knowledge. It is assumed that no underlying world exists which is raised over perception and conceptualizing. In other words, the way phenomena are perceived by the individual constitutes the true world: 'Phenomenological social research takes the embodied, experiencing agent as a starting point and explores the mutually constructed "life-world" of participants, the world of lived experience from which all others derive' (Hackley 2003, p. 112). To exemplify: if a consumer experiences a shopping experience as hurtful, then the shopping experience *is* hurtful, no matter if videotapes or witnesses contest that no harm was done to the customer.

In consumer research, the contrasting views of consumer behaviour in the dominant information-processing perspective (reflected in the consumer-based approach, Chapter 6) and a phenomenological perspective are identified. In Table 8.1, some of the main differences are highlighted. Going through these differences should make it easier to understand why – and how – the relational approach implies such a significant shift in the way brands and consumers are perceived.

Table 8.1 Differences between the information-processing and the experiential consumer perspective

	Information processing	*Experiential/phenomenological*
Products	Objective features, tangible benefits	Subjective features, symbolic benefits
Stimulus properties	Verbal	Non-verbal
Resources	Money	Time
Task definition	Problem-solving	Hedonic response
Type of involvement	Cognitive responses, left-brain	Reaction, arousal, right-brain
Search activity	Information acquisition	Exploratory behaviour
Individual differences	Demographics, socio-economics	Creativity, religion
Cognition	Memory, knowledge structure, beliefs, thought generation	Subconscious, imagery, fantasies, daydreams, free association
Affect	Attitudes, preferences	Emotions, feelings
Behaviour	Buying, purchase decision, choices	Usage, consumption experience, activities
Criteria	Utilitarian, work	Aesthetic, play
	Mentality: economic	Mentality: psychosocial
Output consequences	Function, results, purpose	Fun, enjoyment, pleasure

Source: Hirschman and Holbrook (1992)

By adding the phenomenological (experiential) consumer behaviour perspective to the discipline of brand management, the brand is taken into a whole new era, where brand consumption and brand loyalty are to be understood as closely inter-twined with consumers' 'inner realities'. The focus is not on the mere transaction or the exact moment of choice but on the intricate meanings that lie behind consumption choices. The consumer's whole identity (as perceived by the consumer himself) is to be understood if one wants to gain insight into brand consumption.

Another description of the same paradigm shift (Allen *et al.* 2008) is found in Chapter 2.

Thereby, the emphasis moves away from the domain of the marketer and into the 'chaotic' unstable and idiosyncratic domain of consumers. Even though the managerial implications of the relational approach are not very concrete, the approach leads the way towards new horizons where the role of consumers' social interaction (the community approach) and their cultural context (the cultural approach) are being conceptualized and translated to managerial implications. These approaches also feature a variety of qualitative methods that have become acceptable (valid) by the launch – and immense success – of the relational approach.

It seems that brand management in a way 'lets go' of the brand via this approach. The brand is suddenly 'out there' in a chaotic and ever-changing context. In the previous approaches, the concrete interaction between brand and consumer is being investigated from different angles and there is a focus on defining what a brand is. In the relational, the community and the cultural approaches, brand management research seems to expand focus to different scenarios (consumers' individual lifeworlds, social interaction with other consumers and cultural context, respectively) where the brand is not the 'main character' or the starting point of the research, but merely a factor like many others in complex individual, social and cultural networks.

The relational approach is concerned with understanding the identity projects of consumers. It is important to notice that it is the *individual* identity projects that are investigated in this approach. The cultural approach (Chapter 10) is concerned with *collective* identity projects. So the relational approach beats the drum for integrating knowledge of individual identity projects in the management of a brand, while the cultural approach does the same in favour of our collective identity projects.

The 'brand–consumer exchange'

The brand relationship theory is based on a 'dyadic' brand–consumer relationship, implying an equal exchange between brand and consumer. Both parties contribute to brand value creation, which takes place in an ongoing meaning-based exchange. The fact that the arrows in Figure 8.1 form a circular motion reflects that the development of the brand–consumer relationship is a never-ending process, influenced by the same parameter changes as human relationships.

Even though the focus of the relational approach is the ongoing exchange (or relationship) between brand and consumer, it is important to stress that relationships

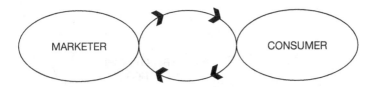

Figure 8.1 'Dyadic' brand–consumer relationship: brand management is perceived as an ongoing meaning-based process

are phenomena influenced by contextual changes. Every relationship is part of an intricate web of other relationships and subject to the small and large changes, we experience on a daily basis. The brand relationship theory also aims at understanding the lives of consumers in a holistic manner, implying that the environment of the consumer is not delimited from analysis. But it is important to understand that the approach focuses on the exchange between brand and consumer, while the understanding of the consumer's social context is the pivotal point of the community approach (Chapter 9) and the impact of the consumer's cultural environment is conceptualized in the cultural approach (Chapter 10).

Summary

The relational approach rests upon assumptions regarding the brand–consumer exchange as a 'dyadic' and cyclical process resembling a human relationship. Brand meaning is constituted through this process to which both parties contribute equally. The relational approach is linked to the tradition of phenomenology implying an existential view of man. 'The inner reality' of the consumer becomes valid by the application of this perspective. The phenomenological perspective emphasizes a holistic view of the consumer and thereby takes an interest in many aspects that are not directly related to the actual consumption choice or behaviour. The relational approach implies a major shift in the academic world of brand management for all of the above reasons, but also for its implied shift from information to meaning as the underlying premise of brand management.

Theoretical framework of the relational approach

It goes without saying that the brand relationship theory is the core theme of the relational approach. Applying the relationship metaphor to a brand–consumer construct requires an abstraction towards regarding the brand as something human. The human propensity to endow inanimate objects or mental constructs with human characteristics is called *animism*. A prerequisite for the relationship theory is the literature dealing with brand personality and therefore animism is the first supporting theme. Animism will be reviewed very briefly; the inquiring reader should refer to Chapter 7: the personality approach. Human relationship theory serves as the second supporting theory of the relational approach (see Figure 8.2).

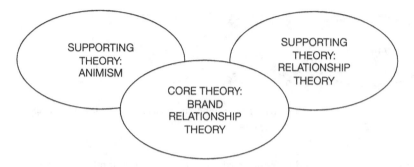

Figure 8.2 Supporting and core theory of the relational approach

Theoretical building block: animism

Human beings have a tendency to endow objects and even abstract ideas with human personality characteristics. Brands can be animated, humanized and personalized. A prerequisite for applying knowledge from the relational approach to the management of a brand is that that brand is perceived as a personality as this furthers the consumer–brand relationship.

When working with brand personality, archetype theories from psychology are also very popular. Simplified versions of what Jung called archetypes are widely used as the basis of brand development and advertising. Empirical studies show a connection between profits and having a brand more or less consciously connected with a personality or archetype.

Supporting building block: (human) relationship theory

It is difficult to imagine life without any relations with other people. Relationships are in many ways how we embed ourselves in the world and are a fundamental part of the way we live our lives. We use relationships for many different things and their importance to us differs significantly. We have lifelong relationships with our siblings that might be characterized by a profound feeling of sharing the same important values stemming from the same family background. You might have a best friend from your kindergarten days. But you also have relationships to fellow students and colleagues knowing that you will only uphold the majority of these relationships in the period of time where you share the same working or university sphere. Long or short, deep or shallow – relationships are instrumental parts of everyone's lives, structuring meaning and adding life content.

Relationships are constituted of our continuous reciprocal exchanges between interdependent relationship partners. For a relationship to exist, active interchanges between relationship partners are required. Relationships can be described as purposive because they add and structure meaning in people's lives. The meaning added and structured by relationships is of a *psychological*, a *sociocultural* and a *relational* nature:

- *Psychological meaning* is linked with the identity of the participants in the relationships. In a consumption context, important research has highlighted the link between consumers and their consumption choices, establishing the central concept of possessions as part of the extended self. The way relationships correspond to the formation of identity is through the way they help solve life themes (central to the core identity and the personal history), important life projects (key life roles) and current concerns (related to daily tasks). It is important to understand the way psychological meaning refers to life themes, life projects and current concerns. These different 'levels' of psychological meaning work as pivotal points in several important brand management and consumer research studies (e.g. Mick and Buhl 1992, Fournier and Yao 1997, Fournier 1998a). A few relationships reflect your *life theme*, which is the core theme (or themes) of your life. A life theme is deeply rooted in personal history and is often difficult to verbalize because it is so fundamental to you that it is often 'buried' in the subconscious (e.g. being free versus not being free). *Life projects* fluctuate more than life themes in accordance with changes in circumstances, and life cycle and relationships are also influenced by the construction, maintenance and dissolution of key roles in life. A life project relates to the most significant choices in our lives – what do we choose as our education and profession – and family priorities. The most practical relationships are the ones spurred by *current concerns* and they are directed towards the completion of tasks in everyday life. An example could be your hairdresser, the employees at your child's day care facility and so on. Besides providing psychological meaning, relationships apply socio-cultural as well as relational meaning to the ones engaged in them.
- *Sociocultural meaning* is linked to changes in our life conditions. Sociocultural meaning can be divided into five broad sociocultural contexts (age/cohort, life cycle, gender, family/social network and culture), which all influence how participants approach relationships. Relationships change as life does – think about college graduation, becoming a parent, getting ready for retirement and so on. Life falls into different eras and so do relationships.
- *Relational meaning* of relationships deals with the fact that all relationships are part of a network of other relationships. The nature of one individual relationship is thereby influenced by the fact that it is part of a jigsaw puzzle of other relationships fitting the requirements of the person having the relationship.

Any relationship is further affected by *contextual* influences. In that sense, relationships grow with us, adjust to our changing lives and influence the changes in our lives as well. In other words, relationships develop over the course of time and are constituted of a series of repeated exchanges between the relationship partners. In that sense, relationships are *process phenomena*, constantly changing.

In sum, relationships add and structure meaning in our lives. Remember that the meaning is of a psychological, sociocultural and relational nature. Furthermore, relationships never stand still and are influenced by an infinite number of contextual factors.

Relationships take place between human beings. But since people tend to endow brands with human-like personalities, the characteristics of a relationship can be applied to brands as well. How this complex notion is conceptualized in the world of brand management will be explained in the next section.

Core theory: the brand relationship theory

Through extensive research into three female informants' lived experiences with brands, Fournier was able to prove that brands can and do serve as viable relationship partners in the sense that they are endowed with human personality characteristics and are used for solving *life themes*, *life projects* and *current concerns* (as well as matching the other characteristics of a relationship).

The characteristics of the human relationships and the way these are connected with the identity of the participants' lives are hence transferred to the customer–brand relationships (CBR) and the concept of brand relationships between brands and consumers is verified; 'Whether one adopts a psychological or socio-historical interpretation of the data, the conclusion suggested in the analysis is the same: brand relationships are valid at the level of consumers' lived experiences' (Fournier 1998a, p. 360).

As explained in the above section, human relationships take on very different forms and so do brand relationships. In the study behind the brand relationship theory, fifteen brand relationships are identified (more about different CBR types later in this section).

The relationship forms resemble human relationships in the way they help fulfil goals and desires at the different life 'levels' of life themes, life projects and current concerns. Some brand relationships last all life and express some of its user's core values and ideas; others mean a lot (the consumer displays brand loyal behaviour) but the consumption of them changes as life progresses, while others deliver on current concerns without being a fundamental part of the consumer's consumption pattern. The system of fifteen brand relationships:

> Illustrates how the projects, concerns, and themes that people use to define themselves can be played out in the cultivation of brand relationships and how those relationships, in turn, can affect the cultivation of one's concept of self. For each woman interviewed, the author was able to identify an interconnected web of brands that contributed to the enactment, exploration, or resolution of centrally held identity issues.
>
> (Fournier 1998a, p. 359)

The pattern of brand relationships resembles the pattern of human relationships in the cases of the three women serving as objects of research. This suggests that the role played by brands in the life of the individual consumer is deeply linked to the overall identity and the way the identity is reflected in their human relationships. A person with few, but deep and lasting human relationships, will also typically display loyalty to a few preferred brands, while a person who prefers to experiment

Box 8.3 Background of the brand relationship theory

The study behind the brand relationship theory involves three female informants: Jean, Karen and Vicki.

Jean is fifty-nine years old, has been married to Henry for most of her life, and tends a bar in her small blue-collar hometown. She is the mother of three grown-up daughters and of Italian descent. Her Catholic faith and family traditions are important to her. When it comes to life themes, affiliation and stability are important in Jean's life. Jean displays brand relationship depicting these life themes as she enjoys using a portfolio of brands for many years. Having been a housekeeper, a mother and a waitress all her adult life, Jean sees herself as a consumer expert, knowing exactly which brands are 'the best'.

Karen's life situation is very different. She is a recently divorced thirty-nine year-old mother of two girls and works full-time as an office manager. She finds herself in a dilemma, on the one hand wanting to pursue new paths in her life, and on the other to create a stable home for her two young children. Karen's life themes are influenced by the transition phase she is experiencing. Karen does not display emotional attachment to brands to the same degree as the other two women. Due to the financial reality of being a single parent she has adopted a very practical approach to brand purchases, going for coupons and other promotions. However, she displays emotional attachment to a few selected brands that are central for upholding her sense of identity in her transitional phase. Karen also displays an experiential approach to brand consumption, reflecting her life situation, where she feels an urge to start over again.

Vicki is the youngest of the three respondents. She is twenty-three years old and in her final year of studying for her master's degree. Vicki is in a transition period between being a dependent child and an independent adult. She uses brands as means in a meaning-based communication system, trying out the potential identities and possible selves typical of the transition phase she is in.

The way the different life situations and life themes of the three women interact with the way they consume is the background of the brand relationship theory. Despite the different nature of their brand consumption, they all relate to brands in a way that is comparable to the way we relate to each other in human relationships. Examples of the three women's brand relationships can be found in Table 8.1.

Source: Fournier (1998a)

more in the people department will also have a tendency to be rather experiential, when it comes to brand choice (Jean displays a behaviour of stability and loyalty, Vicki experiments with own identity, while Karen's preferences mirror the transition phase of divorce, she finds herself in). Human relationships deliver on life themes, life projects and current concerns, and so do brand relationships.

Categorizations of customer-brand relationships

The 1998 research first and foremost firmly established the validity of the customer-brand relationships construct. The publication also presented a framework consisting of 15 different relationship forms – all observed in the study of Jean, Karen and Vicky. These 15 forms are presented in Table 8.2 and will be accompanied by other researchers' and authors' takes on categorizing relationship forms as well as their characteristics. All spring from the same idea but establish more nuances and a deeper understanding on how we can understand a BCR (brand-customer relationship) from different angles suited for different purposes.

It is obvious to employ humanistic metaphors in this context (which is certainly the case), still it might make sense to keep in mind that BCRs are different from interpersonal relationships (IRs) in important aspects; such as the facts that they are all based on monetary exchanges (only some IRs are) and are by nature questionable to 'relationship adverse' segments (Swaminathan and Dommer 2012).

The original 15 relationship forms are based on the study of Jean, Karen and Vicki and are presented below with short examples of the different forms.

Other categorizations of brand relationships have later been created and published to shed more light on the complex metaphor of the brand relationship. In 'The effects of brand relationship norms on consumer attitudes and behavior' (Aggarwal 2004), it is studied how different fundamental perceptions of relationship norms influence the evaluations of marketing actions. In social psychology a distinction is made between two different kinds of relationships with distinctively different relationship norms:

- Exchange relationships are based on economic factors. People in this kind of relationship expect money in return for a favour or expect a comparable favour promptly.
- Communal relationships are based on social factors. Here, money in return for a favour is not expected. Benefits are not compared.

The line of thinking behind this research is that a brand is evaluated as a potential relationship partner in – more or less – the same manner as a human member of society. Certain relationship norms are identified in a brand relationship, as they would be in a human relationship. After having tested how these norms work in the exchange between a brand and a consumer in situations of asking for help, the researcher is able to state that it is very important not to mix the behaviour of the two types of relationships. When a relationship is established, relationship norms (exchange-based and communal) are taken for granted, and violations of these norms are evaluated negatively.

Table 8.2 Eight relationship forms inspired by communal versus exchange relationships

Abusive	*Adversarial*
The brand does not seem to value you as a customer	A brand that you are actively against
Committed	*Communal*
A brand that you are committed to in a lasting way	A brand that you really care about and feel a desire to help succeed
Dependent	*Exchange*
A brand that you 'cannot live without'	A WYSIWYG (what you see is what you get) brand providing straightforward benefits for a reasonable cost
Master-Slave	*Secret affair*
A brand you feel 'stuck with'. You feel that you have no alternative	A relationship you keep hidden from others

Source: Adapted from Miller (2012)

This dichotomy of exchange versus communal is in another study broken down into eight relationship types that are to be understood as being more or less characterized by the rationality of the exchange relationship or the softer and more emotional characteristics of the communal relationship in another study (Miller *et al.* 2012) (see Table 8.2).

Another proposed typology focuses on the CBRs linked to childhood memories and feature relationships characterized as: 'best friends forever', 'forbidden fruits', 'spoiled milk', 'fine wines', 'nefarious seeds', 'long lost friends', 'dearly departed', 'wishful longings' and 'imaginary friends'. Consumers seem to actively use these 'childhood consumption relationships' to reinforce individual identity. Knowledge of these nostalgic and highly emotional relationships can also help marketers create 'intergenerational transfer' and overcome 'long-term biases' (Connell and Schau 2012).

One relationship type given special attention in academia is 'brand love' (Ahuvia *et al.* 2008, Batra *et al.* 2012). Love is here defined as a psychological process applicable to ideas, people, activities – as well as brands. Brand love is a highly desirable state constituting a very strong relationship characterized by repeat purchases and other types of pro-brand behaviour: 'The people and things we love are part of ourselves. We think about them the same way we think about ourselves . . . our relationships with them help define our identity, and we take responsibility for their well-being' (Ahuvia *et al.* 2008, p. 353). The coveted state of a love-based relationship is achieved through the right combination of passion-driven behaviours, self-brand integration, positive emotional connections between brand and customer as well as extending the possibility of a long-term relationship (Batra *et al.* 2012).

Table 8.3 Relationship forms

Relationship form	Definition	Examples
Arranged marriages	Non-voluntary union imposed by preferences of third party. Intended for long-term, exclusive commitment, although at low levels of affective attachment	When married, Karen adopted her husband's favorite brands
Casual friends/ buddies	Friendship low in affect and intimacy, characterized by infrequent or sporadic engagement, and few exceptions for reciprocity or reward	Karen switches between five different detergent brands, buying whatever is on sale
Marriages of convenience	Long-term, committed relationship precipitated by environmental influence versus deliberate choice, and governed by satisfying rules	After a move of residence Vicki cannot buy her favorite brand of baked beans, which makes her reluctantly switch to a competing brand
Committed partnerships	Long-term, voluntarily imposed, socially supported union high in love, intimacy, trust and commitment to stay together despite adverse circumstances. Adherence to exclusivity rules expected	This is the relationship form Jean has with the majority of brands she uses for cleaning and cooking
Best friendships	Voluntary union based on a principle of reciprocity, the endurance of which is ensured through continued provision of positive rewards. Characterized by revelation of true self, honesty and intimacy. Congruity in partner images and personal interests common	In Karen's phase of finding her feet after a divorce, running every morning means a lot to her and has become a symbol of her new self. In this connection Reebok has become a brand that is 'a best friend' to Karen
Compartmentalized friendships	Highly specialized, situationally confined, enduring friendships characterized by lower intimacy than other friendship forms but higher socio-emotional rewards and interdependence. Easy entry and exit	Vicki uses a variety of different perfume brands to display different sides of herself in different situations
Kinships	Non-voluntary union with lineage ties	Vicki and Karen have 'inherited' some brand preferences from their mothers

Relationship form	Definition	Case illustration
Rebounds/avoidance-driven relationships	Union precipitated by desire to move away from prior or available partner, as opposed to attraction to chosen partner per se	At work Karen could choose between a Gateway and an Apple computer. She chose the prior because she does not define herself as an Apple person
Childhood friendships	Infrequently engaged, affectively laden relation reminiscent of earlier times. Yields comfort and security of past self	To Jean the Estée Lauder brand evokes strong memories of her mother
Courtships	Interim relationships on the road to committed partnership contract	Wanting to find the 'right' scent, Vicki and her mother tried out several musk perfumes before settling for the Intimate Musk (a Revlon perfume) brand
Dependences	Obsessive, highly emotional, selfish attractions cemented by feeling that the other is irreplaceable. Separation from others yields anxiety. High tolerance of other's transgressions results	Appearance is important to Karen and she thanks Mary Kay and her running routine for her youthful looks. As this aspect of appearance is crucial for Karen's identity in her transitional phase as recently divorced, she is highly emotional and truly loyal to the Mary Kay brand
Flings	Short-term, time-bounded engagements of high emotional reward but devoid of commitment and reciprocity demands	Vicki tries out several trial-size shampoos and conditioners
Enmities	Intensely involving relationships characterized by negative affect and desire to avoid or inflict pain on the other	Karen has negative feelings towards Diet Coke, as she, taking great pride in not having any weight problems, enjoys being able to drink Classic Coke
Secret affairs	Highly emotive, privately held relationship considered risky if exposed to others	Karen has Tootsie Pops in her office desk and eats them in secret
Enslavements	Non-voluntary union governed entirely by desires of the relationship partner. Involves negative feelings but persists because of circumstances	Karen uses Southern Bell and Cable Vision, as she has no other choice

Source: Fournier (2008)

The variety of these typologies suggests that one can approach the idea of the CBR from many different angles suitable for different purposes. The seminal 1998 publication firmly established the viability of the idea – and since then different typologies have been proposed based on different needs and interests.

A relationship is (also) a process phenomenon

Brand relationships are, however, also process phenomena and as such volatile and intangible: 'Fluctuations in person, brand, and environmental factors trigger relationship evolution, with entropy and stress factors precipitating decline. Relationships are dynamic, temporal phenomena: they require active management over time' (Fournier 2008, p. 16). This section will describe some of the theoretical ideas suited for understanding the volatility and dynamics of a relationship.

The idea of mental accounting (Aggarwal 2012) might be helpful as a point of departure here. At the beginning of a relationship (first encounter, use or buy) a 'mental account' is opened and then 'people keep track of the benefits they receive and the costs they incur in order to assess the well-being of the relationship and the extent to which these relationships actually deliver what people expect them to deliver' (Aggarwal 2012, p. 121). Once opened, the account is continuously balanced – and eventually closed. A positive mental account might lead to a stronger relationship while a negative one might lead, not only to the termination of the relationship, but ultimately to brand-averse, negative customer behaviour damaging to the brand.

The goal of a brand manager applying this theory to his or her work is to make the brand relationship as meaningful, stable and long-lasting as possible. Fournier (1998a) advances the brand relationship theory by putting forward the *Brand Relation Quality* construct. The BRQ (brand relationship quality) construct focuses on the quality, depth and strength of the consumer–brand relationship. Six important relationship factors (love/passion, self-connection, interdependence, commitment, intimacy and brand partner quality) are identified as influencing the durability and quality of the relationship. The relationship is basically meaning-based, reflecting the reciprocal nature of a relationship (read more about the consequences of managing meaning in the section on managerial implications).

The six most important facets, when upholding an important relationship are reflected in the BRQ part of Figure 8.3: love/passion, self-connection, commitment, interdependence, intimacy and brand partner quality. These are important factors when one evaluates a brand relationship and the sum of these factors reflects the perceived quality of the relationship.

The relationship quality is, however, also subject to an ongoing interplay between actions by the brand and the consumer of the relationship. Relationships are in a constant state of flux as the process phenomena they are. Contextual changes as well as changes in the relationship per se determine the stability and durability of the brand–consumer relationship.

The way the brand relationship quality is constantly influenced by the brand actions as well as the consumer actions reflects very well the basic idea of the

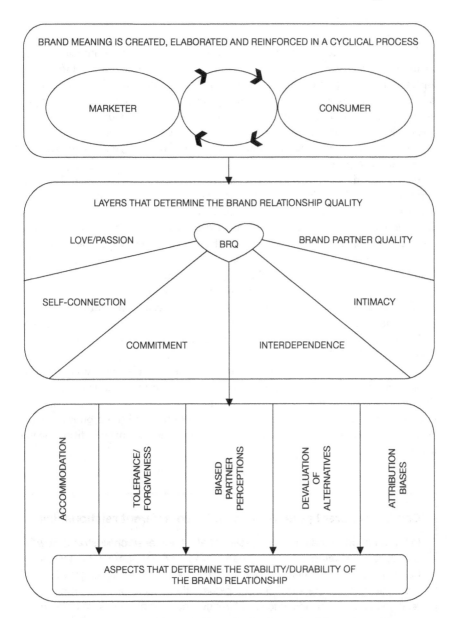

Figure 8.3 Layers and facets of brand relationship quality and stability; adapted from Fournier (1998a)

brand relationship theory: that of a dynamic and dyadic exchange between brand and consumer. The BRQ construct conceptualizes the many and complicated layers of the consumer–brand relationship, outlaying the meaning-based interaction, the six most important facets of an important relationship. These are the most important aspects of the establishment of the relationship, but Fournier adds the understanding of the frailty of any relation as she points towards all the actions from both participants in the relationship that affect the stability and durability of the relationship. Hence, Fournier not only introduces a whole new way of conceptualizing brands, she also introduces the management of the brand as an ongoing, complex and indeed unstable process.

In the world of CBRs, a high level of experienced self-relevance (between customer and brand) is desirable and has to be taken very seriously by the marketer. The level of experienced self-relevance influences how a good relationship gone wrong is likely to develop. If the consumer experiences a high level of self-relevance between himself and the brand, and the relationship somehow goes sour, there is a possibility of a more disappointed reaction, ultimately leading to very negative brand-damaging behaviour from the disappointed customer (e.g. negative word-of-mouth, writing bad online reviews) (Johnson *et al.* 2011).

Another study focuses on the brands that are forgiven by its customers despite transgressions. Customers experiencing 'brand closeness' seem to be more forgiving and willing to continue the relationship despite problems and transgressions (Donovan *et al.* 2012).

Brand closeness or strong self-relevance thereby seem to be a double-edged sword – in some cases the relationship is strong enough to continue even though the mental accounting registers losses, while in other cases, the most loyal and dedicated customers become the worst enemies of the brand (Johnson *et al.* 2011) after having chosen to close the account (to remain in the imagery from mental accounting).

Box 8.4 Different personalities strike up different relationships

In 'When good brands do bad', (Aaker *et al.* 2004) research illustrates how brands are evaluated differently when having different brand personalities, but making the same mistake. The consumers were more forgiving towards the exciting brand personality than towards the sincere brand. The brand relationship was thus influenced differently when the brands were different (read more about this study in Chapter 7).

This line of research extends on the idea that a relationship is a complex and volatile entity. And in the management of a brand relationship, it is beneficial to consider both the brand personality and the implied relationship norms and make all marketing actions consistent accordingly.

Source: Aaker *et al.* (2004)

Summary

Traditionally, we speak of relationships between people. Expanding the notion to brands and consumers implies that consumers have the ability to endow brands with human personality traits. Therefore, animism – or the human propensity to endow inanimate objects or abstract concepts with human personalities – is the first supporting theoretical construct in this chapter. Theory on human relationships serves as the second supporting construct. Human relationships are important factors in all lives and deliver on life themes, life projects and current concerns. They are also process phenomena under influence from many different sources.

The brand relationship theory originates from a study into how consumers experience relationships with brands. This study provides us with a framework consisting of fifteen different brand relationship forms, resembling human relationships. The original typology of the fifteen relationship forms is supplemented by other typologies. But knowing what kind of relationship consumers experience with brands is not enough because we need to take the dynamic qualities of a relationship into account as well.

The theory also provides us with the BRQ construct. It is a model that depicts how relationships are volatile process phenomena constantly under influence of other factors. The brand relationship theory is supplemented by research into how brand personality and relationship norms influence consumers' brand evaluations, the idea of mental accounting and the importance of self-relevance in cases where the relationship is damaged.

Methods and data in the relational approach

The most important methodologies of this approach are based on the scientific tradition of phenomenology. The relational approach takes brand management theory into the domains of experiential consumption. Here, the inner reality of the consumer is investigated and a holistic take on the way the life of the consumer influences consumption is a prerequisite. Accessing the inner reality and thereby understanding the *whole* life of the consumer is primarily done by means of depth interviews and life story methods.

Depth interviews and life stories

One of the most widely used methods of accessing the inner realities of respondents is depth interviews. Often, depth interviews are combined with life story methods, where the respondent's own statements on life transitions and so on are recorded and intertwined with other statements in order to deepen the holistic understanding of the consumer's lifeworld.

The 1998 publication used a combination of these two techniques. The phenomenological interview allows for 'the understanding of the subjective meanings of consumers' lived experiences with brands . . . establishing consumer validity of the brand proposition as a whole' (Fournier 1998a, p. 347).

The life-story case study makes it possible to link the statements put forward in the depth interviews with the stages and themes of the informant's life story, hence linking the consumer experiences with the central themes of consumer identity:

> Identity is reflected in one's life narrative, or life story, capturing various roles including past, present, and anticipated future selves. My life narrative describes the path of my identity development; it defines who I am, who I have been, who I am becoming, and/or who I am no longer.
>
> (Kleine *et al.* 1995, p. 328)

The life-story method is not, as such, separable from the depth interview: 'Phenomenological interviewing can be particularly powerful in chronicling personal transformation and change' (Hackley 2003, p. 122). But being aware of the fact that people structure their understanding of themselves in a narrative linked with the life story enables the researcher to draw more insightful and powerful conclusions based on the analysis of the interview.

The depth interview method involves a turning back to experiencing. Going back to individual and felt experiences supports a reflexive structured analysis that portrays the essence of an experience. By interpreting the retrospective and evident explanations of the respondent's experience with the phenomenon, this approach may reveal underlying structures and concepts. Uncovering these underlying structures opens up a deep understanding of what the experiences really have meant for the respondent. By understanding the experience at the individual level, it is possible to draw more general conclusions.

Box 8.5 Depth is preferred to breadth

As described in Box 8.3, only three informants served as basis of the original brand relationship research in order to secure depth: 'Size restrictions on the informant pool ensured the depth concerning life worlds and brand relationship portfolios necessary for thick description' (p. 347). Each respondent was interviewed for 12 to 15 hours and the interviews were designed to complement the first-person descriptions of the brand use with the contextual details of the informants' lifeworlds: 'To stimulate discussion, kitchen cabinets were opened and informants were instructed to 'tell the story' behind any brand in the inventory' (Fournier 1998a, p. 347). **The life-story information is gathered at a closing interview**. The research design had two purposes: 'Interviews were designed to yield two complementary types of information: (1) a first-person description of the informant's brand usage history and (2) contextual details concerning the informant's life world' (p. 347).

Source: Fournier (1998a)

A depth interview takes several hours and can eventually be conducted in sequence meaning that you return to the same respondent several times in order to go still deeper into understanding his or her lifeworld. Depth is definitely preferred to breadth when collecting data in this tradition.

Life stories often reveal themselves as undercurrents in phenomenological depth interviews. Allowing the respondent to talk for hours will hence often disclose important and recurring themes and values linked with their life history (often the life themes, life projects and current concerns of relationship theory are relevant, when understanding the nature of relationships). Linking these themes with statements about other subjects can deepen the understanding of the *whole* life of the respondent.

Box 8.6 Stories can be helped along

Consumers' unstructured stories about brand consumption can be helped along by the use of images. In a phenomenological study of coffee consumption 'informant-generated' images were used to stimulate stories of brand use. Ten days before the interviews were to take place, the respondents were asked to collect a set of images describing 'how they felt about coffee' (coffee category images) and another set of images capturing their feelings towards their favourite coffee brand.

The interviews (of 2 to 3 or 5 hours) were then structured in three parts:

- Part one centred on the coffee category images. (How do respondents feel about coffee in general?) Central images were identified and laddering techniques were applied, meaning that the interviewee kept asking questions regarding the meaning of the pictures in order to capture the full context of category meaning.
- In part two of the interviews, insight into the use of coffee was obtained. Especially, how coffee consumption has changed over the course of time in the lives of the respondents was highlighted.
- The final part of the interviews focused on the consumers' brand relationships with their favourite coffee brands. The images identified by respondents to depict how they felt about their favourite coffee brands were used to help the stories along.

Deep insight into coffee consumption in general, category use in different stages of life and relationships with favourite brands was obtained through this method. Comparing stage one and stage three of the interviews highlighted the difference between coffee consumption in general and perceived brand relationships specifically.

Source: Fournier and Yao (1997)

Conducting a long interview, the interviewer can apply the techniques of Box 8.6. A depth interview requires a prior agreement and a set time, date and place in order to be successful (remember that a depth interview takes hours and that foreseeable disturbances should be eliminated). It is important that the interviewee is well aware of the magnitude of the task prior to the interview.

The interviewer should be well prepared for the interview, meaning that he or she should be well informed about the topic for the interview, but should still keep an open mind remembering that it is the respondent's *experiences* that are of interest and considered valid in this kind of interview. Below you will find guidelines for the conduction of depth interviews. First, we will explain some of the key terms.

Biographical questions are asked in order to record who the person is, as well as to get the talk going. Grand-tour opening questions are very broad questions opening up for the interview; these will guide the interviewer as to where the interview might be going. Especially in the beginning of the interview, prompting techniques can be applied in order to help the interview along. Prompting techniques are techniques to express interest to help the interviewee along and make them elaborate on the topic. It can be done by raising your eyebrows or repeating the last word of a sentence in an interested way in order to encourage the respondent to explain more. The interviewer is also encouraged to 'play dumb'. It is important not to intimidate the respondent by appearing too clever or superior

---

Box 8.7 Conduct a long interview yourself

- Start out by asking biographical questions. (Ask about age, occupation, family background and so on.)
- Ask 'grand-tour opening questions', for example if you investigate consumption of sports goods, start out by asking broad questions regarding your respondent's interest in sport before going into the more detailed questions about their preferred brands.
- Apply prompting techniques for the grand-tour opening questions, for example repeat the last word of a sentence, and raise your eyebrows in order to make your respondent comfortable about telling his or her stories.
- Listen for key terms, topic avoidance and minor misunderstandings.
- Allow minor changes of subject – they might lead to further insight.
- If not, gently get the interview back on track.
- Eventually 'play dumb'.
- Do not disturb the process by taking notes.
- Record the interview on tape or video.
- Get a verbatim transcript of the interview for analysis.

Source: McCracken (1988)

in other ways. Playing decidedly dumb might not prove necessary but is preferable to the opposite. Remember that you are allowed access into the lifeworld of the respondent and he or she should feel as comfortable as possible about letting you in. A successful depth interview is very much a matter of trust.

The task is not to test some predefined 'truths' but to discover the idiosyncratic truth of your respondent: 'People ascribe meaning to the objects that present themselves in consciousness. The task of the researcher is to explore events or processes by gathering first-hand descriptions of these feelings, thoughts and perceptions' (Hackley 2003, p. 114). And remember that the respondent is always the expert and that we believe in lived experience and inner realities!

Memory elicitation method

A later methodological addition that might prove useful when getting 'under the skin' of consumers is the memory elicitation method. This method probes earliest memories (EM) and defining memories (DM) to gain access to really deep, and in some cases, instrumental insight into even deeper layers of consumers' inner realities. The long interviews and the life story method are upfront with the respondents, who participate in the interview fully aware that they are talking about themselves. The trick is to get the respondents talking and in that process lose themselves a bit and thereby reveal interesting aspects about their lives, values, preferences and so on.

The memory elicitation method is a projective technique and as such built on the idea that 'people are neither able nor willing to provide data about themselves in a self-report fashion because of and ego-defensive reaction' (Braun-LaTour *et al.* 2007, p. 46). This technique qualifies as projective as respondents tend to 'reconstruct' their EMs to fit the values and ideals of their adult self, meaning that the experienced EMs tend to be more of a reflection of the adult self than a truthful memory.

If you want to conduct a study using the memory elicitation method, the following steps are proposed by Braun-LaTour *et al.* (in their studies, themes of respectively Coca-Cola and automobile trucks were presented to their respondents before the gig began):

- Call your respondents some time before they show up for the study and inform them that you are going to probe early memories. Present your theme (brand or product category). Encourage them to activate their memories by talking to family members and looking at childhood photos.
- At the time of the session, place your participants on comfortable mats and offer them relaxation through yoga exercises. The key is to have people relaxing and early memories flowing!
- Next, begin the 'memory walk' and – through breathing and visualization exercises – take your respondents back to their early memories (or their perception of them).

- When early childhood is reached, it is time to access the rich information about the brand or product category of choice. Ask your respondents to write and/or draw images.
- Give respondents a questionnaire with clarifying questions to each EM.
- Encourage them to hold on to the EM and deepen it by writing a story.
- Across participants, you will be able to construct 'memory maps' (looks like association maps (from the consumer-based approach) but all content is memory-based).

The method is quite demanding and complex, but provides insight into deeper mythic and symbolic layers of consumers' psyches:

> By associating themselves with important childhood memory experiences, brands can benefit through the emotions brought forth as consumers relive those memories (in the manner of Proust and his 'petite-madeleine'). Within the EM and DM experiences are similarities and differences that define the generations and suggest segmented communication strategies.
>
> (Braun-LaTour *et al.* 2007, p. 56)

The methods dive into deep layers of the human psyche, suggesting new input to understanding brand relationships (perhaps especially relevant in the case of relationships characterized by nostalgia or in other ways connected to childhood. Think about older brands spanning generations and childhood consumption relationships), but also as strong ties to the symbolism behind brand personalities in general and brand archetypes in specific (see Chapter 7).

Data analysis

The recorded and transcribed depth interviews contain huge amounts of unstructured data. This kind of data is difficult to categorize, but should open up completely new insights. Therefore, the data analysis is a complicated and important part of the process. It requires an 'insider perspective' of the researcher. Since the lived or felt experiences of respondents are considered valid data, the researcher strives for proximity to these experiences. (In positivist research traditions, the researcher strives for distance to the objects of study.)

Repeated analysis is required in order to detect central quotations that can be beneficial in order to pinpoint important themes and metaphors. Repeated analysis also implies the possibility of 'auto-correcting loops', a process of detecting new and central patterns in the interview by going through it repeatedly. These loops ensure the integration of the researcher's and the respondent's perspectives, as well as a holistic approach to the investigation.

Preferably, data collection and analysis should be conducted by the same person to further ensure the holistic perspective.

Summary

The relational approach is founded on the scientific tradition of phenomenology. Phenomenology implies that focus is on the 'inner world' of people, and not the 'outer world'.

Respondents' perceptions of their own experiences are considered valid data as (well as the topic of interest) in this research tradition. Depth interviews combined with life-story methods are the most suitable methods for gaining insight into the life worlds of respondents. The memory elicitation method is a projective method also suitable for research into early brand relationships.

Conducting a phenomenological study, the researcher should strive for proximity to the research process and should ideally collect data as well as analyse them. Data analysis should contain auto-correcting loops in order to detect central themes and metaphors to structure the large and unstructured amounts of data.

Academically striking and managerially a challenge

By now, it should be clear that the relational approach introduces a dyadic brand perspective, an existential view of the consumer, phenomenological methods and a precise conceptualization of key brand relationship concepts (brand relationship forms and the brand relationship quality construct). All these elements draw an accurate and coherent picture of the radical shift in brand management.

The big challenge is, however, to transform the above characteristics of the relational approach into managerial implications that are actually adaptable to real-life situations. Talking about the appropriateness of conceiving the brand as a meaning-based construct created in a dynamic and dyadic process between brand and consumer is much easier than adapting these thoughts to actual branding strategies! The literature behind the relational approach is very accurate and detailed when it comes to methods and scientific background. The same original literature did not, however, give much advice when it comes to managing the brand, nor does it provide insight into best practice case examples: 'Relationship marketing is powerful in theory but troubled in practice' (Fournier *et al.* 1998, p. 44). Even though much research has been done focusing on the management of a relationship. Still, the area remains abstract and complex.

Managerial implications

Wanting to reap the benefits from deepening the loyalty concept through use of the brand relationship theory should be weighed up against the difficulties of managing a consumer–brand relationship. From the literature, we can deduce the following implications: the management has to be founded on meaning; the marketer is offered the opportunity to go far beyond the concept of brand loyalty; a relationship is a volatile entity and the amount of information can be over-whelming. The same literature, however, provides some overall guidelines on how to manage a 'relational' brand successfully. The brand has to act as a true friend.

Getting the management of the relations-based brand right should start by the implementation of the assumptions behind the theory. The brand is perceived as being endowed with a personality, the brand–consumer exchange is assumed to be dyadic, and 'dialogue' and 'friendship' are appropriate metaphors. The personality of the brand as well as the norms and values of the consumer strongly influence the evaluation of the brand's actions. These assumptions should serve as guidelines when managing the brand in question.

If we go back to the origin of this approach, the very notion of meaning holds some interesting managerial implications in itself. An interesting, but a bit neglected, tool is meaning-based segmentation. By investigating the meaning, consumers ascribe to certain brands or consumption objects, one can create meaning-based segmentation opening up for meaning-based brand management based on other insights than traditional segmentation (Fournier 1991).

The fact that the process is dynamic implies that the management of the brand is an ongoing process in which meaning is negotiated on a continuous basis. The marketer should be able and willing to continuously adapt the strategy to fluctuations on the meaning negotiation. Managing meaning thereby requires insight into the lives of the brand's customers as well as a continuous integration of the lived experiences of consumers into the execution of the brand strategy. This condition leads to one of the factors that make the management of the relational brand difficult: the risk of information overload.

Wanting to manage your brand by means of the brand relationship theory, you need real and deep insight into your consumer base: 'True customer intimacy – the backbone of a successful, rewarding relationship – requires a deep understanding of the context in which our products and services are used in the course of our customers' day-to-day lives' (Fournier *et al.* 1998, p. 49). As explained in the methods and data section of this chapter, the methods for acquiring the right kind of data in the relational approach supply the marketer with a vast amount of unstructured data. This data and information complexity in the relational process contains the risk of a standstill. Hence, it is difficult not to get lost in the potential information overload of the relational approach. The deep, and potentially insightful, knowledge of consumers and their lives offer the marketer the main advantage of the relational approach: the opportunity of going beyond brand loyalty.

Still, understanding brand consumption in the light of the relational approach offers the marketer the opportunity to answer questions not answered by measurements of brand loyalty (*if* the brand is consumed on a continuous base versus *how* and *why*), which could balance the workload.

The marketer needs to be open to a truly equal and dyadic relationship. In all aspects, there should be a balance between 'giving' and 'getting'. If over-exploited (for instance by an excessive gathering of data in any encounter with the marketer), the consumer might see the marketer engaged in relationship marketing as an enemy rather than a friend. A friendly marketer respects the basic rules of friendship (to provide emotional support, to respect privacy, to preserve confidences and to be tolerant of other friendships among others) and should apply them to the management of the brand: 'For the brand to serve as legitimate relationship partner, it must surpass the personification qualification and actually behave as an active, contributing member of the dyad' (Fournier 1998a, p. 345).

By entering the 'life worlds' of your consumers, you have the opportunity to gain true insight into how the brand in question fits into the lives of customers. A 'relational' marketer collecting and analysing knowledge about his or her customers runs the risk of having to integrate incompatible knowledge in the branding strategy. The trick is to find some common factors in the meaning negotiation between the brand and key customers and integrate them in the branding strategy:

> Many doubt that something so idiosyncratic can be brought to the level of generalizability that science requires. . . . Individuals and communities manifest relational principles that with dedication can be shown to be generalizable; we just need to apply ourselves to these goals.
>
> (Fournier 2008, p. 18)

Finding the common denominators across respondents might be more accessible when you are dealing with people in a transitional phase of their lives: 'Events such as coming of age, the transition to parenthood, or a change in marital status serve as self-defining moments wherein identity planes experience tectonic shifts. Companies that anticipate these shifts . . . [are] rewarded with strong relationship activity' (Fournier 2008, p. 8). Hence, strong CBRs can be created when tapping into the shifts in sociocultural meanings that relationships are *also* influenced by.

As mentioned in the theory and methodology section of this chapter, we have a typology of 'childhood consumption relationships' as well as special methods for assessing childhood memories related to certain brands and/or product categories. Brands with more than one generation of history on their backs should therefore consider investigating which opportunities these notions hold.

Managers of diverse brand portfolios could also benefit from incorporating relationship thinking and meaning-based segmentation in the management of their portfolios. A deep understanding of the potential of the relational approach opens up for keeping your customers – perhaps through a cradle-to-grave strategy (by knowing at which points in a lifetime consumptions changes are most likely to occur and then easing the customer into a new consumption choice within your portfolio). Another strategy could be to ease business guests into using the leisure hotels within the same brand portfolio through knowing the meaning they ascribe to different usage situations.

An obvious implication of the relational approach is creating strong customer relationship systems (CRM). In an era where more and more consumption transactions are experienced online, new tools have seen the light of day giving the marketer the opportunity to treat people pretty individually (e.g. personified recommendations based on previous browsing and purchasing) despite a complete lack of personal contact. Relying on quantitative data and clever algorithms should, however, be accompanied by the deep and true interest in the individual customer not to have unintended side-effects (Avery and Fournier 2012, Fournier 2008).

The idea of the relational brand – a co-created, meaning-based entity – can also be extended by means of co-creation. Offering customers the chance to co-invent, co-design, co-create their products is a powerful and potentially relationship-building activity.

Collecting deep data of the consumer (also by means of your CRM systems) is a cornerstone in this approach and the marketer needs to tread carefully here. The marketer should be open and honest about the motivation for approaching the consumer and in return offer the consumer benefits corresponding to the inconvenience: 'Robust brand relationships are built not on the back of brands, but on a nuanced understanding of people and their needs, both practical and emotional' (Fournier 2008, p. 6). The marketer should be very aware not to exploit the consumer's confidence and be aware to return any favour in one way or the other. A consumer willing to 'share secrets' should receive some benefits and in all be treated as a friend in order for the brand relationship to develop and grow. Quid pro quo is a fundamental principle in the relational approach.

Keeping track of the experienced self-relevance of your customer is also an important insight when managing your brand. Given a high relevance (or brand closeness), you will be able to communicate in a more personal way by using closeness-implying pronouns (e.g. using 'we' instead of 'you and I') (Sela *et al.* 2012). Brand closeness may help needed forgiveness along, but might also turn devoted relationship partners into active enemies of your brand (Johnson *et al.* 2011).

The idea of the brand personality gives us the opportunity to ask ourselves: how does this type of person look and speak? The relational approach urges us to ask: how do you behave in a specific relationship? How do you approach your best friend?

Summary

The management of a brand relationship is a dynamic process, leaving room for the negotiation of both similar and conflicting views and many different players. The approach is meaning-based, implying brand value is co-created in an ongoing process between brand and consumer. This means that the marketer has to let go of total control of the brand and incorporate the meaning created by consumers in the management of the brand. Furthermore, the management is considered a very dynamic process where the meaning is constantly negotiated under the influence of the many factors influencing both human and brand relationships.

In truly understanding the consumers lies a risk of information overload, leaving the marketer with too much knowledge to incorporate it in the brand communication. The approach, however, also contains the opportunity to go far beyond the notion of brand loyalty and understand *how* and *why* the brand is being consumed on a continuous basis in addition to *if* it is being consumed.

If one wants to reap the benefits of this understanding, it is pivotal to treat customers as true friends. The real-life brand relationship should reflect the pre-requisites of the relational approach in the sense that the brand–consumer exchange is seen as a dyadic and dynamic process. The consumer should accordingly be treated as an equal partner and not just a source of information.

Besides the general potential of letting the management of your brand be influenced by the thoughts of this approach, special opportunities exist for brands related to transitional phases in people's lives (e.g. engagement rings, prams, senior cruises) as well as for brands with a long heritage. CRM systems and co-created products are also compelling tools, but should be handled carefully and with utmost respect for the customers.

The relational approach has some very profound consequences for the future development of the scientific discipline of brand management. It is a clear indicator of a paradigmatic shift for three reasons: it implies a shift towards qualitative methods, it is meaning-based and it emphasizes understanding of the lifeworlds of consumers rather than measuring the mere brand–consumer transactions. In that way, it opens the way to the further development of the discipline embodied in the two approaches to come: the community approach and the cultural approach.

Academic evolution of the relational approach

In this concluding section of the chapter, we outline the evolution of the relational approach in brand management academia. This outline is based on the primary data of the taxonomy of this textbook – articles from the top marketing journals with a primary focus on the brand (read more about methodology and data set in Chapter 2). The supplementary literature included in this chapter is hence not included in this section.

The approach was founded in the 1998 article by Susan Fournier and inspired by the idea of relationship marketing (B2B), which was a marketing buzzword in the 1990s. Fournier adapted the construct to a B2C setting, instigated a completely new brand perspective and opened up brand management academia for more interpretive approaches to the topic.

The approach is full of humanistic metaphors, and in many ways very relatable to the personality approach. In 2004, the approach was expanded through exactly that. Was the distinction (from real life) between communal and exchange relationships applicable to the understanding of brand relationships? (Aggarwal 2004). The two 'founding fathers' of the personality and relational approach teamed up to test the connection between different personalities and relationships exposed to serious transgressions (Aaker *et al.* 2004).

A new data collection method – relevant to the approach – was published in 2007. Probing early childhood memories can yield important insight to older brands (Braun-LaTour *et al.* 2007), while Swaminathan *et al.* (2007) investigated how differences in experienced brand closeness opens up different communication possibilities.

The ideas of closeness and relevance have been further investigated recently. The feeling of brand love and how to create it is explained by Batra *et al.* (2012), while Johnson *et al.* (2011) point out a very interesting dilemma of a close brand relationship. A customer experiencing a high level of self-relevance in the relationship can become the brand's worst enemy if disappointed.

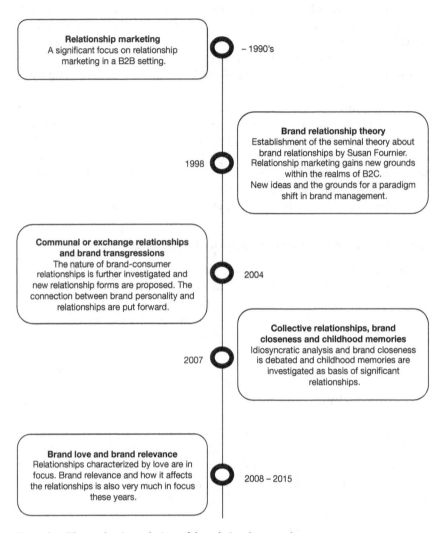

Figure 8.4 The academic evolution of the relational approach

Box 8.8 You are not done!

Don't forget to visit the website for supplementary material such as case examples, student questions and supplementary literature.

Comments from the 'founding fathers'

The value of the relationship approach to the study and management of brands

Susan Fournier, Boston University School of Management

Nearly twenty years ago I was promoted to Vice-president of Consumer–Brand Relationships at Young & Rubicam, an advertising agency in New York. The position was my idea: a translation of the revolutionary B2B relationship marketing paradigm into the B2C world. I quit two weeks later on the heels of a stark realization that the frameworks and concepts I would need to execute my position had yet to be created. So off I went to the University of Florida to pursue the development of consumer–brand relationship theory in consumer research.

The case was not an easy sell to a faculty comprised largely of dyed-in-the-wool experimental cognitive psychologists who thought of brands as economic sources of information. People have relationships with inanimate brands, do they? Do tell! The methods I brought to bear to illuminate my phenomenon were equally troubling. My thesis rested largely on phenomenological interviews among three – yes, three – women. The addition of scale development work and some LISREL modelling surely helped. But, in the end, the brand relationship ideas I generated seemed to sell themselves. My thesis set forth several essential relationship tenets that helped academics and practitioners think about their brands in new and powerful ways.

The first tenet stated that the provision of meaning lay at the core of all consumer–brand relationships. Consumer–brand relationships were purposeful; they were engaged as meaning-laden resources to help people to live their lives. Consumers played active roles as meaning makers in the brand relationship, mutating and adapting brand meanings to fit their life projects and tasks. Significant brand relationships were based not on low or high category involvement levels, but on the significance of the brand's meanings in the person's life. Even mundane goods could foster strong relationships provided their meanings resonated in the personal and cultural world.

A second tenet emphasized the variability of brand relationship types and forms. The relationship perspective forced us to acknowledge that highly committed and emotive brand loyal relationships were not the only meaningful consumer–brand engagements. A broadened view of relationship space included flings, secret affairs, committed partnerships and friendships, not to mention adversaries, enmities and master–slaves. Each of these relationships was governed by a unique set of contract rules: 'do's' and 'don'ts' concerning behaviours in the relationship. Friends should not reveal secrets to others, for example, and marital spouses should not cheat. Brand relationships could be distinguished as strong versus weak, hierarchical versus egalitarian, formal versus informal, positive versus negative. Strong relationships could be qualified beyond loyalty and affect using the brand relationship quality (BRQ) scale and its added facets of self connection, sociocultural connection, interdependence, partner role quality and intimacy. The astute relationship manager recognized that consumer–brand relationships were complex, and managed relationships according to their operative dimensions and rules.

A third tenet supported that relationships were dynamic and reciprocating phenomena that evolved and changed over time. Relationships unfolded through stages, including Initiation, Growth, Maintenance and Decline. They manifested characteristic development trajectories: Biological Life Cycle, Passing Fad, Cyclical Resurgence and Approach Avoidance Curve. Importantly, everything the brand did had the potential to affect the relationship. Brand behaviours – from packaging and logo choices to the salutations on customer service letters – sent 'signals' regarding the type of relationship contract that was in place. These signals controlled inferences and relationship strength levels. Sometimes the consumers' received view of the relationship was not what the managers thought they had in play.

The relationship perspective was powerful in that it forced marketing researchers and practitioners to acknowledge important principles governing consumers' engagements with brands. Co-creation. Personal and Cultural Resonance. Implicit Contracts. Relationship Norms. Brand Relationship Quality and Strength. Consumer Relationship Management. These constructs and essential tenets have helped us to better understand, measure and manage our brands. Recent research continues to build upon basic relationship fundamentals, exploring, for example, the rules and biases associated with communal versus exchange relationship templates, accommodation and tolerance processes in relationship development, relationship transgressions, relationship dissolution processes, personal relationship styles and their influence in the brand relationship space, sociopolitical brand relationships, ethnic and cultural differences in brand relationship behaviours, methods for relationship strength measurement and the functions and provisions of relationships with brands. I am honoured to have participated in this paradigm shift in marketing thought.

References and further reading

Key readings are in bold type

Aaker, J. L. (1997), 'Dimensions of brand personality', *Journal of Marketing Research*, 34 (3): 347–56.

Aaker, J. and Fournier, S. (1995), 'A brand as a character, a partner and a person: Three perspectives on the question of brand personality', *Advances in Consumer Research*, 22: 391–5.

Aaker, J., Fournier, S. and Brasel, S. A. (2004), 'When good brands do bad', *Journal of Consumer Research*, 31 (1): 1–16.

Aggarwal, P. (2004), 'The effects of brand relationship norms on consumer attitudes and behavior', *Journal of Consumer Research*, 31 (1): 87–101.

Aggarwal, P. and Mcgill A. L. (2012), 'When brands seem human, do humans act like brands? Automatic behavioural priming effects of brand anthropomorphism, *Journal of Consumer Research*, 39 (2): 307–23.

Ahuvia, A. C., Batra, R. and Bagozzi, R. P. (2008), 'Love, desire, and identity – a conditional integration theory of the love of things', in D. J. MacInnis, C. Whan Park and J. R. Priester (eds), *Handbook of Brand Relationships*, Armonk, NY: M. E. Sharpe, pp. 341–56.

Allen, C., Fournier, S. and Miller, F. (2008), 'Brands and their meaning makers', in C. Haugtvedt, P. Herr and F. Kardes (eds), *Handbook of Consumer Psychology*, Mahwah, NJ: Lawrence Erlbaum Associates, pp. 781–822.

Avery, J. and Fournier, S. (2012), 'Firing your best customers: How smart firms destroy relationships using CRM', in S. Fournier, M. Breazeale and M. Fetscherin (eds), *Consumer-Brand Relationships*, London: Routledge, pp. 301–16.

Batra, R., Ahuvia, A. and Bagozzi, R. P. (2012), 'Brand love', *Journal of Marketing*, 76 (2): 1–16.

Bitner, M. J., Booms, B. H. and Tetreault, M. S. (1990), 'The service encounter: Diagnosing favorable incidents', *Journal of Marketing*, 54 (1): 71–84.

Braun-LaTour, K. A., LaTour, M. S. and Zinkhan, G. M. (2007), 'Using childhood memories to gain insight into brand meaning', *Journal of Marketing*, 71 (2): 45–60.

Connell, P. M. and Schau, H. J. (2012), 'Examining childhood consumption relationships' in S. Fournier, M. Breazeale and M. Fetscherin (eds), *Consumer-Brand Relationships*, London: Routledge.

Donovan, L. A. N., Priester, J. R., MacInnis, D. J. and Park, C. W. (2012), 'Brand forgiveness: How close brand relationships influence brand forgiveness', in S. Fournier, M. Breazeale and M. Fetscherin (eds), *Consumer-Brand Relationships*, London: Routledge.

Fournier, S. (1991), 'A meaning-based framework for the study of consumer–object relations', *Advances in Consumer Research*, 18 (1): 736–42.

Fournier, S. (1994), '*A Person–Brand Relationship Framework for Strategic Brand Management*', (Ph.D. dissertation, University of Florida).

Fournier, S. (1995), 'Toward the development of relationship theory at the level of the product and brand', *Advances in Consumer Research*, 22: 661–2.

Fournier, S. (1998a), 'Consumers and their brands: Developing relationship theory in consumer research', *Journal of Consumer Research*, 24 (4): 343–73.

Fournier, S. (1998b), 'More than a name: The role of brands in people's lives', *Working Knowledge: A Report on Research at Harvard Business School*, 2 (1): (interview).

Fournier, S. (2008), 'Lessons learned about consumers' relationships with their brands', in D. J. MacInnis, C. Whan Park and J. R. Priester (eds), *Handbook of Brand Relationships*, Armonk, NY: M. E. Sharpe, pp. 5–23.

Fournier, S. and Yao, J. L. (1997), 'Reviving brand loyalty: A reconceptualization within the framework of consumer–brand relationships', *International Journal of Research in Marketing*, 14 (5): 451–72.

Fournier, S., Allen, C. and Miller, F. (2008), '*Mapping Consumers' Relationships with Brands*', working paper, Boston University.

Fournier, S., Avery, J. and Wojnicki, A. (2008), '*Contracting for Relationships*', working paper, Boston University.

Fournier, S., Dobscha, S. and Mick, D. G. (1998), 'Preventing the premature death of relationship marketing', *Harvard Business Review*, 76 (1): 42–51.

Fournier, S., Solomon, M. and Englis, B. (2008), 'When brands resonate', in B. H. Schmitt (ed.), *Handbook of Brand and Experience Management*, Boston, MA: Elgar Publishing, pp. 35–57.

Fournier, S., Tietje, B. and Brunel, F. (2008), '*Measuring Relationship Strength with the Brand Relationship Quality (BRQ) Scale*', working paper, Boston University.

Gürhan-Canli, Z. and Ahluwalia, R. (1999), 'Cognitive and relational perspectives on brand equity', *Advances in Consumer Research*, 26 (1): 343–5.

Hackley, C. (2003), *Doing Research Projects in Marketing, Management and Consumer Research*, London: Routledge.

Hirschman, E. C. and Holbrook, M. B. (1992), *Postmodern Consumer Research: The Study of Consumption as Text*, Newbury Park, CA: Sage Publications.

Holbrook, M. B. and Hirschman, E. C. (1982), 'The experiental aspects of consumption: Consumer fantasies, feelings, and fun', *Journal of Consumer Research*, 9 (2): 132–40.

Johnson, A. R., Matear, M. and Thomson, M. (2011), 'A coal in the heart: Self-relevance as a post-exit predictor of consumer anti-brand actions', *Journal of Consumer Research*, 38 (3): 108–25.

Kleine, S. S., Kleine R. E. III. and Allen, C. T. (1995), 'How is a possession "me" or "not me"? Characterizing types and an antecedent of material possession attachment', *Journal of Consumer Research*, 22 (3): 327–43.

McCracken, G. (1987), 'Advertising: Meaning or information', *Advances in Consumer Research*, 14 (1): 121–5.

McCracken, G. (1988), *The Long Interview*, Newbury Park, CA: Sage Publications.

Mick, D. G. and Buhl, C. (1992), 'A meaning-based model of advertising experiences', *Journal of Consumer Research*, 19 (3): 317–38.

Miller, F. M., Fournier, S. and Allen, C. T. (2012). 'Exploring relationship analogues in the brand space', in S. Fournier, M. Breazeale and M. Fetscherin (eds), *Consumer-Brand Relationships*, London: Routledge, pp. 30–56.

Paulssen, M. and Fournier, S. (2008), '*Attachment Security and the Strength of Commercial Relationships*', working paper, Boston University.

Sela, A., Wheeler, S. C. and Sarial-Abi, G. (2012), 'We are not the same as you and I: Causal effects of minor language variations on consumers' Attitudes towards Brands', *Journal of Consumer Research*, 39 (3): 644–61.

Stern, B. B., Thompson, C. J. and Arnould, E. J. (1998), 'Narrative analysis of a marketing relationship: The consumer's perspective', *Psychology and Marketing*, 15 (3): 195–214.

Swaminathan, V. and Dommer, S. L. (2012), 'When is our connection to brands like our connection to people? Differentiating between consumer-brand relationships and interpersonal relationships', in S. Fournier, M. Breazeale and M. Fetscherin (eds), *Consumer-Brand Relationships*, London: Routledge, pp. 15–29.

Swaminathan, V., Page, K. L. and Gürhan-Canli, Z. (2007), '"My" brand or "our" brand: The effects of brand relationship dimensions and self-construal on brand evaluations', *Journal of Consumer Research*, 34 (2): 248–59.

Thompson, C. J., Locander, W. B. and Pollio, H. R. (1989), 'Putting consumer experience back into consumer research: The philosophy and method of existential phenomenology', *Journal of Consumer Research*, 16 (2): 133–46.

Zahavi, D. (2003), *Fænomenologi*, Frederiksberg, Denmark: Roskilde Universitetsforlag/Samfundslitteratur.

9   The community approach

with a commentary by Associate Professor of Marketing, Albert M. Muniz Jr, De Paul University, and Professor of Marketing Thomas C. O'Guinn, Wisconsin School of Business

> Hello and welcome to our website! Jaguar Clubs of North America (JCNA) is dedicated to the wide range of Jaguar motorcars old and new, and the American, Canadian and Mexican enthusiasts who love them. Incorporated in 1954, the JCNA has become the hub of Jaguar enthusiasts from Canada, Mexico, United States and around the world. As a social organization with a common interest in the Jaguar marque, JCNA strives to provide members with the widest range of services and activities for those with an enthusiasm for all Jaguars, both old and new. We find that the entire family participates in many events because activities span a large cross section of interests.
>
> (Jaguar Clubs of North America, www.jcna.com)

In 2001, a seminal new brand perspective was presented by two American researchers instigating a new take on the conceptual understanding of the brand but also on the meaning creation *among* consumers. The idea of the brand community was inspired by subcultures of consumption, was immediately compelling and soon gathered its own research community, and thereby established a new school of thought within brand management. Despite the immediate interest spurred by die-hard fans of Ford Broncos and their brand-related behaviour, the ideas seemed only applicable to a good handful of high-involvement brands at the time.

The rest is history; it must have been impossible for the founding fathers of this approach to imagine how influential their idea of the 'brand community' later would become. The birth and the wildfire-like influence of Web 2.0 and social media made the idea of the 'community' and 'triangular communication' into something revolutionizing the world of brand management. In brand management academia, the community approach has developed with studies into the transparency of communities, value-creating practices, communities' impact on product adoption and the importance of online word-of-mouth. Basic knowledge of the more casual community behaviour on social media, needs to be found in supplementary research and literature.

In this chapter, we will lay out the foundation of the idea of the brand community and update it with later insights connected to the impact of Web 2.0 and social media. However, it is beyond the scope of this chapter to make an exhaustive presentation of digitalization, social media and their impact.

Googling 'Apple user groups' results in more than 81 million hits (in 2015), indicating the enormous interest consumers have in the sharing of their Apple

---

Box 9.1 Learning objectives

The purpose of this chapter is to:

Understand the assumptions of the community approach

- The idea of a 'triadic' brand relationship is central to the community approach.
- A social brand perspective is introduced to brand management.

Understand the theoretical building blocks and how they are connected

- Community theory
- Subcultures of consumption
- Brand community
- Web 2.0 and social media

Provide insights into the variety of methods used to research brand communities

- Ethnographic methods
- 'Netnography'

Understand the managerial implications

- The marketer as observer
- The marketer as facilitator
- The power of sharing
- Web 2.0 and social media
- eWOM
- Crowdsourcing

Understand the academic evolution of the approach

- The community approach is inspired by theories about subcultures of consumption.
- The 'founding' theory was published in 2001.
- The development of the approach is characterized by a focus on first, online autonomy, then internal and subsequently external potential of communities.

consumption experiences with other Apple users. Consumers form communities around brands. In brand communities, a brand is the focal point of social interaction among passionate consumers. These consumers use the community to share their brand experiences and brand stories. Brand communities may rest entirely on consumer interaction, while others are more or less facilitated by a marketer, but they tend to evolve and thrive around old brands with an interesting history and high involvement products such as cars, motor cycles and computers. Brand communities can be a very powerful force affecting brand value, because the meaning found in the social engagement – the 'dining', 'fun' and 'feasting' of the Sacramento Jaguar Club or the exchange of user tips in Apple user groups – in brand communities adds significantly to brand loyalty. Brand communities have existed for long in practice. The 'breakthrough' research article on the subject was 'Brand community' by Muñiz and O'Guinn (published in 2001 in the *Journal of Consumer Research*). This publication constituted the conceptualization of the brand community in the context of brand management.

This chapter offers insights into the assumptions, key theoretical elements and methods of the community approach and finishes off by providing the managerial guidelines.

Assumptions of the community approach

The brand approaches of the 1990s (the consumer-based approach, the personality approach and the relational approach) dealt with the exchange between one marketer and one consumer. All three approaches fundamentally changed the traditional notion of brand equity as something created entirely in the domain of the marketer. The personality approach and the relational approach further constituted brand value as something co-created in a dialogue between the marketer and consumer (the 'dyadic' brand relationship). The community approach adds meaning found in the social interaction *among* dedicated brand consumers (the 'triadic' brand relationship) to the theories of how brand value can be created: 'The brand communities are social entities that reflect the situated embedded-ness of brands in the day-to-day lives of consumers and the ways in which brands connect consumer to brand, and consumer to consumer' (Muñiz and O'Guinn 2001, p. 418). In other words, the existence of a brand community *also* requires interaction between consumers (see Figure 9.1).

This basic idea of 'triangular communication' is fundamental to the original framework of the community approach. The theory is based on observations among die-hard fans of certain brands. Still, the idea depicted in this model, suits the (often) casual behaviour on social media and other Web 2.0 related activities, which is why the community approach and its brand perspective have proven to have fortune-telling qualities. The levels of commitment are obviously very different, but the basic principles of communicating with more than one consumer at the time, and the consumers being able to communicate with each other, is the same:

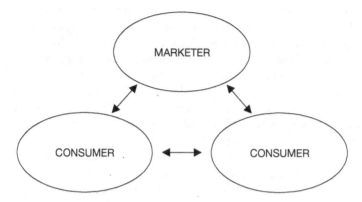

Figure 9.1 The 'brand triad': a brand community exists only when there is interaction
between at least two consumers

'True, in our earlier work we highlighted instances where brand communities
were active, powerful, and large. Certainly such communities exist. . . . But
we do not want other researchers, managers, or readers to believe that
communal brand relationships must always be this strong . . . They do not.'

(O'Guinn and Muñiz 2008, p. 179)

Indeed brand communities can engage consumers in different ways and with a
great variance in the level of either passive commitment or active contributions to
brand communities. These different levels of commitment will be addressed in the
theory section.

The assumptions of the community approach fall into two categories. First, the
'brand triad' notion implies changes in the way the 'brand–consumer exchange' is
perceived. Second, the community approach adds a social brand perspective to
brand management. The methods used to research brand communities borrow from
the scientific tradition of ethnography. These methods reflect the new assumptions
in the context of brand management, since the ethnographic research tradition
builds on a sociocultural rather than individualistic perception of man (or in brand
management, the consumer).

The 'brand–consumer exchange'

[Brands] are social entities experienced, shaped, and changed in communities.
Therefore, although brand meaning might be ascribed and communicated to
consumers by marketers, consumers in turn uncover and activate their
own brand meanings, which are communicated back to marketers and the
associated brand community.

(Brown *et al.* 2003, p. 31)

The community approach adds *groups* of consumers to the picture, which changes the basic premises of the 'brand–consumer exchange'. In the continuous brand–consumer dialogue shaping the brand, the marketer no longer finds himself having a dialogue with only one consumer, but with potentially millions of consumers. These consumers are likely to continue the brand dialogue long after the marketer believes the meeting is over. New rules of the game apply to the management of a brand, when countless consumers are able to share good and bad experiences, their roaring enthusiasm and incredible rumours in face-to-face settings as well as on the Internet. Adding a social consumer perspective to brand management academia was new in 2001. Still, the idea of the meaning-creating social consumer does not fully explain the digital consumer, who is very much the centre of attention post-Web 2.0. (refer to Chapter 12 for an elaboration and additional literature on Web 2.0). The term 'homo connectus' might better explain the 'übersocial' individual who is a citizen of the post-Web 2.0 'technoscape':

> Homo connectus is always on, seeking to know what's going on and what's in, catching up on the latest news and updates. They are versatile, chameleonic, tech-savvy, information junkies, juggling several tasks at the same time, so their attention is fragmented.
>
> (Llamas and Belk 2012, p. 5)

The social benefits experienced by consumers in brand communities add significantly to brand loyalty. Community consumers are extremely loyal and enthusiastic consumers, but at the same time, communities of consumers are also autonomous consumers capable of *collectively* rejecting marketing actions. Many of

---

Box 9.2 Who owns the Apple brand now?

Apple introduced a handheld personal computer – the Apple Newton – in 1993. In 1998, Apple chose to discontinue the Newton and take the Apple brand in new directions with, among other things, the iMac and the iPod.

Even though Apple chose to manage the brand differently, 'autonomous' consumers keep the Apple Newton brand alive in a vibrant grass-roots brand community. Dedicated Newton users have taken over the responsibilities of the marketer and are now running a web-based brand community that has at least 22,000 daily users. Offering technical support, software development and the cultivation of brand meaning, the brand community keeps the abandoned product and brand alive and kicking. Mythical and supernatural narratives are part of the Newton brand community ethos and are used for telling tales of miraculous performance and the survival of the brand, investing the brand with powerful brand meaning.

Source: Muñiz and Schau (2005)

the advantages associated with consuming the brand are created or enhanced *among* the community members, leaving the marketer with limited options of influencing brand meaning. This shift in negotiation power influences the creation of brand meaning and brand equity as the negotiation of brand meaning primarily takes place on consumers' terms.

Due to the shift in negotiation power, communities are difficult to manage. Consumers are able to 'hijack' a brand (Wipperfürth 2005) and endow it with brand meaning very far from that intended by the marketer or choose to overrule management decisions as in the case of the Apple Newton brand.

Besides providing social benefits to consumers, brand communities serve as important information sources. The sharing of brand information can benefit both consumers and marketers. Brand management from the community approach perspective is complex, and the autonomous groups of consumers can be hard to deal with. But the levels of brand loyalty and the depths of brand meaning found in communities can be priceless, making it worthwhile knowing the basic mechanisms ruling this approach.

The sociocultural perspective

The social brand perspective put forward in the community approach draws on the scientific tradition of ethnography. This tradition represents an intellectual framework as well as a set of methodologies. As an intellectual framework, it focuses on the concept of culture and its influence on (consumer) behaviour. The methodological orientation emphasizes a 'real world' approach, which means that researchers participate in the real world of the subjects of investigation. Ethnography stems from the tradition of cultural anthropology.

The publication of the brand community theory in 2001 set off a wave of research. This wave of research introduced the ethnographic perspective in brand management focusing on the consumer as a cultural player in a social setting using the consumption experience as the source of important personal social experiences.

Summary

This new research 'cluster' acknowledges the social nature of brands and the interactive involvement of *groups* of consumers in the creation of brand value and brand meaning. The quantity and importance of these groups have exploded due to the impact of Web 2.0 and social media.

Core to the community approach is the 'triadic' brand–consumer relationship and the social brand perspective. The triadic relationship implies consumers must interact, not only with the brand, but also with each other. The marketer is outnumbered in the brand–consumer exchange, making management of the brand difficult. At the same time, the existence of a brand community represents great advantages such as unforeseen levels of consumer loyalty and the possibility to cultivate deep consumer-driven brand meaning.

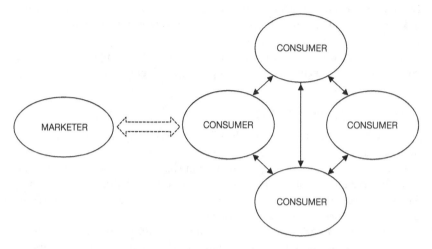

Figure 9.2 Networks of consumers create brand meaning independently of the marketer

The community approach hence represents a social brand perspective and is associated with the scientific tradition of ethnography. The understanding of the social consumer perspective needs to be accompanied by the idea of 'homo connectus' in order to fully grasp the full reach and implication of this new consumer type (see Figure 9.2).

Theoretical framework of the community approach

The key constructs of the brand community theory will be presented in this section. They are the three markers of community: the question of geography, the inter-connectedness with subcultures of consumptions and different variations of the brand community (the brandfest, the brand community and the community brand).

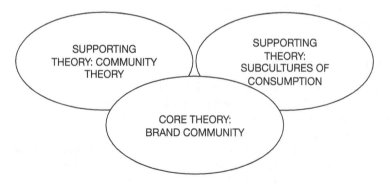

Figure 9.3 Theoretical framework of the community approach

But in order to understand the origin of the brand community concept, it is essential to know the origin of these concepts. The two supporting theories are hence initially presented before the core construct.

The brand community theory draws mainly on two supporting theories: communities and subcultures of consumption (see Figure 9.3).

Supporting theory: community theory

The word 'community' is comprehensible to everybody, but how it is to be understood in the context of brand community requires a more accurate definition. Community is a key concept in sociology and characterized by three markers, or basic characteristics – transcending the countless shapes and forms of a community. The three markers of a community are: consciousness of kind, shared rituals and traditions and a sense of moral responsibility.

If these characteristics are present, a community does exist in theory. In the traditional sense of the word, a community is a geographically bound entity. A community may be geographically bound in a neighbourhood or at the premises of a tennis club. In the same sense it can be formal (the tennis club requiring a membership) or informal (the neighbourhood community feeling is simply there). In the many online communities that have evolved with Web 2.0, however, a community is not geographically bound. They transcend geography and connect humans or consumers who share some kind of common interest.

Supporting theory: subcultures of consumption

The brand community theory is also inspired and influenced by research into *subcultures of consumptions*. Subcultures of consumption were first conceptualized in 1995 by researchers Schouten and McAlexander after a three-year ethnographic study of groups of Harley-Davidson bikers. The level of identification between the Harley-Davidson bikes and their consumers facilitated the emergence of subcultures. These findings added social interaction to concepts such as consumer loyalty, brand meaning and so on, and have inspired a whole new stream of research into the social aspects of consumption. The difference between a subculture of consumption and a brand community will be depicted at the end of this section.

Core theory: the brand community

Researchers Muñiz and O'Guinn pinpointed the existence of brand communities, when they observed: 'active and meaningful negotiation of the brand between consumer collectives and market institutions' (Muñiz and O'Guinn 2005, p. 252). During the course of a two-year study of consumers and their social interaction around three brands (Saab, Ford Bronco and Macintosh). Muñiz and O'Guinn found proof of the existence of brand communities and defined them as 'a specialized, non-geographically bound community, based on a structured set of social relationships among users of a brand' (2001, p. 421).

The research took place in both face-to-face settings and on websites relating to the three brands of study. The three markers of community were displayed in both kinds of environment. Muñiz and O'Guinn were hence able to introduce the brand community notion to the academic world of brand management (see Figure 9.4). Since the three markers of community were displayed in both environments, the brand community notion led to the dissolution of the geographical aspect of the original community definition. Brand communities exist in face-to-face clubs as well as in virtual environments facilitated where 'imagined others' share their passion for a certain brand. A brand community is therefore not restricted by geography, unlike the traditional perception of the community being a geographically bound entity. The community in a brand context relates to a common understanding of a shared identity. The Internet is of course an important vehicle in the formation of communities based on the sense of a shared identity with 'imagined others'.

As regards the first marker of a community: 'consciousness of kind' findings in the research suggest that 'Members feel an important connection to the brand, but more importantly, they feel a stronger connection toward one another. Members feel that they 'sort of know each other' at some level, even if they have never met' (Muñiz and O'Guinn 2001, p. 418).

This feeling of 'sort of knowing each other' is characterized by and enhanced by two aspects: 'legitimacy' and 'oppositional brand loyalty'. 'Legitimacy' is based on observations indicating that members have a feeling of other members either

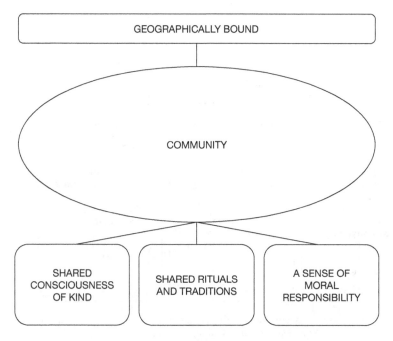

Figure 9.4 Conceptualization of the community in the sociological tradition

being members for the right or the wrong reasons. As expressed by one community member: 'We' are the members 'really knowing' how and why the brand should be consumed, while 'they' consume the brand for the 'wrong reasons'. 'Oppositional brand loyalty' is the other characteristic that can enhance members' 'consciousness of kind'. Brand community members underpin this sense of belonging by sharing a dislike for competing brands. Macintosh community members tend to criticize PCs and Microsoft, while in the Saab brand community, for instance, there is a general tendency to put down the competing Swedish car brand, Volvo. New product adoption might also be facilitated by the existence of a brand community (but only to a certain extent) (Thompson and Sinha 2008).

The second marker of community, 'Shared rituals and traditions' 'typically focus on shared consumption experiences with the brand. All the brand communities encountered in this project have some form of rituals or traditions that function

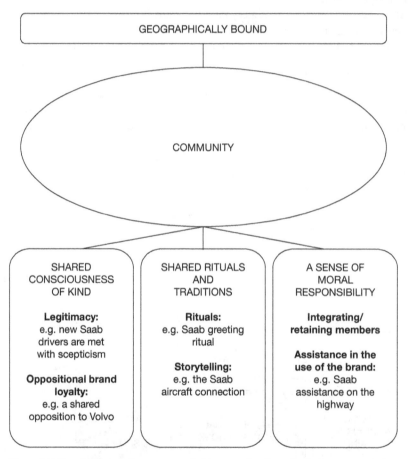

Figure 9.5 Brand community construct (with examples from the Saab community) as conceptualized by Muñiz and O'Guinn, 'Brand community', *Journal of Consumer Research*, 27 (2001), pp. 412–31

to maintain the culture of the community' (Muñiz and O'Guinn 2001, p. 421). These rituals include special greetings, a celebration of the history of the brand and sharing stories of the brand; 'Storytelling is an important means of creating and maintaining community' (ibid., p. 423). The storytelling aspect of the brand community can be very powerful. In the case of the Apple Newton brand community 'Supernatural, religious, and magical motifs are common. . . . There are strong elements of survival, the miraculous, and the return of the creator' (Muñiz and Schau 2005, p. 739).

The third marker of a brand community, 'sense of moral responsibility', is a sense of duty to the community as a whole, and to the individual members of the community, and it 'is what produces collective action and contributes to group cohesion' (Muñiz and O'Guinn 2001, p. 424); these characteristics were also displayed in the social interaction around the three brands in question. The communities display moral systems, but not in a very high-flown sense of the word – they do not relate to life-and-death matters: 'Moral systems can be subtle, and are highly contextualized. Such is the case with brand communities' (ibid., p. 424). These moral systems serve two major purposes: the integration and retention of members and the assistance of members in the proper use of the brand (see Figure 9.5).

Brandfests, brand communities and community brands

The quintessential brand community pivots around an already existing brand and is usually established and run by enthusiastic volunteers. However, the three markers of community can also be observed at so-called brandfests, where a proactive marketer establishes consumer interaction that can facilitate the evolvement of a brand community. McAlexander *et al.*'s (2002) study of the intentional building of brand communities offers insight into the possibilities of a proactive marketer. If the marketer understands and respects the dynamics of a brand community, it is possible to proactively create a platform that facilitates a brand community to evolve: 'Even owners who came to events dwelling on how different they felt from others often left after two or three days believing they belonged to a broader community that understands and supports them in realizing their consumption goals' (ibid. 2002, p. 42). Corporate-sponsored brandfests are often used for recruitment of new members, while the existing communities typically consist of diehard brand enthusiasts.

Brands such as Wikipedia and Linux add a new category to the approach. The Internet-based sharing of, respectively, encyclopaedia articles and an operating system for computers that can be downloaded free of charge is in fact *created* by a community. They are both not only powerful brands but also masters of completely changing the premises of their businesses. MySpace and YouTube are also interesting early examples of social media cases to consider if one wants to gain insight into how the premises of the community approach have in fact changed whole industries by fundamentally changing how consumers interact. These community brands display the same characteristics as the brand communities and brandfests but add another dimension to the scope of the approach, since no marketer (in the traditional sense of the word) exists. Still, it is the principles and mechanisms of the community approach that apply.

Subcultures of consumption and different types of brand communities

As explained above, the formulation of a brand community theory is very much influenced by subcultures of consumption. The two concepts, however, differ significantly and should not be confused. 'A subculture of consumption [is] a distinctive subgroup of society that self-selects on the basis of a shared commitment to a particular product class, brand, or consumption activity' (Schouten and McAlexander 1995, p. 43).

Apart from this self-selection, different markers from the three markers characterizing a brand community are used to characterize a subculture. The markers of a subculture of consumption are:

- a hierarchical social structure;
- ethos is manifested in shared beliefs and values;
- unique jargons and rituals; and
- unique modes of symbolic expressions;

These characteristics are more far-reaching than the 'consciousness of kind', 'rituals and traditions' and 'sense of moral responsibility' that characterize a brand community. In this regard, it is important to notice that the membership of a consumption subculture (being formal or informal) is more demanding than the membership of a brand community. A subculture tends to define itself in opposition to the broader culture, which is not the case with brand communities. 'Brand communities do not typically reject aspects of the surrounding culture's ideology. They embrace them' (Muñiz and O'Guinn 2001, p. 414).

In the subculture, the brand has a socially fixed meaning. In brand communities, brand meaning is socially negotiated rather than delivered unaltered from consumer to consumer. The subculture study is more individually focused on the transformation of self where the brand community approach departs in a social constructionist perspective.

This distinction between different community types stems from the original literature constituting the approach (Schouten and McAlexander 1995, Muñiz and

Table 9.1 Variations of brand community (community in the original understanding)

	Brandfests	*Brand communities*	*Community brands*
Marketer's role	An endorsing marketer	An existing marketer	The community *is* the marketer
Consumers' role	Open to share brand meaning	Co-creators of brand meaning	Creators of brand meaning
Examples	Camp, Jeep, Harley-Davidson rallies	Car clubs, Apple user pages	Wikipedia, Linux

O'Guinn 2001) (see Table 9.1). Since, the need for understanding the true potential of communities has led to the creation of new, interesting definitions and distinctions between different types of communities. A community is a (often loosely organized) group of people held together by shared interests. Communities span (pretty) *stable groups of die-hard fans* (e.g. Harley-Davidson owners) to *casual community behaviour* (e.g. expressed in writing an online review or sharing a message on your Facebook page). Further, community membership (or mere behaviour) can be both *passive* (the reading of the review or noticing your friend's shared message) as well as *active* (the reviewing, sharing, commenting etc.). When it comes to different kinds of community participation, the '90–9–1 principle' is often applied. As a rule of thumb 90 per cent of members are passive 'lurkers', the 9 per cent are 'contributors' posting and participating moderately, while the 1 per cent are 'super-users' and produce the major bulk of community content (Carron-Arthur *et al.* 2014). The common ground is still the basic idea depicted in 'the brand triad' – namely that you are influenced by or actively participate in consumer–consumer communication.

Brand communities (understood broadly) can be broken down into more nuanced categories based on how members actually relate to them. Fournier and Lee (2009) distinguish between three forms of community affiliations: pools, webs and hubs (see Table 9.2).

Across different types of communities, value creation takes place – for the marketer as well as for the consumers. The practices that create the values have been studied by Schau, Muniz and Arnould (2009) and can be divided into the categories of 'social networking', 'community engagement', 'brand use' and 'impression management'. 'Social networking' consists of practices of 'welcoming' new members, 'empathizing' with them as well as 'governing' them, meaning that members instruct new members in the behavioural expectations within the

Table 9.2 Three forms of community affiliation

	Pools	*Webs*	*Hubs*
Members' relationship to community	Strong associations with a shared activity or value, and loose member connections	Strong one-to-one relationships with others with similar needs	Strong connections to a central figure and a weaker association with one another
Key to community affiliation	The shared activity, goal, or values	Personal relationships	A charismatic figure
Examples	Apple enthusiasts, Republicans or Democrats, Ironman triathletes	Facebook, Cancer Survivors Network, Hash House Harriers	Deepak Chopra, Hannah Montana, Oprah

Source: Fournier and Lee (2009)

boundaries of the community. 'Community engagement' is practices of 'documenting' as in creating narratives of the brand's journey, 'badging' as in translating milestones into a symbolic language, 'milestoning' as in noting seminal events in brand ownership and 'staking' as in recognizing the existence of different subgroups within the community. 'Brand use' is another category of value-creating practices and consists of 'customizing', which can be defined as creative modification of the brand; 'grooming', which is caring for the brand and recommending optimal use and 'commoditizing', which is an activity related to the marketplace (e.g. encouragement to buy or not buy). The last category of value-creating practices is labelled 'impression management' and consists of 'evangelizing', 'justifying'. The first is behaviours such as sharing good brand-related news, while the latter is about rationalizing or joking about one's own devotion to the brand and the community.

Web 2.0 and social media

As already explained, the original notion of the brand community is based on observations in physical as well as online communities, with a brand the members are passionate about as the pivotal point of the community. Key findings from these observations are the idea of the triangular communication and the idea of meaning creation in groups of consumers. These ideas apply perfectly to Web 2.0 activities – whether these are 'liking', 'commenting', 'sharing', 'repinning', 'snapping', 'retweeting', 'friending', 'reviewing' or 'blogging'. A true 'homo connectus' does all of the above – and for sure a lot more – all the time. We abstain from the attempt to create an overview of the importance of social media, main platforms or their number of followers in the acknowledgement of how fast this description would be obsolete due to the speed of their development. Figures related to social media tend to become dated in a matter of minutes or days!

Social media can be viewed as just another media – or as something having the potential to dramatically change the communication (Rowley 2008) or even the business strategy (Fournier and Lee 2009) of the company.

If one distinguishes between paid, owned and earned media (Keller 2012; Edelman and Salsberg 2010), a strong social communicator has the opportunity of moving a considerable amount of the media spend from paid media (traditional paid advertising on a variety of media) to earned media (free media through e.g. editorial and social media). A 'like' or a 'retweet' is earned, and thereby 'free media'. But social media are not invented for the good of commercial agents (Fournier and Avery 2011) and marketers therefore need to behave accordingly and post other kinds of communication than traditional brand communication. Content marketing is thereby an important element in a social media-savvy marketer's toolbox (Rowley 2008) (refer to Chapter 12 for elaboration and additional literature on content marketing).

Word-of-mouth (WOM) has long been a central marketing mechanism, one of the brand touchpoints beyond the realms of the marketer that can really propel the popularity of a brand forward (Kozinets *et al.* 2010). The combination of triangular communication, Web 2.0, communities and community behaviour is a godsend in this context! Online WOM (sometimes referred to as word-of-mouse) is a natural outcome of the above-mentioned description of how Web 2.0 and social media have changed both communication channels and content. Pre-social media, you might share your enthusiasm of a delightful shopping experience with the first five people you would meet after the experience took place. Post-social media you can share it with all of your 'friends' and 'followers' in a split second. They might even help with the spreading of the word, and thereby begins the exponential effect of social media and perhaps also the creation of the 'networked narratives' possible in communities (ibid.) (see Table 9.3).

In the original theory coining the idea of the brand community, the interesting notion of 'grass-roots R&D' was mentioned as a potential benefit from a community. The potential and reach of 'grass-roots R&D' is also something that has been amplified tremendously due to the influence of Web 2.0 and is typically called 'crowdsourcing': 'the gathering of online communities whose innovation are beginning to transform the world of marketing' (Kozinets *et al.* 2008, p. 339, read also Hemetsberger 2012). Crowdsourcing seems to truly unfold the potential of the community and fundamentally create new boundaries and roles in the relationship between marketer and consumer(s). A consequence of the assumptions of the relational approach is co-creation, be it in co-authoring the brand or in co-creating brands and experiences. Crowdsourcing takes these premises a step further: 'Collective consumer creativity is qualitatively distinct from individual consumer creativity – it occurs when 'social interactions' trigger new interpretations and new discoveries that consumers 'thinking alone', could not have generated.' (Hargadon and Bechky 2006, p. 489), thereby fully embracing the idea of the service-dominant logic (Vargo and Lusch 2004).

The nature of different 'online creative consumer communities' has been investigated (Kozinets *et al.* 2008) and divided into four different types based on two discriminators: the 'collective innovation orientation' (very goal-oriented

Table 9.3   Typology of online creative consumer communities

	Swarms	*Mobs*	*Crowds*	*Hives*
Collective innovation orientation	Communo-ludic (oriented towards the community)	Communo-ludic (oriented towards the community)	Telo-specific (oriented towards the task at hand)	Telo-specific (oriented towards the task at hand)
Collective innovation concentration	Low (many members)	High (fewer members)	Low (many members)	High (fewer members)
Examples	Amazon, Flickr, Napster, Wikipedia, Google	Slave to Target, The Huffington Post, <alt.coffee>	Crash the Superbowl, Freebeer, Threadless	Skibuilders, Casemodders, Niketalk, New Voyages

Source: Kozinets *et al.* (2008)

versus more community-oriented) and 'collective innovation concentration' (high (few specialized members) versus low (many less-specialized members)).

Summary

The brand community concept is rooted in the sociological notion of community and the idea of subcultures of consumption. Three markers characterize a brand community: 'consciousness of kind', 'rituals and traditions' and a 'sense of moral responsibility'. Brand communities can be geographically bound as well as dispersed. The brand community concept expands into different variations: marketer-facilitated brandfests, typical brand communities run by enthusiasts, and community brands, where the community becomes the marketer. A brand community does not define itself in opposition to the surrounding society, as opposed to a subculture of consumption.

The reality of the original idea of the brand community has been overtaken and the potency of it has been amplified tremendously by a world transformed by Web 2.0 and social media. WOM and crowdsourcing are central aspects of understanding the potential of the community approach.

Having described the theoretical framework of the community approach, the next section provides guidelines for how one can build a research design to explore a brand community. This research is necessary if the aim is to analyse the potential to either facilitate or benefit from a brand community by observing and extracting brand meaning to be used actively in a brand strategy.

Methods and data of the community approach

Research in the community approach borrows from the scientific tradition of ethnography. Ethnography was developed around the turn of the twentieth century as a new approach to the study of cultural and sociological research phenomena. The pioneers of this new scientific approach sought 'fundamental truths about human nature, social affiliation, and the conduct of daily life' (Mariampolski 2006, p. 4). Ethnography has (very roughly) evolved from a methodology used for the study of 'exotic' and 'primitive' people in the early twentieth century to being used increasingly for studies of cultural issues in all kinds of societies, to being applied to the arena of marketing research in the mid-1980s.

Uncovering the sociocultural interaction of a community cannot be done in a laboratory setting or by the use of questionnaires. Research into how meaning is created requires participation and an open mind. Academic ethnographic research designs often span several years, requiring full immersion into the community of interest. Conducting a marketing-based study of a brand community is different from conducting an academic study. The marketing study often needs to be conducted over a much shorter period and with a less explorative aim. But the principles of the ethnographic research tradition can still deliver valuable insights even though the study has to adapt to limited resources and a tight time frame. In this section, these principles will be outlined along with an introduction to the fundamentals of ethnography's twenty-first-century younger sister, 'netnography'.

The ethnographic research tradition

Ethnographic research is also known as field research, observational research or participant observation and is characterized by researcher participation and a variety of data:

> In its most characteristic form [it] involves the ethnographer participating, overtly or covertly, in people's daily lives for an extended period of time, watching what happens, listening to what is said, asking questions – in fact, collecting whatever data are available to throw light on the issues that are the focus of the research.
>
> (Hammersley and Atkinson 1994, p. 1)

The ethnographic research tradition sets no limits on data collection. A participant researcher is free to collect any kind of data that is believed to add to the study of the subject or phenomena of interest. Common data types are interviews (more or less structured), depth interviews, visual impressions, print, video-recording and photographs. Taking notes and photographs/video of all relevant observations also helps memory of minor details that might prove important. A deep understanding of a small sample of data is preferred to the opposite. The participant researcher may collect data incognito or identify himself as he sees fit.

Understanding people in the ethnographic research tradition means under-standing them in their own environment and from the perspective of the participants. In practice, this means that gaining a deep insight into the consumption experiences in a supermarket requires the researcher to be present – in the actual supermarket. If the researcher is subjected to the same consumption experience as

---

Box 9.3 Getting too close?

In a three-year ethnographic study by Schouten and McAlexander (1995) of the Harley-Davidson subculture of consumption, the researchers started out their fieldwork without any specific interest in the biker lifestyle. Their immersion into the biker lifestyle had the consequence that they ended up being motorcycle owners as well as enthusiasts living the lifestyle to the fullest. Getting so fully immersed into the subcultural environment made them ponder one of the classic dilemmas of ethnography: that of the insider/outsider dilemma. Involvement in the social interaction in question – 'going native' – is a prerequisite for understanding the social processes taking place, but over-involvement brings the researcher too close to the phenomena of study to observe and transmit the facts of the research accurately.

Source: Schouten and McAlexander (1995)

the consumer, this sharing of the consumption experience will enable a deeper and more real understanding from the perspective of the subject investigated. The focus on everyday behaviour therefore requires a presence in the natural setting of the research participants.

The researcher needs to get close to the subjects of research. 'Going native' is a term covering the ethnographic research ideal: to live in a certain environment long enough to truly understand the social and cultural phenomena from an 'insider perspective'. One way to solve the insider/outsider dilemma is to team up in pairs, where one researcher adopts an insider role while the other remains an outsider.

In the ethnographic tradition, it is more appropriate to talk about a research draft than a research design, because the researcher must to go with the flow of the research process and adjust continuously. During the exploration of the brand community unexpected observations or information that was not thought to be relevant before collecting data may guide the researcher's attention in new directions. This unstructured collection of data is often characterized by a combination of formal and informal methods. An example could be an interview in a private home, the interview being the formal method. During the course of the interview it becomes clear that the respondent becomes uncomfortable when the interview touches upon certain subjects. Observations of blushing cheeks and a shifty glance might also count as data if they serve the aim of the research (even though these observations are informal and not planned ahead).

Even though the ethnographic research tradition hails qualitative data, it does not reject the use of quantitative data. Qualitative data may be triangulated with quantitative measures if it furthers the deeper understanding of the object of research.

Ethnography allows for creative interpretations. The deep analysis of the sample of data should manifest itself in rich, insightful ('thick') description uncovering as many details as possible in order to provide understanding of as many layers of meaning as possible.

The tradition is suited to the exploration of new themes. As an ethnographic researcher, he or she should attempt to be open-minded in his or her work, unintended knowledge and issues may occur in the process and should not be ignored.

Box 9.4 Solving the insider/outsider dilemma

Researchers Muñiz and Schau solved this dilemma quite easily when researching the Apple Newton brand community. One researcher bought a Newton and used it for writing the research article. He became the insider participant, dependent on the Newton brand community for support in the use of the abandoned (by the marketer) handheld assistant. The other researcher took the outside position, ensuring objectivity in the study.

Source: Muñiz and Schau (2005)

Box 9.5 Quantitative triangulation of qualitative data

Algesheimer *et al*. (2005) conducted ethnographic research in 'The social influence of brand community: evidence from European car clubs', attempting to 'develop and estimate a conceptual model of how different aspects of customers' relationships with the brand community influence their intentions and behaviors' (p. 19). Algesheimer *et al*. identify five central hypotheses in the body of academic literature. During the development of a quantitative research design for studying these hypotheses, the authors conducted exploratory qualitative research through in-depth interviews with car club presidents and focus groups with car club members, experts and graduate marketing students to evaluate and secure the best possible research design. The survey was developed, 282 car clubs were contacted and a potential of 2,440 members were reached with the survey. The survey was made available on line and all participants were contacted via e-mail with additional questions. Through a mathematically based analysis, the five hypotheses were assigned different weights, which made the managerial implications very precise. Including quantitative methods and broadening the range of data to include a large number of members from many different car clubs, ensured that it was possible to derive generally applicable conclusions based on the results of the inquiry.

Source: Algesheimer *et al*. (2005)

Netnography

The Internet-based methodology of netnography plays an important role in several of the community research studies (Kozinets 2010). Applying the principles of ethnography to Internet-related fieldwork is an obvious information source to collect knowledge of the geographically dispersed brand communities. 'Netnography is based in ethnography, and ethnography is insight-generation occurring in the friction between observation, participation, thoughts, actions, language, and representations. Ethnography is pattern recognition under conditions of extreme complexity.' (Kozinets 2012). Netnographic methods are used for gaining insight into Internet-shared brand meaning on community websites and can also be used in combination with a more traditional ethnographic research design. Community members can be contacted and recruited for interviews and/or observation, or e-mail questionnaires can be circulated with the help of the community.

According to Kozinets (2012), netnography has five main characteristics:

- Netnography is naturalistic – the researcher seeks the field, where the culture of interest is unfolded. Data collection takes place in the natural environment (e.g. a digital environment revolving around a specific brand).

- Netnography is immersive – it is not enough to look into a natural online environment of interest. As a true ethnographer, one has to become immersed in the community, extending oneself and not just 'snoop'. Participation is key as in the original ethnographic tradition.
- Netnography requires the ability to translate the insider knowledge to valid 'objective' data and requires quite creative skills in order to convey the 'intense meaning of social life' (Kozinets 2012, p. 97).
- Netnography applies a myriad of methodologies – interviews, documentary analysis, participant-observation, screen shots, quantitative data. When it comes to methods, almost anything goes as long as the research ideal of understanding the lived social reality of interest is being honoured.
- Netnography has to be adaptable – a netnographic study needs to adapt to the nature of the (digital) social world under investigation. Where does the

---

Box 9.6 How to do an ethnographic study of a brand community

- Pair up and let one be an inside observer while the other remains outside the community. This will enable you to gain insight into the deeper structures of the brand community while still being able to analyse the information properly.
- Start with an exploratory phase uncovering all expressions of community. Be creative; everything counts as data (photos, video, etc.).
- Observe – go to the everyday environment of the consumer; watch, listen and learn. Let respondents take the lead, do not interfere and ensure a lot of data. Join a community, go to community face-to-face meetings, sign up as an online user, join discussion forums.
- Be objective, try not to assume anything and put all prejudices aside.
- Be loving – respect your respondents, they are opening their hearts to you! Do not mistreat the information. Start slowly and build confidence.
- Make sure that your presence does not make the respondents change their routine – you need an accurate picture of the true nature of the brand community.
- Start out by being very open and ask questions in an unstructured fashion. Go with the flow and encourage respondents to elaborate and explain statements further.
- Base the more in-depth investigation on the data from the exploratory phase. What seems strange or interesting can in that way be elaborated.
- Rich description and analysis with a variety of media are to be preferred. Consider both verbal and non-verbal sources of data and ways of describing the community and the brand meaning and experiences, traditions and rituals shared in the brand community.

interaction take place? On how many social platforms can we find relevant information and how do we immerse ourselves?

Summary

The community approach represents a social brand perspective and the community concept is a key concept in sociology. Acquiring new knowledge in this perspective requires methods facilitating the understanding of sociocultural interaction and meaning creation. Hence, the methods used to explore brand communities are rooted in the ethnographic tradition departing in a sociocultural perspective on man. Getting close to subjects of interest by participating in their natural environment is key in the brand community approach. The data collection is versatile as all kinds of data shedding light on the phenomena count. Rich and deep analysis with a variety of different expressions in a small sample is preferable to a big sample with little variation. Getting close to the virtual brand communities requires the adaptation of netnography – the ethnographic principles applied to web-based research.

Managerial implications

This section will give a sketchy account of the managerial implications of the community approach. The managerial implications of Web 2.0, social media[1] and the idea of 'homo connectus' are very complex and far-reaching. This section is therefore by no means an exhaustive presentation of these issues, but a brief overview of the implications of the original community theory, how and where these mechanisms have unfolded since.

Can all brands attract communities?

When the ideas of the subculture of consumption and brand community were presented (1995 and 2001 respectively), the theories only applied to a limited number of high-involvement brands. Brand communities evolved around brands with a long and interesting history, high-involvement products, brands threatened by competition, expensive brands or brands with considerable maintenance costs. There was also the 'nerd' factor; very technical and complicated products also had the potential for attracting communities.

Cars and motorcycle brands were among the first to attract communities. Especially iconic brands, representing a certain lifestyle (e.g. Harley-Davidson, Chrysler Jeeps) held the potential for very strong communities and these brands used the communities as an important part of brand ethos. 'Helping each other out' is a big part of community building and is a very good reason for joining both a car/motorcycle as well as a computer brand community. Threatening competition can also be an important factor as 'oppositional loyalty' is something that really entices a community (Muñiz and O'Guinn 2001, Thompson and Sinha 2008). The 'nerd' factor and ideological purposes were evident in the case of some of the *community brands*, for example Linux and Wikipedia.

214 Part II: Seven brand approaches

**Box 9.7 Libresse: the community principles applied to
fast-moving consumer goods**

A line of feminine hygiene products is marketed by Swedish paper product
giant SCA. The products are marketed as Libresse (globally), BodyForm
(UK), Nana (France), Nuvenia (Italy), Libra (Australia), Nosotras (Spain) and
Saba (Mexico and Central America). SCA has successfully managed to apply
the principles of the community approach to an FMCG (fast-moving
consumer goods) in an innovative marketing effort customized for the
youngest of their target audience.

  These websites resemble youth magazines and are devoted more to
emotional subjects and the bodily changes of young teenage girls rather
than to the marketed products. They offer space for interaction about
health and beauty issues, boyfriends, sexuality and puberty, to name a few.
Advice about love, bodily issues and self-esteem is given, chat rooms are
open and horoscopes are provided. Great insight into the psychology of
the target audience has facilitated an innovative platform for brand loyalty.
The Australian website is one of the most innovative ones, encouraging the
user to be a 'Libra girl', get a 'Libra nickname' and thereby access to an
otherwise restricted area of chat rooms, e-diaries and horoscopes. It has
since being launched been elevated to a global platform and by 2015 it had
more than 200,000 active users.

Sources: www.libresse.com; www.libragirl.com

Pretty quickly fast-moving consumer goods caught up on these new ideas and
opportunities; sanitary towel brand Libresse is an early example.

It was thereby proven that brand communities can successfully be facilitated
around low-involvement products. In the case of these not-so-obvious brands, a
community should be based on a deep understanding of the consumption context
rather than the brand itself (the consumption context meaning the psychological
and social concerns of young girls in the Libresse case).

The life-altering, revolutionizing forces of Web 2.0 are all about triangular
communication (in a brand management context). It sets the potential of
this communication model free and holds both enormous potential and challenges.
It also gives a manager of *any* brand the opportunity to embrace these mechanisms
– be it on a small or large scale. In many ways, these opportunities seem to have
had a democratizing effect; new businesses with a good sense of communicating
to 'homo connectus' seem to be equipped with a whole new set of inexpensive
communication opportunities. So this approach has evolved from being mostly
relevant for high-involvement brands with a long history to being of importance
to practically all brands.

The benefits – and threats – of triadic communication

All community activity is a double-edged sword. The positive aspects are value-creating: 'a brand with a powerful sense of community would generally have greater value to a marketer than a brand with a weak sense of community' (Muñiz and O'Guinn 2001, p. 427) but are accompanied by concerns and challenges for any brand marketer: 'However, it should also be recognized that a strong brand community can be a threat to a marketer should a community collectively reject marketing efforts or product change, and then use communal communications channels to disseminate this rejection' (ibid.).

Community members (in the 'real' communities) are diehard fans. They choose to spend leisure time on a brand, cultivating profound brand meaning. Community behaviour (e.g. liking, retweeting, sharing) can be very casual, but still leaves a trace of accessible and valuable information, as well as the influencing of other consumers. A marketer can gain deep insight into these layers of meaning simply by observing the community – be it diehard or casual. This insight can be valuable in the marketing of the brand as online communities in many ways are ongoing, ever-evolving focus groups.

Observations can take place in the face-to-face venues as well as in the virtual communities. A brand manager may enrol in clubs, join rallies or subscribe to user groups, to name a few possibilities. The social interaction in the brand community

---

Box 9.8 Insights from the Volkswagen 'Beetle' community

In 1998 Volkswagen re-launched the legendary 'Beetle'. The original Beetle was launched in 1934. The idea was to produce a car for the people, which at the time was a revolutionary concept. Hugely popular over many generations, the inexpensive VW Beetle surpassed all production records, with more than 20 million cars leaving the VW assembly lines.

In a marketing study on 'retro-branding', researchers Brown *et al.* dived into the brand meaning shared on Beetle-related community websites. By means of a netnographic method, they gained insight into the negotiation and exchange of brand meaning among community members. Adopting a holistic perspective on the community-based brand–consumer exchange, valuable information regarding the delicate matter of re-launching a cult brand was retrieved. Examples are: Beetle fans seem divided on the issue of the technology of the new car. They tend to celebrate an innocent approach to the 'hippie' era of the 1960s and 1970s, with which the Beetle is very much associated. The Beetle is closely linked with family heritage and childhood memories in many cases. Memorable advertising campaigns from the 1960s are still fondly associated with the Beetle.

Sources: www.volkswagen.com; Brown *et al.* (2003)

should be observed applying the appropriate ethnographic (and 'nethnographic') data collection techniques in order to deduce brand meaning.

Brand mystique can be uncovered and used as a source of inspiration for marketing campaigns aimed at the mainstream users of the brand. Brand meaning attached to existing products can be applied to the marketing of new products (see Figure 9.6).

However, any marketer acting as an observer in a brand community should tread extremely cautiously. Community consumers do not like intentional marketing (Fournier and Avery 2011), and they do not like anyone looking over their shoulder. Community members prefer to feel autonomous and in charge of the brand, and would most likely resent being spied on. Another potential danger is the dilution of brand mystique, which ultimately can lead to the brand losing its appeal.

Social media are not invented with the wellbeing of commercial agents in sight and therefore the social media brand manager (essentially a 'party crasher' (ibid.)) should be aware of his place in this 'landscape of open source branding'. The party crashing brand manager is met by and with (ibid.):

- the social collective – Web 2.0 is a powerful nurturer of social collectives. Likeminded beings can seamlessly connect to share and create meaning in all areas of life. Some of the most successful online brand communities (Nutella and Coca-Cola) are established and run by fans;
- transparency (or 'What happens in Vegas stays on YouTube'). Dove hired a fashion photographer retoucher for the 'Campaign for Real Beauty' (a campaign exposing the digital manipulation of the looks of models) who later exposed the job. Examples of companies not being able to hide unwanted information are countless;

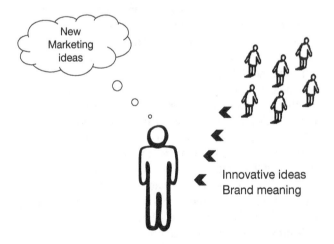

Figure 9.6 The marketer as observer of a brand community

- criticism – the democratic access to publicly evaluating every action of any company has created a dramatic shift in the power relationship between marketer and consumer; and
- parody – friendly spoofs or highly political online attacks on brands and their communication are also part of this new age within brand management. A more democratic access to digital production tools, social media and the easy access to likeminded individuals create a – sometimes loving, sometimes toxic – supplementary meaning creation of the brand. Consumer activism (Albinsson and Perena 2012, Handelman 2012) is in extreme cases part of this brand management landscape of open source branding.

Still, in this challenging environment, the opportunities of Web 2.0 are extremely powerful in brand management. Community engagement nurtures loyalty, offers the opportunity of crowdsourcing, viral branding (social media as free media), WOM as a positive force. In the next section, we will go more into detail with the proposed management of these areas.

Facilitating a community

As a general rule of thumb, the marketer facilitating a brand community should be just as cautious as the observing marketer. A brand community is a powerful force and, in order for a community to thrive, the facilitating marketer is advised to adopt a 'behind the scenes' approach (Muñiz and O'Guinn 2001, Fournier and Avery 2011).

An Internet-based user group, a face-to-face club or a well-orchestrated brandfest can proactively facilitate valuable consumer interaction. Facilitating a brand community can be a great retention tool, but caution and very discreet marketer presence is essential. It is important to note that it is, in fact, the social interaction around the consumption of the brand that spurs brand loyalty and contributes to the building of brand meaning. A marketer must hence engage members, not only with the brand, but also with each other. A photo or design contest is not enough, no matter the number of participants (that would essentially be a relationship-building activity). A community requires interaction in the lower part of the brand triad model, meaning consumers need to interact independently (see Figure 9.1 on p. 196).

If we look at the basic types of communities that exist under the umbrella of the brand triad, the brandfest requires active management by the marketer. The activities and events of this category of community go hand in hand with the importance of social media. Inviting customers to join a party, a product launch, a test drive, a fashion show or other events typically spurs a lot of activities on social media – as well as creating the coveted brand-related meaning on site. A company like Burberry has excelled in creating online brandfests and thereby expanding the number of attendees to their events limitlessly (Ahrendts 2013).

When managing a brand community, it is advisable to consider the value-creating practices that can be observed across different communities: 'if firms give consumers the opportunity to construct brand communities and the freedom to modify their products, they will' (Schau *et al.* 2009, p. 41). Facilitating and (discreetly) encouraging the practices of 'social networking', 'community engagement', 'brand use' and 'impression management' support and nurture a meaningful community. Schau *et al.* (2009) propose that the community should be built on transparency rather than 'lurking' – post-web 2.0 community members know the game. It is also advisable to find out if your community is a 'web', a 'hub' or a 'pool' (Fournier and Lee 2009) (see Table 9.2 on p. 205) and adapt your part of the communication accordingly.

Crowdsourcing takes place in online creative consumer collectives and is the post-Web 2.0 version of 'grass-roots R&D' mentioned in the original theory. Knowing the four types of online creative consumer collectives (swarms, mobs, crowds and hives) (see Table 9.3 on p. 207) will help you structure the online facilities supporting the online creative consumer collective needed for your purpose. Do you have a specific task that needs solving (consider creating a crowd or a hive) or do you want the steady, casual reviewing/commenting of e.g. Amazon (a swarm)?

'Seeding' (giving product samples to opinion leaders, e.g. central community members or influential bloggers) is a central management tool in this approach (Kozinets 2010). Research shows that it activates a lot of the value-creating practices mentioned above (Schau *et al.* 2009). In the case of word-of-mouth management (WOMM), it is also of utmost importance. Measuring the 'amplification' (the quantitative spread of the WOM) is not enough. A strong and successful online WOM campaign needs to take into account qualitative measures as well; it needs to be congruent with the ongoing character narrative and respect communal norms (Kozinets *et al.* 2010).

WOMM is an important tool in the social brand manager's toolbox: 'Until the early 2000s, WOM was largely considered a side effect of marketing activity. Today, marketers are trying to develop a systematic approach to manage it' (Lovett *et al.* 2013, p. 440). The trick is to create a 'talkable' brand – one that makes consumers talk. Research finds social, emotional and functional drivers behind this willingness to talk about a certain brand. Social drivers are quality, differentiation, premium/ value, relevance and visibility. Emotional drivers are excitement, satisfaction, perceived risk and involvement, while functional drivers are age, complexity, type of good, knowledge, perceived risk and involvement (the latter two are hybrid characteristics found in both emotional and functional). A strong combination of these brand characteristics leads to many WOM mentions (offline as well as online) (Lovett *et al.* 2013). Studies show a correlation between eWOM (online WOM) and sales, and consumers are more influenced by WOM if the brand is weak (low equity) than if the brand is strong (with high equity) (Ho-Dac *et al.* 2013). Finding and addressing the 1 per cent 'super-user' of your community is important in any case of brand community management.

Wanting to create a strong community requires more than changes in the marketing agenda. Truly embracing the 'networked narratives' of community branding requires a fitting mindset – and should optimally be a business strategy rather than just a marketing strategy (Fournier and Lee 2009).

Welcome to the vortex of triadic brand management

The community approach and the influence of Web 2.0 are indeed revolutionary forces instigating very different rules of the game in many areas. In this concluding section, we will touch upon some of the changes brought about in recent years – all explainable by the brand triad. We will touch upon the ownership of the brand, the power of platform brands, the sharing economy, networked narratives and networked innovation, and an industry-altering tendency of demand predicting supply. Last but not least a few words about balancing the stable and the unstable brand elements.

The ownership of the brand is severely challenged (or changed) by this approach. Communicating to and with *groups* of consumers changes the game and 'homo connectus' is never alone and is therefore a desirable friend and a terrifying friend. Consumer activism and collective rejection of marketing activities are great challenges for any marketer. 'Homo connectus' participates in an infinite number of meaning exchanges with an infinite number of networks. Therefore, the meaning originally created by the marketer is mixed with meaning from many different actors: 'in reality marketers neither own nor control the brand. They do not create the brand: society does. The marketer is a relatively powerful social actor, but by no means the only one' (O'Guinn and Muñiz 2008).

The term 'networked narratives' (Kozinets *et al.* 2010) might be the best expression when describing the maelstrom of meaning creation the brand participates in. Networked R&D – or crowdsourcing – is taking the participation of consumers one step further and erupts the boundaries between companies and consumers dramatically. The implications of open innovation are far-reaching (Davenport *et al.* 2006).

The transparency of brand communities also imply that the followers of a brand become a more visible aspect of the brand, which has proven to be more challenging for brands with a homogeneous group of followers than ones with heterogeneous followers (Naylor *et al.* 2012).

When describing the management of brandfests versus brand communities in the above section, we skipped the community brands. Community brands are not manageable as they come into existence outside corporate control, but have been game-changing forces, and as such something you have to take into consideration – either as a collaborator, a competitor or a new medium. Many of the community brands are so-called 'platform brands', simply facilitating online interaction among people (consider Etsy, eBay, Airbnb, Facebook).

The platform brands have a significant say in the fast-growing 'sharing economy'. Why buy when we can share? In these cases, we not only share meaning and likes, but products, holiday homes, cars and so on. Airbnb is a striking example of a 'platform brand' that in few years has managed to change the behaviour of people on vacation – to an extent where the service is a real threat to the hotel industry.

Another interesting and far-reaching tendency instigated by the power of sharing is a democratic one. Suddenly artists can attract their audience before they are signed by a record label (as in the case of Justin Bieber to name an example

(Pamentier and Fischer 2012)). This fundamentally rocks the boat in many industries, where demand suddenly predicts supply. Bloggers who attract big audiences are turning the blog into a solid business, same basic mechanism, where the ownership of brand communication is turned upside down.

The vortex of 'networked brand narratives' is extremely important in contemporary brand management, but we would like to end this account of the community approach with a remark about finding the right balance between the networked, co-authored brand and the stable brand carefully communicated by the marketer. The right mix between stable and unstable elements is essential and will be different from company to company and brand to brand (Da Silveira *et al.* 2013).

Summary

Marketers can benefit from a brand community in many ways. The marketer can reap benefits either by observing brand communities and extracting brand meaning or by facilitating consumer interaction through a brand community. Both roads

---

Box 9.9 Dos and don'ts of the community approach

Do	Don't
Acknowledge the power of the 'networked narrative'	Don't let go of your own narrative – be precise in order to not let everything flow
Consider involving your followers in crowdsourcing	Don't neglect criticism and parody from online movements
Create possibilities for the value-creating practices among your followers	Don't be too present as a marketer – adopt a 'behind the scenes' presence
Build brand communities that enhance shared customer experiences	Don't forget that competitors can 'snoop' easily through the community
Consider changing the content of your communication	Don't think of social media as just another type of media
Use brand communities to tap into brand meaning	Don't exploit the trust of your community
Use community ethos to develop and vitalize the brand	Don't overuse the unique ethos of the community and thereby dilute brand mystique

to obtaining the benefits of a brand community require the discretion of the marketer who should adopt a 'behind the scenes' presence. Neither selling nor the recruitment of new consumers should be attempted. Managerial discretion is key in the community approach. The focus should be on facilitating the sharing of consumption experiences and value-creating practices between consumers.

The landscape of open source branding holds opportunities of viral branding, WOM and crowdsourcing, as well as the challenges of being subject to the challenges of being unwelcome, the transparency of the Internet as well as criticism and parody.

The community approach holds some very far-reaching implications as well. New power relations, platform brands, networked narratives and the opportunity for individuals to attract an audience before even launching a career: those are the new rules of the game.

Academic evolution of the community approach

In this concluding section of the chapter, we outline the evolution of the community approach in brand management academia. This outline is based on the primary data of the taxonomy of this textbook – articles from the top marketing journals with a primary focus on the brand (read more about methodology and data set in Chapter 2). The supplementary literature included in this chapter is hence not included in this section.

The main theory was introduced in 2001, drawing heavily on knowledge and inspiration from the notion of subcultures of consumption. The theory about subcultures of consumption was published in 1995 by researchers Schouten and McAlexander and offered new insight into brand-related social meaning found in the Harley-Davidson Owner Groups.

Fuelled by this inspiration and intrigued by own experiences, Muñiz and O'Guinn took a point of departure in a sociological understanding of what a community is, and researched online and offline communities – and came up with a solid and compelling theory about what a brand community is. A new brand perspective, consumer perspective, and scientific inspiration became part of the academic brand management canvas – as is explained in detail in this chapter.

This knowledge was then expanded through insight into an 'unintended' community. Researchers Muñiz and Schau published in 2005 a study of the vibrant community of an otherwise abandoned product and subbrand – the handheld Apple Newton computer. This focus raises interesting questions regarding some of the game-changing dimensions of the community, consumer autonomy and the possibility of 'brand hijacking'. The world's most valuable brand and powerful marketer – Apple – cannot decide to effectively abandon a product that is not deemed interesting in their portfolio if a community decides otherwise.

In the publications from the following years, there is an interest in the 'internal' mechanisms of a community and it seems that the underlying question is whether or not communities are really worthwhile. Are community members more loyal and do they adopt new products than non-community members? Which practices are truly value-creating? The focus has shifted from the community as an (also) offline entity to online consumer behaviour.

In the last period of time covered in this textbook, focus is on the way community members influence the communication of the brand. eWOM and online reviews are aspects of the 'networked narrative' that the brand in many ways has become since the idea of the brand community was introduced. The visibility of community consumers and overall transparency of communities are also addressed.

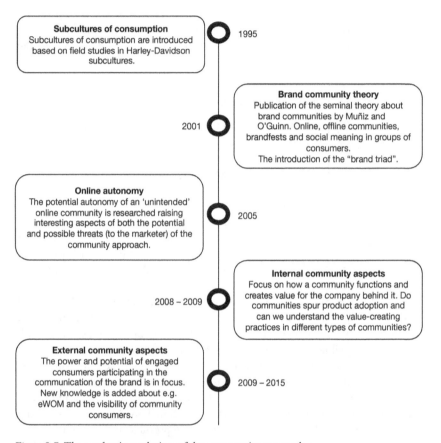

Subcultures of consumption
Subcultures of consumption are introduced based on field studies in Harley-Davidson subcultures.

1995

Brand community theory
Publication of the seminal theory about brand communities by Muñiz and O'Guinn. Online, offline communities, brandfests and social meaning in groups of consumers.
The introduction of the "brand triad".

2001

Online autonomy
The potential autonomy of an 'unintended' online community is researched raising interesting aspects of both the potential and possible threats (to the marketer) of the community approach.

2005

Internal community aspects
Focus on how a community functions and creates value for the company behind it. Do communities spur product adoption and can we understand the value-creating practices in different types of communities?

2008 – 2009

External community aspects
The power and potential of engaged consumers participating in the communication of the brand is in focus. New knowledge is added about e.g. eWOM and the visibility of community consumers.

2009 – 2015

Figure 9.7 The academic evolution of the community approach

Box 9.10 You are not done!

Don't forget to visit the website for supplementary material such as case examples, student questions and supplementary literature.

Comments from the 'founding fathers'

Brands and communities

Albert M. Muñiz, Jr, De Paul University, and Thomas C. O'Guinn, University of Wisconsin School of Business

Like many successful collaborations, this one began over food and drink. We had both been talking for some time about the lack of sociological thought in mainstream consumer behaviour. We had both used brands in debates and discussions with our psychologist friends. Brands seemed such as an obvious product of social forces and constructs. If brands could have personalities (actually, we 'don't think they do), could they not be the centre of a meaningful social aggregation, a community? Meaning, objects and meaningful objects are often at the centre of communities. Brands were the perfect extension of contemporary social thought. So went our academic argument.

So over food and wine more than a decade ago, we coined the term 'brand community'.

In truth, we were also both drawn to this topic by our own personal brand community experiences. We both had (somewhat) vintage Saabs in the early 1990s. While driving these cars, we were frequently stopped by complete strangers who wanted to talk to us about our Saabs, the brand's history, where we had them serviced and our advice on very Saab-centric problems. We quickly came to realize that these weren't complete strangers stopping us; they were fellow members in a community of Saab enthusiasts. When we looked at the behaviours of these self-proclaimed Saabists, we realized that they were a lot like the Apple Macintosh enthusiasts that we had encountered at various points of our lives. We also realized that the fields of branding and consumer behaviour, as they existed then, could not adequately explain this phenomenon. The social aspects of consumption, particularly with regard to the consumption of brands, were almost completely unexplored. Thus a research calling was revealed.

Brand research had been bound up in what was a sometimes useful, but very limited, idea of brands as summations of attitudes. To be clear: it was an unarguably impoverished view of brands. It was worse than incomplete. It did not and could not properly capture the social nature of brands. Brands are about meaning: meaning clearly left open by summations of attitude. Further, brand meaning derives from society, its forces, agents and institutions, among them marketers and consumers. It is an essentially communal process.

What we saw among users of brands reminded us of what we saw in cohesive neighbourhoods: a sense of community. We began to think that community might be a useful way to think about the relationships between users or admirers of brands. As we thought about it more, and collected more data, and read more of the classical sociological literature on community, we became convinced that we were on to something. Human beings living in consumer cultures aggregate around brands in a manner similar to those occurring in traditional face-to-face communities. It was a novel idea that made perfect sense.

Obvious cases came first. In our earliest work, we studied mostly small-share brands. We initially gave some the impression that brand communities occurred only with a small fraction of consumers and represented marginal populations. More than a decade later, we are delighted to observe that the brand community construct and its application have proven to be quite mainstream in both theory and application. Social network marketing, often through brand communities, is now commonplace. Large-share multinational brands (as well as start-ups) now use the construct, the essential dynamics we revealed (e.g. desired marginality, communal legitimacy, oppositional brand loyalty, the communication structures of communities, essential communal metaphors, communal co-creation, community-generated content, narratives and language). We are honoured through our modest connection to canonic social thought.

Note

1   A recommended read is Kietzmann *et al.* (2011).

References and further reading

Key readings are in bold type

Ahrendts, A. (2013), 'Burberry's CEO on turning an aging British icon into a global luxury brand', *Harvard Business Review* 91 (1): 39–42.
Albinsson, P. A. and Perena, B. Y. (2012), 'Consumer activism 2.0: Tools for social change' in R. Llamas and R. Belk (eds), *The Routledge Companion to Digital Consumption*, London: Routledge.
Algesheimer, R., Dholakia, U. M. and Herrmann, A. (2005), 'The social influence of brand community: Evidence from European car clubs', *Journal of Marketing*, 69 (3): 19–34.
Brown, S., Kozinets, R. V. and Sherry, J. F., Jr (2003), 'Teaching old brands new tricks: Retro branding and the revival of brand meaning', *Journal of Marketing*, 67 (3): 19–33.
Carron-Arthur, B., Cunningham, J. A. and Griffiths, K. M. (2014), 'Describing the distribution of engagement in an Internet support group by post frequency: A comparison of the 90-9-1 Principle and Zipf-s law', *Internet Interventions*, 1 (4): 165–8.
Da Silveira, C., Lages, C. and Simoes, C. (2013), 'Reconceptualizing brand identity in a dynamic environment', *Journal of Business Research*, 66 (1): 28–36.
Davenport, T. H., Leibold, M. and Voelpel, S. (2006), *'Strategic Management in the Innovation Economy'*, New Jersey, NJ: Publicis/Wiley.
Edelman, D. and Salsberg, B. (2010), 'Beyond paid media: Marketing's new vocabulary', *McKinsey Quarterly*, pp. 1–8. Retrieved from www.mckinsey.com/insights/marketing_sales/beyond_paid_media_marketings_new_vocabulary (accessed 2 October 2015).
Fournier, S. and Avery, J. (2011), 'The uninvited brand', *Business Horizons*, 54 (3): 193–207.
Fournier, S. and Lee, L. (2009), 'Getting Brand Communities Right', *Harvard Business Review*, 87: 105–11.
Hackley, C. (2003), *Doing Research Projects in Marketing, Management and Consumer Research*, London: Routledge.
Hammersley, M. and Atkinson, P. (1994), *Ethnography: Principles in Practice* (2nd edn), London: Routledge.

Handelman, J. M. (2012), 'Online consumer movements', in R. Llamas and R. Belk (eds), *The Routledge Companion to Digital Consumption*, London: Routledge, pp. 386–96.

Hargadon, A. B. and Bechky, B. A. (2006), 'When collectives of creatives become creative collectives. A field study of problem-solving at work', *Organization Science*, 17 (4): 484–500.

Hemetsberger, A. (2012), 'Crowdsourcing', in R. Llamas and R. Belk (eds), *The Routledge Companion to Digital Consumption*, London: Routledge, pp. 159–71.

Ho-Dac, N. N., Carson, S. J. and Moore, W. L. (2013), 'The effects of positive and negative online customer reviews: Do brand strength and category maturity matter?' *Journal of Marketing*, 77 (6): 37–53.

Keller, K. L. (2012), *'Strategic Brand Management'*, Harlow, UK: Pearson Education.

Kietzmann, J. H., Hermkens, K. and McCarthy, I. P. (2011), 'Social media? Get serious! Understanding the functional building blocks of social media', *Business Horizons*, 54 (3): 241–51.

Kozinets, R. V. (1997), '"I want to believe": A netnography of the X-philes' subcultures of consumption', *Advances in Consumer Research*, 24: 470–5.

Kozinets, R. V. (2002), 'The field behind the screen: Using netnography for marketing research in online communities', *Journal of Marketing Research*, 39 (1): 61–72.

Kozinets, R. V. (2010), *Netnography: Doing Netnographic Research Online*, Thousand Oaks, CA: Sage Publications.

Kozinets, R. V. (2012) 'Netnography and the digital consumer', in R. Llamas and R. Belk (eds), *The Routledge Companion to Digital Consumption*, London: Routledge, pp. 93–102.

Kozinets, R. V., Hemetsberger, A. and Schau, H. J. (2008), 'The Wisdom of Consumer Crowds', *Journal of Macromarketing*, 28 (4): 339–54.

Kozinets, R. V., de Valck, K., Wojnicki, A. C. and Wilner, S. J. S. (2010), 'Networked narratives: Understanding word-of-mouth marketing in online communities', *Journal of Marketing*, 74 (1): 71–89.

Llamas, R. and Belk, R. (2012), 'Living in a digital world', in R. Llamas and R. Belk (eds), *The Routledge Companion to Digital Consumption*, London: Routledge, pp. 3–13.

Lovett, M. J., Peres, R. and Shachar, R. (2013), 'On brands and word of mouth', *Journal of Marketing Research*, 50 (4): 427–44.

McAlexander, J. H. and Schouten, J. W. (1998), 'Brandfests: Servicescapes for the cultivation of brand equity', in J. Sherry, Jr (ed.), *ServiceScapes*, Chicago, IL: NTC Business Books, pp. 377–402.

McAlexander, J. H., Schouten, J. W. and Koenig, H. F. (2002), 'Building brand community', *Journal of Marketing*, 66 (1): 38–55.

Mariampolski, H. (2006), *Ethnography for Marketers: A Guide to Consumer Immersion*, Thousand Oaks, CA: Sage Publications.

Muñiz, A. M., Jr and O'Guinn, T. C. (1995), *'Brand Community and the Sociology of Brands'*, paper presented to the 1995 Association for Consumer Research annual conference. Minneapolis, MN.

Muñiz, A. M. Jr and O'Guinn, T. C. (2001), 'Brand community', *Journal of Consumer Research*, 27 (4): 412–31.

Muñiz, A. M., Jr and Schau, H. J. (2005), 'Religiosity in the abandoned Apple Newton brand community', *Journal of Consumer Research*, 31 (4): 737–47.

Muñiz, A. M., Jr and Schau, H. J. (2007), 'Vigilante marketing and consumer-created communications', *Journal of Advertising*, 36 (3): 35–50.

Naylor, R. W., Lamberton, C. P. and West, P. M. (2012), 'Beyond the "Like" button: The impact of mere virtual presence on brand evaluations and purchase intentions in social media settings', *Journal of Marketing*, 76 (6): 105–20.

O'Guinn, T. C. and Muñiz, A. M., Jr (2005), 'Communal consumption and the brand', in S. Ratneshwar and D. G. Mick (eds), *Inside Consumption: Consumer Motives, Goals, and Desires*, London: Routledge, p. 252.

O'Guinn, T. C. and Muñiz, A. M., Jr (2008), 'Collective brand relationships', in D. J. MacInnis, C. Whan Park and J. R. Priester (eds), *Handbook of Brand Relationships*, Armonk, NY: M. E. Sharpe, pp. 173–94.

Pamentier, M. and Fischer, E. (2012), 'Interactive online audiences', in R. Llamas and R. Belk (eds), *The Routledge Companion to Digital Consumption*, London: Routledge, pp. 171–82.

Rowley, J. (2008), 'Understanding digital content marketing', *Journal of Marketing Management*, 28 (5–6): 517–40.

Schau, H. J., Muñiz, A. M. Jr and Arnould, E. J. (2009), 'How brand communities create value', *Journal of Marketing*, 73 (5): 30–51.

Schouten, J. W. and McAlexander, J. (1995), 'Subcultures of consumption: An ethnography of the new bikers', *Journal of Consumer Research*, 22 (1): 43–61.

Thompson, S. A. and Sinha, R. K. (2008), 'Brand communities and new product adoption: The influence and limits of oppositional loyalty', *Journal of Marketing*, 72 (6): 65–80.

Vargo, S. L. and Lusch, R. (2004), 'Evolving to a new dominant logic for marketing, *Journal of Marketing*, 68 (1): 1–17.

Wipperfürth, A. (2005), *Brand Hijack: Marketing without Marketing*, New York: Portfolio.

10 The cultural approach

with a commentary by Founder and President of Cultural Strategy Group, former Professor Douglas B. Holt

Starbucks is often referred to as an iconic brand. In 1971, Starbucks was founded as one single coffee shop in Seattle; by 2014, the American corporation owned more than 20,500 coffee shops and stores around the world. Starbucks initiated what subsequently has been referred to as the 'Starbucks Revolution', which is an expression of how much Starbucks has changed the way coffee is consumed all around the world. The financial success is substantial and Starbucks is one of the global 'brand icons' serving as a common frame of reference.

Starbucks is, however, also subjected to criticism for acting as a cultural imperialist and a quencher of local coffee shops. This dualism – the tremendous success of the Starbucks brand and the concerns it spurs – is characteristic of the cultural approach. The approach was founded in 2002, when a new brand perspective was presented in the article 'Why do brands cause trouble? A dialectical theory of consumer culture and branding' by Douglas B. Holt. The new perspective is a cultural one; encompassing both the mechanisms behind cultural branding (how brands become iconic) and an ideological, critical brand perspective. The 2002 article relates to both perspectives of cultural branding.

The cultural approach has since evolved into two very different streams of literature. The theory of how to deliberately use cultural sources to build iconic brands is managerial by nature, while the ideological stream definitely is not. Managerial, ethical, political and philosophical discussions rage in the cultural approach alongside research into to what extent consumers can or cannot liberate themselves from consumer culture.

Still, the two streams of literature have the same point of departure, the same brand perspective, consumer perspective and thereby they adhere to the same paradigmatic assumptions about the brand–consumer exchange – and hence the same approach. However, for pedagogical reasons, we will present the two streams of literature separately; therefore, this chapter will feature two sub-chapters reflecting the two streams of research literature activated to explore: 'iconic brands' and 'ideological issues'.

The theory about how to build an iconic brand is very much the doing of researcher and author Douglas B. Holt. The managerial aspects of the cultural brand perspective articulated in the seminal 2002 article are elaborated greatly in *How to Build an Iconic Brand* (2004) and *Cultural Strategy* (2010).

The ideological discourse has very much developed through the publication of several academic articles. The most recent literature deals with global, ideological issues with both positive and negative stances towards global, Western brands. Though critical and ideological by nature, these articles (or their subject of analysis, critical consumers) have led to new managerial practices, namely that corporate social responsibility has become a must in the toolbox of any contemporary brand manager. Corporate social responsibility is also investigated in the research, and concrete managerial implications are deduced.

These two streams of literature are in many respects opposing, still the founding 2002 article presents the most logical bridge between the two with the concept of the citizen–artist brand; a brand *both* communicating relevant cultural meaning and acting as a responsible citizen. Hence, this article both establishes the approach and bridges the contained dilemmas of it.

Box 10.1 Learning objectives

The purpose of this chapter is to:

Understand the assumptions of the cultural approach

- The brand is perceived as a cultural artefact and a cultural brand perspective is hence introduced in brand management.

Understand the main supporting theories and how they are connected

- The theory of cultural branding – a study into how brands become icons.
- An ideological movement.
- The citizen-artist brand prospect – a viable brand scenario for the future of cultural branding.

Provide insights into the variety of methods used to research cultural consumption

- In order to understand cultural consumption, macro-level analysis is applied to a variety of micro-level data.

Understand the managerial implications

- The management of an iconic brand requires the ability to think and act like a cultural activist.
- The management of all brands requires consideration of corporate social responsibility.

Understand the academic evolution of the cultural approach

The last approach of this book is called the cultural approach, because it is based on analysis of brands and branding in the light of cultural influences. The approach emphasizes the cultural forces in society and how these can be used to build iconic brands, as well as the impact of branding practices on the globalized culture and marketplace.

As mentioned in the introduction, this chapter will be structured a bit differently from the other approaches. First, we will present the general assumptions of the approach; they are the same for the two streams of literature (why it is one approach and not two). After that, we will first present the theories, methods and managerial implications of the 'iconic brands' and after that the same topics related to the 'ideological issues'. The notion of the citizen-artist brand will be presented at the end of the chapter as a natural bridge between the two traditions within the same mindset (see Figure 10.1).

Assumptions of the cultural approach

The individual brand perspectives introduced in the 1990s (the consumer-based approach, the personality approach and the relational approach) had different takes on understanding the exchange between a marketer and a consumer. The consumer-based approach turned the spotlight on the consumer, while the personality approach and the relational approach further constituted brand value as something co-created in a dialogue between marketer and consumer (the 'dyadic' brand relationship). The community approach added meaning found in the social interaction *among* dedicated brand consumers (the 'triadic' brand relationship) to the main theories of brand value creation. Inspired by cultural studies, the cultural brand perspective adds the exchange between macro-level culture and brands to the picture. The literature deals with the way marketers can deliberately use cultural forces to build strong brands (ultimately brand icons) and what brands and branding do to culture.

It is consumer culture rather than the individual consumer that is researched in the cultural approach. One could argue that the pivotal point is still the brand meaning found in groups of consumers just as in the community approach, but the focus of analysis is completely different:

> In contrast [to research in communities], this article focuses on brand co-creation in a context where brands are not the central focus; thus, it is necessary to unpack the meanings and sociocultural processes that continually problematize and ensure a brand's legitimacy to its various consumer groupings.
>
> (Kates 2004, p. 455)

Consumer Culture Theory[1] (CCT) (Arnould and Thompson 2005) is very much the foundation of the streams of literature melting together in this approach. CCT, 'refers to a family of theoretical perspectives that address the dynamic relationships between consumer actions, the marketplace, and cultural meaning' (Arnould and Thompson 2005, p. 868).

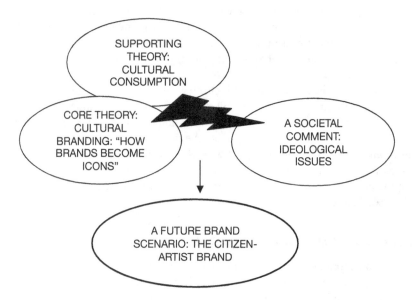

Figure 10.1 The core and supporting theories (cultural consumption), the societal
          comment on brand icons (the No Logo movement) and the future brand
          scenario (the citizen-artist brand)

Box 10.2 Macro-level culture defined

The identity approach (Chapter 5) is also concerned with cultural aspects
of branding. In the identity approach, culture is defined as culture at a
micro level – specifically organizational culture. The cultural approach
focuses on culture in a macro perspective, applying findings from the
culture surrounding us all to branding practices.

In this approach, macro-level culture is defined as the *social* definition
of culture. In this definition, culture is closely intertwined with meaning and
communication. In specific cultures, specific meanings and values are
shared (as collective representations) and it is through this common ground
of understanding that a culture can be said to exist. Cultural studies
departing from this definition of culture hence attempt to clarify the explicit
and implicit meanings of the culture in question, as well as understanding
how meaning is produced and circulated.

Source: du Gay *et al.* (1997)

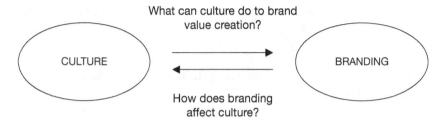

What can culture do to brand
value creation?

CULTURE

BRANDING

How does branding
affect culture?

Figure 10.2 Scope of the cultural approach

CCT (and the cultural approach) does *not* refer to the homogenous understandings of national culture (e.g. Danish culture, British culture, American culture spilling into country-of-origin effects on brands associated with the country in question), but rather, 'explores the heterogeneous distribution of meanings and the multiplicity of overlapping cultural groupings that exist within the broader sociohistoric frame of gloablization and market capitalism.' (Arnould and Thompson 2005, p. 869).

The 'brand–consumer exchange'

In the cultural approach, the brand is analysed as a 'cultural artifact moving through history' (Holt 2004, p. 215) and is as such comparable to, for example, a Hollywood movie, a Pulitzer Prize-winning novel or a music festival concert. The brand is a storyteller, endowed with cultural meaning and an important factor in the intricate web of cultural meanings used in the collective identity projects of consumers. In that sense, the brand is 'a vessel of meaning', successful only if it resonates with consumers' collective identity projects of the time. Understanding the brand–consumer exchange in the relational approach also requires an understanding of the collective identity projects of consumers. It is, however, important to note that the understanding and focus of consumers' identity projects is different in the two approaches. In the cultural approach, consumers' identity projects are analysed at a (macro) collective level. The relational approach is concerned with the understanding of individual identity projects as important contributors to brand meaning (refer to Chapter 12 for elaboration and additional literature about identity projects).

In the macro-level focus of culture, the brand is also a significant political and financial power and is at the centre of debate when it comes to issues and discussion surrounding globalization issues:

> With the growing impact of market institutions on almost all aspects of our lives, it does not take much imagination to see 'brands' and 'branding' as part of an increasingly dominant market economic and commercial ideoscape carried by organizations such as WTO, by marketing and management practices

and by the contemporary sovereign status of the liberal market economy. As [part of] such an ideoscape, branding is becoming central to the structuring of commercial and economic activities in still larger parts of the world.

(Askegaard 2006, p. 92)

One may argue that brands are among the most significant ideoscapes in the globalization processes.

(Askegaard 2006, p. 94)

(Please refer to Chapter 12 for elaboration and additional literature about ideoscapes.)

The cultural brand perspective assumes a consumer who is very much embedded in the symbolic universes of branding:

Branding also causes a new consumer to form, a consumer who is brand conscious in the largest sense: a consumer for whom these new symbolic universes gradually become some of the most central parts of his or her identity formation, both individually and in groups.

(Askegaard 2006, p. 100)

The consumer of the cultural approach is a 'no man is an island' man. Embedded in and influenced by the surrounding culture, the cultural brand perspective assumes that it is the collective brand meaning creation that is important and relevant to the consumer: *homo mercans* or market man (Askegaard 2006) is deeply embedded – or trapped, depending on the point of view – in consumer culture:

Market man is forged out of the interplay between different technologies: technologies of production, which allow us to transform and manipulate things; of sign systems, which allow us to use meanings, symbols or significations; of power, which directs the conduct of individuals; and of the self, which allows us to affect our way of being so as to reach a certain state of being.

(Garsten and Hasselström 2004, p. 213)

The role of the marketer implies bird perspective, and brand value is created through playing an active role in mainstream culture. The brand is subjected to social and cultural changes and thereby influenced by changes completely outside the brand manager's control. On the one hand, this means that the marketer is not the only author behind the brand meanings. On the other, a brand manager who manages to understand the most relevant cultural currents will be able to write the proper 'manuscript' for the brand to benefit from pervasive cultural issues of the time. In that sense, the brand gains competitive power by providing the consumer with the appropriate web of cultural meanings and the most powerful myths of its time.

The cultural perspective focuses a lot on advertising and its symbolic meanings: 'Consumer culture theory explores how consumers actively rework and transform symbolic meanings encoded in advertisements, brands, retail settings, or material goods to manifest their particular personal and social circumstances and further their identity and lifestyle goals' (Arnould and Thompson 2005, p. 871).

Even though both streams of literature held in this approach potentially put a lot of strain on the organization behind the brand (either if communicating like an iconic brand or committing wholeheartedly to corporate social responsibility), the organizational aspects of the brand are not mentioned in the literature. The cultural approach has a strong focus on the symbolic language of brands.

The cultural perspective

The perspective of the cultural approach embeds brand consumption in a macro-level cultural context and it is linked to the tradition of cultural studies. The culture researched in the cultural approach surrounds us all; subcultural, national and global are all valid analysis levels and concerns of the cultural brand perspective. No matter the level of analysis, the point of departure is conflict substance and not the country-of-origin culture of the brand.

Viewing consumption through the cultural lens means that all aspects of consumption experiences are analysed in their respective cultural context. The approach 'borrows' methods from different scientific traditions, such as phenomenological interviews, ethnographic field studies and netnography. The macro level of analysis, however, makes the interpretation of the data different from other approaches. The following quote illustrates well how data derived from phenomenological interviews are interpreted in the cultural approach:

> This hermeneutic mode of interpretation is premised on the idea that a given consumer is not expressing a strictly subjective viewpoint. Instead, he or she is articulating a culturally shared system of meanings and beliefs, personalized to fit his or her specific life goals and circumstances.
>
> (Thompson *et al.* 2006, p. 55)

This is a typical example of how the researchers of the cultural approach use methodologies from different scientific traditions for data collection (in this case, the phenomenological/existentialist tradition behind the relational approach) and 'elevate' their findings to a cultural level through a macro-level analysis. This will be explained in more detail in the methods and data section of this chapter.

Summary

This 'cluster' of brand literature introduces the cultural brand perspective, where the brand acts as a cultural artefact, broadening the focus of analysis from an individual consumer level to a macro level about the role brands play in consumer culture. The approach focuses on what brands do to culture and what culture can do to brands. Core to the cultural approach are brand icons and the countercultural anti-branding movements. Iconic brands are the ones that have managed to integrate themselves in culture more skilfully than others. At the same time, brand icons are also subjected to the greatest concerns (regarding cultural imperialism, cultural standardization and globalization). Core to the cultural approach is also the idea of the marketer deliberately endowing the brand with cultural meaning and through that playing an active role in consumer culture. The brand is seen as 'a storied product' and the cultural approach reveals the mechanisms behind brands becoming icons. At the same time, the approach also relates to a consumer culture increasingly concerned with the branded products, pressuring for changes in the way brands behave. The consumer of this approach is a *homo mercans*, a market man woven into the intricate meaning found in cultural consumer objects. How these assumptions rub off on to theories, methods and managerial implications will be explained in the following sections.

Iconic brands: theoretical framework

The theory on cultural branding by Douglas B. Holt (elaborated in the textbooks *How Brands Become Icons* (2004) and *Cultural Strategy* (2010)) is a cornerstone in the cultural approach and serves as the core theory. Different from the majority of the publications with a cultural perspective, this theory is focused on the *management* of brands, and the overall recommendation is to understand brands as cultural entities, 'storied products' able to tell relevant, interesting stories instead of being restricted to traditional commercial communication. The cultural branding model is closely related to the theory on cultural consumption formulated by Grant McCracken. Understanding the basic way of thinking about consumption in a cultural context facilitates the further reading of the theory on how brands become icons, which is why a basic understanding of cultural consumption serves as the supporting theory.

Supporting theory: cultural consumption

Canadian anthropologist Grant McCracken conceptualized a cultural perspective on consumption in the 1980s. His theories have since become central to the understanding of consumption in a cultural context. If one considers the culture definition behind this approach, it is obvious that McCracken's theory is a prerequisite for understanding the production and circulation of cultural meaning through consumption goods. It is important to notice that cultural consumption is not about the consumption of cultural objects (books, music, etc.) but is applied to all consumer goods that are regarded as equal circulators of meaning.

Pivotal in the theory of cultural consumption is the notion of culture and consumption operating as a system. This cultural consumption paradigm acknowledges that goods not only have a utilitarian character, they are also able to carry and communicate cultural meaning. The cultural meaning is mobile, flowing and always in transition. Meaning is transferred from the culturally constituted world into consumer goods and through the consumption of goods integrated into the lives of consumers. In this fashion, cultural meaning is integrated into the lives of consumers through consumption.

Cultural meaning from the culturally constituted world is incorporated into consumer goods by the advertising and fashion system. The idea is that the advertising system and the fashion system pick fragments of meaning and bestow them on products through advertising and the media. These fragments are found in the everyday life that makes up the culturally constituted world. Hence, the fashion and advertising systems function as producers of meaning. Consumer goods are hence in the cultural approach circulators of meaning recognizable to the 'enculturated' (being a member of a culture endows you with the ability to read the right kind of meaning into the goods) consumer. The consumer thereby chooses meaning, adequate for his or her life by making consumption choices. If a certain consumer good delivers a meaningful take on your specific life situation, you adopt this meaning through consumption of that good. This is how goods become carriers of cultural meaning besides possessing a utilitarian value. In the consumption of goods, consumers thereby also choose to consume the cultural meaning, which seems most appropriate to suit their lives. The cultural consumer system supplies humans with the cultural materials to realize their various ideas of what it is to be, for example a man or a woman, middle-aged or elderly, a parent, a citizen or a professional:

> All of these cultural notions are concretized in goods, and it is through their possession and use that the individual realizes the notions in his own life.
>
> (McCracken 1988, p. 88)

This conceptualization of the transfer of cultural meaning draws heavily on semiotics. Semiotics is the study of signs and symbols in communication. Signs and symbols are considered able to communicate meaning differently from the word, picture (or a composition of words, images and sound as in an advertisement, for example) itself. The interpretation of the sign systems is dependent on the interpreter and his cultural and personal background: 'The meaning of signs is arbitrary. In principle, anything could stand for anything else. It is the cultural context that frames the interpretation of signs and imbues particular signs with localized meanings' (Hackley 2003, p. 162). Intertextuality is an important aspect of semiotics; meaning that a 'text' refers to another 'text' which again refers to something else. It is obvious that the level of cultural 'literacy' and general cultural knowledge (enculturation) very much determine the interpretation of the 'text'. The marketing system is therefore the creator of a 'string of signs'; marketing communications are composed of multiple layers of meaning. The production and circulation of meaning has no beginning and no end.

Core theory: cultural branding

By now, the assumptions of, and logic behind, a cultural understanding of consumption should be clear. Douglas B. Holt is the researcher and author

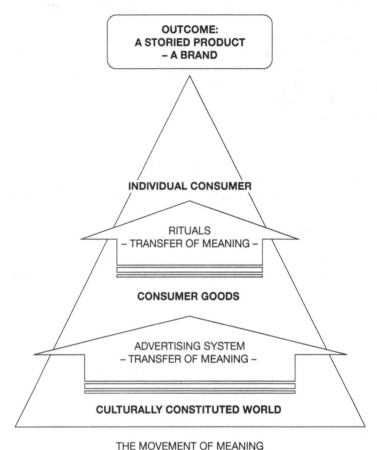

Figure 10.3 Movement of meaning from culture to consumer goods to individuals create
brands; adapted from McCracken (1988)

catapulting this understanding into the world of brand management through a
stream of journal articles (Holt 2002, 2003a, 2003b) and elaborated on in two
textbooks (Holt 2004, 2010). In an extensive empirical study of iconic brands,
Holt has conceptualized a new way of perceiving and managing brands. Cultural
branding is the strategic principles behind how to create and manage a brand and
alter it into an icon. Here, we do not tell stories related to either sender or receiver
of a message, but focus on stories related to cultural substance found elsewhere.

How Brands Become Icons presents a new recipe for success in brand management
based on extensive studies of the communication practices of iconic brands; and
Cultural Strategy translates the theories into very accessible managerial advice if one
wants to try out cultural branding.

Table 10.1 A comparison between the mindshare branding model and the cultural branding model

	The mindshare branding model	The cultural branding model
Brand communication	*Persuasion* – the purpose of advertising is to influence consumer perception of the brand through rhetoric	*Myth making* – communication is the centre of consumer value. The brand is a 'storied' product and the product is merely a means to embracing the story
Brand components	*Abstract associations* – the brand consists of a set of associations that is the brand's purified essence (brand DNA)	*Cultural expressions* – the brand's value is found in the cultural contents of the brand's myth. The brand has a reputation for performing certain myths
Brand management	*Consistency* – brand management is about upholding consistency in communications over time	*Historical fit* – brand management is about adapting the brand's myth to cultural changes in order to remain relevant

Source: Adapted from Holt (2004)

How Brands Become Icons

How Brands Become Icons presents research into the creation of the inspired and talented brand communication behind the iconic brands and is the first comprehensive research on branding in a cultural perspective. The theory is built from case studies of a selection of American iconic brands representing different industries, different company histories, competitive situations and consumer bases. Despite their differences, the brand icons under the microscope displayed definitive commonalities, which have led to their success. These success stories are the foundation of the cultural branding model; the theory of how brands become icons.

The point of departure is the same as McCracken's in the sense that brands and/or products are seen as endowed with cultural meaning, but Holt's theory is more precise and demanding. He pinpoints the need for addressing certain powerful cultural issues and contradictions before one is able to create myths that are so powerful and resonant that the brand becomes iconic.

What is an iconic brand?

A brand icon is an identity brand approaching the identity value of a cultural icon. An identity brand is a 'storied' brand, whose value to consumers (and, thus, its brand equity) derives primarily from identity value. Identity value is the aspect of a brand's value that derives from the brand's contributions to the self-expression of the consumer.

A cultural icon is a person or thing regarded as a symbol, especially of a culture or a movement – a person, institution and so forth – considered worthy of admiration or respect (definitions, Holt 2004, p. 11). An icon is an *exemplary* symbol. The cultural icons are exemplary symbols, resonant to a majority of people and offering the most potent and relevant solution to the cultural situation of their time. The same goes for brand icons; they have to address the most general concerns of the time in the most skilful way. In that sense, they have to *perform more representative and powerful myths to mainstream culture* than the identity brand (the brand strong enough to be used for self-expressive purposes).

Reebok, Pepsi and IBM are hence considered identity brands, meaning that they as brands are strong enough to contribute significantly to their consumers' self-expression. John Wayne, J.F.K. and Bruce Springsteen are considered cultural icons serving as exemplary and powerful symbols to a majority of people. And Apple, Nike and Harley Davidson are representatives of the brand icons: the few brands approaching the identity value of the cultural icons (see Table 10.2).

How does a brand become iconic?

Having established what a brand icon is, we now turn to the mechanisms behind the rise to iconic status. The empirical studies behind the cultural branding model establish that the rise to icon status happens mainly through advertising and can be aided by cultural industries (via product placement) and populist worlds (via viral branding):

> Identity brands must be very good at product quality, distribution, promo-
> tion, pricing, and customer service. But these attributes are simply the
> ante that marketers must pony up to be competitive. They aren't drivers of
> business success. Identity brands live or die on the quality of their com-
> munications.
>
> (Holt 2004, p. 225)

Table 10.2 Iconic brands are brands that have become cultural icons

	Identity brands	*Iconic brands*	*Cultural icons*
Definition	Brands strong enough to be used for self-expressive purposes	Brands strong enough to be considered exemplary symbols	People (real-life or fictional) who have become icons and are perceived as exemplary symbols
Identity value	Low	Medium	High
Examples	Reebok, Pepsi, IBM	Nike, Coca-Cola, Apple	J.F.K, Rambo, Oprah, Bruce Springsteen

Source: Adapted from Holt (2004)

There are four common denominators of how iconic brands communicate:

- *Target a cultural contradiction.* The iconic brands have been able to target cultural contradictions in society and perform a powerful myth to accommodate the tensions: 'Cultural branding works when the brand's stories connect powerfully with particular contradictions in American society' (Holt 2004, p. 224).
- *Act as a cultural activist.* Aspiring to the identity value of a cultural icon, radical action needs to be taken: 'Icons act as cultural leaders, as activists encouraging people to think and act differently through their stories' (Holt 2003b, p. 7).
- *Create original expressive culture as an artist.* Also, when it comes to aesthetics, the brand must lead the way and not just follow trends. The brand icons have managed to provide their own unique visual expression and thereby have provided consumers with something entirely new and original.
- *Develop an authentic populist voice.* A brand must be perceived as a credible representative of a 'populist epicentre' (a non-commercial place; e.g. subculture, folk culture or a social movement), that is where new non-commercial culture is being created. The brand must display a deep understanding of the point of view it represents.

Moving through time and cultural changes and still staying relevant is one of the great challenges of the iconic brands. The powerful myth has to be reinvented over and over again in congruence with the socio-political-economic-cultural changes: 'Iconic brands remain relevant when they adapt their myths to address the shifting contradictions that their constituents face' (Holt 2004). The cultural branding model is essentially very different from the mindshare branding model (Holt's term; in this book the consumer-based approach) as the mindshare model establishes that consistency in brand communication is what builds a strong brand. The aim of this book is the side-by-side presentation of the seven 'ideal types', not to discuss if one approach is superior to another. Emphasizing the differences between the mindshare model (the consumer-based approach) and the cultural model (this approach), however, facilitates the understanding of both approaches, which is why their most fundamental differences are depicted in Table 10.1.

Cultural strategy

The knowledge presented in *How Brands Become Icons* is translated into concrete recommendations in *Cultural Strategy* (2010) – again framed in opposition to the consumer-based approach: 'Our goal then was to transform the practice of brand management, challenging the psychology-driven model that has gained favour in the 1970's' (Holt and Cameron 2010, p. ix). The book emphasizes the possibility of making radical (brand) innovation by means of diving into the rich material of mainstream culture. Mindshare branding creates 'red oceans' while cultural branding can create 'blue oceans'[2] (in a branding-context) and is proposed to be a better

Box 10.3 How Snapple became an iconic brand

In 1972, healthy fruit drink brand Snapple saw the light of day in Brooklyn. In 1993, Snapple's sales had climbed to an annual $516 million and the company was bought by Quaker Oats for $1.7 billion. The marketing strategy behind the huge financial success encompassed the four steps mentioned above:

- *Target a cultural contradiction.* During the 1980s, the United States led by President Reagan was going through hard times in order to become a more dynamic economy. The labour market was marked by constant restructuring and downsizing. Around 1990, the labour market had become quite unbalanced, with companies and elites profiting well but also large parts of the population left with 'McJobs', sparking a current of discontent and disbelief in corporate America as well as among elected officials. Snapple managed to address this societal imbalance – or cultural contradiction – by authoring a myth about a company run by amateurs, indirectly suggesting that the 'overpaid' elites in marketing departments of other companies were not needed at all. Consuming a bottle of Snapple became a way of embracing that cultural meaning.
- *Act as a cultural activist.* Before the rest of the world became truly aware of the powerful tensions in US society, Snapple acted as an instigator of the new myths regarding the company run by a bunch of playful amateurs, giving vent to deep societal frustration. Thereby, Snapple managed to comment on an important tension before most people managed to even verbalize the problems.
- *Create original expressive culture as an artist.* Snapple's branding activities (new product development, advertising, design and promotion) were radically new in aesthetics, and yet unified in the expression of the brand's political voice. All these activities displayed an ironic comment on the society at the time through a credible aura of amateurism. Tennis player Ivan Lendl became a spokesperson because he was a fan, even though he mispronounced the brand name in the television ads. 'Wendy the Snapple lady' became a star of many television ads. Wendy was a clerk working at Snapple who had taken up the job of answering letters from consumers. Wendy, who was quite far from the beauty standards of advertising, became very popular as 'the real thing'. To mock the celebrity events sponsored by competing companies such as Coca-Cola and Pepsi, Snapple became the sponsor of events like cherry spitting in Minnesota and yo-yo tossing in New York.
- *Develop an authentic populist voice.* Snapple hired two radio hosts as endorsers of the brand. Rush Limbaugh and Howard Stern could not be more different, coming from both ends of the political spectrum, but both represented defiance against the establishment and expressed a genuine affection for Snapple. Their endorsement is one example of how Snapple gained credibility from a populist epicentre.

Source: Holt (2003b)

strategy than trying to grow through traditional innovation ('building a better mousetrap' in the terminology of *Cultural Strategy*) (Holt and Cameron 2010).

Instead of stressing minor product innovation and communicating a set of associations, the culturally relevant brands tap into the relevant cultural fabric of the time. The cultural fabric might be very innovative and the perfect background for conducting the cultural strategy. One example is how the world of food consumption has changed in the first decade of the twenty-first century:

> [F]armer-cookbook-author-television host Hugh Fearnley-Whittingstall, author Michael Pollan, the international Slow Food movement, and the American grocery retailer Whole Foods Market, amongst others, have transformed food consumption for the upper middle class. [. . .] Relying upon what we term *myth* and *cultural codes*, these cultural innovators have massively transformed food preferences.
>
> (Holt and Cameron 2010, p. 2)

This is cultural innovation and what every imaginative brand manager should either tap into or try to participate in. One of the cases, often referred to in the groundwork in *How Brands Become Icons* is Corona and their success is explained as based on their ability to tap into an ideology of a given time – and not the product itself: 'These beers were me-too product offerings . . . But as brands, they offered very innovative cultural expressions that resonated perfectly with the ideological needs of their target' (Holt and Cameron 2010, p. 6).

The six-stage strategic framework

Cultural Strategy presents a six-stage strategic framework, which is a hands-on interpretation of the findings from *How Brands Become Icons*. In this section, we will first outline the framework and thereafter exemplify the six steps through the case of Clearblue pregnancy tests.

- *Map the category's cultural orthodoxy* – get an overview of the conventional cultural expression (ideology, myth and cultural codes) of the category. How do competitors communicate? Which stories and tendencies do they convey in their brand communication?
- *Identify the social disruption that can dislodge the orthodoxy* – here, we have to get a hold of the conflict substance in society (think about the 'cultural and social contradictions' explained in the section about iconic brands). In this social disruption, you will find the changes that have the potential to change the ideology of the category.
- *Unearth the ideological opportunity* – here, you unearth the identity projects of the relevant consumers (collective, remember?). Look for 'collective desires' and 'collective anxieties'.
- *Cull appropriate source material* – it is time to sample relevant material in order to energize the strategy. Cultural expressions lurk in subcultures, social

movements and media myths (read more about data collection methods later in this chapter).

- *Apply cultural tactics* – the authors have established a 'laundry list' of powerful tactics (provoking ideological flashpoints, mythologizing the company, resuscitating reactionary ideology, cultural capital trickle-down, crossing the cultural chasm and cultural jiujitsu). In order to truly understand these tactics, one needs to read the cases of *Cultural Strategy*.
- *Craft the cultural strategy* – the cultural brief is different from traditional branding briefs. The briefs are full and detailed descriptions of the cultural strategy: 'Cultural strategies are detailed documents that specify nuanced direction in terms of ideology, myth, and cultural codes. In cultural innovation, details matter' (Holt and Cameron 2010, p. 199).

The idea of brands benefitting from tapping into mainstream/subcultural meaning is in recent research extended by the idea of brands benefitting from even *producing cultural material themselves*. In a study of the toy brand American Girl (chosen because of its innovative brand management), the researchers propose that: 'As an original producer of cultural meaning, it may be viewed as a prototypical "future brand"' (Diamond *et al.* 2009, p. 131). American Girl not only becomes relevant by tapping into relevant cultural issues but has taken upon itself the task of – through their products and a lot of other well-managed touchpoints – telling American history to young (mostly) girls, their mothers and grandmothers.

Methods and data in the cultural approach

In order to understand the production and circulation of cultural meaning central to the cultural approach, a certain approach to data collection is required. The cultural approach displays a variety of methods and data 'borrowed' from different interpretive research traditions. What binds the studies together is that all data are interpreted in a macro perspective. Furthermore, the basics of semiotics are important to understand if one is considering gathering knowledge about cultural consumption.

Semiotics

Understanding the production and circulation of meaning fundamental to the cultural consumption perspective requires insight into semiotic methods. When conducting semiotic marketing studies one deconstructs the meaning displayed in commercial communication. Samples of commercial communications (e.g. brand logos, television advertisements, print ads, package designs and shopping malls) are the objects of study and should be deconstructed accordingly. The objects are supposed to be made strange and unfamiliar in order to go beyond the 'taken-for-granted' meanings. Semiotic codes should then be decoded and the intertextual strings of signs deconstructed.

Box 10.4 The case of Clearblue pregnancy tests

A number of cases carried out by the two (consulting) authors form a large part of *Cultural Strategy*. The case of Clearblue is used here to exemplify *the six-stage strategic framework* (consult the textbook for all case details).

- **Cultural orthodoxy** – through analysis of the rhetoric of Clearblue's competition, the term *Patriarchal Medicine* became a pivotal point in the process of creating the cultural strategy of Clearblue. In the existing symbolic context, women are passive and married, and a woman taking a pregnancy test always (!) crosses her fingers anxiously in the hope of a positive result. Male doctors are the authoritative figures in this communication and husbands are somewhat patronizing figures cut after a 1950s mould.
- **Social disruption/Source material** – the authors looked for relevant subcultural material and discourses among the target segment of women between 16 and 40 – preferably material picked up by media and turned into a media myth. To make a long (and very interesting) story short, they ended up with the idea of *Body-Positive Feminism*, a third wave of feminism shared among definitely not shy nor prudish, active confident women and expressed in its pure form via publications like Bust, Bitch and Nerve.com. The passive and married woman of the cultural orthodoxy was definitely a figure of the past!
- **Ideological opportunity** – the authors held identity interviews with representatives from the target segment, and the women confirmed the relaxed and playful attitude towards body issues and sexuality. The data from the interviews was triangulated with the cultural tapestry described as Body-Positive Feminism. Powerful media expressions of interest were *Sex and the City* and *The Vagina Monologues* and the ideological opportunity became clear; 'Clearblue should **champion body-positive feminism in women's reproductive health**' (Holt 2010, p. 213, our highlight).
- **Cultural tactics/Cultural strategy** – A manifesto was created, for example featuring these lines: *'Clearblue champions a body-positive feminist view of reproduction and women's health. Clearblue celebrates women's bodies. We are not embarrassed by them. We see reproductive health as playful and fun, not "sinful" or "unladylike".'* (Holt 2010, p. 214). Further, the tactic of 'provoking an ideological flashpoint' was chosen because of the controversy still held in body-positive feminism. This ideological flashpoint was the point of departure for the central, creative idea; **puncturing a lot of taboos by addressing the fact that you have to pee on a pregnancy test, openly**. A playful, ironic way of communication to the body-positive third-wave feminists was crafted on this foundation.

Source: Holt and Cameron 2010

Box 10.5 Doing semiotics

Questions to ask

- What does X signify to me?
- Why does X signify this to me?
- What might X signify for others?
- Why might X signify this for others?

Sources of X

- Objects, for example clothes, hairstyle, make-up, logos, graphic design
- Gesture, for example body types, faces, expressive gestures, postures
- Speech, for example accent or dialect, use of metaphor, tone or volume of speech, use of humour

Source: Hackley (2003)

Intertextuality is an important aspect of semiotics. The commercial message (the brand in this case) is regarded as a cultural 'text' like other cultural expressions. Intertextuality is the idea of texts referring to other texts. When, for instance, a cosmetics brand signs a famous actress as their 'face', the brand becomes related to the movies the actress has starred in. These movies are linked with other cultural 'texts', such as the book behind the script, other actors and the famous director who once won an Oscar and so on and so on.

These 'strings of signs' and 'strings of text' can be deconstructed individually or in focus groups. It is important to understand that all ends are open-ended in semiotics; meaning that there are no right or wrong answers and that the deconstruction of a 'text' will depend entirely on the enculturation of the respondent. Still, different interpretations add up to a more varied interpretation of the text.

Other methods

Other methods are used to collect knowledge of the production and circulation of cultural meaning. Cultural brand research displays a wide variety of data collection. Ethnographic, phenomenological interviews and case methods are the most important ones; creativity is key and a one-fits-all approach to data collection does not exist.

- Ethnographic studies are suitable for understanding the consumer in a cultural setting. In general, the ethnographic research tradition is aimed at understanding man in his cultural setting and is, as such, important if one is collecting data on the cultural aspects of consumption. Conducting an ethnographic field study requires a high degree of immersion and no delimitations when it comes to data sources. Here, the researcher is supposed to participate in consumption practices and not delimit himself from any kind of data source. Please refer to the methods section of Chapter 9 for a more full description of the ethnographic research tradition.

- Phenomenological interviews are also viable methods in the cultural approach. The approach is very much concerned with understanding the collective identity projects of consumers. Phenomenological interviews are excellent for the inquiry into individual identity projects, and through a macro-level analysis and interpretation the data from the individual interviews can be applied to a cultural setting, shedding light on the collective identity projects of consumers. Please refer to the methods section of Chapter 8 for guidelines on how to master the technique of the long, unstructured interview.

- In the American Girl case research, a plethora of methods was applied in order to understand the multigenerational aspect of the brand. In-home interviews were conducted, families were approached in buses going to the American Girl store and researchers went to the store with the families. Participation, observations and participant playing with the dolls took place in the retail environment. Videos, audios and notes supported the three-year long data collection process. Organization members were interviewed and articles in the press were also consulted (Diamond *et al.* 2009). This is the research method behind an academic study, but goes to show that a very creative and all-encompassing research design is recommendable when wanting to grasp the cultural aspects of a given brand.

- As explained in the section about the ideological issues of this approach, the Internet is an ideological battlefield where alternative brand agendas are cultivated and negotiated. Please refer to the section about netnography in Chapter 7 in order to find inspiration for this type of research.

- The 'extended case method' is a discovery-oriented method of anthropological descent where a relatively small sample of informants is studied closely through loosely structured, long interviews and observations in their homes and environments. The cultural approach is focused on understanding the most important cultural contradictions of the time. Investigating relevant consumer groups by means of this method might provide great insight into these contradictions. This is the research method behind the citizen-artist brand prospect.

- In the rich case collection of *Cultural Strategy*, it is stressed that data collection should be customized for each project. The curious exploration of the cultural tapestry of a given category as well as the very different historical potential of each brand in question is essential:

> For the Nike case, we relied on the extensive documentation of Nike, including oral histories, archived at the Smithsonian Museum in Washington, DC. For the Marlboro case, we analyzed the entire collection of Marlboro advertising held in the Library of Congress archives, as

well as the oral history accounts of the campaign offered by Phillip
Morris and Leo Burnett executives, also collected by the library. . . . The
Starbucks and Vitaminwater cases relied upon secondary materials in
the public domain.

(Holt and Cameron 2010, p. xi)

The interpretation of the collected data is very important, because the focus of
analysis is unique to the cultural approach. A 'bottom-up' interpretation of data is
applied; the informants are not expected to express idiosyncratic meanings, but
rather to be acting as mouthpieces of the surrounding culture: 'To study how
consumer culture operates, I examine the phenomena that it structures, people's
everyday consumption practices. In methodological terms, I will use microlevel
data – people's stories about their consumption – to investigate macrolevel
constructs' (Holt 2002, p. 73).

Box 10.6 Doing a cultural study yourself

- Immerse yourself in the environment of research like a true ethnographer.
- Conduct long phenomenological interviews.
- Deconstruct the 'strings of signs' of commercial communication.
- Test the enculturation of relevant cultural groups by having them deconstruct the same commercial texts.
- Sample cultural knowledge of the relevant cultural context.
- Conduct extended case studies of individuals of specific interest.
- Consider analysing historical sources of symbolism and discourse.
- Most important: feel free to pick the most suitable methods for your research design,
- . . . but be sure to submit all your micro-level data to a macro-level interpretation . . .
- . . . as you bear in mind the golden rule of regarding your informants as mouthpieces of their cultural context!

Summary

The cultural approach 'borrows' methods and data from other approaches to science.
Phenomenological interviews, ethnographic immersion, case methods and the
semiotic decoding of commercial and cultural manifestations are all legitimate data
in this approach when attempting to shed light on the cultural aspect of brands
and branding. What makes the methods and data stand out compared with their
use in the other approaches is the macro-level interpretation they are subjected to.
The informants are not assumed to speak entirely idiosyncratic beliefs and

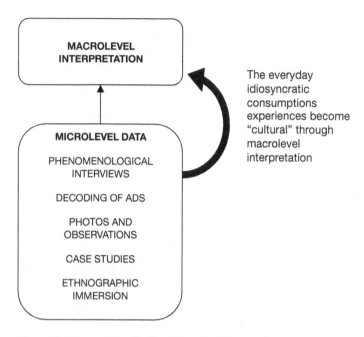

Figure 10.4 Research methods of the cultural approach

opinions, but rather they are considered representatives of the surrounding culture (see Figure 10.4).

The management of an iconic brand

The brand manager of an iconic brand – or an identity brand striving for iconic status – should get ready for a rather complicated work agenda. The brand is regarded as a medium for cultural expression and the path to icon status requires the ability to create radical cultural expressions. Supposed to act as a cultural activist quite far from the standard business school type, the brand manager is above all the composer of the brand's myth: 'As cultural activists, managers treat their brand as a medium – no different from a novel or a film – to deliver provocative creative materials that respond to society's new cultural needs' (Holt 2004, p. 219). The activist managers should not only be able to understand the legacy of the brand as a myth creator but also be able to be a cultural trend setter by *not* exploiting what is hot and happening right now but rather be the one *defining* hot and happening.

The cultural brand management process consists of two stages: gathering and analysing cultural knowledge and composing the cultural brand strategy. The gathering of relevant cultural knowledge is required; cultural contradictions must be identified and uncovered. The identification of emerging cultural contradictions requires a thorough understanding of the cultural context, and the empathetic

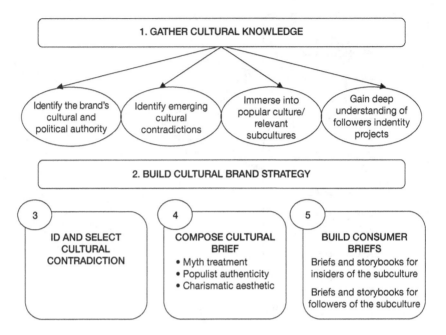

Figure 10.5 Gather cultural knowledge to build a cultural brand strategy

understanding of the identity projects of consumers is different from the gathering of traditional consumer research data. A different kind of consumer knowledge is required: 'Rather than static, microscopic research that delivers a snapshot of individual consumers, genealogy is macroscopic and dialectical' (Holt 2004, p. 214) (see Figure 10.5).

The building of great myths requires an empathetic and deep (macro-level) understanding of the collective identity projects of the relevant consumer segment. The manager needs to deeply understand the cultural contradictions of the time and how they feed the hopes and anxieties of, for example, a generation of American urban middle-class people: 'Resonant myths spring from an understanding of people's ambitions at work, their dreams for their children, their fears of technology, their difficulties in building friendships, and so on' (Holt 2004, p. 212).

The brand manager also has to understand the reputation of the brand. In the cultural approach, the brand's reputation is considered to be the reputation for telling certain kind of stories – for competing in a certain myth market. This reputation endows the brand with a cultural and political authority, meaning that the brand has a reputation for telling stories/performing myths about a certain notion (e.g. freedom, cultural authority) aimed at certain cultural segments (political authority). In order for the brand manager to document the brand's cultural and political authority, he should look back in time to comprehend what historic activities constrain or enhance the future mythmaking ability of the brand.

Where one looks for the empathic understanding is also important. It cannot be found on the periphery of brand loyalists; it is the nucleus of brand insiders/ followers that can reveal the most significant 'outlets' of the cultural contradictions. Full immersion – or preferably a 'cultural membership' – in the relevant populist worlds is therefore required.

After having identified the most relevant cultural contradiction to target, the myth has to be composed and executed in the right way. A traditional positioning statement should be substituted by a 'myth treatment' (as in the film industry) in which the brand's proposed cultural role is clarified. The execution of the brand communication should elevate itself from being a parasite on popular cultural trends; it should rather develop a 'populist authenticity' on its own terms. Furthermore, the brand should communicate by means of its own charismatic aesthetics. In sum, the brand communication should adopt its own independent voice and play a proactive role in the culture of its time (eventually, re-refer to the Snapple case in Box 10.3). The successful brand is the most skilful commentator and provider of relevant cultural 'text' addressing the sociocultural tensions of the time.

Holt's ideas of managing the cultural brand are very oriented towards communication and advertisements – and thereby hold an interesting dilemma. Even though the theories are far-reaching, complex and demanding, they are also based on a very traditional idea of the brand. More recent ideas of the brand being dependent on every action of the company (as in the identity approach) are neglected. Organizational issues, co-creation and touchpoint management are neglected even though taking on a cultural strategy is a very opinionated and ambitious choice. The case study of American Girl is more focused on how the management of all touchpoints creates the future-proof brand and also on the co-creation taking place between the brand and its customers. The brand is described as a gestalt and a (somewhat) open source brand which affects the 'ownership' of the brand:

> marketers can retain a significant degree of control while choreographing coauthorship opportunities and that all four aspects of a brand – physical, textual, meaning and experience – can be 'opened' to consumer input, thus enhancing consumer value, while primary brand ownership remains with the corporation and value to the corporation is undiminished.
>
> (Diamond *et al.* 2009 p. 132)

Ideological issues: the societal response to brand icons (and branding in general)

Having understood the logic behind cultural consumption, the mechanisms of iconic brands, and how to work with cultural strategy, one needs to understand the other side of the ideological spectrum as well in order to understand the full scope of the cultural approach. The founding article from 2002 addresses both the need for communicating in a culturally relevant way as well as the need for being a responsible 'pillar of society'. The data collection in this article is conducted among people living on the brink of established consumer society and thereby investigates ideological and critical stances to branding and popular (consumer) culture.

Box 10. 7 The versatile brand manager of the cultural approach

Being a brand manager/cultural activist requires a distinct talent for multitasking. Holt proposes that the abilities of the brand manager should encompass:

- *The mindset and work methods of a genealogist.* A genealogist goes back in time in order to piece together a family tree. In much the same fashion, the brand manager is supposed to go back in time in order to understand the brand heritage and the brand's possibilities versus constraints for performing certain kinds of myths
- *A cultural historian's understanding of ideology.* National shifts in ideology are closely intertwined with cultural, political and economic changes. The brand manager who is able to understand the ideological shifts and the cultural changes they cause is skilled at targeting the most relevant tensions in society
- *A sociologist's charting of the topography of social contradictions.* Social contradictions are inevitably linked with cultural, economic and political changes. Developing an empathetic understanding of social contradictions enables the brand manager to perform powerful myths.
- *The willingness and ability to take on a literary expedition into popular culture.* Managing an iconic brand is all about developing a deep cultural understanding – and being able to deliver on it as a cultural activist. Having one's ear to the ground and understanding the cultural web is therefore a prerequisite.
- *The sensitivity and empathetic antennae of a writer.* Just like a writer is often able to observe life more than participate and still be the one who pinpoints the exact feelings of other people, the brand manager needs to have a sixth sense of what goes on beneath the surface of people's lives.

Source: Holt (2004)

In this section, we will present brief insights into the notion of 'doppelgänger brands', anti-branding discourse, corporate social responsibility and brands as part of the global ideoscape.

As mentioned in the introduction, Starbucks is emblematic of the dualism of the cultural approach, on one hand often referred to as an iconic brand, on the other often subject to criticism for acting as a cultural imperialist and for not taking interest and paying enough attention to fair trade, local coffee shops and so on. Its success hence goes hand in hand with being one of the brands that is most fiercely criticized by the anti-brand movement: 'Starbucks has become a cultural icon for all the rapacious excesses, predatory intentions, and cultural homogenizations that social critics attribute to globalizing corporate capitalism' (Thompson and Arsel 2004, p. 631).

Doppelgänger brands

Cultural agendas aimed negatively at your brand can be used as inspiration or warning signs of the branding strategy losing its appeal. Therefore, Thompson *et al.* (2006) introduce the term 'Doppelgänger brand image' as a theoretical term to describe the negative autonomous brand images circulating in our culture. Where Holt views the tension between brand icons and the global brand culture in the bigger picture (in the research behind the citizen-artist brand prospect), Thompson *et al.* view the tensions in a more concrete light, presenting the 'doppelgänger brand construct'. The 'doppelgänger brand' is a brand that has been subjected to 'culture jamming' and can provide hints about the need for a change of brand strategy. Therefore, any brand manager should be very conscious of anti-brand activities and take them as warning signs of a brand strategy losing its appeal. (Refer to Chapter 12 for elaboration and additional literature about doppelgänger brand image). A doppelgänger image should be seen as an early indication regarding flaws and imperfections in a brand's image and strategy:

> the analysis of a doppelgänger brand image can (1) call attention to cultural contradictions that potentially undermine the perceived authenticity of a firm's emotional-branding strategy, (2) provide early warning signs that an emotional-branding story is beginning to lose its value as an authenticating narrative for consumers' identity projects, and (3) offer insights into how an emotional-branding strategy can be reconfigured to fit better with changing cultural times and shifting consumer outlooks.
>
> (Thompson *et al.* 2006, p. 51)

A study into the case of Botox shows that there has been a continuous exchange between the intended communication from Botox and the accompanying negative cultural agenda created in mainstream culture. The contestation by mainstream culture has been instrumental in driving the intended image of Botox forward as Botox has kept updated its communication to overcome the 'doppelgänger' brand image (Giesler 2012).

Deep insight can be found in studying the ideological debates spurred by brands (intentionally and unintentionally), and the Internet is in this regard an ideological battlefield. Whether one wants to adjust an existing branding strategy or wants insight into ideological issues, the brand-related cultural issues tell us a lot about the symbolism and ideologies found in the 'brandscape' or 'ideoscape' that our consumer society is sometimes described as.

Big questions are linked to discussions about brands, which for example are studied in the case of the Hummer brand. This car brand whirls up 'underlying mythic dimensions of consumers' moralistic identity work' (Luedicke *et al.* 2010,

p. 1017). Some people love this brand, while others hate it and the meanings aired in the online as well as offline debates reveal that the people attacking Hummer think that Hummer drivers are 'mainstream consumers, who are frequently stereotyped as self-centered materialist and/or mesmerized dupes of the corporate system' (ibid., p. 1017). On the other hand, the defenders of the Hummer attack their ideological opponents for being anti-American and un-patriotic. By diving into the shared opinions about value-laden brands, one is able to understand a lot about the roles played by brands in our society. In a case study such as this one, we dive into bigger questions and more complex webs of symbolism and can learn a lot of value from a managerial perspective, but also understand how their symbolism triggers interesting opinions, ideas and values: 'By invoking the myth of the moral protagonist, consumers can frame ideological differences in terms of an essentially Calvinistic distinction between the elect (or saved) and the sinners' (ibid., p. 1028).

It goes without saying that the mechanisms described in the community approach (Chapter 9) are important in this context and make cultural movements and ideological debates spread like wildfires. Online consumer activism (Albinsson and Perena 2012, Handelman 2012) and the ages of transparency, criticism and parody (Fournier and Avery 2011) are phenomena fuelling these types of debates.

Anti-branding discourse

No Logo by Naomi Klein (2000) is the most well-known publication representing many of the concerns of the anti-brand movement. The managerially oriented theory on how brands become icons is faced with the societal response from the No Logo movement.

In the No Logo movement, branding efforts are critically analysed and linked with environmental issues, human rights and cultural degradation. The book is also a moral rebellion against the idea of corporations outsourcing production while focusing on the production of images. In that sense, No Logo is a serious attack on the idea of branding in itself and seriously questions whether the iconic brands

---

Box 10.8 Just another legal case or an early warning sign?

In 1999, San Francisco-based cartoonist Kieron Dwyer made comic books, t-shirts and stickers with his 'Consumer Whore' version of the Starbucks logo and sold them in the anti-Starbucks milieu. The year after, Starbucks sued him for copyright and trademark infringement. Dwyer claimed that his work was meant as a parody and as such should be protected by the US constitutional amendment of free speech. In 2000, the court decided that Dwyer was allowed to continue displaying his logo but only in extremely limited circumstances.

Sources: www.illegal-art.org, www.wikipedia.org

are selling something of real value or only empty images and promises (refer to Chapter 12 for an elaboration and additional literature about No Logo).

Kalle Lasn is another significant voice in the anti-brand movement. Founder of Adbusters and advocating the 'uncooling', 'unswooshing' and 'demarketing' of America, Lasn's overall concern (1999) is that culture is not 'bottom-up' any more (significant cultural issues stemming from the people), but rather 'top down', reversed by big companies and global branded corporations. Thereby, culture is no longer created by 'the people', but by 'corporate America'. Brands, products, fashions, celebrities, entertainments have moved from being spectacles surrounding culture to become the main constituents of culture. Human desires are manipulated through advertising; thereby an authentic life is no longer possible.

The activist agenda of Adbusters encourages 'the people' to fight 'the cool machine'. This can be done through 'culture jamming' (the distortion of commercial signs and mediums), by joining 'buy nothing days' and sticking to 'TV turnoff weeks'. Through these actions people can change the way cultural meaning is created in society. Adbusters is also linked to and helped instigate the anti-capitalist movement Occupy Wall Street (refer to Chapter 12 for elaboration and additional literature on Adbusters). Activist anti-brand movements also monitor corporations closely and thereby pressure for corporate social responsibility (so-called corporate watch). This pressure for more corporate social responsibility has created increasing attention in management circles for the display of corporate social responsibility.

The ideology behind this discourse is vividly displayed online, while it is not very clearly formulated in brand management academia. One academic article explaining the logical underlying argumentation of these movements is '*Brands – a critical perspective*' (Arvidsson 2005). In this critical Marxist analysis, the contemporary co-creating, community-building, symbolism-consuming, dialogue-participating consumers are pointed out as – not autonomous nor powerful – being exploited by the symbol-owning capitalist manipulating them into doing immaterial labour for the brand. The 'capital' is pointed out as not only linked to the production facilities of former days, but very much found in the symbolic world of brands and brand management.

CSR

The harsh criticism raised in the anti-branding movement is the extreme version of a more broad change of mind making corporate social responsibility (CSR) a mainstream phenomenon: 'brands across industries and markets are investing in CSR with unprecedented momentum' (Torelli *et al.* 2012, p. 948). CSR has hence become an integrated element in a large number of branding strategies as well as an area attracting more and more theoretical attention (Jutterström and Norberg 2013). Corporate social responsibility is the company's integrated responsibility for environment, working conditions and human rights. CSR is typically understood as either an organizational reform or charity; this first being intimately linked to the activities of the company (changing for instance working conditions internally), identity and values of the corporation, while the idea of 'charity' is linked to using

---

Box 10.9: Does CSR benefit all brands?

Implementing a CSR (corporate social responsibility) initiative in the overall branding strategy influences the brand identity and work differently for different types of brands. In 'Doing Poorly by Doing Good: Corporate Social Responsibility and Brand Concepts', the consumer response to CSR initiatives of different brand concepts is investigated. Consumer response to 'self-enhancing' brand concepts (e.g. luxury brands) was significantly more negative than towards brands with other concepts. A CSR concept of Rolex was evaluated much more negatively than CSR initiatives of Apple iTunes, Aunt Jemima and Tom's Shoes. Deducing that luxury brands should not be involved in CSR initiatives would most likely be jumping to the wrong conclusion, but this research highlights interesting aspects of *why* we buy certain categories of brands, *what* we want them to do for us and – then – *which types of CSR* initiatives could enhance and not dilute these benefits.

Source: Torelli 2012

---

the transactions with customers to raise contributions to external charities (Jutterström and Norberg 2013). The traditional bottom line (reflecting only financial measures) is in this regard substituted by the idea of the triple bottom line[3] (financial, social and environmental measures (or the easy-to-remember version; profit, people and planet)).

In this stream of literature, one finds concrete research about incorporating CSR into the branding strategy, but one also finds articles articulating abstract and complex issues such as the relationship between first and third world countries. An interesting example is a study of a much-praised CSR initiative by Nike (Boje and Khan 2009). One of Nike's subcontractors faced criticism over working conditions in Sialkot, a very poor area of Pakistan. Footballs were stitched by primarily women and under-age children and often in the homes of the stitchers. Nike reacted quickly to the criticism and demanded action of their subcontractor while bringing CSR issues to the political arena ending with the signing of 'The Atlanta Agreement' in 1997. The American sporting goods industry signed the agreement and presented it as the final solution to child labour, then-President Clinton praised the initiative publicly, and Nike stood out as a highly socially responsible brand and company.

The two researchers behind the article were faced with another reality when they investigated the impact of the initiative among the Sialkot stitchers. Families had lost an important part of their income due to the banning of child labour, and women experienced huge risks having to walk from their homes to the new soccer ball stitching factory. There were reports of sexual harassment and even rape. Furthermore, the football stitchers experienced social stigma as the job was seen as somewhat humiliating and hence preferably carried out in the privacy of the home. This article raises very important and critical issues of power relations between rich and poor countries and addresses the tremendous power held by the ones having the public attention and hence the opportunity to brand themselves – sometimes at the expense of the ones being 'helped' (refer to Chapter 12 for an elaboration and additional literature on CSR).

Global ideoscapes

Interesting research in the role played by brands in the global ideoscape has also been published in recent years. In *The Use of Western Brands in Asserting Chinese National Identity*, researchers Dong and Tian (2009) present a study of the roles played by Western brands in the personal national identity negotiation by Chinese consumers. China and Chinese identity has changed a lot over a short period of time and Western brands play an interesting role in the imagination and dreams of Chinese citizens/consumers. Historically, the idea of the West has encompassed the USA, Western Europe and Japan in Chinese imagination. In the symbolic and ideological context of the cultural approach, brands from these geographical areas hence represent the West and certain Western ideas. Going back in Chinese history, central narratives of the West as either an oppressor or a liberator are found. Traces of these central narratives are found in the dreams of Chinese consumers and used in the personal identity formation taking place in the largest and fastest evolving country in the world. The themes at play in this article are linked to the contribution made by consumption in the making of a nation.

The research presented in *Unveiling Alternative Meanings of Global Brands at the Nexus of Globalization* (Izberk-Bilgin 2012) is based on the same understanding of the brand as a central part of the global ideoscape. Here, field studies and analysis of Islamist discourses of Western brands display value-laden positions to central Islamistic narratives and prove that: 'transnational corporations' associations with powerful nation states, coupled with their immense financial resources and cultural influence, tangle global brands in a complex web of sociopolitical dynamics, subjecting these brands to religiously charged interpretations such as 'infidels' (ibid., p. 663). Members of the Islamist society actively use their disgust of Western brands to establish and confirm their religious and cultural beliefs. The idea of 'consumer jihad' is presented and the rhetoric among respondents goes as far as to state that, for example, Nestlé kills Palestinians.

Both articles build on comprehensive historical accounts revealing central narratives that form religious and national identities – and pinpoint how brands and their symbolism play different and very potent roles in forming these identities. The roles are both oppositional ('consumer jihad') and positive (e.g. 'Western brands as liberators').

Managerial implications of the ideological issues

A brand manager fully embracing the cultural perspective needs to get ready for a complex and dynamic work agenda. Negative cultural agendas or even 'doppelgänger brands' need to be monitored in order to adjust the brand communication. An implication that applies to most brands is the need for considering a CSR initiative, and it is highly recommended to thoroughly consider the impact of the initiative on the brand in question. A CSR initiative needs to fit the purpose and identity of the brand.

Studies of the global ideoscapes prove that global brands are (also) associated with geo-political issues, which might influence management of the brand in certain geographic areas.

Concluding thoughts – a future brand scenario: the citizen–artist brand

None of the other brand approaches holds opposing views in the same manner as the cultural. The fact that the absolute champions of the branding process (the brand icons) are also subjects to a 'revolutionary' agenda aiming at their downfall is, however, important to understand. But maybe the two views are not so opposite as they first appear. Just like critical voices can comment on the impact of the iconic brands, management can benefit from an analysis of the tension between the two sides of the spectrum in the cultural branding literature.

One research article delivers an interesting take on the tensions between brand icons and the anti-brand 'No Logo' movement ('Why do brands cause trouble? A dialectical theory of consumer culture and branding', Holt 2002). It is the article that is mentioned as a key reading in the introduction to this approach. Holt's analysis provides a new logic to the opposites as he analyses 'the emerging anti-branding movement to understand tensions between the current branding paradigm and consumer culture to speculate on their future directions' (Holt 2002, p. 71).

The brand icons are the champions of the postmodern branding paradigm (the branding techniques that have proven efficient since the 1960s). The pressure and criticism they are exposed to by the anti-brand movement should, according to Holt's analysis, be seen as the beginning of a paradigm shift. The same thing happened in the 1960s, when cultural changes implied a new marketing/branding paradigm to emerge. The pressure on the champions of the postmodern branding paradigms is hence nothing more than an indication that things are about to change. Below is an illustration with a short description of the postmodern branding paradigm and the post-postmodern paradigm of Holt's (2002) analysis. Changes in consumer culture have led to changes in the marketing function, and branding techniques have changed accordingly. The move from one dominant paradigm to another has been instigated by rebellion against the dominant marketing techniques. In that sense: 'Consumers are revolutionary only insofar as they assist entrepreneurial firms to tear down the old branding paradigm and create opportunities for companies that understand emerging new principles' (Holt 2002, p. 89).

If a new branding agenda is about to emerge, it is relevant to look at the major differences between the existing and the new. 'Authenticity' is central to understanding the proposed shift from the postmodern to the post-postmodern branding paradigm. In the postmodern branding paradigm postmodern, 'stealth' branding (where the profit motive is disguised behind disinterested, ironic brand communication) is perceived as being authentic. In the post-postmodern paradigm, openness about profit motives should be accompanied by an engaged citizenship. The authenticity problem of disguising profit motives behind a laid-back, ironic brand attitude is what is being revealed by the anti-brand movement.

In the post-postmodern branding paradigm the citizen-artist brands should be frank about profit motives, act as responsible citizens *and* be able to deliver original and relevant cultural material:

> As consumers peel away the brand veneer, they are looking for companies that act like a local merchant, as a stalwart citizen of the community. What consumers will want to touch, soon enough, is the way in which companies treat people when they are not customers. Brands will be trusted to serve as cultural source materials when their sponsors have demonstrated that they shoulder civic responsibilities as would a community pillar.
>
> (Holt 2002, p. 88)

To reflect one final time on this somewhat different review of the theoretical building blocks of the approach: brand icons are brands capable of telling powerful myths commenting on the central cultural contradictions of the time. The basic understanding of consumption of goods as the consumption of cultural meaning facilitates the understanding of the cultural brand perspective and thereby serves as a supporting theme. How the culturally savvy brands influence mainstream culture is fiercely resisted by the anti-branding agenda. Even though it is not a supporting theme, but rather a societal comment, it is important to understand some of the challenges facing the branding champions. Evoking thoughts about the future of brand management, the future scenario of the citizen-artist brand is a central and managerially relevant comment on the societal resistance by the No Logo movement. Even though it seems contradictory at first glance, the core elements of the cultural approach fit nicely together.

Table 10.3 The postmodern and the post-postmodern branding paradigm

	Postmodern branding paradigm	*Post-postmodern branding paradigm*
Time frame	1960s and onwards	Emerging (c. 2000)
Consumer culture	Seeking personal sovereignty and identity construction through brands	Cultivating self through consumption of brands
Marketing function	In constant negotiation with consumer culture	Providers of original and relevant cultural material
Branding paradigm characteristics	1 Authentic cultural resources 2 Ironic, reflexive brand persona 3 Coat-tailing on cultural epicenters 4 Lifeworld emplacement 5 Stealth branding	The brand as a cultural resource in its own right + a community pillar + honest about profit motive

Source: Adapted from Holt (2002)

Box 10.10 A citizen-artist brand?

When reading the following case example of PRODUCT (RED), take into consideration the whole scope of the cultural approach. Consider the nature of the brand icon, the urge for corporate social responsibility and, not least, the citizen-artist brand prospect.

In 2006, the (RED) initiative was founded by Bono, U2 and Bobby Shriver, CEO of Debt, AIDS, Trade in Africa (DATA) and was first introduced to the world media at the World Economic Forum in Davos. (RED) is a new business model and could be an indicator of a new brand agenda.

The new fund-raising business model of the (RED) brand works like this. Iconic brands have the opportunity to license the (PRODUCT) RED mark and use it for specific products co-branded by (RED) and the original product brand. The corporations commit themselves to sending a fixed portion of the profits made on (RED) products directly to the Global Fund to fight AIDS in Africa (established in 2002 with the support of several world leaders, among them then UN Secretary General Kofi Annan). The sole purpose of the Global Fund is to raise funds and make grants to countries, organizations and communities that need financial help to allow them to respond to epidemics of AIDS, tuberculosis and malaria.

Iconic brands such as American Express, Converse, Apple, Emporio Armani and Gap have licensed the right to create, market and sell specially designed (RED) products. Apple has designed a (RED) iPod. Gap has, among other things, designed an entire collection of red t-shirts imprinted with words such as INSPI(RED), EMPOWE(RED), WI(RED) and ADMI(RED). A bodysuit collection from BabyGap spells out words like DIAPE(RED) and ADO(RED). Gap has further committed to the cause by having more products made in Africa. If you use an American Express (RED) credit card, 1 per cent of your total spending is sent to the Global Fund. (RED) Motorola phones are available, as is a whole collection of clothing and fashion accessories by Emporio Armani. That is just to name a few of the initiatives.

These corporations commit themselves to refunding a percentage of the (RED) turnover to the Global Fund. A main point is that the consumer does not pay extra for his or her (RED) purchase – the company does. The licensing fee received by (RED) for use of the (PRODUCT) RED mark is used to manage and market the (RED) brand. By early 2008 (RED) purchases had generated more than $100 million for the Global Fund.

(RED) was created not only to raise money for, but also to create awareness of, the Global Fund and the severe issues it addresses. On 15 May (with Bono serving as guest editor) and 21 September (Giorgio Armani as guest editor) of 2006, the *Independent* went (RED). The newspaper promoted the Global Fund and 50 percent of the day's revenue was donated to the cause. Internationally well-known personalities like Tony Blair, Nelson Mandela, Bill Gates, Arnold Schwarzenegger, Condoleezza Rice and George

Clooney contributed to the (RED) editions of the newspaper. An entire army of international celebrities have supported the (RED) cause by modelling the clothes and backing the projects in all kinds of ways. Check out the website below for new (RED) initiatives.

By combining the marketing power of the world's leading consumer brands with the accountability, scale and pace of Global Fund grant making, (PRODUCT) RED has created a new global brand and a new business model. Even though (RED) was created in order to raise awareness and money for the good of African women and children affected by AIDS, it is important to notice that (RED), in its own words, is not a charity. It is a commercial initiative designed to create awareness and a sustainable flow of money from the private sector into the Global Fund to fight the AIDS pandemic in Africa.

Source: www.joinred.com

The citizen-artist brand manager

As explained in the section on theoretical building blocks, the seemingly contradictory clash between the brand icons and the anti-branding movement might indicate a shift towards a new branding paradigm. The citizen-artist brand is supposed to accommodate the new requirements of an increasingly critical consumer culture by supplying the relevant cultural material (already skilfully done by the iconic brands) *and* acting as a responsible citizen, shouldering its corporate social responsibilities. The management of this future brand scenario requires an even more versatile work agenda than the management of a brand icon; not only is the brand supposed to deliver potent cultural material but at the same time lead the way towards new dimensions in corporate citizenship.

Summary

Core to the cultural approach is the theory on how brands become icons. So-called identity brands (strong on self-expressive benefits) have the potential for becoming brand icons by adapting to the cultural branding model. The cultural branding model is closely related to McCracken's classic theory about cultural consumption. In this view of consumption, the consumption objects are seen as cultural artefacts carrying meaning from the culturally constituted world to the consumers. Brands are regarded as cultural resources just like movies, social movements, books, magazines and so on. In this brand perspective, the tools for building iconic brands are found. Through addressing the pressing cultural contradictions as a viable cultural 'text', and being able to reinvent as changes in societal contradictions occur, the brand can approach the identity value of a cultural icon. The anti-brand movement is concerned with what branding and globalization do to culture. The encouragers of civil activism, they also raise important political questions and push for corporate social responsibility. The tensions between brand icons and the anti-brand movement can be understood as a phenomenon indicating the beginning of a new branding paradigm. In this prospect of a post-postmodern branding paradigm, the brand should act as a citizen-artist, meaning being able to deliver relevant cultural material while shouldering its social and civic responsibilities.

Summary

Marketers can benefit from cultural branding insight in different ways. The brand manager can engage fully in the cultural branding model in order to pursue the path to icon status (or learn from the best). Going down this road, the brand manager needs to adapt to an agenda of cultural activism and get ready for a rather complicated work method. The brand manager needs to gain a deep insight into cultural issues in society and be able to use this insight to perform brand myths connecting to the most important cultural contradictions of the time.

Insights from this approach can also be used to become aware of the importance of monitoring if the brand is being subjected to criticism or even 'culture jamming'. This can be an early warning sign of a branding strategy losing its appeal or a pressure towards displaying more corporate social responsibility.

The implications of the citizen-artist brand prospect should also be taken into consideration by brand managers.

Box 10.11 Dos and don'ts in the cultural approach

Do	Don't
Acknowledge the powerful forces in consumer culture	Don't believe that the brand communication happens just between you and your customer
Use cultural feedback – also negative – to adjust your brand strategy	Don't ignore critical voices: things might spin out of control
Be open to inspiration from many different sources	Don't focus too much on spreadsheets from business school guys
Acknowledge that the brand changes over the course of time	Don't believe that the brand is made up of consistent associations
Regard your brand's reputation as a reputation for performing myths	Don't ignore political, social and ideological changes

Academic evolution of the cultural approach

Research published in the journals from the data set used as primary data for this book indicates how the academic focus of the brand personality approach has started and developed with regards to assumptions, theory, methodology and managerial guidelines over time.

In 2005, Arnould and Thompson published a 20 years review of literature said to be constituting a new stream in brand management, Consumer Culture Theory. The area is wide but *also* encompasses literature about branding with a (macro-level) cultural perspective. Hence, the groundwork for the cultural approach emanated during the 1990s.

In 2002, Holt published the article *Why do brands cause trouble? A dialectical theory of consumer culture and branding*, which became the founding article of a new brand perspective. Here, both the managerial possibilities of using cultural material in brand communication and the emerging anti-branding discourse were researched

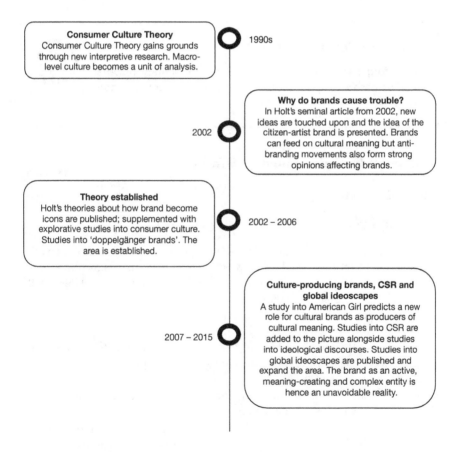

Figure 10.6 The academic evolution of the cultural approach

and discussed, and the future brand scenario of the citizen-artist brand was presented as a notion bridging the duality of the approach.

In the years that followed, Holt's theories about how brands become iconic were presented (e.g. Holt 2003b) and explorative studies into this new branding domain were published, broadening and deepening the understanding of the complexity of macro-level culture and branding (e.g. Kates 2004, Kozinets 2002, Thompson and Arsel 2004, and Thompson *et al.* 2006).

Most recently, studies of CSR and branding have been added to the picture with clear implications for brands willing to meet the new requirement from critical consumers (e.g. Torelli *et al.*). An interesting study into 'American Girl' predicts a future, where brands are not only using cultural material in their communication but work as producers of cultural meaning as well. The same study bridges the gap between emotional and cultural branding (Diamond *et al.* 2009). Two new studies investigate cultural meaning creation on a global scale: Western brands in an Islamist context and as part of national identity among Chinese consumers (Dong and Tian 2009, Izberk-Bilgin 2012).

Box 10.12 You are not done!

Don't forget to visit the website for supplementary material such as case examples, student questions and supplementary literature.

Comments from the 'founding fathers'

Cultural branding

Douglas B. Holt, Founder and President of Cultural Strategy Group

I developed the cultural branding model to explain how brand symbolism works. I'm also concerned with how brand symbolism influences other dimensions of the brand such as perceived quality, distinctive benefits and trust (Holt 2002). Conventional theories of branding do a particularly poor job of theorizing brand symbolism (Holt 2005). So I've spent the last decade conducting research to address this gap.

Conventional brand theories have yoked brand symbolism to the dominant psychological models without considering its distinctive qualities. This is a major weakness, because outside of certain technology- and service-driven categories, where brands are built largely through reputation effects, branding's big stakes are decided increasingly by cultural symbolism.

Branding has been dominated by these psychological assumptions for nearly four decades. In this view, which I call the mindshare model, the brand is a set of valued associations in the individual consumer's mind. So branding is reduced to being actions that systematically reinforce these associations. The American ad man Rosser Reeves developed the foundational intuition for this idea in the 1950s with his idea that each brand required a Unique Selling Proposition that should be repeated over and over to install it in consumers' minds. Al Ries and Jack Trout made this idea hegemonic with the publication of a series of *Ad Age* articles that culminated in the 1981 publication of *Positioning the Battle for your Mind*. They introduced a powerful metaphor that won over the marketers worldwide: we live in a world that has far too many messages for people to process, so branding is a battle for mental real estate. The firm needs to identify a cognitive gap in the benefits and associations important to the product category and then seek to own this mental real estate through ultra-simple ultra-consistent brand communications. Beginning in the 1980s, consumer psychologists have published scores of academic articles, textbooks and management books that rely on this foundational intuition to advance a general theory of branding that paralleled what Reeves, Ries and Trout had previously developed for practitioners. The goal of branding is to claim valued cognitive associations in a product category, and consistently communicate these associations in everything the brand does over time to sustain the brand's hold on this cognitive territory.

The mindshare model works fine for certain aspects of branding, but it is fundamentally flawed as a theory of brand symbolism. Mindshare branding – as well as its various New Age cousins such as emotional branding, brand personality, brand archetypes, relationship branding – is but one model for branding, as this book makes clear. The mindshare approach is a basic tool for the day-to-day brand management of established brands – the incremental and rote aspect of branding. When it comes to the most important, exciting and strategically crucial role of branding – using branding to build extraordinary new businesses and drive economic value – mindshare is a dead end.

To address this gap, I developed a cultural theory of branding. Cultural branding is conceived specifically to explain how branding works as an innovation engine, to drive significant new domains of customer value. To do so requires an entirely different theory of consumer motivations and desires: moving from the essentialist, static, individual-level constructs of mindshare theory to social and cultural constructs that are grounded in historical contexts. And the application of this new theory in practice demands different research techniques and different conceptions of strategy.

Cultural branding overview

To build the cultural branding model, I conducted detailed cultural histories (i.e. brand genealogies) of many iconic brands, including Budweiser, Marlboro, Volkswagen, Mountain Dew, Nike, ESPN, Jack Daniels, Coca-Cola, Corona, Snapple and Patagonia. Most of these brands are American, but I have expanded the research since then to Europe, Japan, Latin America and also global brands.

Brand symbolism delivers customer value by providing culturally resonant stories and images that groups of consumers use to buttress their identities. The collective need for such stories arises in response to major shifts in society. Cultural theorists term stories that provide this functional role a myth. The most important and valued brand stories respond to – and often help to lead – major shifts in society and culture. My theory seeks to explain why particular branded stories and images are so valued at particular historical junctures.

Brands establish powerful durable symbolism (i.e. become iconic) when they perform powerful identity myths: simple fictions that address cultural anxieties from afar, from imaginary worlds rather than from worlds that the consumer lives in. Identity myths are useful fictions that stitch back together otherwise damaging tears in the cultural fabric of the nation. These tears are experienced by people in their everyday life as tensions or anxieties. People use myths to smooth over these collective tensions, helping them to create purpose in their lives, to cement their desired identity in place when it is under stress. Academic research has demonstrated that the extra-ordinary appeal of the most successful cultural products has been due to their mythic qualities—from Horatio Alger's rags-to-riches dime novels of the nineteenth century to John Wayne westerns, to Harlequin romance novels, to the action-adventure films of Willis, Schwarzenegger and Stallone. Iconic brands work the same way.

Brands become iconic when they address societal desires, not individual ones. Iconic brands perform myths (through any customer touchpoint) that symbolically resolve the identity desires and anxieties stemming from an important cultural tension. Iconic brands earn extraordinary value because they address the collective anxieties and desires of the nation (and sometimes beyond). We experience our identities – our self-understandings and aspirations – as intensely personal quests. But, when scholars examine consumer identities in the aggregate, they find that identity desires and anxieties are widely shared across a broad swathe of a nation's citizens. These similarities result because, even though they may come from different walks of life, people construct their identities in response to the same historical changes that impact the entire nation, and sometimes regions or the entire globe.

Over time, as the brand performs its myth, consumers come to perceive that the myth resides in the product. The brand becomes a symbol, a material embodiment of the myth. So as customers drink or drive or wear the product they experience a bit of the myth. This is a modern secular example of the *rituals* that anthropologists have documented in every human society. But, rather than religious myth, in modern societies the most powerful myths have to do with identities. Customers use iconic brands as symbolic salves. Through the products in which they are embedded, customers grab hold of the myth and use it in their lives to make their identity burdens a bit less burdensome. Great myths provide for their consumers little epiphanies—moments of recognition that put images and sounds and feelings on barely perceptible desires. Customers who make use of the brand's myth for their identities forge powerful emotional connections to the brand.

To understand some of the basic features of cultural branding, it is useful to contrast the cultural branding with the conventional mindshare model.

From building associations to performing myths

The mindshare model assumes that brand symbolism consists of abstract associations in the consumer's mind. Thus the purpose of advertising is to influence these associations. The communication content is treated as instrumental rhetoric. Consumers are assumed to discard this rhetorical material and only absorb (or not, depending on the success of the ad) associations to the brand.

The cultural branding model turns this view of brand communications on its head. For iconic brands such as Coke and Nike and Budweiser, the brand's communications are the centre of customer value. Customers buy the product primarily to experience the stories that the brand performs. The product is simply a conduit through which customers get to experience the stories that the brand tells. When consumers sip a Coke, or Corona, or Snapple, they are imbibing more than a beverage. Rather they are drinking in identity myths that have become imbued in those drinks. The brand is a *storied product:* a product that has distinctive brand markers (trademark, design, etc.) through which customers experience identity myths. Because the mindshare model ignores the particular contents of the brand's communications, the model is unable to decipher how brand symbolism works.

From abstractions to cultural expressions

The mindshare model proposes that the brand consists of a set of abstractions. Descriptions of brands are full of abstract adjectives and nouns such as security and performance and quality and ruggedness. In cultural branding, in contrast, the brand's value is located in the particulars of the brand's cultural expression: the particular cultural contents of the brand's myth and the particular expression of these contents in the communication. For Corona the brand exists on the Mexican beach and the evocative expression of the beach in its 'nothing's happening' style of advertising. For Coke in 'Teach the world to sing' the brand existed in the idea that in the hippy counterculture could be found the seeds of peace and racial harmony. For Snapple's early 1990s breakthrough '100% natural' campaign the brand was centred in loud-mouthed Wendy telling silly stories of Snapple drinkers, and in the barbed political soliloquies of Howard Stern and Rush Limbaugh. Abstracting these cultural expressions to 'relaxation' and 'friendship' and 'quirky', respectively, strips these brands of their most valuable assets.

The mindshare model abstracts away the messiness of society and history in search of the brand's purified essence. This distilled model denies the brand a role as an historical actor in society. In its insistence that brands forge a transcendental identity lodged in consumers' minds, the mindshare model ignores that identity value is created and transformed in particular historical contexts. A theory of brand symbolism must detail the brand's stakes in the transformation of culture and society and the particular cultural expressions the brand uses to push for these transformations.

From transcendental consistency to historical fit

In the mindshare model, the brand's associations transcend time and space. Therefore explanations of the evolution of brands boil down to whether or not the brand maintains consistency in the face of organizational and competitive pressures that push for zigging and zagging. Brand management is about stewardship: finding the brand's true 'identity' and maintaining this compass point come hell or high water.

Yet the brands I have studied succeed by moving away from their initial branding – their supposed DNA at the time – to address shifting currents in American society. In fact, all of the iconic brands that I've studied, with histories extending more than a decade, have had to make significant shifts in order to remain iconic. Brands that haven't adjusted properly – such as Pepsi, Levi's and Cadillac – have lost much of the brand equity. These reinterpretations of the brand are necessary because, for a myth to generate identity value, it must directly engage the most acute cultural tensions of the day. Coke celebrated America's triumphs against Nazi Germany in World War II but then suddenly shifted to dramatize ways to heal internal strife around war in the early 1970s and then racial divisions in the early 1980s. Corona, originally a brand that represented collegiate hedonism, later was retooled to provide a soothing antidote to the compression and anxieties of the networked free agent work that came to a head in the 1990s.

Iconic brands are built using a philosophy the opposite of that espoused by the mindshare model. The brand is an historical entity whose desirability comes from performing myths that address the most important social tensions that pulse through the nation. For iconic brands, success depends upon how well the brand's myth is modified to fit historical exigencies, not by its consistency in the face of historical change.

Much work remains to be done on cultural branding. To develop this area, the discipline of marketing must embrace theories and methods that it has for decades pushed to the margins, rather than continue to insist against all evidence that its favoured psychological assumptions are universally applicable to resolve all important branding questions.

Notes

1 The CCT construct also relates to literature from relational and community approaches. The literature behind this approach is interested in understanding macro-level culture and branding.
2 A reference to Kim and Mauborgne's *Blue Ocean Strategy*.
3 A phrase coined by John Elkington in 1994 and used in his book *Cannibals with Forks: The Triple Bottom Line of 21st Century Business* (1997).

References and further reading

Key readings are in bold type

Albinsson, P. A. and Perena, B. Y. (2012), 'Consumer activism 2.0: Tools for social change' in R. Llamas and R. Belk (eds), *The Routledge Companion to Digital Consumption*, London: Routledge.
Alden, D. L., Steenkamp, J-B. E. M. and Batra, R. (1999), 'Brand positioning through advertising in Asia, North America, and Europe: The role of global consumer culture', *Journal of Marketing*, 63 (1): 75–87.

Allen, C. T., Fournier, S. and Miller, F. (2006), 'Brands and their meaning makers', in C. P. Haugtvedt, P. M. Herr and F. R. Kardes (eds), *Handbook of Consumer Psychology*, Mahwah, NJ: Lawrence Erlbaum Associates, pp. 718–822.

Arnould, E. J. and Thompson, C. J. (2005), 'Consumer Culture Theory (CCT): Twenty years of research', *Journal of Consumer Research*, 31 (4): 868–82.

Arvidsson, A. (2005), 'Brands: A critical perspective', *Journal of Consumer Culture*, 5 (2): 235–58.

Askegaard, S. (2006), 'Brands as a global ideoscape', in J. E. Schroeder and M. Salzer-Morling (eds), *Brand Culture*, London: Routledge, pp. 91–102.

Boje, D. M. and Khan, F. R. (2009), 'Story-branding by empire entrepreneurs: Nike child labour and Pakistan's soccer ball industry', *Journal of Small Business and Entrepreneurship*, 22 (1): 9–24.

Diamond, N., Sherry, J. F. Jr, Muniz, A. M. Jr., McGrath, M. A., Kozinets, R. V. and Borghini, S. (2009), 'American girl and the brand gestalt: Closing the loop on socio-cultural branding research', *Journal of Marketing*, 73 (3): 118–34.

Dong, L. and Tian K. (2009), 'The use of western brands in asserting Chinese national identity', *Journal of Consumer Research*, 36 (3): 504–23.

Elkington, J. (1997), *Cannibals with Forks: The Triple Bottom Line of 21st Century Business*. Mankato, MN: Capstone.

Frank, T. (1997), *The Conquest of Cool: Business Culture, Counterculture, and the Rise of Hip Consumerism*, Chicago, IL: University of Chicago Press.

Fournier, S. and Avery, J. (2011), 'The Uninvited Brand', *Business Horizons*, 54: 193–207.

Garsten, C. and Hasselström, A. (2004), 'Homo mercans and the fashioning of markets', in C. Garsten and M. L. de Montoya (eds), *Market Matters: Exploring Cultural Processes in the Global Marketplace*, New York: Palgrave Macmillan, pp. 209–32.

Gay, P. du., Hall, S., Janes, L., Mackay, H. and Negus, K. (1997), *Doing Cultural Studies: The Story of the Sony Walkman*, London: Sage Publications.

Giesler, M. (2012), 'How doppelgänger brand images influence the market creation process: Longitudinal insights from the rise of Botox Cosmetic', *Journal of Consumer Research*, 76 (6): 55–68.

Hackley, C. (2003), *Doing Research Projects in Marketing, Management and Consumer Research*, London: Routledge.

Handelman, J. M. (2012), 'Online consumer movements', in R. Llamas and R. Belk (eds), *The Routledge Companion to Digital Consumption*, London: Routledge, pp. 386–96.

Holt, D. B. (2002), 'Why do brands cause trouble? A dialectical theory of consumer culture and branding', *Journal of Consumer Research*, 29 (1): 70–90.

Holt, D. B. (2002), *Brands and branding* (Harvard Business School Note 503–045), Cambridge, MA: Harvard Business School Publishing (hbsp.com).

Holt, D. B. (2003a), 'What becomes an icon most?' *Harvard Business Review*, 81 (3): 43–9.

Holt, D. B. (2003b), 'How to build an iconic brand', *Market Leader*, 21 (summer): 35–42.

Holt, D. B. (2004), *How Brands Become Icons: The Principles of Cultural Branding*, Boston, MA: Harvard Business School Press.

Holt, D. B. (2005), 'How societies desire brands: Using cultural theory to explain brand symbolism', in S. Ratneshwar and D. G. Mick (eds), *Inside Consumption: Consumer Motives, Goals, and Desires*, London: Routledge, pp. 273–91.

Holt, D. B. (2006), 'Jack Daniels's America: Iconic brands as ideological parasites and proselytizers', *Journal of Consumer Culture*, 6 (3): 355–77.

Holt, D.B. and Cameron, D. (2010), *Cultural Strategy: Using innovative ideas to build breakthrough brands*, Oxford: Oxford University Press.

Holt, D. B., Quelch, J. and Taylor, E. (2004), 'How global brands compete', *Harvard Business Review*, 82 (9): 68–75.

Izberk-Bilgin, E. (2012), 'Infidel brands: Unveiling alternative meanings of global brands at the nexus of globalization, consumer culture, and Islamism', *Journal of Consumer Research*, 39 (4): 663–87.

Jutterström, M. and Norberg, P. (2013), 'CSR as a management idea', in M. Jutterström and P. Norberg (eds), *CSR as a Management Idea*, Cheltenham, UK: Edward Elgar Publishing.

Kates, S. M. (2004), 'The dynamics of brand legitimacy: An interpretive study in the gay men's community', *Journal of Consumer Research*, 31 (2): 455–64.

Klein, N. (2000), *No Logo*, London: Flamingo.

Kozinets, R. V. (2002), 'Can consumers escape the market? Emancipatory illuminations from Burning Man', *Journal of Consumer Research*, 29 (1): 20–38.

Lasn, K. (1999), *Culture Jam: The Uncooling of America*, New York: Eagle Brook.

Luedicke, M. K., Thompson, C. J. and Giesler, M. (2010), 'How myth and ideology animate a brand – Mediated moral conflict', *Journal of Consumer Research*, 36 (6): 1016–1032.

McCracken, G. (1988), *Culture and Consumption: New Approaches to the Symbolic Character of Consumer Goods and Activities*, Bloomington and Indianapolis, IN: Indiana University Press.

McCracken, G. (2005), *Culture and Consumption II: Markets, Meaning, and Brand Management*, Bloomington and Indianapolis, IN: Indiana University Press.

Mick, D. G. (1986), 'Consumer research and semiotics: Exploring the morphology of signs, symbols, and significance', *Journal of Consumer Research*, 13 (2): 196–213.

Ries, A. and Trout, J. (1981) *Positioning: The Battle for your Mind*. New York: McGraw-Hill Professional.

Schroeder, J. E. (2005), 'The artist and the brand', *European Journal of Marketing*, 39 (11–12): 1291–1305.

Thompson, C. J. and Arsel, Z. (2004), 'The Starbucks brandscape and consumers' (anticorporate) experiences of glocalization', *Journal of Consumer Research*, 31 (3): 631–42.

Thompson, C. J., Rindfleisch, A. and Arsel, Z. (2006), 'Emotional branding and the strategic value of the doppelgänger brand image', *Journal of Marketing*, 70 (1): 50–64.

Torelli, C. J., Monga, A. B. and Kaikati, A. M. (2012), 'Doing poorly by doing good: Corporate social responsibility and brand concepts', *Journal of Consumer Research*, 38 (5): 948–63.

Willmott, M. (2001), *Citizen Brands: Putting Society at the Heart of your Business*, Chichester, UK: Wiley.

Websites

www.adbusters.org
www.bp.com
www.corporatewatch.org.uk
www.corpwatch.org
www.debeerscompany.com
www.joinred.com
www.nologo.org
www.starbucks.com

Part III

Other perspectives

11 Other categorizations of brand management

Box 11.1 Learning objectives

The purpose of this chapter is to:

Compare the proposed taxonomy of this book with other categorizations of brand management

Other categorizations of brand management

Other writers have also proposed different frameworks with the attempt to pin down the elusive nature of the brand by systemizing the field into different categories. In this section, we will relate the categorization and taxonomy of this book to other categorization frameworks of brand management and reflect upon the relevance of the framework categorization of this book in comparison with the other categorizations.

The analysis underlying our proposed taxonomy stems from a Kuhnian mindset and reflects Kuhn's philosophy of science and its theories on how formalized knowledge in scientific disciplines evolves. The results of the analysis and the taxonomy are hence tightly connected with the data of the approach, namely research articles. In the review of each approach, other relevant literature has been added to enable a full and accurate picture of each approach, but it is important to point out that the *identification* of the seven brand approaches is solely based on research articles. The other frameworks stem from other analyses with other backgrounds and use other denominators for categorizing brand management. It is not our intent to add confusion by these comparisons; our aim is rather to enhance clarity by pointing out the similarities between ours and other frameworks – even though they stem from different mindsets and analyses there are significant similarities in the end result.

We will review the study 'Divided by a common language: diversity and deception in the world of global marketing' by Mary Goodyear (1996) that focuses on different brand roles in different markets; an identification of four brand management paradigms based on using two main discriminators on brand management and strategy literature 'Brand Management Paradigms' by Louro and Cunha (2001). The final categorization of brand approaches is Holt's *How Brands Become Icons* (2004), which is a comparison of four practical branding models.

The role of brands

In 'Divided by a common language: diversity and deception in the world of global marketing' Mary Goodyear (1996) investigates the marketing and branding confusion in terms of linguistics and asks the question: how can branding be defined if one does not consider the many different roles of brands in different economies, time eras and phases of market maturation? Considering these macro-level factors, Goodyear comes up with the definitions of the roles of brands shown in Table 11.1. The model reflects the different roles played by brands as markets evolve. In that sense, the Goodyear framework reflects the life cycle of a brand – how branding techniques become more sophisticated as consumers become more and more accustomed to marketing techniques.

This categorization pivots around the evolution of branding techniques (and hence, different brand roles) in the context of maturing market places. In a non-industrialized economy, the majority of goods are unbranded and the mere fact that goods are packaged may be a vehicle of consumer preferences. In low-consumerized and undersupplied countries, the primary role of the brand is to serve as a reference. The manufacturer need not apply sophisticated marketing tools to sell his goods. This brand role is more or less comparable to the economic approach.

In a more mature market, the marketer is faced with more competition and, hence, has to apply other branding techniques in order to differentiate the products. This situation requires the 'three-dimensional brands' where product quality is supported by emotive advertising, where the brand's most important role is to act as a personality. As the branding techniques relate to emotions and connotations, this role is comparable to the individualistic brand approaches of our taxonomy (the consumer-based approach, the personality approach and the relational approach).

In an even more saturated market place, the consumer becomes the main driver in the branding process; the consumer 'owns' the brand and plays an active part in endowing it with commonly held values, catapulting a few brands to iconic status (as found in the cultural approach of our taxonomy).

In Goodyear's categorization, she differentiates between classic branding and postmodern branding. The postmodern consumer lives in a highly literate consumer culture and is – through sophisticated brand literacy – able to see through the classic roles of brands. The highly empowered postmodern consumer will demand responsibility and identity from the corporation behind the brands; hence the two latter roles of brands apply. The brand as organization is comparable to the identity approach while the brand as policy is comparable to the CSR-related aspects of the cultural approach.

Table 11.1 The role of brands

Marketing era	Role of brands	
Classic branding	Unbranded	Commodities, packaged goods Major proportion of goods in nonindustrialized context Minor role Europe/United States Supplier has power
	Brand as reference	Brand name often name of maker Name used for identification Any advertising support focuses on rational attributes Name over time becomes guarantee of quality/consistency
	Brand as personality	Brand name may be 'stand-alone' Marketing support focuses on emotional appeal Product benefits Advertising puts brand into context
	Brand as icon	Consumer now 'owns' brand Brand taps into higher-order values of society Advertising assumes close relationship Use of symbolic brand language Often established internationally
Postmodern branding	Brand as company	Brands have complex identities Consumer assesses them all Need to focus on corporate benefits to diverse 'customers' Integrated communication strategy essential through-the-line
	Brand as policy	Company and brands aligned to social and political issues Consumers 'vote' on issues through companies Consumers now 'own' brands, companies and politics

Source: Goodyear (1996), Figures 2 (classic branding) and 5 (postmodern branding)

Four brand management paradigms

In 'Brand Management Paradigms' (Louro and Cunha 2001), four ruling branding paradigms are identified by the use of two discriminators: the role of the consumer in the branding process (customer centrality) and whether the brand should hold a tactical or strategic position in the company (brand centrality). These two dimensions provide four 'ideal types' of approaches to brand management (see Figure 11.1).

The product paradigm reflects an approach to branding where the brand is a low strategic priority and the customer is seen as a passive player in the branding process.

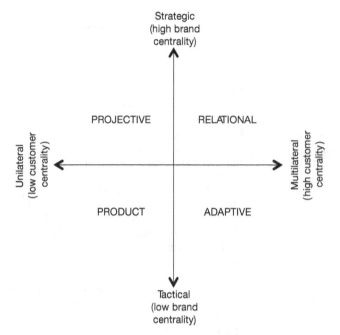

Figure 11.1 Four brand paradigms along two dimensions; adapted from Louro and Cunha (2001)

If the brand strategy is perceived as central for the overall strategy of the organization, but with the same conception of the customer, Louro and Cunha label it as a projective paradigm. The third paradigm is characterized by the brand having a low strategic priority and a tactical focus supplemented by a conception of the customer as an active and primary co-creator of value, called the adaptive paradigm. The fourth and last brand paradigm in the Louro and Cunha categorization of branding is the relational paradigm. Here the brand is perceived to be key in relation to the overall strategy, and consumers are assumed to be active co-creators of the brand.

The product paradigm reflects a product-centred approach to brand management. The product and its functional benefits are central to the profitability of the organization in the product paradigm. The brand holds two primary functions: as the statement of legal ownership and as a communicative tool upholding visual identification of differentiation in the marketing of the products of the company. In this brand management paradigm, brand equity is seen as something created by having the optimal marketing mix: the right price, right product, price, placement and promotion. The product paradigm is comparable to the economic approach of this book.

The projective paradigm of the Louro and Cunha categorization resembles the identity approach in our framework. It focuses on the usefulness of the brand on a strategic level as opposed to the tactical approach to branding reflected in the product paradigm. The brand is seen as a strategic entity that should be used as a template for the overall business model. Thus, the brand reflects purpose and ethics, as well as core competences in an organization and vice versa. The theoretical background of the projective paradigm is the resource-based perspective. The consequence of this is that value and brand meaning are found internally. In this paradigm, competitiveness of the business is based on the organization's ability to find its own internal strengths and cultivate them with the purpose of creating a unique business culture and unique competences difficult to imitate. This idea of creating unique concepts based on sender identity is the foundation of the projective paradigm in brand management.

Where the projective paradigm stresses the internal business resources and competences as the source of brand meaning, the adaptive paradigm stresses the consumer as the source of brand meaning: 'The power of the brand resides in the minds of the consumer' (Keller 2003, p. 59). The adaptive brand management paradigm thereby resembles the consumer-based approach in the taxonomy of this book.

The relational brand management paradigm in the Louro and Cunha framework is the opposite of both the lack of review of the actions of the customers in the projective paradigm and the 'excessive' focus on the active customer in the adaptive paradigm. The relational paradigm conceptualizes brand management as a dynamic, dyadic process, in which an interaction between the creation of brand value (internally) and brand meaning (externally) on a strategic level results in a strong and relevant brand equity through an experienced meaningful relation between consumer and brand. In this paradigm, the marketer can benefit from constructing the brand as a personality because it furthers the consumer–brand relationship. This is done by implementing the acknowledgement of the consumer's active contribution to the creation of brand meaning and at the same time making brand management and brand identity the kernel of the formulation of strategy and the external business communication. In that way, both customer and brand centrality are high-ranking priorities in this paradigm. It goes without saying that this brand management paradigm covers the personality and the relational approach.

The categorization by Louro and Cunha is created through the use of other discriminators and using an entirely different way of sorting existing brand models, but the proposed brand management paradigms are indeed comparable to the taxonomy of this book. As described above, the first five approaches are covered by the four brand management paradigms, and the latter two emerged around and after the publication of 'Brand Management Paradigms' in 2001.

Four branding models

In *How Brands Become Icons* (2004), Holt proposes four different branding models; cultural branding, mind-share branding, emotional branding and viral branding. Holt does not embed the four branding models in a chronological context, but focuses on presenting and comparing the most widely used (in practice) branding models. Holt labels the mind-share branding model the dominant branding model since the 1970s. In the 1990s, emotional branding became a managerial priority

Table 11.2 Four brand management paradigms

		The product paradigm	The projective paradigm	The adaptive paradigm	The relational paradigm
Brand–consumer exchange metaphor		Silence	Monologue	Listening	Conversation
Marketing focus		Product orientation	Brand logic	Customer orientation	Relationship
Brand management	Brand management focus	Marketing mix	Brand identity	Brand image	Relationship
	Brand definition	Logo, legal, instrument	Identity system, company	Image, shorthand device, risk reducer, adding value, value system	Relationship, personality, evolving entity
	Brand roles	Product-centred roles supporting communication, advertising and legal protection	Firm-centred roles associated with the unilateral creation and sustenance of competitive advantage through the differentiation and/or efficiency (cost leadership)	Consumer-centred roles facilitating decision-making, reducing risks inherent to product acquisition and providing emotional value	Symbolic partner co-configuring the relational domain for firm–customer interaction
	Dimensions of brand management	Marketing programme, brand elements as residual decisions	Organizational strategy, brand identity charter, brand elements, marketing programme	Brand image, brand elements, marketing programme	Organizational strategy, brand identity charter, brand image, brand history, brand elements, marketing programme
	Performance metrics	Product-based (financial perspective)	Brand-based (internal perspective)	Consumer-based (customer perspective)	Process-based (balanced scorecard)
	Brand management structure	Functional, product/ brand management, product market	Functional, product/ brand management, product market	Functional, product/ brand management, product market	Customer management, entrepreneurial brand management
Strategy formation	Strategic orientation	Internal	Internal	External	Internal/external
	Strategic focus	Product and positions	Resources and capabilities	Contexts and consumers	Integrations and interactions

Source: Adapted from Louro and Cunha (2001). p. 857

Table 11.3 A comparison across four branding models

	Cultural branding	Mind-share branding	Emotional branding	Viral branding
Key words	Cultural icons	DNA, brand essence, genetic code, USP (unique selling point) benefits, onion model	Brand personality, experiential branding, brand religion, experience economy	Stealth marketing, coolhunt, meme, grass-roots, infections, seeding, contagion, buzz
Brand definition	Performer of, and container for, an identity myth	A set of abstract associations	A relationship partner	A communication unit
Required for a successful brand	Performing a myth that addresses an acute contradiction in society	Consistent expression of associations	Deep interpersonal connection	Broad circulation of the virus
Company's role	Author	Steward: consistent expression of DNA in all activities over time	Good friend	Hidden puppet master: motivate the right consumers to advocate for the brand
Source of customer value	Buttressing identity	Simplifying decisions	Relationship with the brand	Being cool, fashionable
Consumers' role	Personalizing the brand's myth to fit individual biography	Ensuring that benefits become salient through repetition	Interaction with the brand	'Discovering' brand as their own, DIY
	Ritual action to experience the myth when using product	Perceiving benefits when buying and using product	Building a personal relationship	Word of mouth

Source: Adapted from Holt (2004)

as well, and with the rise of the Internet viral branding techniques also became applied to branding practices. The cultural branding model is based on Holt's research into how brands become icons (please refer to Chapter 10).

It is obvious that the cultural branding model is the equivalent of the cultural approach of our taxonomy; the mind-share branding model is comparable to the consumer-based approach; the emotional branding model sums up the personality and the relational approach; while the viral branding model resembles the community approach (see Tables 11.2 and 11.3).

Overview

A new taxonomy of brand management is proposed in this book. It is based on an exhaustive analysis of the most influential research in brand management covering the last thirty years; it hence offers a research-based categorization of brand management. A comparison with other categorizations of brand management indicates that, despite different starting points, the frameworks and especially the results of the categorizations are comparable in many ways (see Table 11.4).

It is interesting to compare our analysis with the Goodyear categorization, because the starting point of the two frameworks is so different. Goodyear's analysis provides insight into how brands play different roles as a market evolves

Table 11.4 Comparison of brand management categorizations

Categorization	This taxonomy	Goodyear (1996)	Louro and Cunha (2001)	Holt (2004)
Discriminators	A Kuhnian analysis of 500+ research papers	Macro-level analysis of market evolution	Customer centrality and strategic priority (in literature)	Widely used branding models (in literature and practice)
Comparable brand categories	The economic approach	Brands as reference	The product paradigm	
	The identity approach	Brand as company	The projective paradigm	
	The consumer-based approach	Brand as personality	The adaptive paradigm	Mind-share branding
	The personality approach	Brand as personality	The relational paradigm	Emotional branding
	The relational approach	Brand as personality	The relational paradigm	Emotional branding
	The community brand categories approach			Viral branding
	The cultural approach	Brand as icon + brand as policy		Cultural branding

and its consumers become more sophisticated, which is quite different from the Kuhnian approach used in this book. The proposed brand roles are, however, highly comparable to the evolution of brand management as a scientific discipline. Hence, the macro-level analysis of evolving market places is comparable to the analysis of how the academic discipline has evolved (even though the proposed evolution of brand roles does not fit the chronology of the taxonomy).

In Louro and Cunha's framework, the most influential brand management literature is categorized using two discriminators (brand centrality and customer centrality). The four brand management paradigms identified in that framework more or less cover five approaches of our taxonomy.

Holt compares axioms of the four most popular branding models. The side-by-side presentation of these models is very much comparable to the five latest approaches of the taxonomy in this book.

Concluding remarks

The proposed taxonomy of the seven approaches hence complements existing frameworks or categorizations of brand management even though it stems from a different background. The taxonomy provides much detail to enhance under-standing of brand management, both when it comes to width and when it comes to depth. The fact that the taxonomy proposes seven approaches to brand manage-ment provides a very detailed insight into the subject. Furthermore, the chosen background of research articles and Kuhnian philosophy of science (Bjerre *et al.* 2008) has provided the taxonomy with a detailed and logical structure based on the interconnectedness between assumptions, theories, methods and data and managerial implications.

References and further reading

Bjerre, M., Heding, T. and Knudtzen, C. (2008), 'Using the dynamic paradigm funnel to analyse brand management', in K. Tollin and A. Caru (eds), *Strategic Market Creation: A New Perspective on Marketing and Innovation Management*, Chichester, UK: Wiley, pp. 27–48.

Goodyear, M. (1996), 'Divided by a common language: Diversity and deception in the world of global marketing', *Journal of the Market Research Society*, 38 (2): 105–23.

Holt, D. B. (2004), *How Brands Become Icons: The Principles of Cultural Branding*, Boston, MA: Harvard Business School Press.

Keller, K. L. (2003), 'Brand synthesis: The multidimensionality of brand knowledge', *Journal of Consumer Research*, 20 (4): 595–600.

Louro, M. J. and Cunha, P. V. (2001), 'Brand management paradigms', *Journal of Marketing Management*, 17 (7–8): 849–75.

12 Keywords in brand management

This chapter introduces the reader to keywords often used in brand management but not covered by this textbook. It also elaborates on concepts mentioned in the approach chapters, but not granted the same attention as the theoretical building blocks of each approach. The concepts explained in further detail here are all marked in the approach chapters.

This chapter hence provides a list of keywords that readers will often stumble upon when reading this and other brand management texts. These keywords are provided with references to recommended supplementary reading and will enable the reader to fully understand the many concepts mentioned in the approach chapters as well as providing a guide to some of the most common concepts in brand management.

The keywords are listed alphabetically.

Adbusters

As mentioned in the ideological perspective on cultural brand management, Adbusters is a non-profit, anti-consumerist organization. Adbusters was founded by Kalle Lasn and Bill Schmalz. The higher aim of the organization is anti-capitalism and it is devoted to anti-consumerism by provoking people to reflect on the pervasive influence of advertising and consumer culture. In his most influential book *Culture Jamming*, Lasn portrays consumerism as the fundamental evil of the modern era. The organization has launched numerous international campaigns to raise awareness, including 'buy nothing day', 'TV turnoff week' and Occupy Wall Street. It is also known for its so-called 'subvertisements', satirical reinterpretations of popular advertisements. For further insights into Adbusters, we recommend this article: Rumbo, J. D. (2002) 'Consumer resistance in a world of advertising clutter, the case of Adbusters', *Psychology & Marketing*, vol. 19 (2) or read the books by Kalle Lasn: *Culture Jam* (2000), *Design Anarchy* (2005) and *Meme Wars: The Creative Destruction of Neoclassical Economics* (2012), *www.adbusters.org*

Blue Ocean

Blue ocean strategy is a management concept developed by professors W. Chan Kim and Renée Mauborgne from INSEAD in France. The strategy revolves around the idea that the company should not waste too much attention on the competition but rather focus all efforts to build the uniqueness of the company or brand. It should create market advantages by creatively innovating new products and ways to reach the consumer. The company should hence instead of operating in an ocean red with blood from the heavy competition, focus on creating a blue ocean free from competitors, thus keeping the company always ten steps ahead of the competition. For more information we recommend the original book *Blue Ocean Strategy* by W. Chan Kim & Renée Mauborgne (2005).

Brand

The brand is and has been defined in many different ways over the years, depending on the perspective and school of thought from which the brand is defined. Hence the focus and scope of the definition often depends on the academic background of the author/originator. In the classical definition, the brand is linked to the identification of a product and the differentiation from its competitors, through the use of a certain name, logo, design or other visual signs and symbols. The American Marketing Association (AMA) defined the brand in 1960 as:

> A name, term, sign, symbol, or design, or a combination of them which is intended to identify the goods or services of one seller or a group of sellers and to differentiate them from those of competitors.

Other more recent definitions of branding also include internal and organizational processes. Many brand management books today feature extremely broad definitions, because they aim at covering all the different aspects and facets of the brand and how it has developed over time. In 2013, the American Marketing Association (AMA) defined the brand as:

> A brand is a customer experience represented by a collection of images and ideas; often, it refers to a symbol such as a name, logo, slogan, and design scheme. Brand recognition and other reactions are created by the accumulation of experiences with the specific product or service, both directly relating to its use, and through the influence of advertising, design and media commentary. A brand often includes an explicit logo, fonts, colour schemes, symbols, sound, which may be developed to represent implicit values, ideas and even personality.

This book is all about understanding the core of different brand perspectives and their implications for how the brand is understood, explored and managed. The seven approaches offer seven quite different understandings of the brand and would hence result in seven different definitions. We will therefore not give any definite brand definitions, but will provide the reader with different perspectives on the nature of the brand. From there, it will then be up to the reader, after having read the seven brand approach chapters, to create their own definitions.

Brand architecture

Brand architecture is the structure organizing the brand portfolio. It defines brand roles and relationships among a company's brands, for example the role between a car brand and the model brand (as in Volkswagen Golf). Some corporations choose to communicate the corporate brand to the market while others choose to market product brands to specific segments and keep the corporate brand in the background. According to Olins (1990), brand architecture can be structured in three main ways. Monolithic brand structure equals a structure where the company relies solely on a corporate brand; at the other end of the spectrum there are the individually branded products, and finally the brand architecture can consist of endorsed brands, which are a hybrid, where a corporate brand is used to endorse the corporate brands in the portfolio. If interested in more information about brand architecture, we recommend *Brand Leadership* by Aaker and Joachimsthaler (2002), Part III and *Strategic Brand Management: Creating and Sustaining Brand Equity Long Term* by Kapferer (1997), Chapter 7. They both offer very good treatments of this subject. The main differences between product and corporate branding are explained in Table 5.1 of this book.

Brand audit

A brand audit assesses the health of a brand. Typically, it consists of a brand inventory and a brand exploratory. The brand inventory is a detailed internal description of exactly how the brand has been marketed. The brand exploratory is an external investigation of what the brand means to consumers (through focus groups and other marketing research techniques). Brand audits are most useful when conducted on a regular basis (Keller 2000). The seven brand approaches do not go into depth with how to conduct a brand audit in practice, but inspiration for how to conduct a brand exploratory in the seven different brand perspectives can be found in the methods and data sections of the seven approach chapters. For a practical guide to conducting a brand audit, we recommend: *Strategic Brand Management: Building, Measuring, and Managing Brand Equity* by Kevin Lane Keller.

Brand culture

Brand culture is a term that has been increasingly used over the last few years. It sometimes refers to the organizational culture of the brand (micro-level culture) and sometimes to the brand as part of the broader cultural landscape (macro-level culture). For insight into the organizational perspective of brand culture, the reader can turn to the identity approach (Chapter 5). How brands affect macro-level culture and how they can benefit from playing an active role in mainstream culture are the topics of Chapter 10. For further insight into the different meanings of brand culture, we recommend the anthology *Brand Culture* by Schroeder and Salzer-Morling (2006).

Brand equity

Fundamentally, the goal for any brand manager is to endow products and/or services with brand equity (Park and Srinivasan 1994, Farquhar 1989). Brand equity defines the value of the brand and can refer to two understandings of brand value, namely a strategic, subjective understanding or brand equity as a financial, objective expression of the value of the brand.

In the financial understanding of brand equity, the concept is a way to account for how much value a brand holds. Brand equity is one of the intangible entries on the balance sheet (such as *goodwill* and *know-how*). Being able to account for how much the brand holds is extremely important, both in relation to financial statements, mergers, acquisitions and as a tool for brand managers to argue their case.

The subjective understanding of brand equity refers to the consumers' perception of the brand and is strategically valuable for brand management. Consumers are the ones who experience the brand, and their perception of brand equity can be defined as: 'A consumer perceives a brand's equity as the value added to the functional product or service by associating it with the brand name' (Aaker and Biel 1993, p. 2).

A good introduction to the concept of brand equity can be found in Kapferer (1997), Chapter 1. For more information about the financial approach to brand equity Simon and Sullivan (1993) and Lindemann (2004) offer good explanations. More literature about strategic approaches to brand equity can be found in Aaker (1991) and Keller (1993). Creation of brand equity is at the heart of brand management, and the seven brand approaches feature seven varied perspectives on how to work strategically with brand equity optimization.

Brand essence

Most academic brand management authors agree that every brand has an identity and that every brand identity contains an essence (DNA or kernel) that is the very core of the brand. The brand essence is most often an abstract idea or sentence summarizing what is the heart and soul of the brand. In order for the brand not to become compromised, the brand essence should stay the same over the course of time and no marketing actions that will compromise the brand essence should be allowed. We believe that finding the right brand essence requires insight into as many facets of the brand as the seven approaches provide. For an introduction to brand essence, turn to the brand identity system in Aaker and Joachimsthaler (2002) and Kapferer (1997, where the same notion is called brand kernel), and in Keller (2003, where it is called brand mantra).

Brand extensions

A brand can be extended into new product categories. Brand extensions are often necessary when adapting to changes in the environment or in order to reap the full benefits of a strong brand. Extensions have many benefits. In the beginning, brand extensions were used as a strategic tool mainly to enter new markets (Aaker and Keller 1990). Today, brand extensions are also used to underpin and develop the brand to meet market changes.

A successful brand extension should respect the brand essence and thereby be based on the core of the brand and be true to the brand vision. If a brand is extended to a product category or to clients in a way that does not at all consider the core of the original brand, both brands risk dilution. We do not address the subject in this book: excellent treatments can be found in Kapferer (1997), Chapter 8 and Keller (2003), Chapter 12, or in the classic article: 'Consumer evaluations of brand extensions' by David Aaker and Kevin Lane Keller.

Brand genealogy

A genealogist goes back in history, uncovers family histories and constructs family trees. Brand genealogy is a managerial mindset introduced in the cultural branding model (Holt 2004) where the brand manager goes back and uncovers the brand's history. In the cultural approach, it is assumed that brands play important roles in mainstream culture and that the ways they play these roles determine their level of success. An introduction to this managerial mindset is found in Chapter 10 (this book), for the full treatment turn to *How Brands Become Icons* by Douglas B. Holt.

Brand icon

An exclusive elite of valuable brands can claim icon status, which is considered the holy grail of brand management. An iconic brand holds references that most people agree upon and it obtains that status by playing an active role in contemporary culture. An introduction to brand icons is found in Chapter 10 of this book, for the full treatment turn to *How Brands Become Icons* by Douglas B. Holt.

Brand loyalty

Achieving a high degree of loyalty is an important goal in the branding process. Loyal consumers are valuable consumers because it is much more expensive to recruit new customers than nursing and keeping existing ones. Brands are important vehicles when building consumer loyalty as they provide recognizable fix points in the shopping experience. The concept of brand loyalty has been elaborated in the relational approach (Chapter 8) that seeks to answer *how* and *why* loyal brand consumers consume the brand of choice. For more insights into brand loyalty, we recommend Chapter 5 in *Strategic Brand Management* by Kevin Lane Keller (2003) that offers a good overview and explanation of how to develop loyalty programs. Or a classic from this field is Arjun Chaudhuri and Horris B. Hoolbrook's article: 'The chain of effects from brand trust and brand affect to brand performance: The role of brand loyalty', published in the *Journal of Marketing* (2001).

Brand portfolio

A brand portfolio is the range of brands a company has in the market. How the brand portfolio is managed relates to strategic issues of brand architecture, market segmentation and product versus corporate branding. *Brand Management: Research, Theory and Practice* does not touch upon this subject. We recommend Kapferer 1997, Chapter 9 and Aaker and Joachimsthaler (2002), Part III, for book treatments of this topic. New theories suggest that a brand portfolio should be analysed in three-dimensional molecule systems, including also the brand portfolios of competitors. For more about this perspective, we recommend: *The Infinite Asset* by Hill and Lederer (2001).

Brand positioning

The idea of brand positioning is based on the assumption that consumers have limited mind space for commercial messages and that the most successful brands hence are the ones able to position themselves in the minds of consumers by adapting the most congruent and consistent commercial message. The idea is linked to the information-processing theory of consumer choice that is the basis of the consumer-based approach in Chapter 6 of this book. Another recommended reading is *Positioning: the Battle for your Mind* by Ries and Trout (2001).

Brand recall and recognition

Brand recall is a measurement term closely linked to brand awareness that provides a way to measure how well brand identities are embedded in consumers' memory and to what extend consumers can identify a brand under various conditions. Brand recall refers to the ability of the consumers to generate and retrieve the brand in their memory when, for example thinking of the brand category. Techniques to uncover recall and recognition are surveys and interviews, where consumers are asked to recall as many brands they can from a specific category. Brand recognition refers to the ability of the consumers to correctly differentiate a brand they previously have been exposed to from other brands in the same category. This does not necessarily require that the consumers identify the brand name, but that they are able to respond to a certain brand after viewing, for example. the visual packaging images. Recall and recognition are often used to measure the effect of mass communication and advertising campaigns. For more on brand awareness, recall or recognition, we recommend *Strategic Brand Management: Building, Measuring and Managing Brand Equity* by Kevin Lane Keller (2003).

Brand revitalization

A brand sometimes ages and declines in strength because as time goes by it loses its relevance and attractiveness for consumers. There can be different reasons for that ageing or decline in brand relevance, for example the brand may not have adapted to changes in the environment or to changes in consumer preferences. Sometimes the situation occurs where the brand simply ages along with the ageing of its core consumers.

The solution for an ageing brand or a brand in decline can be revitalization. The key for brand management when revitalizing a brand is always to start the process by identifying or reviving an existing brand vision and finding new and innovative ways of making that brand vision relevant once again for existing or new consumers. This book does not elaborate the topic, but we recommend Chapter 11 in *Strategic Brand Management: Creating and Sustaining Brand Equity Long Term* by Kapferer (1997).

Brand strategy

The majority of brand management textbooks feature generic 'one size fits all' guidelines for building a brand strategy. It is our conviction that every brand is unique and requires its own unique recipe for success.

The aim of a brand strategy is to enhance the internal and external opportunities of the brand. The brand strategy must be strategic, visionary and proactive rather than tactical and reactive. Each brand must find its own holy grail to success – in the shape of a unique and relevant brand identity and brand vision; these are the first elements that must be in place when developing a brand strategy. The brand vision is brought to life through a customized brand strategy able to release the full potential of the brand. Brand managers must have long-term rather than a short-term focus. If the performance of the brand is based on quarterly sales figures, chances are that the brand strategy will end up being much more tactical than strategic, without enough visionary thinking to drive the growth and the strength of the brand in the future.

A prerequisite for making the brand strategy work is that it is closely linked to the business strategy. This means that the brand and the brand strategy should not be perceived as something other than or as an addition to business strategy developed at late stages in a product launch for example. In an ideal world, business and brand strategy should be developed simultaneously and support each other. The brand vision must also resonate with consumers and differentiate the brand from competitors. Once the brand vision has been established, a customized range of elements that comprise the brand strategy should be prioritized and developed. The brand strategy will typically consist of a customized range of elements from the seven brand approaches. Each of the seven brand approaches has certain strengths and weaknesses which is why a customized combination of elements from the relevant approaches that matches the specific challenges and opportunities the brand faces will provide a foundation for the right brand strategy.

Great guidelines for the implementation of the brand strategy can be found in the managerial implications of each approach. Here, it is possible to evaluate which managerial steps are in line with the approaches on which the brand identity and brand vision are based.

Brand stretch

It is assumed that all brands have a core that should stay the same over the course of time (see the section about brand essence). When a brand is extended into new product categories, or joins co-branding ventures, its identity is stretched. The trick is to stretch it enough to be able to go in new directions, but never to stretch it to such an extent that the essence is diluted. Since this book does not go into more detail with brand stretch, for a more thorough review of the subject we recommend Chapter 8 in *Strategic Brand Management: Creating and Sustaining Brand Equity Long Term* by Kapferer (1997).

Co-branding

Co-branding occurs when two or more brands are combined in a joint product or brand. This phenomenon is also called brand alliance or brand bundling. The two companies should consider carefully what their strategic alliance means for their respective brand portfolios, as their brands will become more associated in the future through the new product. Keller (2003) in Chapter 7 describes this phenomenon in more detail. A good article highlighting the effects co-branding has on brand equity and customer trials, while also offering a good review of the concept of co-branding, is: 'Co–branding: Brand equity and trial effects' by Washburn, Till and Priluck (2000).

Content marketing

The rationale of content marketing is that consumers have turned off the traditional world of marketing and advertising; therefore, consumers can no longer be reached by using these traditional marketing tools. Content marketing tries to solve this by providing a strategic marketing approach focused on creating and distributing valuable, relevant and consistent content or information to attract and retain customers. It is a key in digital marketing and viral branding and very practitioner-led. A key reading on the subject is: 'The rise of storytelling as the new marketing', by Joe Pulizi, *Publishing Research Quarterly* (2012) or *EPIC Content Marketing – How to Tell a Different Story, Break Through the Clutter, and Win More Customers by Marketing Less* also by Joe Pulizi (2013). The book *Brand Journalism* (Andy Bull 2013) also provides a good-practice guide for how to use content marketing to build stronger brands. For additional best practice and tools for content marketing, we recommend the digital resources at: *www.contentmarketinginstitute.com*.

Corporate brand

When the corporation is branded instead of the individual products, a corporate brand is the case. In most literature on corporate branding, it is assumed that the energy and inspiration of the brand stem from within the organization and that a branding strategy, in order to be successful, requires the engagement of the whole corporation. Read more in Chapter 5 (this book) about the identity approach. For additional literature, we recommend the comprehensive anthology: *Revealing the Corporation: Perspectives on Identity, Image, Reputation, Corporate Branding, and Corporate-Level Marketing* edited by Balmer and Greyser (2003) or the research article by another pioneering duo on the subject: 'Bringing the corporation into corporate branding' by Hatch and Schultz (2003).

CSR – Corporate Social Responsibility

CSR – corporate social responsibility became popular in the 1960s and has since become an integral part of business strategy relevant to many companies. The term refers to a corporation's legal, social and moral responsibility towards the community or environment in which it operates – without legal obligation. CSR, hence provides a set of ethical business guidelines that a corporation will live by. Advocates of CSR argue that corporations increase long-term profits by operating with a CSR perspective or as an indisputable part of the business model. Critics of CSR question the benefits of CSR on profitability and argue that CSR is merely 'window dressing', which is not necessarily reflected in operating procedures. CSR is a culturally very heterogeneous concept and living up to CSR standards means very different things when operating in, for example the United States versus China or Europe. The fair trade system is a good example of CSR, where an ethical marketing organization attempts to organize a social movement to ensure fair trade for producers in developing countries. For more literature on corporate social responsibility, we recommend *Corporate Social Responsibility: Readings and Cases in a Global Context*, by Andrew Crane *et al.* (2013).

Doppelgänger brand image

A doppelgänger brand image refers to an assembly of the disapproving negative stories or images of a brand circulated in popular culture in a loosely organized network of consumers, brand activists and opinion leaders, and it represents a serious threat to emotional branding especially for large multinational companies. The doppelgänger brand image is however not just a threat, it can also be used as a diagnostic tool to monitor and understand the cultural vulnerability of a brand. To gain more insights into the doppelgänger brand construct, we recommend the article: 'Emotional branding and the strategic value of the doppelgänger brand image' by Thompson *et al.* (2006) or 'How myth and ideology animate a brand – Mediated moral conflict' (Luedicke *et al.* 2010).

Employee branding

Employee branding is defined as 'the process by which employees internalize the desired brand image and are motivated to project the image to customers and other organizational constituents' (Miles and Mangold 2004 p. 68). It is a notion resembling the 'living the brand' concept a lot; turn to Chapter 5 (this book) about the identity approach, Miles and Mangold (2004) and the references mentioned under 'living the brand' for further insight.

Employer branding

The term 'employer branding' relates to strategies for communicating about a company as an attractive employer to both current and potential employees. It is a hot management topic at the moment with a corresponding number of books and articles. On the subject, we recommend: *The Employer Brand: Bringing the Best of Brand Management to People at Work* (Barrow and Mosley 2005). It emphasizes the interrelationship between HR, communication and top management. For more about the emotive and tangible benefits for both potential and actual employees, when a corporation engages in employer branding, we recommend the article 'The relation of instrumental and symbolic attributes to a company's attractiveness as an employer' by Lievens and Highhouse (2003). For a good scholarly framework to study of employer branding, we recommend: 'Conceptualizing and researching employer branding' by Backhous and Tickoo (2004).

Identity projects – individual and collective

In consumer culture theory, consumers' individual and collective identity projects are key to understanding how consumers use brands to fulfil identity needs and as a mode of individual self-expression. In this perspective in the consumer, objects or brands are viewed as an extension of self and it is believed that brands or certain objects can on a functional and emotional level contribute to the consumer achieving the goal of their identity project – either on an individual or collective level. Individual identity projects are a focal point for the relational approach (Chapter 8), while the collective identity projects are central to the cultural approach in Chapter 10. An interesting article covering both approaches is the great introduction to consumer culture theory by Arnould and Thompson (2005). For another article with an interesting study of identity projects we recommend: 'A meaning-based model of advertising experiences' by Mick and Buhl (1992).

Ideoscape

Social-cultural anthropologist Appadurai proposes five dimensions that contribute to the global exchange of ideas and information and the way culture and ideas are shaped and dispersed through global cultural processes: ethnoscape, technoscape, finanscape, mediascape and ideoscape.

Within each of the five 'scapes', multiple realities exist. An idea or image changes along with its context depending on the spectator. The rationale behind this theoretical construct is that the meaning attributed to an idea changes depending on the person. It hence acknowledges the existence of an 'imagined world', in which there is no fixed reality – your reality is no more real than the reality of your neighbour. The idea of the 'ideoscape' has been briefly touched upon in the cultural approach, and it describes how ideologies and those that oppose it are highly dependent on the context of the spectator. A picture of, for example, Nelson Mandela will mean very different things to a European child, a black South African or a white South African. For more information about 'ideoscapes', we recommend the book *Brand Culture* (Askegaard 2006) or the article 'Disjuncture and difference in the global cultural economy' in *Cultural Theory: An Anthology* by Appadurai (2010).

Living the brand

Employees are important bearers of the brand, especially when it comes to service brands. 'Living the brand' is an end-goal in the process of engaging employees in the branding process. Making employees live the brand means that employees incorporate and live brand values and thereby deliver the brand promise fully to consumers. The concept is briefly reviewed in the identity approach, Chapter 5 of this book. Other recommended readings are *Living the Brand* by Ind (2001) or 'Living the brand' in *Corporate Branding: Purpose, People, Process* by Karmark (2005).

No Logo

'No logo: Taking Aim at the Brand Bullies' is an international bestseller published by Naomi Klein in 1999. It has been an important driver for the alter-globalization movement. The book focuses on branding and addresses the deeds and misdeeds of big multinational brands, who cover up Asian sweatshops, corporate censorship and culture jamming with glittery and picture-perfect brands. *No Logo* describes movements in resistance to consumerism and big brands, such as Adbusters (also explained in this chapter). The book has become a cultural manifest for alter-globalisation and anti-consumerist movement, but it also paradoxically became a very influential business bestseller because it helped managers to understand the risks of resistance and how to deal with phenomena such as doppelgänger brand images (also explained in this chapter).

Persona

In marketing, personas are fictional characters used along with market segmentation to describe the different target groups or user types of a product. They are a way for the marketer to gain insights into more detailed knowledge about the behaviours, thoughts and feelings of potential customers. They can help marketers to understand, for example customers' decision-making processes when considering and purchasing a product or brand in more depth than a traditional demographic customer description. The concept persona was originally developed by C. G. Jung as a description of the social mask linking and communicating self with the outer and social world. The construct is closely related to the concept of archetypes, described in Chapter 7. For more about personas in marketing, *The New Rules of Marketing* by David M. Scott provides a good overview.

PR – public relations

The Public Relations Society of America defined PR as: 'Public relations is a strategic communication process that builds mutually beneficial relationships between organizations and their publics' (from 2012). Two overriding theories of relationships are predominantly used in PR: systems theory and situational theory. Systems theory underpins the interdependence of organizations with their environment, organizations are part of a greater environment made up of systems, PR is in this perspective a way for organizations to communicate properly and ensure good relations with all system components – politician, supplier or the general public. In the situational theory perspective, the system is also acknowledged, but further it argues that not all 'members' of the system are equally likely to communicate with an organization. Therefore, the organization must identify specific public subgroups to communicate with, based on their relative importance and likelihood to respond to communication. For a comprehensive guide to public relations, we recommend: *Excellence in Public Relations and Communications Management* edited by James E. Grunig (2013).

Product brand

A product brand is a brand linked to the product and not to the corporation and describes a situation where each individual product has its own brand. Choosing to brand the corporation or the product is a question of brand architecture. Marketing a product brand holds several advantages, such as the liberty to market to different segments, the ability to close unsuccessful brands without harming the mother brand and so on. To get an overview of product branding versus corporate branding go to Table 5.1 in this book.

Projective techniques

Projective techniques refer to data collecting methods for activating subconscious feelings or thoughts about a product or brand. Participants are invited (not asked directly) to project their thoughts and feelings for at brand or product into other things: for example if this detergent was an animal, what animal would that be? The idea is that using projection can help uncover and articulate unconscious levels of responses to brands and products and help respondents give up ego-defensive mechanisms. Getting behind these projections, and understanding why one would have a specific projective association, is necessary to gain an understanding of the connection of how a projection relates to that brand or product – probing is used for this step when doing a projective study. Specifically different projective tools can be used such as memory elicitation, sentence or cartoon completion, stereotyping and brand personification. Projective techniques have their origin in psychoanalytical psychology. To gain more insight into projective techniques and for an interesting case study, we recommend: 'Using childhood memories to gain insight into brand meaning' by Braun-LaTour *et al.* (2007) or 'Projective techniques for brand image research: Two personification methods explored' by Hofstede *et al.* (2007).

Push versus pull marketing

In push marketing, the strategy is to push the products to consumers through heavy advertising and ever-present sales channels. The idea is that if only the products are pushed to be visible for consumers, they will also end up choosing a product. Pull strategies on the other hand refer to a marketing strategy approach where the marketer is attempting to pull customers in. Push marketing measurement is more concerned with short-term sales, whereas pull marketing adversely tries to create loyal consumers and encourage word of mouth referrals. Push marketing is focused on creating supply to create demand while pull marketing aims at creating demand before the consumer is presented with supply, hence, creating a preference before the consumer browses consumption choices – basically, what branding is all about.

Service brand

Service brands are brands that sell services instead of physical products. This means that the brand is experienced in the process of consuming the service and that the employee delivering the service becomes a central bearer of the brand. Service brands can benefit from all the same insights as product brands, but as the service encounter requires dedicated employees and human interaction, service brand managers might benefit more from the identity approach and the relational approach (Vallaster and de Chernatony 2005, de Chernatony and Drury 2004). For an overview of the differences between product and service branding, we recommend: 'From goods to service branding: An integrative perspective' by Brodie (2009) or the key publication: 'Cultivating service brand equity' by Berry (2000).

Social media

Social media allow people to create, share or exchange information, ideas and pictures/videos in virtual communities and networks. Kaplan and Haenlein (2010) defined social media as 'a group of Internet-based applications that build on the ideological and technological foundations of Web 2.0, and that allow the creation and exchange of user-generated content'. The users are hence in focus, they are the ones creating and exchanging content on platforms made available to them and that for the most part have evolved into big multinational corporations. Social media can take many shapes and forms such as Facebook, Twitter, LinkedIn, Flickr, Snapchat and blogs. For more reading on social media as phenomenon, we recommend: 'Users of the world, unite! The challenges and opportunities of social media' by Kaplan and Hanlein (2010) or for a key reading about how social media affects branding, we recommend: 'Social media in branding: Fulfilling a need' by Yan (2011).

Storytelling

Storytelling refers to the use of narrative techniques, when communicating about, for example a brand or product. In a brand management context, storytelling is useful, because stories are easier to remember than facts while also adding humanity to brands. This enhances consumers' ability to connect emotionally and create relations with brands. Stories generate empathy, and we can more easily see ourselves in a story and thereby relate to brands telling stories. Research has documented that consumers who have been exposed to story-driven as opposed to fact-driven traditional branding develop much more positive brand associations, and they are willing to pay a higher price for the product. (Lundqvist *et al.* 2013). For more literature on storytelling, we recommend: *Legendary Brands: Unleashing the Power of Storytelling to Create a Winning Market Strategy* by Laurence Vincent (2002).

Transgressions

Transgressions are defined as violations of consumer-brand relationship norms. A transgression occurs when breaches of the implicit or explicit rules guiding the relationship between the brand and the consumer happen (Aaker *et al.* 2004). A research focus for many consumer behaviour scientists is to uncover how brand personality and transgressions made by the brand affect consumer behaviour and consumers' emotional attachments to brands (Steinman 2012). A classic publication about consumer responses to brand transgressions is the article 'When good brands do bad' by Aaker *et al.* (2004).

User imagery

User imagery describes who or what type of person might use a product or brand. It communicates the lifestyle of the user that rubs off on the brand personality. User imagery is hence closely connected to the creation and evolution of brand personality and also the creation of consumer identity (Chapter 7). Often user imagery can be used actively in advertising portraying an ideal or typical user consuming or in some kind of connection with the brand. Having consumers describe a typical user and measurement of these results in relation to the self-image consumers have can help consumption researchers uncover self-brand congruity. A suggested reading is: 'You are what they eat: The influence of reference groups on consumers' connections to brands' by Escalas and Bettman (2003).

Viral branding

The term covers mechanisms where consumers help or in some cases take over the marketing of the brand. A marketer who applies a certain amount of 'coolness' to the brand often initiates viral branding, and the coolness starts a process where consumers spread the brand like a virus. Having consumers support the marketing process, and by their autonomy giving the brand a higher level of authenticity, can be beneficial for the marketer. Still, viral branding implies a risk of a contrary marketing effort, where the brand is 'hijacked' and taken in unintended directions through autonomous meaning-making among consumers (the brand turns into a networked narrative). Even though a brand community is a narrower concept than viral branding, the mechanisms behind the two concepts are comparable; they are described in the community approach, Chapter 9. Another suggested read is *Brand Hijack: Marketing without Marketing* by Wipperfürth (2005).

Web 2.0

In 2001, the dot-com bubble burst and it was the beginning of the end to what many referred to as Web 1.0. Many concluded that the web was overhyped, but instead the dot-com collapse instigated a new technological revolution with the development of business models and services with user-driven content. Hence the shift from Web 1.0 to 2.0 is a move from servers and platforms towards applications, services and social interaction with users creating content as opposed to developers and marketers. For more literature about Web 2.0, we recommend the book: *Groundswell. Winning in a World Transformed by Social Technologies* by Li and Bernoff (2008) and for insights into the consequences Web 2.0 has for branding, we recommend: 'Counterbrand and alter-brand communities: The Impact of Web 2.0 in tribal marketing approaches' by Cova and White (2010). Tim O'Reilly is often referred to as the inventor of Web 2.0 and the inquiring reader might turn to his website and publications: www.oreilly.com.

References and further reading

Aaker, D. A. (1991), *Managing Brand Equity*, New York: Free Press.

Aaker, D. A. and Biel, A. L. (1993), *Brand Equity and Advertising: Advertising's Role in Building Strong Brands*, Hillsdale, NJ: Lawrence Erlbaum Associates.

Aaker, D. A. and Joachimsthaler, E. (2002), *Brand Leadership*, Sydney, Australia: Free Press Business.

Aaker, D. A. and Keller, K. L. (1990), 'Consumer evaluations of brand extensions', *Journal of Marketing*, 54 (1): 27–41.

Aaker, J., Fournier, S. and Brasel, S. A. (2004), 'When good brands do bad', *Journal of Consumer research*, 31 (1): 1–16.

Abratt, R. (1989), 'A new approach to the corporate image management process', *Journal of Marketing Management*, 5 (1): 63–76.

Appadurai, A. (2011), 'Disjuncture and difference in the global cultural economy 1990', in I. Szeman and T. Kaposy (eds), *Cultural Theory: An Anthology*, Chichester, UK: John Wiley and Sons, pp. 282–95.

Arnould, E. J. and Thompson, C. J. (2005), 'Consumer Culture Theory (CCT): Twenty years of research', *Journal of Consumer Research*, 31 (4): 868–82.

Askegaard, S. (2006), 'Brands as a global ideoscape', in J. E. Schroeder and M. Salzer-Morling (eds), *Brand Culture*, London: Routledge.

Backhaus, K. and Tikoo, S. (2004), 'Conceptualizing and researching employer branding', *Career Development International*, 9 (5): 501–17.

Bahl, S. and Milne, G. R. (2010), 'Talking to ourselves: A dialogical exploration of consumption experiences', *Journal of Consumer Research*, 37 (1): 176–95.

Balmer, J. M. T. and Greyser, S. T. (2003), *Revealing the Corporation: Perspectives on Identity, Image, Reputation, Corporate Branding and Corporate-Level Marketing*, London: Routledge.

Barber, J. F. (2008), 'Design Anarchy by Kalle Lasn', *Leonardo*, 41 (2): 193–4.

Barrow, S. and Mosley, R. (2005), *The Employer Brand: Bringing the Best of Brand Management to People at Work*, Chichester: Wiley.

Berry, L. L. (2000), 'Cultivating service brand equity', *Journal of the Academy of Marketing Science*, 28 (1): 128–37.

Braun-LaTour, K. A., LaTour, M. S. and Zinkhan, G. M. (2007), 'Using childhood memories to gain insight into brand meaning', *Journal of Marketing*, 71 (2): 45–60.

Brodie, R. J. (2009), 'From goods to service branding: An integrative perspective', *Marketing Theory*, 9 (1): 107–11.

Bull, A. (2013), *Brand Journalism*, London: Routledge.

Chan Kim, W. and Mauborgne, R. (2005), 'Value innovation: a leap into the blue ocean', *Journal of business strategy*, 26 (4): 22–28.

Chaudhuri, A. and Holbrook, M. B. (2001), 'The chain of effects from brand trust and brand affect to brand performance: the role of brand loyalty', *Journal of Marketing*, 65 (2): 81–93.

Chernatony, L. de and Drury, S. (2004), 'Identifying and sustaining services brands' values', *Journal of Marketing Communications*, 10 (2): 73–93.

Crane, A., Matten, D. and Spence, L. J. (2013), 'Corporate social responsibility in a global context', in Crane, A., Matten, D., and Spence, LJ, *Corporate Social Responsibility: Readings and Cases in a Global Context, 2*: 3–26.

Cova, B. and White, T. (2010), 'Counter-brand and alter-brand communities: the impact of Web 2.0 on tribal marketing approaches', *Journal of Marketing Management*, 26 (3–4): 256–70.

Escalas, J. E. and Bettman J. R. (2003), 'You are what they eat: The infulence of reference groups on consumers' connections to brands', *Journal of Consumer Psychology*, 13 (3): 339–48.

Farquhar, P. H. (1989), 'Managing brand equity', *Marketing Research*, 1 (3): 24–33.

Fischer, E., Otnes, C. C. and Tuncay, L. (2007), 'Pursuing parenthood: Integrating cultural and cognitive perspectives on persistent goal striving', *Journal of Consumer Research*, 34 (4): 425–40.

Gray, E. R. and Schmeltzer, L. R. (1987), 'Planning a face-lift: Implementing a corporate image programme', *Journal of Business Strategy*, 8 (1): 4–10.

Grunig, J. (1993) 'Image and substance: From symbolic to behavioural relationships', *Public Relations Review*, 19 (2): 121–39.

Grunig, J. E. (ed.), (2013), *Excellence in public relations and communication management*, London: Routledge.

Hatch, M. J. and Schultz, M. (1997), 'Relations between organizational culture, identity and image', *European Journal of Marketing*, 31 (5–6): 356–65.

Hatch, M. J. and Schultz, M. (2003), 'Bringing the corporation into corporate branding', *European Journal of Marketing*, 37 (7–8): 1041–64.

Hill, S. and Lederer, C. (2001), *The Infinite Asset*, Boston, MA: Harvard Business School Press.

Hofstede, A. (2007), 'Projective techniques for brand image research: Two personification-based methods explored', *Qualitative Market Research: An International Journal*, 10 (3): 300–309.

Holt, D. B. (2004), *How Brands become Icons: The Principles of Cultural Branding*, Boston, MA: Harvard Business School Press.

Ind, N. (2001) *Living the Brand*, London: Kogan Page.

Kapferer, J-N. (1997), *Strategic Brand Management: Creating and Sustaining Brand Equity Long Term*, London: Kogan Page.

Kaplan, A. M. and Haenlein, M. (2010), 'Users of the world, unite! The challenges and opportunities of social media', *Business Horizons*, 53 (1): 59–68.

Karmark, E. (2005), 'Living the brand', in M. Schultz, Y. M. Antorini and F. F. Csaba (eds), *Corporate Branding: Purpose, People, Process*, Copenhagen, Denmark: Copenhagen Business School Press, pp. 103–24.

Keller, K. L. (1993), 'Conceptualizing, measuring, and managing customer-based brand equity', *Journal of Marketing*, 57 (1): 1–22.

Keller, K. L. (2000), 'The brand report card', *Harvard Business Review*, 78 (1): 147–57

Keller, K. L. (2003), *Strategic Brand Management: Building, Measuring, and Managing Brand Equity* (2nd edn), Upper Saddle River, NJ: Pearson.

Kennedy, S. H. (1977), 'Nurturing corporate images', *European Journal of Marketing*, 11 (3): 119–64.

King, S. (1991), 'Brand building in the 1990s', *Journal of Marketing Management*, 7 (1): 3–13.

Klein, N. (1999), *No Logo: Taking Aim at the Brand Bullies*, New York: Picador.

Lasn, K. (1999), *Culture Jam*, New York: Quill.

Lasn, K. (2012), *Meme Wars: The Creative Destruction of Neoclassical Economics: A Real World Economics Textbook*, New York: Seven Stories Press.

Li, C. and Bernoff, J. (2008), *Groundswell: Winning in a World Transformed by Social Technologies*, Boston, MA: Harvard Business Press.

Lievens, F. and Highhouse, S. (2003), 'The relation of instrumental and symbolic attributes to a company's attractiveness as an employer', *Personnel Psychology*, 56 (1): 75–102.

Lindemann, J. (2004), 'Brand valuation', in R. Clifton (ed.), *Brands and Branding*, London: Economist.

Luedicke, M. K., Thompson, C. J. and Giesler, M. (2010), 'How myth and ideology animate a brand – Mediated moral conflict', *Journal of Consumer Research*, 36 (6): 1016–1032.

Lundqvist, A. (2013), 'The impact of storytelling on the consumer brand experience: The case of a firm-originated story', *Journal of Brand Management*, 20 (4): 283–97.

Mick, D. G. and Buhl, C. (1992), 'A meaning-based model of advertising experiences', *Journal of Consumer Research*, 19 (3): 317–38.

Miles, S. J. and Mangold, G. (2004), 'A conceptualization of the employee branding process', *Journal of Relationship Marketing*, 3 (2–3): 65–88.

Olins, W. (1990), *The Wolff Olins Guide to Corporate Identity*, London: Design Council.

Park, C. S. and Srinivasan, V. (1994), 'A survey-based method for measuring and understanding brand equity and its extendibility', *Journal of Marketing Research*, 31 (2): 271–88.

Pulizi, J. (2012), 'The rise of storytelling as the new marketing', *Publishing Research Quarterly*, 28 (2): 116–23.

Pulizi, J. (2013), *Epic Content Marketing: How to Tell a Different Story, Break Through the Clutter and Win More Customers by Marketing Less*. New York: McGraw-Hill Professional.

Ries, A. and Trout, J. (1983, 2001), *Positioning: The Battle for Your Mind*, New York: McGraw-Hill.

Rumbo, J. D. (2002), 'Consumer resistance in a world of advertising clutter: The case of Adbusters', *Psychology & Marketing*, 19 (2): 127–48.

Schroeder, J. E. and Salzer-Morling, M. (eds) (2006), *Brand Culture*, London: Routledge.

Scott, D. M. (2007), *The New Rules of Marketing and PR: how to use news releases, blogs, podcasting, viral marketing and online media to reach buyers directly*, New York: John Wiley & Sons.

Simon, C. J. and Sullivan, M. W. (1993), 'The measurement and determinants of brand equity: A financial approach', *Marketing Science*, 12 (1): 28–52.

Steinman, R. B. (2012), 'Brand Personality, Brand Transgression and Consumer Behavior', *International Journal of Business and Commerce*, 2 (1): 76–83.

Thompson, C. J., Rindfleisch, A. and Arsel, Z. (2006), 'Emotional branding and the strategic value of the doppelgänger brand image', *Journal of Marketing*, 70 (1): 50–64.

Yan, J. (2011), 'Social media in branding: Fulfilling a need', *Journal of Brand Management*, 18 (9): 688–96.

Vallaster, C. and de Chernatony, L. (2005), 'Internalisation of services brands: The role of leadership during the internal brand building process', *Journal of Marketing Management*, 21 (1–2): 181–203.

Vincent, L. (2002), *Legendary Brands: Unleashing the Power of Storytelling to Create a Winning Market Strategy*, Sydney, Australia: Kaplan Business.

Washburn, J. H., Till, B. D. and Priluck, R. (2000), 'Co-branding: Brand equity and trial effects', *Journal of Consumer Marketing*, 17 (7): 591–604.

Wipperfürth, A. (2005), *Brand Hijack: Marketing without Marketing*, New York: Portfolio.

Author index

In this index, b denotes box, f denotes figure and t denotes table.

Aaker, D. A. 4, 49, 282–5
Aaker, J. 20–1f, 112, 120, 122–3, 125–6,
133–6, 138–9, 141–2, 150, 151b, 154–5,
176b, 187, 293
Abratt, R. 45
Aggarwal, P. 170–1, 187
Ahuvia, A. C. 128, 171
Alba, J. W. 107–8b
Albert, S. 54b
Algesheimer, R. 211b
Allen, C. T. 11t, 11–12
Arsel, Z. 251, 261
Arvidsson, A. 253
Askegaard, S. 232, 290
Atkinson, P. 209
Avery, J. 185, 216

Balmer, J. M. T. 46, 55, 61–2, 63b, 70, 79,
288
Barrow, S. 289
Batra, R. 122, 154, 171, 187
Belk, R. W. 122, 127–8, 153, 197
Bettman, J. R. 85, 93, 115, 293
Biel, A. L. 283
Bitner, M. J. 46, 58, 77b, 79, 160b
Bjerre, M. 4, 18
Borden, N. 20–1f, 27, 33
Braun-LaTour, K. A. 182, 187
Bouwman, M. 92b, 98b
Brasel, A. 150
Brown, S. 196, 215b
Buhl, C. 167, 289

Cameron, D. 241–2, 243b, 246
Cunha, P. V. 87, 110, 272–5, 276t, 278t,
279

de Chernatony, L. xiv (foreword by), 292
Dong, L. 255, 261
Drury, S. 292

Escalas, J. E. 293

Farquhar, P. H. 283
Fournier, S. 11, 20–1f, 112, 150, 158,
160–2, 167–8, 169b, 171, 173t, 174,
175f, 176–7, 178b, 179b, 183–7, 188f,
189–90 (comment by)
Franzen, G. 92b, 98b

Garsten, C. 232
Gay, P. du 229b
Gioia, D. 54b
Goodyear, M. 271–2, 273t, 278t
Greyser, S. E. 46, 61, 63b, 70, 288
Grönroos, C. 34
Grunig, J. 291

Hackley, C. 162–3, 178, 181, 235, 244b
Hammersley, M. 209
Hanby, T. 10–1
Hasselström, A. 232
Hatch, M. J. 20–1f, 46, 51b, 52–3, 55,
57b, 58, 61–2, 72, 77b, 79, 288
Heding, T. 4, 18
Highhouse, S. 289
Hill, S. 285
Holt, D. B. 20–1f, 87, 113, 227, 231,
234, 236–9, 240b, 241–2, 243b, 246–9,
250b, 251, 256–7, 257t, 261–6
(comment by)
Hultman, C. M. 33
Hutchinson, J. W. 107–8b

Izberk-Bilgin, E. 255, 261

James, W. 127
Joachimsthaler, E. 282–3, 285
Jung, C.J. 136b, 166, 290

Kapferer, J.-N. 4, 49, 120, 282–7
Kaikati, A. M. 253, 254b, 261
Karmark, E. 58, 290
Kates, S. M. 230, 261
Keller, K. L. 14, 20–1f, 85, 87, 94–5, 97,
    102, 103b, 108, 109b, 111–12, 115–17
    (comment by), 206, 275, 282–5, 287
Kennedy, S. H. 49b
Klein, N. 252, 290
Kleine, S. S. 178
Knudtzen, C. 4, 18
Kotler, P. 39
Kozinets, R. V. 206–7, 211–12, 218–19,
    261
Kuhn, T. S. 4, 10, 12, 18, 23, 271,
    278–9

LaTour, M. S. 182, 187
Lederer, C. 285
Lee, L. 205, 205f, 206, 218
Lehman, D. R. 112
Lievens, F. 289
Lindemann, J. 283
Llamas, R. 197
Louro, M. J. 87, 110, 272–5, 276t, 278t,
    279

McAlexander, J. 200, 203–5, 209b, 221
McCarthy, E. J. 20–1f, 27, 34
McCracken, G. 180b, 234–5, 236f, 237
Mangold, G. 288–9
Mariampolski, H. 208
Mark, M. 136–7b
Martin, J. 66t
Mick, D. 167, 289
Miles, S. J. 288–9
Miller, F. 11t, 11–12
Monga, A. B. 253, 254b, 261
Mosley, R. 289

Muñiz, A. M. Jr. 20–1f, 112, 195–6, 197b,
    200–1, 203–5, 210b, 213, 215, 217, 219,
    221, 223–4 (comment by)

O'Guinn, T. C. 20–1f, 19, 112, 195, 196f,
    200–1, 204–5, 213, 215, 219, 221, 222f,
    223–4 (comment by)
Olins, W. 49b, 56, 78, 282

Park, C. S. 283
Park, C. W. 95
Pearson, C. S. 136–7b
Plummer, J. 122, 131b, 135, 153, 154–5
    (comment by)

Ries, A. 85, 263, 285

Salzer-Mörling, M. 51b, 282
Schouten, J. W. 200, 204–5, 209b, 221
Schroeder, J. E. 51b, 282
Schultz, M. 20–1f, 46, 50t, 51–3, 55, 57b,
    58, 61–2, 72, 75t, 76b, 79, 79–82
    (comment by), 288
Shau, H. J. 171, 197b, 203, 205, 210b,
    218, 221
Shaw, E. 33
Simon, C. J. 283
Srinivasan, V. 283
Sullivan, M. W. 283
Sung, Y. 122, 133, 154

Thompson, C. J. 202, 213, 233, 251, 261,
    288–9
Tian, K. 255, 261
Tinkham, S. F. 122, 133, 154
Torelli 253, 254b, 261
Trout, J. 85, 263, 285

Vallaster, C. 292

Wipperfürth, A. 294, 198

Yao, J. L. 167, 179b

Zinkham, G. M. 182, 187

Subject index

In this index, b denotes box, f denotes figure and t denotes table.

'90-9-1 principle' 205

AC4ID framework 62–5
adaptive paradigm 274–6
Adbusters 253, 280, 290
advertising 35, 59, 103, 105, 120–2, 135, 144–6, 153–5, 206, 233, 235–6
American Girl 242, 245, 249, 261
American Marketing Association (AMA) 281
animism 165
anthropological research 53, 64, 198, 245
anti-brand activities 234, 250–60
Apple 120, 173, 194–5, 197, 204–5, 221, 238, 258
Apple Newton brand community 198, 203, 210, 221
archetypes 135–7, 142, 166, 182, 290
associations 14, 53, 87–8, 91, 94–110, 130–4, 141–2, 237, 255, 277, 291
Atlanta Agreement, the 254

Big Five personality, modified 125, 132–3, 138
blog 206, 218, 220
Blue Ocean 280–1
Body Shop 63
Botox 251
brand, definition of 281
brand architecture 282
brand attitudes 96, 122
brand audit 282
brand awareness 94, 96, 98, 101–2, 105–8
brand communities: anthropological research 15; brands attracting 213–14; 'consciousness of kind' 200–4, 208;

construct 202; facilitation of 217; geographical dispersion 201; legitimacy 201–2; observing 217; oppositional brand loyalty 201, 189; 'sense of moral responsibility' 200–4; 'shared rituals and traditions' 201f; subcultures of consumption 200, 204; see also community approach
brand–consumer exchange: community approach 196f; consumer-based approach 88f; cultural approach 231f; economic approach 30–2; identity approach 53–4; personality approach 125f; relational approach 164f
brand culture 282; see also cultural approach
brand equity, customer-based (CBBE) 89, 94f
brand equity, definitions of 283; brand equity pyramid 4
brand essence 283
brand extensions 283
brand genealogy 284
brand icons 15, 145, 230, 237f, 284; see also cultural branding; iconic brands, management of
brand identity 4, see also identity approach
brand identification 58, 77b, 78
brand image 68, 71f, 94f, 106, 162, 276; see also consumer-based approach and doppelgänger brand image
brand knowledge 94f, 96, 101f, 107, 109, 111f
brand loyalty 12, 125, 132, 160, 164, 183f, 195–8, 214, 217, 284; oppositional 201f
brand love 171, 187

brand management paradigms 273f;
adaptive paradigm 274–6; brand
centrality dimension 274; customer
centrality dimension 274; product
paradigm 274–6; projective paradigm
274–6; relational paradigm 274–6
brand meaning 11, 92, 132, 165, 175, 188,
196–8, 204, 208, 211, 215–17, 230–3,
275
brand mystique 216
brand myths 260
brand name choice 107b
brand ownership 107, 206, 249
brand personality 13; appeal 143; and
archetypes 130–2; brand-self exchange
127–8, 143; communication platform
142–3; construct 118, 119–20;
consumer-brand relationships 144–6;
direct sources 140, 141; exciting
personality type 141b, 145; expression of
self 128, 129f, 130, 132; indirect sources
140, 141–42; management 139, 140t;
measurement of 134, 137; sincere
personality type 141b, 145; target groups
143, 148; *see also* personality approach
brand perspective 11, 13–17, 19–20, 22,
29, 85–7, 111–13, 128, 158, 183, 187,
193–9, 206
brand portfolio 185, 282, 285, 287
brand positioning 144, 285
brand prism model 4
brand recall 94f, 102, 106, 285
brand recognition 94f, 106, 281, 285
brand relation 112, 131–2, 143, 149–51,
158, 160–2, 164–70, 174–8, 182–4,
186–8, 275; *see also* personality *and*
relational approach
brand reputation 45, 51–6, 57, 59–64,
67–73, 237, 248
brand revitalization 285
brand stories 195, 264
brand strategy 106, 108, 184, 195, 20–21f,
251, 264, 286
brand stretch 287
brand symbolism 263–5
brand value creation 20–2, 48, 54, 87–8,
104, 164, 229, 231
brandfests 199, 203–4, 217, 219
branding models 113, 275; cultural
branding 277; emotional branding 277;
mindshare branding 277; viral branding
277

brands, roles of: classic branding 256, 257t;
postmodern branding 256, 257t; post-
postmodern branding 256, 257t

citizen-artist brand: anti-brand movement
256–60; manager 256–7;
postmodern/post-postmodern paradigms
256–7
Clearblue 243b
classic branding 256, 257t
co-branding 287
Coca-cola 107b, 137b, 181, 216, 238t,
240b
'cognitive man' 88
cognitive perspective: associative networks
91; brand choice 91; brand-consumer
exchange 88–9; cognitive mechanisms
99; computer metaphor 89–90, 97;
higher cognitive processes 90; memory
processes 85; *see also* consumer choice
theory
cognitive psychology *see* cognitive
perspective
collective unconscious 136b
communal relationships (versus exchange)
170
communication: personality approach 125,
131b, 134–5, 136b, 138, 144–5, 148–50;
consumer-based approach 87–8, 104–6;
community (triangular communication)
193, 195, 206–7, 214; cultural branding
234–9, 241–3, 20–1fb, 249, 257; iconic
brands, management of 259; identity
approach 48–50, 53–4, 59–60, 65–7, 68,
73t, 81
community affiliations 205, 205t
community approach 3, 21f; '90-9-1
principle' 205; blog 206, 218, 220;
brand, collective rejection of 219; brand-
consumer exchange 20–1f, 196–8; brand
loyalty 198; brand meaning 198; brand
perspective 20–1f, 198; brandfests 203–4;
community affiliations 205, 205t;
community brands 203–4; community
theory 200, 201f; consumer perspective
20–1f, 197; crowdsourcing 207, 217–21;
dos and don'ts of 220b; eWOM
(electronic word of mouth) 218, 222;
'grassroots R and D' 218; 'homo
connectus' 197, 199, 206, 213–14, 219;
hubs 205, 205t; key reading 20–1f, 225;
key words 20–1f, 227; methods 20–1f,

208–13; networked narrative 207, 218–19, 293; platform brands 219, 221; pools 205, 205t; 'seeding' 218; scientific tradition 20–1f, 198; 25; sharing economy 219; social media 193–5, 203, 206–8, 213–17; subcultures of consumption 200, 204; supporting themes 200; time of origin 20–1f; triadic brand relationship 193, 195, 206–7, 214; Web 2.0 193–5, 197, 200, 206–8, 213–17, 219, 292, 294; webs 205, 205t; WOMM (word of mouth management) 218; *see also* brand communities; ethnographic methods

competition, identifying 108

consumer-based approach 3, 20–1f; adaptive paradigm 274–6; brand associations 87, 292; brand awareness 94, 285; brand-consumer exchange 88; brand equity 86–7, 89–90; brand knowledge 94–7, 101–4, 107b, 109b; brand name choice 107b; brand perspective 20–1f; brand positioning 86, 285; brand recognition *versus* recall 285; brand value creation 20–1f; 'cognitive man' 20–1f, 88; communication 87–8, 104–6; consumer behaviour, study of 88, 116; consumer collectives, online creative 207, 207t, 218; consumer perspective 20–1f; data collection 100–4; don'ts; dos and don'ts 111b; inside-out *versus* outside-in approach 87; key reading 20–1f; key words 20–1f; managerial guidelines 104–10; 'market sensing' priority 110; methods 20–1f; multidisciplinary approach 115; non-cognitive issues 116; organizational vision 110; scientific tradition 20–1f; strategy, emphasis on 108; supporting themes 20–1f; time of origin 20–1f; *see also* brand equity; cognitive perspective; consumer choice theory

consumer choice theory 85, 88–90, 93–4, 97, 106, 285

consumer collectives, online creative 207, 207t, 218

'consumer jihad' 255

consumer perspective 12, 20–1f

content marketing 287

corporate brand 287

corporate branding 13, 46, 48–51, 54, 71, 74, 81–2, 282, 285, 287

corporate identity 13, 20f, 49b, 50, 52–7, 60ft, 61, 63–6, 69b, 70, 73t

corporate social responsibility (CSR) 253–5, 288

crowdsourcing 207, 217–21

cultural approach 3, 16; anti-brand activities 234, 250–60; brand, definition of 210; brand-consumer exchange 231–3; brand perspective 20–1f, 233; brand value creation 20–1f; citizen-artist brand 229–30, 245, 256–9; consumer culture 230; 'consumer jihad' 255; consumer perspective 20–1f, 232; corporate social responsibility (CSR) 253–5; cultural consumption theory 230; cultural studies 20–1f, 229, 229b, 231b, 233; Doppelgänger brand image 251; dos and don'ts 260; ethnographic studies 244; identity projects, cultural 231–2, 242, 245, 248; ideological issues 249–55; ideological issues, managerial implications of 255–6; ideoscape 289; ideoscapes, global 232, 250–1, 255–6; key reading 20–1f; key words 20–1f; macro-level culture 229b, 230; 'market man' (*homo mercans*) 232–4; Marxist analysis 253; methods 20–1f, 242–7; No Logo movement 252–3; phenomenological interviews 233, 244–6; scientific tradition 20–1f; semiotics 242–4; six-stage strategic framework 241, 243b; supporting themes 20–1f; time of origin 20–1f; *see also* cultural branding; iconic brands, management of

cultural branding: advertising 238; brand icons 237–9, 249, 251; brand myths 260; brand symbolism 263–5; change, moving through 231; communication 234–9, 241–3, 20–1fb, 249, 257; cultural histories 263; cultural icons 238t; definition of 238; iconic status, rise to 238–40; identity brands 238; and mindshare model 237t, 239, 262–6, ; societal desires 264; *see also* iconic brands, management of

cultural branding model 276t

cultural consumption theory 230

customer centrality dimension 274

data collection: chronometric analysis 101; consumer-based approach 100–4;

cultural approach 242–7; economic
approach 36–9; ethnographic methods
208–11; input-output methods 100;
matrix arrays 100, 101t; memory
elicitation method 181–2; process-
tracing approaches 101; prompted
protocols 100; verbal protocols 100
data interpretation, macro-level culture
234, 245
depth interviews 167–70, 177; biographical
questions 180, 180b; conducting 180,
180b; depth *versus* breadth 179; felt
experiences 182; grand-tour opening
questions 180, 180b; life story methods
177; playing dumb 180b; prompting
techniques 180, 180b
Doppelgänger brand image 251, 288
Dr Pepper 155
dyadic brand relationship 14, 22, 125, 164,
176, 183

economic approach 3, 20–1f; behaviour of
optimization 30; brand-consumer
exchange 31f, 30–32; brand perspective
20–1f; brand value creation 20–1f;
classical marketing theory 27; consumer
perspective 20–1f; data collection 36–9;
'economic man' 29–31, 35; functional
utility 30, 36; functionalist brand
perspective 13; 'invisible hand' principle
30–2, 36, 42b; key reading 20–1f; key
words 20–1f; managerial tasks 39; market
forces 29; marketing mix concept 28–9,
31f, 32–40; microeconomic theory
29–31; price elasticity 32, 34, 41; push–
versus pull-oriented approaches 39;
quantitative methods 30, 36–9, 41, 43b;
rational choice 30; regression analysis
38b, 43b; scanner panel data 34, 38–9,
41; scientific tradition 20–1f; stockpiling
42; supporting themes 20–1f; time of
origin 20–1f; transaction cost theory 30,
32–4
'economic man' 29–31, 35
emotional branding model 277
employee branding 288
employer branding 289
enterprise branding 52, 72, 77, 82
ethnographic methods: creative
interpretation 210; cultural approach
244–5; data collection 209; ethnographic
studies 209–10; 'going native' 209b;

insider/outsider dilemma 209b, 210,
210b; organizational culture, study of 67;
researcher participation 209
eWOM (electronic word of mouth) 218,
222
exchange relationships (versus communal)
170
experiential consumer perspective (versus
information-processing consumer
perspective) 163t
extended case method 245

factor analysis 139
fast moving consumer goods (FMCGs) 27,
214b
Ford 101, 193, 200
Four Ps 28–9, 33–41; identity approach 48;
as 'infallible' guide 34
functional utility 30, 36

'grassroots R and D' 218

Harley-Davidson bikers 200
heuristic methods 11, 20–1f, 64, 70, 93b,
94, 105–6
'homo connectus' 197, 199, 206, 213–14,
219
hubs 205, 205t

iconic brands, management of: brand
manager abilities 247–9, 250b; brand
reputation 248; communication 249;
cultural contradictions 249; cultural
knowledge 247, 248f; strategy,
composing 247, 248f; *see also* cultural
branding
identity approach 3, 12, 20–1f; AC4ID
framework 62–5; anthropological studies
65, 70; brand-consumer exchange 52–4;
brand identification 58, 76b, 78; brand
identity 48, 49b, 50–74, 75t, 76b, 77–9;
brand perspective 20–1f; brand value
creation 20–1f; communication 48–50,
52–4, 59–60, 64–7, 68, 73t, 81;
company, total experience of 48, 49b;
consumer perspective 20–1f; corporate
branding 48–9, 50t, 51b, 81–2;
corporate identity 48, 49b, 50, 52–8,
60f, 61, 63–5, 69b; corporate image
57–9; employee involvement 77b;
enterprise branding 52, 72, 76, 82;
heuristic methods 64, 70; identity gaps,

aligning 61–4, 70–3, 75t; image/reputation, study of 62; key reading 20–1f; key words 20–1f; laddering techniques 67; 'living the brand' 57, 77b; multidimensional approach 53, 76; organizational identity 52–9, 60f, 60t, 61, 63–6, 67f; organizational structure 74; projective paradigm 274f, 274–5; quantitative/ qualitative methods 20–1f; reputation 59–60; service encounters 76b, 79; social brand identity 46, 80; social media 45, 72, 79; scientific tradition 20–1f; supporting themes 20–1f; time of origin 20–1f
identity projects - individual and collective 289
identity projects: collective 231–2; individual 164
ideological issues 249–55
ideological issues, managerial implications of 255–6
ideoscape 289
ideoscapes, global 232, 250–1, 255–6
information-processing consumer perspective (versus experiential consumer perspective) 163t
information-processing theory *see* consumer choice theory
information sources 198
intentional marketing, consumer dislike of 216
intertextuality 235, 244
interviews *see* depth interviews
'invisible hand' principle 30, 32, 34

key readings, for approaches 20–1f
key words, in brand management, *chapter 12*
Lego 51b
Libresse, and FMCGs 214b
life story methods 177
Likert scale 141
Linux 203–4
'living the brand' 57, 77b, 290

macro-level culture 229b, 230
malleability 154
'market man' *(homo mercans)* 232, 234
marketing mix concept 28–9, 31f, 32–41
Marxist analysis 253
memory elicitation method 181–2

memory processes 85
mental accounting 171, 176–7
methods, of approaches 20–1f
MTV 148
MySpace 203

Napster 207t
national culture 122, 138, 142b
'nerd' factor 213
netnographic methods 211
networked narrative 207, 218–19, 293
No Logo movement 252–3, 256–7, 290

Occupy Wall Street 253, 280
Oil of Olay 131b
online creative consumer collectives 207, 207t, 218
organizational culture: three-perspective approach 66

paradigm concept 10
Pepsi 155, 238, 238b, 266
persona 290
personality approach 3, 14; brand-consumer exchange 125; brand perspective 20–1f; brand-self congruence 126, 130, 132, 141, 145; brand value creation 20–1f; consumer behaviour research 122, 124; consumer perspective 20–1f; dos and don'ts of 152b; early adopters 144, 146; emotional bonding 121b; expression of self 123–30, 134, 138, 144; free association methods 142; human psychology 121–4, 127, 132; interactive process 125; key reading 20–1f; key words 20–1f; malleability 154; national culture 122, 138, 142b; personality research 121; personality traits 125, 127, 130, 133, 135f, 139, 141, 142b, 143, 146, 148, 149, 150; scaling techniques 139; scientific tradition 20–21f; self, layers of 122, 145, 154; supporting themes 20–1f; symbolic benefits 123, 125–6, 144, 163t; time of origin 20–1f; *see also* brand personality
phenomenological perspective: individual identity projects 164; 'inner reality' 161–2, 165, 177; 'lived experience' 161–3, 168, 177, 181, 184; meaning 162, 164; methods 177–82; *see also* depth interviews
platform brands 219, 221

pools 205, 205t
positivistic stance 10
postmodern branding 256, 257t
postpostmodern branding 257, 257t
price elasticity 32, 34, 41
Procter & Gamble 27
product brand 291
product paradigm 273, 274f, 276t
PRODUCT (RED), and Global Fund 258–9b
projective paradigm 273, 274f, 276t
projective techniques 102, 103b, 291
public relations (PR) 59, 291
pull marketing (versus push) 292
push marketing (versus pull) 292

Quiksilver 77b

regression analysis 38b
relational approach 3, 14; academic implications 161–4; animism 165–6, 165; birth of 11; brand-consumer exchange 164–5; brand loyalty 160, 164, 183–4; brand love 171, 187; brand perspective 20–1f; Brand Relationship Quality 174, 175f, 183; brand relationship theory 168, 174, 183–4; brand value creation 20–1f; communal relationships (versus exchange) 170; consumer perspective 20–1f; data analysis 182; depth interviews 167–70, 177; exchange relationships (versus communal) 170; experiential consumer perspective 183t; holistic perspective 182; information overload 184; 'inner reality' 161–2, 165, 177; key reading 20–1f; key words 20–1f; 'lived experience' 161–3, 168, 177, 181, 184; memory elicitation method 181–2; mental accounting 171, 176–7; paradigm shift to 11, 15; qualitative methods 20–21f, 162, 164; relationship marketing 160b; scientific tradition 20-21f; supporting themes 20–1f; time of origin 20–1f; true friend, brand as 183, 186; *see also* phenomenological perspective; relationship theory
relational paradigm 273, 274f, 276t
relationship forms 170, 172t, 174t
relationship theory 179; current concerns 167, 179; life projects 161, 167–8, 170; life themes 168, 169b, 170; process

phenomena 171, 174; psychological meaning 167; relational meaning 167

Sacramento Jaguar Club 195
sales channels 80, 292
scaling techniques: brand personality scale 141; interval scales 140; nominal scales 139; ordinal scales 140; ratio scales 141
scanner panel data 34, 38–9, 41
scientific traditions, of approaches 20–1f
'seeding' 218
self, consumer 122, 124, 127, 129f, 129-30, 138, 143–4, 146, 147f
self, layers of 122, 145, 154
semiotics, and deconstruction of meaning 242–4
service encounters 76b, 79
sharing economy 219
six-stage strategic framework 241, 243b
Snapple, iconic brand 240b
social brand identity 46, 80
social brand perspective 196, 198–9
social media 45, 72, 79, 193–5, 203, 206–8, 213–17, 292
Starbucks 227, 246, 250, 252b
stockpiling 41
storytelling 203, 292
subcultures of consumption 200, 204

taxonomy, of brand management: brands, roles of 272; categorizations, comparison of 278t; community approach 20–1f; consumer-based approach 20–1f; cultural approach 20–1f; economic approach 20–1f; four brand management paradigms 273–5, 274f, ; four branding models 275–8; identity approach 20–1f; personality approach 20–1f; relational approach 20–1f; seven approaches, overview of 20–1f
transaction cost theory: brand-consumer exchange 30–3; economic man concept 29–31, 35; 'invisible hand' principle 30, 32, 34; rational choice 30; transaction costs 30–3
transgressions 151b, 173t, 176, 293
triadic brand relationship 195
triangulation, data 211b

user imagery 95, 98-99f, 134, 293

viral branding 217, 221, 238, 275, 293

viral branding model 277t
Virgin 148
Volkswagen, associations 91-92
Volkswagen 'Beetle' community 215b

Web 2.0 193–5, 197, 200, 206–8, 213–17,
  219, 292, 294

webs 205, 205t
WOMM (word of mouth management)
  218

Young & Rubicam 135
YouTube 203

Taylor & Francis eBooks

Helping you to choose the right eBooks for your Library

Add Routledge titles to your library's digital collection today. Taylor and Francis ebooks contains over 50,000 titles in the Humanities, Social Sciences, Behavioural Sciences, Built Environment and Law.

Choose from a range of subject packages or create your own!

Benefits for you

>> Free MARC records
>> COUNTER-compliant usage statistics
>> Flexible purchase and pricing options
>> All titles DRM-free.

Benefits for your user

>> Off-site, anytime access via Athens or referring URL
>> Print or copy pages or chapters
>> Full content search
>> Bookmark, highlight and annotate text
>> Access to thousands of pages of quality research at the click of a button.

REQUEST YOUR **FREE** INSTITUTIONAL TRIAL TODAY

Free Trials Available
We offer free trials to qualifying academic, corporate and government customers.

eCollections – Choose from over 30 subject eCollections, including:

Archaeology	Language Learning
Architecture	Law
Asian Studies	Literature
Business & Management	Media & Communication
Classical Studies	Middle East Studies
Construction	Music
Creative & Media Arts	Philosophy
Criminology & Criminal Justice	Planning
Economics	Politics
Education	Psychology & Mental Health
Energy	Religion
Engineering	Security
English Language & Linguistics	Social Work
Environment & Sustainability	Sociology
Geography	Sport
Health Studies	Theatre & Performance
History	Tourism, Hospitality & Events

For more information, pricing enquiries or to order a free trial, please contact your local sales team: www.tandfebooks.com/page/sales

 Routledge
Taylor & Francis Group

The home of
Routledge books

www.tandfebooks.com